EASY COOKING FOR TODAY

EASY COOKING FOR TODAY

Chef Pol Martin

BRIMAR PUBLISHING

The author wishes to thank Melissa du Fretay
for her invaluable assistance

Graphic Design
Robert Doutre for Graphus

Photographs by
Pol Martin (Ontario) Ltd Studio

BRIMAR PUBLISHING INC.
8925 Saint-Laurent Boulevard
Montreal, Canada   H2N 1M5
Telephone: (514) 384-8660
Telex: 05-826756

Legal deposit: Fourth Quarter 1986
Bibliothèque nationale du Québec
National Library of Canada

The information in this book is true and complete to the best of our knowledge. All recommendations are made without any guarantees on the part of the author and the publisher. They disclaim all liability in connection with the use of this information.

ISBN: 2-920845-07-1

Printed and bound in Canada

2009-A
 3 4 5 6 7 8 9

CONTENTS

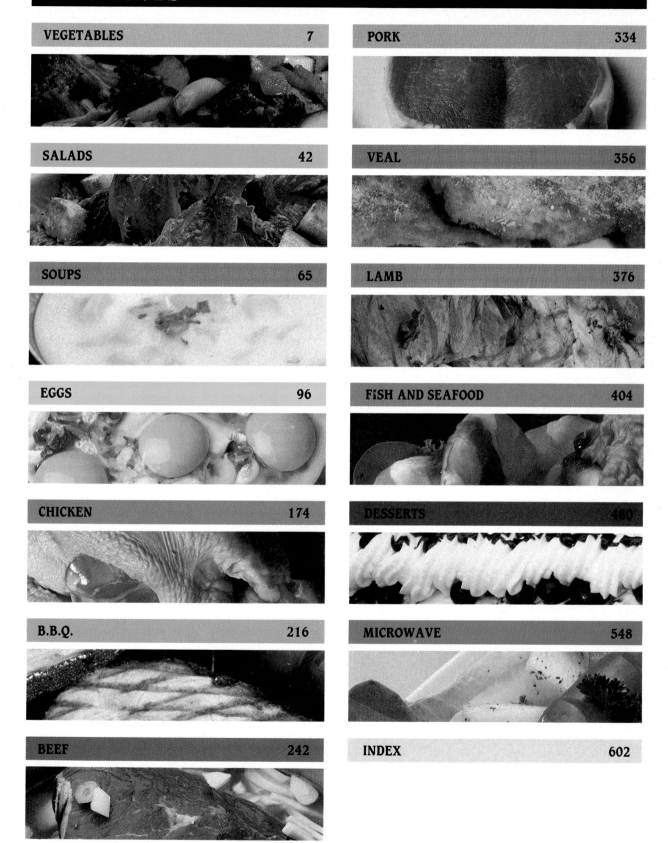

VEGETABLES	7
SALADS	42
SOUPS	65
EGGS	96
CHICKEN	174
B.B.Q.	216
BEEF	242

PORK	334
VEAL	356
LAMB	376
FISH AND SEAFOOD	404
DESSERTS	480
MICROWAVE	548
INDEX	602

VEGETABLES

Lemon Beans and Mushrooms *(serves 4)*

1 ½ lb	(750 g) green beans, washed and trimmed
2 tbsp	(30 ml) butter
½ lb	(250 g) fresh mushrooms, cleaned and sliced
	rind and juice 1 lemon
	salt and pepper

Place beans in boiling salted water; cook 10 minutes.

Cool beans under cold running water; drain and set aside.

Heat butter in frying pan or sauté pan. When hot, add mushrooms and cook 2 to 3 minutes over high heat. Do not stir.

Season generously with salt and pepper; mix well. Continue cooking 2 minutes.

Add beans, lemon rind and juice; cover and cook 3 minutes.

Serve.

8

Potato Purée   *(serves 4)*

4	large potatoes, cooked in skins
¼ cup	(50 ml) commercial spicy tomato sauce, heated
1 tbsp	(15 ml) butter
2 tbsp	(30 ml) 35% cream
	pinch nutmeg
	salt and pepper

Peel potatoes. Purée through food mill; place in serving bowl.

Add tomato sauce and butter; incorporate well.

Add cream and remaining ingredients; mix until combined.

Correct seasonings and serve.

1 SERVING	193 CALORIES	33 g CARBOHYDRATE
4 g PROTEIN	5 g FAT	1.0 g FIBER

Winter Vegetable Mix   *(serves 4)*

2 tbsp	(30 ml) vegetable oil
1	onion, peeled and chopped
2	carrots, pared and sliced
1	zucchini, sliced ¼ in (0.65 cm) thick
2	stalks broccoli (stalks and flowerets) sliced
1	garlic clove, smashed and chopped
3 tbsp	(45 ml) soya sauce
	lemon juice
	salt and pepper

Heat oil in wok (or large frying pan). When hot, add onion and carrots; season well. Cover and cook 4 minutes over high heat; stir occasionally.

Add remaining vegetables and garlic; continue cooking 8 to 10 minutes.

Mix in soya sauce and lemon juice to taste. Serve immediately.

1 SERVING	115 CALORIES	10 g CARBOHYDRATE
3 g PROTEIN	7 g FAT	1.4 g FIBER

Sautéed Okra   *(serves 4)*

½ lb	(250 g) frozen whole okra
1 tbsp	(15 ml) butter
1 tsp	(5 ml) chopped fresh parsley
2 tbsp	(30 ml) pine nuts
	salt and pepper
	few drops lemon juice

Bring 1 cup (250 ml) salted water to boil in saucepan. Add okra and cover; cook 10 minutes.

When okra is cooked, cool under running water. Drain well.

Heat butter in frying pan. When hot, add okra and parsley; mix and add pine nuts. Cook 2 minutes over medium heat; season well.

Sprinkle with lemon juice and serve.

1 SERVING	69 CALORIES	4 g CARBOHYDRATE
2 g PROTEIN	5 g FAT	0.7 g FIBER

Baked Leeks *(serves 4)*

8	leeks, cut in four and washed*
1 tbsp	(15 ml) lemon juice
2 cups	(500 ml) heated light white sauce**
¼ tsp	(1 ml) nutmeg
⅓ cup	(75 ml) grated Gruyère cheese
	salt and pepper
	dash paprika

Preheat oven to 350°F (180°C).

Place leeks in 2 cups (500 ml) boiling salted water. Add lemon juice and cook 16 minutes over medium heat.

Drain leeks and transfer to buttered baking dish.

Season generously and pour in white sauce. Sprinkle with nutmeg and add cheese; top with dash paprika. Bake 20 minutes in oven.

* See following technique.
** See Light White Sauce, page 14.

1 SERVING	204 CALORIES	16 g CARBOHYDRATE
8 g PROTEIN	12 g FAT	0.7 g FIBER

TECHNIQUE: BAKED LEEKS

1 Cut leeks into four leaving about 1 in (2.5 cm) from bottom. Wash well in cold water.

2 Place leeks in 2 cups (500 ml) boiling salted water. Add lemon juice and cook 16 minutes over medium heat.

3 Drain leeks and transfer to buttered baking dish.

4 Season generously and pour in white sauce. Sprinkle with nutmeg.

Continued next page.

5 Add cheese and top with dash paprika.

6 Bake 20 minutes in oven until golden brown.

Light White Sauce

2 cups	(500 ml) milk
2 tbsp	(30 ml) butter
2½ tbsp	(40 ml) flour
	salt and white pepper

Pour milk into saucepan and bring to boiling point. Remove and set aside.

Heat butter in separate saucepan. When hot, add flour and mix well. Cook 2 minutes over low heat.

Incorporate milk into flour very slowly; stir constantly. Season sauce well and continue cooking 10 minutes over low heat. Mix frequently.

1 SERVING	73 CALORIES	5 g CARBOHYDRATE
2 g PROTEIN	5 g FAT	0 g FIBER

Asparagus with Butter   *(serves 4)*

2	bunches asparagus, pared and washed
¼ cup	(50 ml) melted clarified butter
2	hard-boiled eggs, chopped
	lemon juice to taste
	chopped fresh parsley
	salt

Place asparagus in saucepan of boiling salted water. Add few drops lemon juice; cook 7 to 8 minutes over high heat.

Prick asparagus with knife to test if cooked. Stalks should be tender. Drain well.

Arrange asparagus on serving platter and add melted butter. Sprinkle with lemon juice and season with salt.

Top with eggs and chopped parsley. Serve.

Asparagus au Parmesan   *(serves 4)*

5 cups	(1.2 L) cold water
2	large bunches asparagus, pared and washed
¼ cup	(50 ml) grated parmesan cheese
1½ cups	(375 ml) heated light white sauce*
¼ tsp	(1 ml) nutmeg
	juice 1 lemon
	salt and white pepper
	paprika

Preheat oven to 375°F (190°C).

Pour water into roasting pan; add lemon juice and salt. Bring to boil on stove top.

Add asparagus to hot water and cook 8 to 10 minutes over medium heat.

When asparagus is cooked, remove and transfer to baking dish.

Mix half of cheese into white sauce; add nutmeg and pour over asparagus. Sprinkle top with remaining cheese and paprika.

Cook 7 to 8 minutes in oven.

Correct seasoning and serve.

*See Light White Sauce, page 14.

1 SERVING	173 CALORIES	15 g CARBOHYDRATE
8 g PROTEIN	9 g FAT	0.7 g FIBER

Sautéed Potatoes and Leeks   *(serves 4)*

2 tbsp	(30 ml) butter
2	leeks, white section only, washed and sliced
4	large potatoes, cooked in their skins
¼ tsp	(1 ml) celery seed
	chopped fresh parsley
	salt and pepper

Heat butter in frying pan. Add leeks and cover pan; cook 8 to 10 minutes over low heat.

Peel potatoes and cut into thick slices; add to frying pan. Season and sprinkle in celery seed; mix well and cook, uncovered, 7 to 8 minutes over medium heat.

Sprinkle with chopped parsley and serve immediately.

Artichokes with Vinaigrette   *(serves 4)*

4	fresh artichokes, washed
4	lemon slices
1	shallot, finely chopped
1 tbsp	(15 ml) Dijon mustard
¼ tsp	(1 ml) thyme
2 tbsp	(30 ml) white wine vinegar
5 tbsp	(75 ml) olive oil
1 tbsp	(15 ml) chopped fresh parsley
	salt and pepper
	lemon juice

Cut off artichoke stems and snap off tough leaves around bottom. Cover artichoke base with lemon slice; secure with string.

Bring water to boil in saucepan; add salt and lemon juice. Add artichokes and cook 35 to 40 minutes.

When cooked, cool artichokes in cold water. Drain and set aside.

Place shallot, mustard, thyme and vinegar in small bowl. Season and mix with whisk.

Add oil in thin stream while mixing constantly with whisk. Correct seasoning.

Sprinkle with parsley and set aside.

Separate artichoke leaves and arrange on attractive platter.

Remove artichoke heart from base. Using small knife cut out fuzzy 'choke' and discard. Do not attempt to eat choke!

Place hearts alongside leaves and serve with prepared vinaigrette.

1 SERVING	214 CALORIES	10 g CARBOHYDRATE
3 g PROTEIN	18 g FAT	2.4 g FIBER

TECHNIQUE

1 Cut off artichoke stems and snap off tough leaves around bottom.

2 Cover artichoke base with lemon slice.

3 Secure with string to keep lemon and leaves in place during cooking.

4 Place artichokes in salted boiling water with lemon juice; cook 35 to 40 minutes.

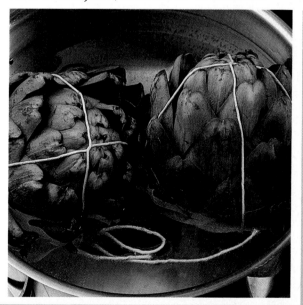

Continued next page.

5 To serve, separate leaves and arrange on attractive platter. Remove artichoke heart from base.

6 Using small knife cut out fuzzy 'choke' and discard! Do not attempt to eat choke.

Cheese White Sauce

4 tbsp	(60 ml) butter
4 tbsp	(60 ml) flour
2½ cups	(625 ml) hot milk
¼ tsp	(1 ml) nutmeg
½ cup	(125 ml) grated cheddar cheese
¼ cup	(50 ml) grated mozzarella cheese
	salt and white pepper

Heat butter in saucepan. When hot, add flour and mix well. Cook 1 minute over low heat.

Add half of milk and incorporate; continue cooking 3 to 4 minutes over low heat.

Pour in remaining milk and spices; cook 10 minutes over low heat.

Mix in both cheeses and cook 3 to 4 minutes over low heat.

Serve this sauce with almost any vegetable.

1 SERVING	199 CALORIES	9 g CARBOHYDRATE
7 g PROTEIN	15 g FAT	0 g FIBER

Spinach with Cream and Melted Cheese *(serves 4)*

4	bunches fresh spinach, washed and dried
2 cups	(500 ml) white sauce*
⅓ cup	(75 ml) grated Gruyère cheese
	butter
	salt, pepper and paprika

Place spinach in boiling salted water and add some pepper. Cover and cook 3 minutes.

Cool spinach under cold water. Drain and squeeze leaves dry; chop.

Butter baking dish and add chopped spinach; dab with a bit of butter. Season with salt, pepper and paprika.

Pour white sauce over spinach and sprinkle with cheese. Broil 10 minutes in oven.

Serve hot.

*See White Sauce, page 23.

See Technique next page.

1 SERVING	275 CALORIES	16 g CARBOHYDRATE
10 g PROTEIN	19 g FAT	0.5 g FIBER

TECHNIQUE: SPINACH WITH CREAM

1 Place spinach in boiling salted water and add pepper. Cover and cook 3 minutes.

2 Cool spinach under cold water. Drain and squeeze leaves dry. The best way is to form spinach into several balls and squeeze out excess water.

3 Chop spinach.

4 Butter baking dish and add chopped spinach; dab with a bit of butter. Season with salt, pepper and paprika.

5 Pour white sauce over spinach.

6 Sprinkle with cheese; broil 10 minutes in oven.

White Sauce

4 tbsp	(60 ml) butter
4 tbsp	(60 ml) flour
2½ cups	(625 ml) hot milk
	pinch nutmeg
	salt and white pepper

Heat butter in saucepan. When hot, mix in flour and cook 1 minute over medium heat.

Incorporate half of milk with whisk.

Add remaining milk, nutmeg, salt and pepper; stir well. Bring sauce to boil; cook 10 to 12 minutes over low heat. Stir several times during cooking.

Remove saucepan from heat and set aside.

1 SERVING	181 CALORIES	11 g CARBOHYDRATE
5 g PROTEIN	13 g FAT	0 g FIBER

Fava Beans and Zucchini   *(serves 4)*

2 cups	(500 ml) water
2 cups	(500 ml) fava beans
1	zucchini, diced
1 tbsp	(15 ml) butter
1 tbsp	(15 ml) chopped green onion
1 tbsp	(15 ml) chopped lemon rind
	few drops lemon juice
	salt and pepper

Pour water, lemon juice and salt into saucepan. Bring to boil.

Add fava beans and cook 3 minutes over medium heat.

Add zucchini; continue cooking 3 minutes.

Drain vegetables and cool in cold water.

Drain and replace vegetables in saucepan; add butter, onion and lemon rind; season well. Mix and cook 2 minutes.

Serve immediately.

1 SERVING	87 CALORIES	14 g CARBOHYDRATE
1 g PROTEIN	3 g FAT	0 g FIBER

Castle Potatoes *(serves 4)*

5	cooked potatoes, mashed
2 tbsp	(30 ml) soft butter
2	egg yolks
¼ cup	(50 ml) hot milk
2 tbsp	(30 ml) heavy cream
¼ tsp	(1 ml) nutmeg
	salt and pepper

Preheat oven to 400°F (200°C).

Butter and flour cookie sheet; set aside.

Add butter to mashed potatoes and mix well. Add remaining ingredients and mix until incorporated.

Spoon mixture into pastry bag fitted with star nozzle. Form small 'castles' about 1½ in (4 cm) high on cookie sheet.

Cook 15 minutes in oven or until browned.

Serve with roasts or steaks.

1 SERVING	199 CALORIES	20 g CARBOHYDRATE
5 g PROTEIN	11 g FAT	0.6 g FIBER

Scalloped Potatoes   *(serves 4)*

3½ tbsp	(55 ml) butter
1	onion, peeled and finely chopped
2½ tbsp	(40 ml) flour
2 cups	(500 ml) hot milk
¼ cup	(50 ml) heavy cream
¼ tsp	(1 ml) nutmeg
¼ tsp	(1 ml) thyme
¼ tsp	(1 ml) basil
4	medium-size potatoes, peeled and sliced
	salt and pepper

Preheat oven to 375°F (190°C).

Butter baking dish and set aside.

Heat remaining butter in saucepan. When hot, add onion; cover and cook 3 to 4 minutes over medium heat.

Add flour and mix well. Cook 1 minute, uncovered, over low heat.

Pour in half of milk and incorporate. Add remaining milk, cream and spices; stir well. Cook 10 minutes, uncovered, over low heat.

Arrange half of sliced potatoes in baking dish; pour in half of sauce.

Repeat procedure. Season well and cover top with foil. Cook 40 to 45 minutes in oven.

Remove foil and continue cooking 15 minutes to brown top.

If desired, serve with chopped fresh parsley.

1 SERVING	264 CALORIES	27 g CARBOHYDRATE
3 g PROTEIN	16 g FAT	0.8 g FIBER

Special Cauliflower with Cheese Sauce *(serves 4 to 6)*

¼ cup	(50 ml) milk
1	head cauliflower
1	recipe cheese white sauce*
	salt and white pepper

Fill large saucepan about half full with cold water; add milk and salt. Bring to boil.

Meanwhile, remove green leaves from cauliflower. Cut off stem.

Place cauliflower (whole) in saucepan upside down. Cover saucepan and cook 8 minutes.

Remove and drain well.

Transfer to serving platter and pour some of cheese sauce over top. Reserve remaining sauce for individual portions.

Serve.

* See Cheese White Sauce, page 20.

1 SERVING	256 CALORIES	17 g CARBOHYDRATE
11 g PROTEIN	16 g FAT	1.3 g FIBER

O'Brien Potatoes   *(serves 4)*

3	slices bacon, diced
4	potatoes, peeled and diced
1	onion, peeled and diced
1 tbsp	(15 ml) chopped parsley
	salt and pepper

Place bacon in frying pan and cook 3 to 4 minutes over medium heat.

Remove bacon with slotted spoon and set aside.

Add diced potatoes to hot bacon fat; season well. Partially cover and cook 6 to 7 minutes over medium-high heat. Stir occasionally.

Add onion and bacon to pan; cook 3 to 4 minutes, uncovered, on medium-high.

Sprinkle with parsley and serve at once.

1 SERVING	151 CALORIES	23 g CARBOHYDRATE
8 g PROTEIN	3 g FAT	0.6 g FIBER

Baked Potato Skins *(serves 4)*

4	baking potatoes, baked
½ cup	(125 ml) grated cheddar cheese
½ cup	(125 ml) grated Gruyère cheese
4	slices cooked bacon, diced
	salt and pepper
	dash paprika

Slice potatoes in half lengthwise. Scoop out about ¾ of flesh and set aside for other recipes.

Set skins on cookie sheet and place in oven about 4 in (10 cm) away from top element. Broil 8 minutes.

Remove skins from oven and sprinkle with both cheeses. Season well and add bacon and paprika. Broil another 4 to 5 minutes.

Serve hot, with sour cream if desired.

1 SERVING	273 CALORIES	22 g CARBOHYDRATE
17 g PROTEIN	13 g FAT	0.5 g FIBER

Stir-Fried Vegetables   *(serves 4)*

2 tbsp	(30 ml) vegetable oil
2½ lb	(1.2 kg) broccoli
3	green onions, sliced
1	celery stalk, sliced
2	carrots, pared and thinly sliced
6	mushrooms, cleaned and cut in half
½	green pepper, cut into large pieces
½	zucchini, cut in half lengthwise and sliced
5	water chestnuts, sliced
1	garlic clove, smashed and chopped
	salt and pepper

Heat oil in wok or large frying pan. Meanwhile, separate broccoli into flowerets and split stalks; slice if large.

Add broccoli and green onions to wok; stir-fry 2 minutes over medium-high heat.

Add celery and carrots; stir-fry 2 to 3 minutes.

Season well and add remaining ingredients; continue to stir-fry 6 to 7 minutes.

Serve immediately.

1 SERVING	208 CALORIES	23 g CARBOHYDRATE
11 g PROTEIN	8 g FAT	4.8 g FIBER

Mushrooms Provençale *(serves 4)*

2 tbsp	(30 ml) butter
1 tsp	(5 ml) vegetable oil
1 lb	(500 g) fresh mushrooms, cleaned and sliced ¼ in (0.65 cm) thick
1 tbsp	(15 ml) chopped fresh chives
1 tsp	(5 ml) chopped fresh parsley
2	garlic cloves, smashed and chopped
	salt and pepper
	juice ¼ lemon

Heat butter and oil in frying pan. When hot, add mushrooms and season generously. Cook 3 to 4 minutes over medium-high heat; stir occasionally.

Add chives, parsley, garlic and lemon juice; continue cooking 2 minutes.

Correct seasoning and serve.

This dish is very nice with steak.

Tasty Vegetable Mix *(serves 4)*

3 cups	(750 ml) cold water
12	baby carrots, pared, ends trimmed, and cut in half lengthwise
8 oz	(227 g) yellow beans, ends trimmed
½	red pepper, cut in long strips
1 tbsp	(15 ml) butter
1 tsp	(5 ml) chopped chives or parsley
	salt and pepper
	few drops lemon juice

Place water in saucepan; add salt and lemon juice. Bring to boil.

Add carrots; cover and cook 6 minutes over medium heat.

Drop in beans and continue cooking, covered, 6 minutes.

Add red pepper; cover and finish cooking 2 minutes.

Drain vegetables and cool in cold water. Drain again and set aside.

Heat butter in frying pan. When hot, add vegetables and sprinkle with chives; cover and cook several minutes over medium heat.

Season and serve.

1 SERVING	63 CALORIES	7 g CARBOHYDRATE
2 g PROTEIN	3 g FAT	1.1 g FIBER

Broccoli au Gratin *(serves 4)*

2½ lb	(1.2 kg) broccoli flowerets
1	recipe cheese white sauce*, heated
½ cup	(125 ml) grated cheddar salt and pepper

Steam broccoli 5 to 6 minutes or until done to taste.

Transfer to ovenproof dish and pour on hot cheese sauce. Sprinkle with grated cheese and season lightly.

Broil 7 to 8 minutes in oven.

*See Cheese White Sauce, page 20.

1 SERVING	456 CALORIES	28 g CARBOHYDRATE
23 g PROTEIN	28 g FAT	3.8 g FIBER

Ratatouille   *(serves 4)*

3 tbps	(45 ml) vegetable oil
1	eggplant, cut in half lengthwise and sliced
1	onion, peeled and diced
2	garlic cloves, smashed and chopped
½	zucchini, sliced
2	tomatoes, cored and diced large
¼ tsp	(1 ml) thyme
¼ tsp	(1 ml) oregano
½ tsp	(2 ml) basil
	salt and pepper

Heat oil in deep frying pan. When hot, add eggplant and season; cover and cook 15 minutes over medium heat. Stir occasionally.

Add onion and mix well; cook 4 to 5 minutes, uncovered, over high heat.

Add garlic and zucchini; partly cover and cook 10 minutes over medium heat.

Add tomatoes and spices; partly cover and cook 15 minutes over very low heat.

Serve.

1 SERVING	159 CALORIES	12 g CARBOHYDRATE
3 g PROTEIN	11 g FAT	1.5 g FIBER

Vegetarian Lasagna *(serves 4 to 6)*

1 lb	(500 g) package lasagna noodles
3 tbsp	(45 ml) butter
1	onion, peeled and diced small
2	carrots, pared and diced small
½	cauliflower, chopped
1	green pepper, diced small
½	zucchini, diced small
2	tomatoes, cored and diced small
½ lb	(250 g) mushrooms, cleaned and diced small

see next page

Preheat oven to 375°F (190°C).

Butter 12 × 9 in (31 × 22 cm) lasagna dish; set aside.

Cook pasta in plenty of boiling salted water with a bit of oil added. Be sure pot is wide enough to allow noodles to lie flat. Follow directions on package and remove pasta when 'al dente'.

Drain pasta and carefully lay out strips on paper towels. Cover with more paper towels.

Heat butter in large saucepan. When hot, add onion; cover and cook 3 minutes over low heat.

Add carrots and mix; continue cooking 3 to 4 minutes over low heat, covered.

1 SERVING	726 CALORIES	87 g CARBOHYDRATE
27 g PROTEIN	30 g FAT	1.7 g FIBER

Vegetarian Lasagna (continued)

1 tbsp	(15 ml) chopped lemon rind
¼ tsp	(1 ml) nutmeg
½ tsp	(2 ml) ground clove
½ tsp	(2 ml) oregano
¼ tsp	(1 ml) thyme
1 cup	(250 ml) grated Gruyère cheese
1 cup	(250 ml) grated mozzarella cheese
4 cups	(1 L) light white sauce, heated
	salt and pepper

Add cauliflower, green pepper and zucchini; season generously. Cover and cook 4 to 5 minutes over low heat.

Stir in tomatoes, mushrooms, lemon rind and spices; cover and continue cooking 3 to 4 minutes.

Remove saucepan and set aside.

Arrange first layer of pasta in lasagna dish.

Add layer of vegetables, layer of cheese and layer of sauce. Repeat until most of ingredients are used. Finish with layer of pasta.

Add some sauce and top with cheese. Bake 45 minutes in oven.

Serve hot and reserve any leftovers, which reheat easily in oven.

Tomatoes Stuffed with Castle Potatoes (serves 4)

4	large tomatoes
1 tbsp	(15 ml) olive oil
½	recipe castle potatoes*
1 tbsp	(15 ml) chopped chives
	salt and pepper

Preheat even to 400°F (200°C).

Slice off the top from each tomato. Use spoon and scoop out pulp and seeds; discard.

Place shells in baking dish and sprinkle insides with oil; season well.

Spoon mashed potatoes into pastry bag fitted with star nozzle. Fill tomato shells and sprinkle with chives.

Broil 15 minutes in oven.

Serve with melted butter to taste.

*See Castle Potatoes, page 25.

1 SERVING	209 CALORIES	19 g CARBOHYDRATE
4 g PROTEIN	13 g FAT	1.3 g FIBER

Stuffed Vegetables *(serves 4)*

2 tbsp	(30 ml) butter
½ cup	(125 ml) finely chopped onion
2	garlic cloves, chopped
2 tbsp	(30 ml) chopped parsley
1 tsp	(5 ml) chopped fresh tarragon
1 tbsp	(15 ml) chopped chives
1¾ oz	(50 g) can anchovy filets, drained and chopped
3 tbsp	(45 ml) breadcrumbs
2	tomatoes, partially hollowed
1	zucchini, cut in 2 in (5 cm) lengths and blanched 4 minutes
3	small potatoes, cooked in jackets, cut in two and partially hollowed
2	onions, peeled, partially hollowed and blanched 8 minutes
	olive oil, salt and pepper

Preheat oven to 425°F (220°C).

Heat butter in saucepan. When hot, add chopped onion and garlic; cook 3 to 4 minutes over low heat.

Add parsley, tarragon and chives; mix well and continue cooking 2 to 3 minutes. Season well.

Add anchovies and breadcrumbs; stir and cook 2 minutes. Remove saucepan from heat and set aside.

Sprinkle insides of tomatoes with some oil; season with pepper.

Scoop out the flesh from zucchini lengths and set standing up on ovenproof platter. Add tomatoes, potatoes and onions.

Stuff vegetables with anchovy mixture and sprinkle all with olive oil. Cook 10 to 12 minutes in oven.

If desired, serve with Zesty Tomato Sauce, page 40.

1 SERVING	250 CALORIES	27 g CARBOHYDRATE
4 g PROTEIN	14 g FAT	1.4 g FIBER

Braised Fennel Root in Chicken Stock   *(serves 4)*

4	large fennel roots
2 tbsp	(30 ml) lard
4	garlic cloves, peeled
1½ cups	(375 ml) hot chicken stock
	salt and pepper
	chopped chives to taste

Preheat oven to 375°F (190°C).

Remove green leaves from fennel and cut bulbs in two; clean.

Heat lard in large frying pan with ovenproof handle. When hot, add garlic and fennel (flat side down). Cook 12 to 15 minutes over medium heat. Season and turn fennel over once during cooking.

Pour in chicken stock and cover frying pan. Cook 40 to 45 minutes in oven, depending on size.

Sprinkle with chives before serving.

1 SERVING	95 CALORIES	5 g CARBOHYDRATE
3 g PROTEIN	7 g FAT	0.5 g FIBER

Chinese Cabbage   *(serves 4)*

1	Chinese cabbage, washed
2 tbsp	(30 ml) butter
1 tbsp	(15 ml) chopped ginger
1 cup	(250 ml) hot chicken stock
1 tbsp	(15 ml) cornstarch
2 tbsp	(30 ml) cold water
	salt and pepper

Slice cabbage into 1 in (2.5 cm) pieces.

Heat butter in large frying pan. When hot, add cabbage and ginger; cook 3 to 4 minutes over high heat. Stir occasionally.

Season well and pour in chicken stock; cover and cook 6 to 7 minutes over medium heat.

Mix cornstarch with water; incorporate in sauce. Simmer 1 minute to thicken sauce and serve.

1 SERVING	94 CALORIES	8 g CARBOHYDRATE
2 g PROTEIN	6 g FAT	1.2 g FIBER

Leftover Cauliflower and Zesty Tomato Sauce *(serves 4)*

½	leftover cooked cauliflower
2 cups	(500 ml) zesty tomato sauce*
½ cup	(125 ml) grated cheddar cheese
	salt and pepper

Slice cauliflower into ¾ in (2 cm) pieces. Place in buttered baking dish and pour in tomato sauce.

Season and sprinkle with cheese. Broil 8 to 10 minutes in oven.

Serve hot.

*See Zesty Tomato Sauce, page 40.

1 SERVING	139 CALORIES	11 g CARBOHYDRATE
8 g PROTEIN	7 g FAT	1.5 g FIBER

Broccoli with Garlic *(serves 4)*

3 cups	(750 ml) salted water
2 lb	(900 g) broccoli flowerets, washed
3 tbsp	(45 ml) butter
2	garlic cloves, smashed and chopped
¼ cup	(50 ml) slivered almonds, browned in butter
	juice 1 lemon
	salt and pepper

Place water in saucepan and add half of lemon juice. Bring to boil.

Add broccoli and cover; cook 8 minutes.

Cool in cold water and drain.

Heat butter in frying pan. When hot, add broccoli and cook 4 to 5 minutes over medium heat.

Stir in garlic and almonds; sprinkle with remaining lemon juice. Cook 3 minutes over medium heat.

Correct seasoning and serve.

1 SERVING	244 CALORIES	15 g CARBOHYDRATE
10 g PROTEIN	16 g FAT	3.6 g FIBER

Zesty Tomato Sauce

1 tbsp	(15 ml) olive oil
2 tbsp	(30 ml) finely chopped onion
1	garlic clove, smashed and chopped
28 oz	(796 ml) can tomatoes, drained and chopped
2 tbsp	(30 ml) tomato paste
	pinch oregano
	few drops Tabasco sauce
	salt and pepper

Heat oil in large saucepan. When hot, add onion and garlic; stir and cook 3 minutes.

Add spices, tomatoes, tomato paste and Tabasco sauce. Cook 10 to 12 minutes over medium heat.

Remove saucepan from heat. Transfer mixture to blender and purée.

This sauce is good with many vegetable recipes.

1 SERVING	84 CALORIES	10 g CARBOHYDRATE
2 g PROTEIN	4 g FAT	0.9 g FIBER

TECHNIQUE: JULIENNE VEGETABLES

1 The term 'julienne' refers to cutting ingredients in matchstick shapes.

2 Julienne vegetables are an attractive garnish to almost any dish.

Julienne Vegetables *(serves 4)*

2 tbsp	(30 ml) butter
1 cup	(250 ml) hot chicken stock
2	medium-size potatoes, peeled and cut in julienne
2	large carrots, pared and cut in julienne
1	small zucchini, cut in julienne
	juice ¼ lemon
	salt and pepper
	chopped chives

Heat butter in saucepan and pour in chicken stock; add lemon juice and bring to boil.

Add potatoes and cook, uncovered, 3 minutes over medium heat.

Add remaining vegetables and season well; continue cooking 3 minutes.

Drain vegetables and arrange on plate. Sprinkle with chives and serve with butter.

1 SERVING	126 CALORIES	16 g CARBOHYDRATE
2 g PROTEIN	6 g FAT	1.0 g FIBER

41

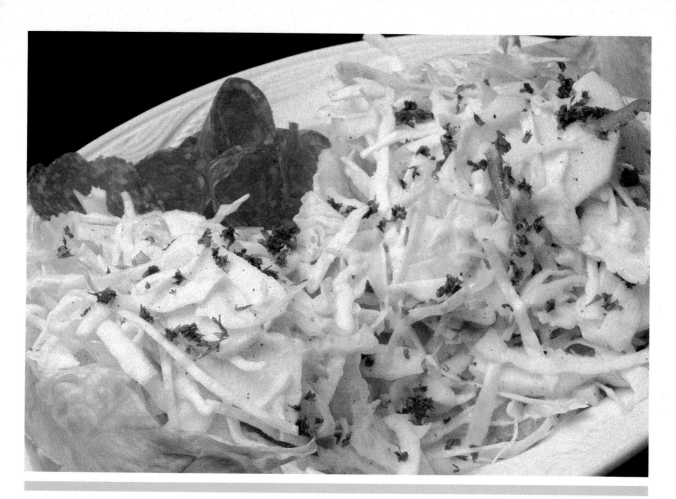

Cold Cabbage Salad *(serves 4)*

½	head cabbage
1	apple, peeled and sliced
½	green pepper, sliced
2 tbsp	(30 ml) grated onion
½ cup	(125 ml) white vinegar
2 tbsp	(30 ml) brown sugar
2 tbsp	(30 ml) vegetable oil
¼ cup	(50 ml) cold water
¼ tsp	(1 ml) celery seed
2 tbsp	(30 ml) mayonnaise
2 tbsp	(30 ml) sour crean
	dash paprika
	salt and pepper

Finely shred cabbage and place in bowl.

Add apple, green pepper and onion; season with salt and pepper. Set aside.

Place vinegar, brown sugar, oil, water and celery seed in saucepan. Cook 5 minutes over medium heat.

Pour marinade over cabbage; toss until evenly coated. Add remaining ingredients and mix again. Season well.

Marinate 3 hours in refrigerator before serving.

1 SERVING	210 CALORIES	19 g CARBOHYDRATE
2 g PROTEIN	14 g FAT	1.4 g FIBER

Light Vegetable Salad *(serves 4)*

4	large ripe tomatoes, cut in half and sliced
20	large fresh mushrooms, cleaned and sliced
1 tsp	(5 ml) chopped fresh tarragon
1	shallot, finely chopped
1 tsp	(5 ml) Dijon mustard
3 tbsp	(45 ml) wine vinegar
6 tbsp	(90 ml) olive oil
	several drops lemon juice
	salt and pepper
	small marinated pickles
	prosciutto slices
	lettuce leaves, washed and dried

Place tomatoes and mushrooms in large bowl; season generously. Sprinkle with tarragon and set aside.

Place shallot in separate bowl. Add mustard and vinegar; mix well with whisk.

Add oil in thin stream while mixing constantly with whisk. Season to taste.

Pour vinaigrette over tomatoes and mushrooms; toss until evenly coated. Add lemon juice and toss again. Marinate 15 minutes.

Serve on lettuce leaves and decorate platter with pickles and prosciutto.

1 SERVING	282 CALORIES	15 g CARBOHYDRATE
6 g PROTEIN	22 g FAT	2.0 g FIBER

Potato and Endive Salad *(serves 4 to 6)*

4	large potatoes, cooked with skin and still hot
2	large Belgian endives, washed and dried
12	cherry tomatoes, washed and cut in half
3	large hard-boiled eggs, sliced
2	shallots, finely chopped
1 tbsp	(15 ml) chopped fresh parsley
1 tbsp	(15 ml) Dijon mustard
4 tbsp	(60 ml) cider vinegar
7 tbsp	(105 ml) olive oil
1 tsp	(5 ml) chopped fresh chives
	several cooked asparagus tips
	salt and pepper from mill

Peel hot potatoes and cut into cubes; place in large bowl. Add endive leaves, tomatoes and eggs; season with salt and pepper.

Place shallots and parsley in small bowl; season generously. Add mustard and vinegar; mix well.

Add oil in thin stream while mixing constantly with whisk.

Pour vinaigrette over salad ingredients; mix well. Correct seasoning and sprinkle with chives.

Decorate with cooked asparagus before serving.

1 SERVING	321 CALORIES	25 g CARBOHYDRATE
8 g PROTEIN	21 g FAT	1.3 g FIBER

Rotini Salad *(serves 4)*

3 cups	(750 ml) cooked rotini noodles
3	tomatoes, cut into small wedges
10 oz	(284 ml) can mandarin orange segments
1	celery stalk, diced small
1 tbsp	(15 ml) chopped fresh chives
½ cup	(125 ml) plain yogurt
1 tsp	(5 ml) lemon juice
¼ tsp	1 ml dry mustard
	dash paprika
	salt and pepper

Place noodles, tomatoes, mandarin segments and celery in large serving bowl. Sprinkle with chives.

Mix yogurt with lemon juice in small bowl. Add mustard and paprika; mix thoroughly.

Season dressing generously and pour over salad ingredients. Toss well.

Chill salad and serve.

1 SERVING	182 CALORIES	35 g CARBOHYDRATE
6 g PROTEIN	2 g FAT	0.7 g FIBER

Fresh Fruit Salad *(serves 4)*

½	cantaloupe
½	honeydew melon
1	grapefruit
1 tbsp	(15 ml) liquid honey
½ tsp	(2 ml) cinnamon
3 tbsp	(45 ml) plain yogurt
2 tbsp	(30 ml) sultana raisins

Cut cantaloupe and melon in sections; remove seeds and fibers. Cut off rind. Slice flesh in large pieces and place in bowl.

Cut grapefruit in half; scoop out flesh and add to bowl.

Mix in honey and cinnamon; toss fruit to coat evenly.

Add yogurt and mix well.

Sprinkle salad with raisins and serve.

1 SERVING	92 CALORIES	21 g CARBOHYDRATE
18 g PROTEIN	0 g FAT	0.6 g FIBER

Spicy Cheese Dip and Vegetables *(serves 4)*

¼ lb	(125 g) blue cheese
1 tbsp	(15 ml) chopped fresh chives
4 tbsp	(60 ml) sour cream
	few drops Tabasco and Worcestershire sauce
	pinch nutmeg
	white pepper
	zucchini sticks
	green and red pepper sticks
	sliced fresh mushrooms
	carrot sticks
	celery sticks
	several tomatoes

Place cheese in food processor; add chives, sour cream, Tabasco, Worcestershire and spices. Mix about 1 minute.

Arrange vegetables on large serving platter; set aside.

Cut tomatoes in half and scoop out insides. Place hollowed tomatoes alongside vegetables and fill with cheese dip.

Serve with cocktails.

1 SERVING	160 CALORIES	5 g CARBOHYDRATE
8 g PROTEIN	12 g FAT	0.3 g FIBER

Tomato Salad   *(serves 4)*

4	ripe tomatoes, sliced
½ lb	(250 g) fresh mushrooms, cleaned and sliced
2	green onions, sliced
2 tbsp	(30 ml) capers
6 tbsp	(90 ml) olive oil
3 tbsp	(45 ml) wine vinegar
1 tsp	(5 ml) chopped fresh tarragon
	lemon juice to taste
	salt and freshly ground pepper

Place tomatoes and mushrooms in large salad bowl. Add onions and toss; season well.

Add capers and sprinkle with oil; toss well.

Pour in vinegar and toss again.

Add tarragon and lemon juice. Correct seasoning and toss.

Serve on lettuce leaves and decorate with hard-boiled eggs and red onion rings.

1 SERVING	250 CALORIES	10 g CARBOHYDRATE
3 g PROTEIN	22 g FAT	1.3 g FIBER

Fresh Cucumber Salad   *(serves 4)*

2	large cucumbers
1	bunch radishes, washed and sliced
1	green onion, sliced
1	hard-boiled egg, sliced
1	recipe curry vinaigrette*
	salt and petter

Peel cucumbers and cut in two lengthwise. Remove seeds and slice.

Place cucumbers in bowl; add onion and radishes. Season generously and mix well.

Add sliced egg and curry vinaigrette; toss gently.

If desired, serve on lettuce leaves.

*See Curry Vinaigrette, page 58.

1 SERVING	149 CALORIES	5 g CARBOHYDRATE
3 g PROTEIN	13 g FAT	0 g FIBER

California Vegetable Salad   *(serves 4)*

½	cauliflower, in flowerets
½ lb	(250 g) green beans, ends trimmed
1 tbsp	(15 ml) vegetable oil
1	zucchini, sliced
1	red pepper, cut in large pieces
½	green pepper, cut in strips
1 tbsp	(15 ml) chopped hot pepper
½	red onion, cubed
1	garlic clove, smashed and chopped
¼ tsp	(1 ml) oregano
4 tbsp	(60 ml) olive oil
2 tbsp	(30 ml) wine vinegar
1 tbsp	(15 ml) chopped fresh parsley
2	hard-boiled eggs, coarsely chopped
	lettuce leaves, salt and pepper

Cook cauliflower and beans together in salted boiling water. Drain and set aside.
Arrange lettuce leaves on serving platter.

Heat oil in deep frying pan. When hot, add zucchini, peppers, onion and garlic; cover and cook 5 to 6 minutes over medium-high heat. Season well and stir occasionally.

Mix in cauliflower and beans; sprinkle with oregano. Cover and continue cooking 2 to 3 minutes.

Remove pan from burner and transfer vegetables to large bowl. Pour in olive oil and vinegar; toss until combined. Sprinkle with parsley.

Correct seasoning and spoon salad over arranged lettuce leaves. Decorate with hard-boiled eggs and serve immediately.

1 SERVING	250 CALORIES	14 g CARBOHYDRATE
8 g PROTEIN	18 g FAT	2.4 g FIBER

Fresh Mint Salad   *(serves 4)*

½ cup	(125 ml) mayonnaise
4	fresh mint leaves, washed, dried and finely chopped
2 tbsp	(30 ml) lemon juice
1 tbsp	(15 ml) wine vinegar
1	celery stalk, sliced
2	¼ in (0.65 cm) slices Black Forest ham, cut in strips
1	cooked chicken breast, cut in strips
½	cucumber, peeled, hollowed and sliced
3	small tomatoes, quartered
2	hard-boiled eggs, sliced
8	large stuffed green olives, sliced
⅓ lb	(150 g) cooked yellow beans several drops Tabasco sauce

Place mayonnaise, mint and lemon juice in small bowl; mix together well.

Add vinegar, Tabasco sauce, salt and pepper; mix again.

Place remaining ingredients in large salad bowl. Pour in mint dressing and toss until combined.

Serve.

1 SERVING	344 CALORIES	8 g CARBOHYDRATE
15 g PROTEIN	28 g FAT	1.1 g FIBER

Aiolli with Vegetables   *(serves 4)*

5	garlic cloves, peeled
2	egg yolks
1 cup	(250 ml) olive oil
¼ lb	(125 g) fresh mushrooms, cleaned and sliced
3	carrots, pared and cut in sticks
½ lb	(250 g) yellow beans, blanched
1	small zucchini, sliced in sticks
½ lb	(250 g) asparagus tips, blanched
	few drops Tabasco sauce
	few drops lemon juice
	salt and pepper

Place garlic in mortar and add Tabasco sauce; mash with pestle.

Add egg yolks and mix until incorporated. Season with pepper.

Add oil in steady stream while mixing constantly with electric hand beater.

Add some lemon juice and correct seasoning; set aside.

Place mushrooms in bowl and add some lemon juice; marinate 5 minutes.

Arrange vegetables on attractive platter and serve with aiolli.

See technique next page.

1 SERVING	611 CALORIES	14 g CARBOHYDRATE
6 g PROTEIN	59 g FAT	2 g FIBER

TECHNIQUE: AIOLLI WITH VEGETABLES

1 Place garlic in mortar and add Tabasco sauce. Mash with pestle.

2 Add egg yolks.

3 Mix until incorporated and season with pepper.

4 Add oil in steady stream while mixing constantly with electric hand beater.

Vegetable Chicken Salad *(serves 4)*

½	Iceberg lettuce, washed and dried
1 lb	(500 g) cooked asparagus, cut into 3
1	large cooked chicken breast, sliced
8 to 10	leaves Chinese cabbage, washed, dried and cut in strips
4	whole baby corn
4	artichoke hearts, drained and cut in 2
	salt and pepper
	dressing to taste*
	sliced tomatoes for decoration

Arrange lettuce leaves on large platter; set aside.

Place asparagus, chicken, cabbage, corn and artichoke hearts in large bowl. Toss to combine and season generously.

Pour dressing over salad ingredients and toss again.

Spoon salad onto arranged lettuce leaves and decorate with sliced tomatoes.

*Use your own or use Garlic Mustard Vinaigrette, page 58.

1 SERVING	372 CALORIES	16 g CARBOHYDRATE
23 g PROTEIN	24 g FAT	2.3 g FIBER

Boiled Beef Salad *(serves 4)*

1½ lb	(750 g) leftover boiled beef, cut in strips
½	red pepper, sliced
1 tbsp	(15 ml) chopped parsley
3 tbsp	(45 ml) chopped red onion
1	cucumber, peeled and sliced
1	hot cherry pepper, finely chopped
3 tbsp	(45 ml) wine vinegar
⅓ cup	(75 ml) sesame oil
	several drops Tabasco sauce
	salt and pepper

Place beef, parsley and vegetables in large bowl; season well. Mix until combined.

Pour in vinegar, oil and Tabasco sauce; mix well.

Refrigerate salad 30 minutes.

Correct seasoning, toss and serve.

1 SERVING	846 CALORIES	2 g CARBOHYDRATE
43 g PROTEIN	74 g FAT	0.4 g FIBER

Spinach Salad   *(serves 4)*

3	large bunches fresh spinach
3	hard-boiled eggs, sliced
1 cup	(250 ml) garlic croutons*
¼ lb	(125 g) Gruyère cheese, cut in strips
1 tbsp	(15 ml) chopped fresh chives
4	slices cooked ham, cut in strips
	salt and pepper

Wash spinach carefully in cold water. Dry leaves and place in large salad bowl.

Add sliced eggs and croutons; toss gently.

Add cheese and chives; toss again. Correct seasoning.

Arrange ham decoratively on top and pour in dressing. Serve.

*See Homemade Garlic Croutons, page 63.

Dressing

1 tbsp	(15 ml) Dijon mustard
1 tbsp	(15 ml) chopped fresh chives
½ cup	(125 ml) olive oil
	juice 1 large lemon
	salt and pepper

Place mustard and chives in bowl; season well. Mix with whisk and add lemon juice; mix again.

Add oil in thin stream while mixing constantly with whisk. Correct seasoning and set aside.

1 SERVING	546 CALORIES	5 g CARBOHYDRATE
19 g PROTEIN	50 g FAT	0.5 g FIBER

Garlic Mustard Vinaigrette

1 tbsp	(15 ml) strong mustard
1	egg yolk
1 tbsp	(15 ml) chopped fresh parsley
1	garlic clove, smashed and chopped
3 tbsp	(45 ml) lemon juice
⅓ cup	(75 ml) olive oil
	several drops Tabasco sauce
	several drops wine vinegar
	salt and pepper

Place mustard, egg yolk and parsley in bowl; mix together with whisk. Season generously.

Stir in garlic and lemon juice.

Incorporate oil in steady stream while mixing constantly with whisk.

Add Tabasco sauce and vinegar; correct seasoning.

Mix again and refrigerate until use.

1 SERVING	72 CALORIES	0 g CARBOHYDRATE
0 g PROTEIN	8 g FAT	0 g FIBER

Curry Vinaigrette

1 tsp	(5 ml) curry powder
3 tbsp	(45 ml) mayonnaise
¼ cup	(50 ml) light cream
	juice ½ lemon
	salt and pepper
	dash paprika

Place curry powder, paprika, salt and pepper in bowl; mix well.

Add lemon juice and mix with whisk.

Add mayonnaise and cream; mix until well incorporated. Correct seasoning. Refrigerate until use.

1 SERVING	54 CALORIES	0 g CARBOHYDRATE
0 g PROTEIN	6 g FAT	0 g FIBER

Club Salad   *(serves 4)*

2 tbsp	(30 ml) wine vinegar
1 tbsp	(15 ml) soya sauce
6 tbsp	(90 ml) olive oil
1	Boston lettuce, washed and dried
1	romaine lettuce, washed and dried
12	thin slices garlic sausage or salami, cut in strips
6 to 8	slices Gruyère cheese, cut in strips
¼ lb	(125 g) liver paté, cubed
4	hard-boiled eggs, sliced
	few drops lemon juice
	salt and pepper

Mix vinegar, soya sauce, and oil together; season and set aside.

Tear lettuce leaves into pieces; place in large bowl. Add remaining ingredients and toss.

Pour in dressing and mix well. Correct seasoning and serve.

Note: If desired, top with Homemade Garlic Croutons, page 63.

1 SERVING	527 CALORIES	8 g CARBOHYDRATE
18 g PROTEIN	47 g FAT	1.3 g FIBER

Caesar Salad *(serves 4)*

2	garlic cloves, smashed and chopped
1	shallot, chopped
1 tbsp	(15 ml) strong mustard
1 tbsp	(15 ml) chopped fresh parsley
3 tbsp	(45 ml) wine vinegar
1	egg yolk
¾ cup	(175 ml) olive oil
1	large romaine lettuce, washed and dried
6	anchovy filets, drained
¼ cup	(50 ml) grated parmesan cheese
	lemon juice
	salt and pepper
	homemade garlic croutons*

Place garlic, shallot, mustard and parsley in bowl; season well.

Pour in vinegar and mix well with whisk. Incorporate egg yolk.

Add oil, in steady stream, while mixing constantly with whisk. Correct seasoning and add few drops lemon juice.

Tear lettuce leaves into large pieces and place in large salad bowl. Toss in croutons and season well.

Add anchovy filets and pour in vinaigrette; toss until combined.

Sprinkle salad with cheese, toss and serve immediately.

* See Homemade Garlic Croutons, page 63.

1 SERVING	580 CALORIES	12 g CARBOHYDRATE
7 g PROTEIN	56 g FAT	0.6 g FIBER

TECHNIQUE: CAESAR SALAD

1 Place garlic, shallot, mustard and parsley in bowl; season well.

2 Pour in vinegar and mix well with whisk. Incorporate egg yolk.

3 Add oil, in steady stream, while mixing constantly with whisk. The dressing should thicken.

4 Begin placing salad ingredients in bowl.

Roquefort Salad *(serves 4)*

1	Boston lettuce, washed and dried
½	curly lettuce, washed and dried
½	cucumber, peeled and sliced
2	Italian tomatoes, sliced
¼	red onion, sliced
	some chopped parsley
	pine nuts (optional)
	sliced Roquefort cheese
	salt and pepper

Place lettuce, cucumber, tomatoes and onion in large bowl; toss.

Add parsley and season well. Pour in vinaigrette dressing and toss until combined.

Sprinkle with pine nuts and top with cheese before serving.

1 SERVING	459 CALORIES	8 g CARBOHYDRATE
10 g PROTEIN	43 g FAT	1.1 g FIBER

Vinaigrette

¼ lb	(125 g) Roquefort cheese, coarsely chopped
1 tbsp	(15 ml) chopped parsley
1	shallot, finely chopped
2 tbsp	(30 ml) wine vinegar
1 tbsp	(15 ml) strong mustard
8 tbsp	(120 ml) oil
3 tbsp	(45 ml) sour cream
	lemon juice
	salt and pepper

Place cheese in bowl. Add parsley, shallot and vinegar; season and mix very well.

Mix in mustard. Add oil in steady stream while mixing constantly with whisk.

Stir in sour cream and lemon juice to taste. Correct seasoning and set aside until use.

1 SERVING	72 CALORIES	0 g CARBOHYDRATE
0 g PROTEIN	8 g FAT	0 g FIBER

Homemade Garlic Croutons

3	thick slices French bread
3 tbsp	(45 ml) olive oil
2	garlic cloves, smashed and chopped

Toast bread until light brown. Cut bread in cubes and set aside.

Heat oil in frying pan. When hot, add bread cubes and cook 1 minute over high heat.

Stir in garlic and turn bread cubes over; continue cooking 1 minute.

Let cool and store in airtight container until use.

1 RECIPE	548 CALORIES	33 g CARBOHYDRATE
5 g PROTEIN	44 g FAT	0 g FIBER

Cold Vegetable Loaf *(serves 6 to 8)*

4	slices white bread, trimmed of crusts and cubed
½ cup	(125 ml) milk
2 tbsp	(30 ml) butter
2 cups	(500 ml) sliced carrots
1	green pepper, diced small
1	cucumber, diced small
2 cups	(500 ml) diced cauliflower
1	large celery stalk, diced small
1	garlic clove, smashed and chopped
¼ tsp	(1 ml) thyme
½ tsp	(2 ml) oregano
½ tsp	(2 ml) powdered ginger
½ tsp	(2 ml) basil
¼ tsp	(1 ml) nutmeg
6	eggs
	salt and pepper

Preheat oven to 375°F (190°C).

Generously grease 6 cup (1.5 L) loaf pan. Placed bread in small bowl and cover with milk; set aside.

Heat butter in large frying pan. Add carrots, green pepper, cucumber, cauliflower, celery and garlic; season well.

Sprinkle in herbs and cover pan; cook 8 to 10 minutes over medium heat.

Remove pan from heat and transfer vegetables to bowl of food processor. Blend until pureed. Add soaked bread and blend again.

Transfer mixture to bowl. Mix in eggs using whisk. Correct seasoning.

Pour mixture into loaf pan and cover with sheet of foil. Place mold in roasting pan containing 1 in (2.5 cm) hot water. Cook 1 hour and 10 minutes in oven.

20 minutes before end of cooking, remove foil. Cool slightly, then refrigerate 2 hours.

1 SERVING	153 CALORIES	11 g CARBOHYDRATE
7 g PROTEIN	9 g FAT	0.9 g FIBER

Puréed Potato Soup *(serves 4)*

2 tbsp	(30 ml) butter
1	small onion, peeled and finely chopped
2	small leeks, white section only, washed and finely chopped*
5	potatoes, peeled and sliced
¼ tsp	(1 ml) chervil
6 cups	(1.5 L) hot chicken stock
¼ cup	(50 ml) hot heavy cream
	pinch thyme
	salt and pepper

Heat butter in large saucepan. When hot, add onion and leeks; cover and cook 8 minutes over low heat.

Add potatoes and spices; season generously. Mix and continue cooking, covered, 3 minutes.

Add chicken stock and season well; bring to boil. Cook soup, uncovered, 30 to 35 minutes over low heat.

Purée soup in food processor or food mill; correct seasoning. Stir in cream and serve.

*See Farmer's Potage, page 76.

1 SERVING	190 CALORIES	22 g CARBOHYDRATE
3 g PROTEIN	10 g FAT	0.9 g FIBER

Cream of Green Split Peas   *(serves 4)*

4½ oz	(125 g) side bacon, diced
1	onion, peeled and diced
2	carrots, pared and diced
¼ tsp	(1 ml) thyme
½ tsp	(2 ml) sweet basil
1	clove
1	bay leaf
1 cup	(250 ml) green split peas
5 cups	(1.2 L) hot chicken stock
½ cup	(125 ml) hot light cream
	salt and pepper
	croutons

Cook bacon in saucepan 2 minutes.

Add onions; cover and continue cooking 2 minutes over medium heat.

Add carrots and all spices; cover and cook 2 minutes.

Add split peas and pour in chicken stock. Bring to boil and continue cooking, partly covered, 1½ hours over low heat.

Purée soup with cream in food processor. Serve with croutons.

Cream of Asparagus *(serves 4)*

4 tbsp	(60 ml) butter
1	onion, peeled and finely chopped
1 lb	(500 g) fresh asparagus, washed, pared and diced (reserve some tips for garnish)
5 tbsp	(75 ml) flour
4½ cups	(1.1 L) hot chicken stock
1 tbsp	(15 ml) chopped chives
½ cup	(125 ml) hot light cream
	dash celery seed
	dash nutmeg
	pinch paprika
	salt and pepper
	few drops lemon juice

Heat butter in saucepan. When hot, add onion; cover and cook 4 minutes over medium heat.

Add asparagus and stir; continue cooking, covered, 8 minutes. Stir several times during cooking process.

Mix in flour and cook 2 minutes, uncovered, over low heat.

Pour in chicken stock and add all spices. Season generously and bring to boil. Cook soup, uncovered, 25 minutes over medium heat.

Before soup is done, blanch reserved asparagus tips in boiling salted water with lemon juice added.

Purée soup with cream in food processor. Serve hot or cold and garnish with blanched asparagus tips.

1 SERVING	216 CALORIES	14 g CARBOHYDRATE
4 g PROTEIN	16 g FAT	0.6 g FIBER

Cream of Mushroom *(serves 4)*

4 tbsp	(60 ml) butter
1	onion, peeled and finely chopped
½ lb	(250 g) mushrooms, cleaned and thinly sliced
¼ tsp	(1 ml) basil
5 tbsp	(75 ml) flour
5 cups	(1.2 L) hot chicken stock
¼ cup	(50 ml) hot light cream
	juice ¼ lemon
	pinch celery seed
	dash paprika
	salt and pepper

Heat butter in saucepan. When hot, add onion; cover and cook 4 minutes over medium heat.

Add mushrooms, spices and lemon juice; mix well. Cover and cook 4 minutes over medium-high heat.

Mix in flour and cook 1 minute, uncovered, over low heat.

Pour in chicken stock and season; bring to boil. Cook soup, uncovered, 12 minutes over medium heat.

Purée soup with cream in food processor. Sprinkle with paprika and serve with croutons.

1 SERVING	190 CALORIES	13 g CARBOHYDRATE
3 g PROTEIN	14 g FAT	0.7 g FIBER

Versatile Cucumber Soup *(serves 4)*

3 tbsp	(45 ml) butter
2 tbsp	(30 ml) finely chopped onion
½	English cucumber, with skin, thinly sliced
1	cucumber, peeled, seeded and thinly sliced
¼ tsp	(1 ml) marjoram
¼ tsp	(1 ml) basil
4 tbsp	(60 ml) flour
4 cups	(1 L) hot chicken stock
1	egg yolk
¼ cup	(50 ml) heavy cream
	dash fennel seed
	salt and pepper

Heat butter in saucepan. When hot, add onion; cover and cook 2 minutes over medium heat.

Add cucumbers and season generously. Add herbs, cover and cook 5 to 6 minutes over low heat.

Mix in flour and cook 1 minute, uncovered, over low heat.

Pour in chicken stock, stir and bring to boil. Cook soup, uncovered, 16 minutes over low heat. Meanwhile, mix egg yolk with cream; set aside.

Put soup through sieve, using pestle or back of spoon, into another saucepan.

Replace saucepan on stove top over medium heat. Incorporate egg mixture; mixing constantly with whisk. Cook 2 minutes, whisking constantly!

Serve.

This soup is equally good served cold. In that case, do not include egg mixture.

1 SERVING	170 CALORIES	9 g CARBOHYDRATE
2 g PROTEIN	14 g FAT	0 g FIBER

Cream of Turnip *(serves 4)*

2 tbsp	(30 ml) butter
1	small onion, peeled and finely chopped
4	turnips, peeled and sliced
2	large potatoes, peeled and sliced
5½ cups	(1.3 L) cold chicken stock
¼ tsp	(1 ml) tarragon
1	bay leaf
¼ tsp	(1 ml) thyme
	salt and pepper

Heat butter in saucepan. When hot, add onion; cover and cook 2 to 3 minutes over medium heat.

Add turnips and potatoes; mix well. Continue cooking, covered, 2 minutes.

Add remaining ingredients and mix well. Season to taste and bring to boil. Cook soup, partly covered, 30 minutes over medium heat.

Purée soup in food processor or food mill. If desired, sprinkle with chopped parsley before serving.

This soup will keep 4 to 5 days in refrigerator, covered with sheet of wax paper.

1 SERVING	162 CALORIES	24 g CARBOHYDRATE
3 g PROTEIN	6 g FAT	1.4 g FIBER

Yellow Split Pea Soup *(serves 4)*

6	slices bacon
1	onion, peeled and diced
2	carrots, pared and diced
¼ tsp	(1 ml) oregano
½ tsp	(2 ml) chervil
1	clove
1	bay leaf
1 cup	(250 ml) yellow split peas
5 cups	(1.2 L) hot chicken stock
¼ cup	(50 ml) heavy cream, heated
	salt and pepper

Place bacon in saucepan and cook 2 minutes.

Add onions, cover and cook 2 minutes over medium heat.

Add carrots and all spices; cover and cook 2 minutes.

Add split peas and pour in chicken stock; bring to boil. Continue cooking, partly covered, 1½ hours over low heat.

Purée soup with cream in food processor.

1 SERVING	327 CALORIES	37 g CARBOHYDRATE
20 g PROTEIN	11 g FAT	1.4 g FIBER

Okra Soup *(serves 4)*

4 tbsp	(60 ml) butter
½	onion, peeled and finely chopped
1	celery stalk, thinly sliced
½ lb	(250 g) frozen whole okra, cooked
2 tbsp	(30 ml) pine nuts
¼ tsp	(1 ml) sweet basil
¼ tsp	(1 ml) marjoram
4 tbsp	(60 ml) flour
4 cups	(1 L) hot chicken stock
	pinch thyme
	few crushed red peppers
	salt and pepper

Heat butter in saucepan. When hot, add onion and celery; cover and cook 3 minutes over medium heat.

Add okra, pine nuts and spices; correct seasoning. Cover and continue cooking 4 minutes.

Mix in flour and cook, uncovered, 1 minute over low heat.

Pour in chicken stock and bring to boil. Cook, partly covered, 18 to 20 minutes over low heat. Stir occasionally.

Pass soup through sieve pressing okra with back of spoon.

Serve.

1 SERVING	186 CALORIES	12 g CARBOHYDRATE
3 g PROTEIN	14 g FAT	0.9 g FIBER

Corn Soup   *(serves 4 to 6)*

4 tbsp	(60 ml) butter
1	onion, peeled and chopped
12 oz	(350 g) package frozen corn kernels
4 tbsp	(60 ml) flour
4 cups	(1 L) hot chicken stock
¼ tsp	(1 ml) nutmeg
1 tsp	(5 ml) chopped chives
¼ cup	(50 ml) hot light cream
	salt and pepper

Heat butter in saucepan. When hot, add onion; cover and cook 4 minutes.

Add corn and continue cooking 2 minutes over medium heat.

Mix in flour; cook, uncovered, 1 minute over low heat.

Pour in chicken stock and season well. Add nutmeg and chives; bring to boil. Cook soup, uncovered, 18 minutes over medium heat. Stir occasionally.

About 2 minutes before and of cooking, mix in cream.

Serve hot.

1 SERVING	264 CALORIES	26 g CARBOHYDRATE
4 g PROTEIN	16 g FAT	0.6 g FIBER

Light Watercress Soup *(serves 4)*

2 tbsp	(30 ml) butter
½	onion, peeled and finely chopped
5	potatoes, peeled and thinly sliced
¼ tsp	(1 ml) tarragon
5 cups	(1.2 L) cold chicken stock
6	sprigs watercress, washed and chopped
	pinch thyme
	pinch rosemary
	salt and pepper

Heat butter in saucepan. When hot, add onion; cover and cook 2 minutes over medium heat.

Add potatoes and herbs; mix well. Continue cooking, covered, 3 minutes over low heat.

Pour in chicken stock, season and stir well. Bring to boil and continue cooking, partly covered, 5 minutes over medium heat.

Add watercress to soup; cook 5 minutes.

Serve soup with sandwiches if desired.

1 SERVING	146 CALORIES	20 g CARBOHYDRATE
3 g PROTEIN	6 g FAT	0.7 g FIBER

Cauliflower and Apple Soup *(serves 4)*

2 tbsp	(30 ml) butter
½	onion, peeled and finely chopped
1	medium cauliflower, coarsely chopped (reserve some for garnish)
3	potatoes, peeled and thinly sliced
1	apple, peeled, cored and sliced
1 tsp	(5 ml) chopped parsley
1 tsp	(5 ml) chopped chives
6 cups	(1.5 L) cold chicken stock
2 tbsp	(30 ml) plain yogurt
	few drops lemon juice
	few drops Tabasco sauce
	salt and pepper

Heat butter in saucepan. When hot, add onion; cover and cook 2 minutes over medium heat.

Add cauliflower, potatoes and apple; mix well. Sprinkle with parsley, chives, lemon juice and Tabasco sauce; season well. Cover and cook 8 minutes over medium heat. Stir twice during cooking.

Pour in chicken stock and mix well. Cook, partially covered, 20 minutes over medium-low heat.

Purée with yogurt in food processor. Correct seasoning and garnish with reserved cauliflower.

1 SERVING	140 CALORIES	22 g CARBOHYDRATE
4 g PROTEIN	6 g FAT	1.6 g FIBER

Farmer's Potage *(serves 4)*

1	leek, white section only
2 tbsp	(30 ml) butter
1	onion, peeled and diced
½ tsp	(2 ml) basil
1	bay leaf
1 tsp	(5 ml) chopped parsley
2	carrots, pared and diced
2	turnips, peeled and diced
2	potatoes, peeled and diced
6 cups	(1.5 L) cold chicken stock
	pinch thyme
	salt and pepper

Cut leek into four lengthwise sections leaving the bottom end connected about 1 in (2.5 cm). Wash well in cold water and thinly slice.

Heat butter in saucepan. When hot, add onion and leek; sprinkle with herbs. Cover and cook 4 minutes over medium heat.

Add remaining vegetables and season well. Stir, cover and continue cooking 3 minutes.

Pour in chicken stock and bring to boil. Cook soup, uncovered, 15 to 18 minutes over low heat.

Serve hot.

1 SERVING	130 CALORIES	17 g CARBOHYDRATE
2 g PROTEIN	6 g FAT	1.3 g FIBER

Tomato Soup with Egg Noodles   *(serves 4)*

2 tbsp	(30 ml) butter
1	onion, peeled and chopped
1	celery stalk, diced small
8	tomatoes, peeled and chopped
¼ tsp	(1 ml) oregano
1	garlic clove, smashed and chopped
4 cups	(1 L) hot chicken stock
2 oz	(60 g) fine egg noodles
	few crushed chili peppers
	salt and pepper

Heat butter in saucepan. When hot, add onion and celery; cover and cook 5 minutes over low heat.

Add tomatoes, oregano and garlic; season well. Mix and continue cooking, uncovered, 5 minutes over medium heat.

Pour in chicken stock and season with remaining spices. Mix well and bring to boil. Cook soup, partly covered, 1 hour over low heat.

Add noodles and stir; continue cooking 10 minutes.

Serve hot.

1 SERVING	195 CALORIES	27 g CARBOHYDRATE
6 g PROTEIN	7 g FAT	1.1 g FIBER

Creamy Lobster Soup   *(serves 4)*

2 tbsp	(30 ml) butter
1	onion, peeled and finely chopped
3	potatoes, peeled and diced small
2 cups	(500 ml) hot light cream
2 cups	(500 ml) hot milk
¼ lb	(125 g) mushrooms, cleaned and diced
1 lb	(500 g) frozen lobster meat, thawed and diced
1 tbsp	(15 ml) chopped chives
	salt and pepper
	dash paprika

Heat butter in saucepan. When hot, add onion; cover and cook 2 minutes over medium heat.

Add potatoes and season well; pour in cream and milk; season again.

Bring to boil and cook 10 minutes over low heat.

Add mushrooms and continue cooking 5 minutes.

Stir in lobster meat and simmer 3 to 4 minutes over low heat.

Sprinkle with chives and paprika before serving.

1 SERVING	520 CALORIES	24 g CARBOHYDRATE
34 g PROTEIN	32 g FAT	0.8 g FIBER

Old-Time Favorite Chicken Noodle Soup *(serves 4)*

1 tbsp	(15 ml) butter
2	celery stalks, diced
2	carrots, pared and diced
5 cups	(1.2 L) cold chicken stock
1½ cups	(375 ml) turret noodles
1½	chicken breasts, skinned, deboned and diced
	pinch basil
	salt and pepper

Heat butter in saucepan. When hot, add celery and carrots; cover and cook 3 minutes over medium heat.

Stir and pour in chicken stock; add basil and season. Bring to boil.

Add noodles and stir. Cook, partly covered, 12 minutes over medium heat, stirring twice.

Meanwhile, put chicken in separate saucepan. Cover with salted water and bring to boil; cook 4 minutes.

Drain chicken and immediately add to cooking soup.

Test noodles for desired firmness before serving. Adjust cooking time to taste.

1 SERVING	365 CALORIES	24 g CARBOHYDRATE
47 g PROTEIN	9 g FAT	0.6 g FIBER

Chicken and Rice Soup *(serves 4)*

1 tbsp	(15 ml) butter
1½ cups	(375 ml) diced celery
5 cups	(1.2 L) cold chicken stock
¼ tsp	(1 ml) savory
1 cup	(250 ml) long grain rice, rinsed and drained
1	large chicken breast, skinned, deboned and diced
	salt and pepper

Heat butter in saucepan. When hot, add celery; cover and cook 5 minutes over medium heat.

Pour in chicken stock and add savory; season well. Mix and bring to boil.

Add rice and stir; cook, partly covered, 10 minutes over medium-low heat.

Meanwhile, put chicken in separate saucepan. Cover with salted water and bring to boil; cook 4 minutes. Drain and set aside.

Add chicken to soup; continue cooking, partly covered, 8 minutes.

Serve.

Quick Chicken Soup *(serves 4)*

4 tbsp	(60 ml) butter
2 tbsp	(30 ml) chopped onion
5 tbsp	(75 ml) flour
4½ cups	(1.1 L) hot strong chicken stock
1	chicken breast, skinned, deboned and diced
	dash paprika
	pinch nutmeg
	salt and pepper
	chopped parsley

Heat butter in saucepan. When hot, add onion; cover and cook 2 minutes over medium heat.

Mix in flour and cook, uncovered, 1 minute over low heat.

Pour in chicken stock and add spices; mix well and bring to boil. Cook soup, uncovered, 18 minutes over low heat.

About 8 minutes before soup is done, put chicken in separate saucepan. Cover with salted water and bring to boil; cook 4 minutes.

Drain chicken and add to soup.

Sprinkle with chopped parsley and serve.

1 SERVING	287 CALORIES	8 g CARBOHYDRATE
30 g PROTEIN	15 g FAT	0 g FIBER

Quick Leftover Soup *(serves 4)*

2 tbsp	(30 ml) butter
2	celery stalks, thinly sliced on the bias
1	small cucumber, peeled and sliced on the bias
¼ lb	(125 g) mushrooms, cleaned and sliced
1	tomato, sliced
4 cups	(1 L) hot chicken stock
1 tsp	(5 ml) soya sauce
	few drops lemon juice
	salt and pepper

Heat butter in saucepan. When hot, add celery, cucumber and mushrooms; sprinkle with lemon juice and season. Cover and cook 5 minutes over medium heat.

Add tomato and pour in chicken stock; season well. Bring to boil and continue cooking 10 minutes, uncovered, over low heat.

Add soya sauce, mix and correct seasoning. Simmer several minutes over low heat.

Serve soup with toasted bread or crackers.

Lentil Soup *(serves 4)*

1 tbsp	(15 ml) butter
1	celery stalk, diced
½	onion, peeled and finely chopped
1	carrot, pared and diced
½ tsp	(2 ml) basil
¼ tsp	(1 ml) celery seed
1 tsp	(5 ml) chopped fresh parsley
1	garlic clove, smashed and chopped
1 cup	(250 ml) lentils
6 cups	(1.5 L) hot chicken stock
¼ cup	(50 ml) long grain rice, rinsed and drained
	salt and pepper

Heat butter in saucepan. When hot, add celery and onion; cover and cook 3 minutes over medium heat.

Add carrot, spices and garlic; cover and continue cooking 3 minutes.

Add lentils and chicken stock; season well and mix. Bring to boil. Cook soup, partially covered, 2 hours over low heat.

Sixteen minutes before end of cooking, add rice and finish cooking.

Serve.

1 SERVING	239 CALORIES	40 g CARBOHYDRATE
13 g PROTEIN	3 g FAT	2.3 g FIBER

Mixed Vegetable Soup   *(serves 4)*

1 tbsp	(15 ml) butter
½	onion, peeled and chopped
1	small leek, white section only, washed and thinly sliced*
¼ tsp	(1 ml) oregano
¼ tsp	(1 ml) thyme
¼ tsp	(1 ml) basil
1	bay leaf
1 tbsp	(15 ml) chopped chives
1	turnip, peeled and diced
¼	cabbage, thinly sliced
2	carrots, pared and diced
2	potatoes, peeled and diced
5 cups	(1.2 L) cold chicken stock
1 tbsp	(15 ml) soya sauce
1	tomato, peeled and diced
1 cup	(250 ml) diced mushrooms

Heat butter in saucepan. When hot, add onion and leek; cover and cook 3 minutes over medium heat.

Add herbs, turnip, cabbage, carrots and potatoes; season and mix well. Cover and cook 6 minutes over low heat.

Pour in chicken stock and soya sauce; stir. Season and bring to boil. Cook soup, partially covered, 13 minutes over low heat.

Stir in tomato and mushrooms; continue cooking 5 minutes.

Serve with sandwiches for lunch or with green salad for dinner.

* See Farmer's Potage, page 76.

1 SERVING	127 CALORIES	21 g CARBOHYDRATE
4 g PROTEIN	3 g FAT	1.8 g FIBER

Chicken Broth and Rice *(serves 4)*

2 tbsp	(30 ml) butter
½	onion, peeled and diced small
1	leek, white section only, washed and thinly sliced*
1	carrot, pared and diced small
1	turnip, peeled and diced small
½	celery stalk, diced small
6 cups	(1.5 L) cold chicken stock
½ cup	(125 ml) long grain rice, rinsed and drained
2 tbsp	(30 ml) pine nuts
	pinch thyme
	large pinch basil
	dash celery seed
	chopped parsley
	salt and pepper

Heat butter in saucepan. When hot, add onion and leek; sprinkle with herbs. Cover and cook 3 to 4 minutes over medium heat.

Add remaining vegetables and season well. Continue cooking, covered, 3 to 4 minutes.

Pour in chicken stock and bring to boil.

Add rice and pine nuts; mix well. Cook, partially covered, 16 minutes over medium heat.

If desired, sprinkle with parsley before serving.

* See Farmer's Potage, page 76.

1 SERVING	168 CALORIES	19 g CARBOHYDRATE
3 g PROTEIN	8 g FAT	0.7 g FIBER

Carrot Soup *(serves 4)*

2 tbsp	(30 ml) butter
½	onion, peeled and finely chopped
5	large carrots, pared and thinly sliced
½ tsp	(2 ml) chervil
1 tsp	(5 ml) chopped fresh dill
6 cups	(1.5 L) cold chicken stock
¾ cup	(175 ml) long grain rice, rinsed and drained
	pinch mint
	salt and pepper

Heat butter in saucepan. When hot, add onion; cover and cook 2 minutes over medium heat.

Add carrots and herbs; continue cooking, covered, 4 minutes over medium heat.

Pour in chicken stock, season and mix. Bring to boil.

Add rice, stir and partially cover. Cook 16 minutes over medium heat or until rice is cooked.

Serve with croutons.

1 SERVING	456 CALORIES	28 g CARBOHYDRATE
23 g PROTEIN	11 g FAT	1.5 g FIBER

Cream of Pumpkin Soup *(serves 6 to 8)*

½	small pumpkin
4 cups	(1 L) milk
4 cups	(1 L) water
3 tbsp	(45 ml) rice flour *or* all purpose flour
3 tbsp	(45 ml) butter
2-3 tbsp	(30-45 ml) sugar
	salt and pepper

Seed pumpkin, then pare off skin. Cut pumpkin flesh into 1 in (2.5 cm) pieces.

Place in a saucepan.

Pour enough water to cover; bring to a boil. Simmer until tender and very well done. Strain and purée.

Place puréed pumpkin in a saucepan.

Reserve ¼ cup (50 ml) of milk, then add remaining milk and water to saucepan.

Bring to a simmer.

Mix flour with reserved milk. Stir mixture into saucepan.

Continue to simmer over low heat for 15 to 20 minutes. Stir occasionally.

Blend in butter, season with salt and pepper.

To serve, pour soup into bowls and springkle a bit of sugar over each serving.

1 SERVING	119 CALORIES	20 g CARBOHYDRATE
3 g PROTEIN	3 g FAT	1.0 g FIBER

Vichyssoise   *(serves 4 to 6)*

2 tbsp	(30 ml) butter
1	large onion, peeled and sliced
1 tbsp	(15 ml) chopped fresh parsley
2	large leeks, (white section only) cut in four and washed
½ tsp	(2 ml) basil
¼ tsp	(1 ml) thyme
¼ tsp	(1 ml) tarragon
5	potatoes, peeled, washed and sliced
6 cups	(1.5 L) hot chicken stock
½ cup	(125 ml) whipping cream
1 tbsp	(15 ml) chopped fresh chives
	dash paprika
	salt and white pepper

Heat butter in large saucepan. When hot, add onion and parsley; cover and cook 3 minutes over medium-low heat.

Add leeks and herbs; mix well. Season with salt and pepper; cover and continue cooking 7 to 8 minutes over medium-low heat.

Mix in potatoes and cook 2 minutes.

Pour in chicken stock, stir and season to taste. Bring to boil and continue cooking, uncovered, 25 to 30 minutes.

When potatoes are cooked, pass soup through food mill. Cool and refrigerate.

Just before serving stir in cream and sprinkle with chives.

This soup will keep 3 to 4 days in refrigerator but do not add cream until serving.

See Technique next page.

1 SERVING	251 CALORIES	25 g CARBOHYDRATE
4 g PROTEIN	15 g FAT	0 g FIBER

TECHNIQUE: VICHYSSOISE

1 Add onion and parsley to hot butter; cover and cook 3 minutes over medium-low heat.

2 Add leeks and herbs; mix well. Season, cover and continue cooking 7 to 8 minutes. Mix in potatoes and cook 2 minutes.

3 Pour in chicken stock, stir and season. Bring to boil and continue cooking, uncovered, 25 to 30 minutes.

4 When potatoes are cooked, pass soup through food mill.

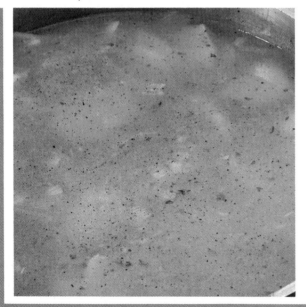

Mussel Soup à la Sonja   *(serves 4)*

3 lb	(1.4 kg) unshucked fresh mussels, bearded and scrubbed
1 tbsp	(15 ml) chopped parsley
¼ cup	(50 ml) dry white wine
2 tbsp	(30 ml) butter
1	medium onion, peeled and finely chopped
4	potatoes, peeled and diced
1	celery stalk, diced
2¼ cups	(550 ml) hot light cream
2¼ cups	(550 ml) hot milk
	juice ¼ lemon
	dash paprika
	salt and pepper

Place mussels, parsley, lemon juice and wine in saucepan. Add pepper; cover and cook until mussels open.

Shuck mussels and strain cooking liquid through cheesecloth; set both aside.

Heat butter in saucepan. When hot, add onion; cover and cook 3 minutes over medium heat.

Add potatoes and celery; season and pour in reserved cooking liquid. Cover and cook 6 to 7 minutes over low heat.

Mix cream with milk; incorporate into soup. Season and bring to boil. Cook, partially covered, 15 to 18 minutes over low heat.

Add mussels, paprika and correct seasoning. Simmer several minutes and serve.

1 SERVING	576 CALORIES	28 g CARBOHYDRATE
26 g PROTEIN	40 g FAT	1.3 g FIBER

Creamy Pearl Onion Soup   *(serves 4)*

4 tbsp	(60 ml) butter
3	medium onions, peeled and thinly sliced
5 tbsp	(75 ml) flour
5 cups	(1.2 L) hot chicken stock
¼ tsp	(1 ml) nutmeg
1	beaten egg yolk
¼ cup	(50 ml) heavy cream
1 cup	(250 ml) cooked pearl onions
	salt and pepper

Heat butter in saucepan. When hot, add sliced onions and season; cover and cook 10 minutes over low heat. Stir occasionally and avoid browning onions.

Mix in flour and cook, uncovered, 1 minute over low heat.

Add chicken stock and nutmeg; stir and bring to boil. Cook soup, partially covered, 18 to 20 minutes over low heat.

Mix egg yolk with cream; incorporate into soup. Simmer 2 minutes over low heat.

Add pearl onions, mix and simmer several minutes.

Serve hot with croutons.

1 SERVING	241 CALORIES	18 g CARBOHYDRATE
4 g PROTEIN	17 g FAT	0.8 g FIBER

Minestrone *(serves 4 to 6)*

2 tbsp	(30 ml) butter
1	onion, peeled and diced small
¼	cabbage, sliced
1	leek, white section only
¼ tsp	(1 ml) basil
¼ tsp	(1 ml) oregano
1	turnip, peeled and diced small
1	potato, peeled and diced small
1	carrot, pared and diced small
1	tomato, diced
1	garlic clove, smashed and chopped
1 tsp	(5 ml) chopped parsley
7 cups	(1.8 L) cold chicken stock
5½ oz	(160 ml) can tomato juice
2½ oz	(71 g) spaghetti
	pinch celery seed and thyme
	grated Parmesan cheese to taste

Heat butter in large saucepan. When hot, add onion, cabbage and leek; season well. Add basil, oregano and remaining spices. Cover and cook 4 minutes over low heat.

Add turnip, potato and carrot; mix well. Continue cooking, covered, 3 to 4 minutes over medium heat.

Add tomato, garlic, parsley; pour in chicken stock and tomato juice. Stir and bring to boil.

Season soup well and cook, uncovered, 5 minutes over low heat.

Break spaghetti in three and add. Season and continue cooking 12 minutes over medium heat or until pasta is cooked.

Sprinkle with cheese and serve.

1 SERVING	124 CALORIES	19 g CARBOHYDRATE
3 g PROTEIN	4 g FAT	0.9 g FIBER

Gazpacho *(serves 4)*

1	cucumber, peeled, seeded, and thinly sliced
5	garlic cloves, smashed and finely chopped
¼ tsp	(1 ml) cumin seeds
¼ cup	(50 ml) ground almonds
2 tbsp	(30 ml) wine vinegar
¼ cup	(50 ml) olive oil
3	tomatoes, peeled, seeded, and cut in two
6½ cups	(1.6 L) cold basic brown beef stock
	freshly ground pepper
½	green pepper, seeded and thinly sliced
1 tbsp	(15 ml) fresh parsley, finely chopped

Place cucumber slices in a mixing bowl. Sprinkle with salt and set aside for 30 minutes.

Drain.

Put garlic, cumin seeds, and almonds in blender. Mix.

Add vinegar and oil; blend again.

Add cucumbers and tomatoes; blend well. Thoroughly blend in beef stock. Season to taste.

Cover soup with buttered wax paper and refrigerate for at least 4 to 5 hours.

Pour the gazpacho into a soup tureen and garnish with the green pepper and parsley.

1 SERVING	157 CALORIES	8 g CARBOHYDRATE
2 g PROTEIN	13 g FAT	0 g FIBER

Onion Soup au Gratin   *(serves 4)*

2 tbsp	(30 ml) butter
4	white onions, peeled and sliced
1 tbsp	(15 ml) flour
¼ cup	(50 ml) dry white wine
5 cups	(1.2 L) cold beef stock
½ cup	(125 ml) grated Gruyère cheese
4	toasted rounds French bread
	pinch thyme
	pinch marjoram
	bay leaf
	several drops Tabasco
	salt and pepper

Heat butter in saucepan. When hot, add onions; cook, uncovered, 15 minutes over medium-low heat. Stir often scraping bottom of pan to brown onions.

Add flour and mix well; continue cooking 2 minutes over low heat.

Pour in wine and cook 2 minutes over high heat. Stir occasionally.

Pour in beef stock, season and add all herbs. Stir and bring to boil. Cook soup, partially covered, 20 minutes over low heat. Stir occasionally.

Place 2 tbsp (30 ml) cheese in botton of ovenproof soup bowls. Pour in soup and top with toasted bread. Cover with remaining cheese, adding more if necessary.

Broil in oven 5 minutes or until lightly browned 6 in (15 cm) from top element. Serve immediately.

1 SERVING	227 CALORIES	21 g CARBOHYDRATE
11 g PROTEIN	11 g FAT	0.6 g FIBER

Chilled Mexican Soup *(serves 4 to 6)*

4	fresh tomatoes, peeled and seeded, finely chopped
1 cup	(250 ml) celery, finely chopped
2	scallions, finely chopped
2	medium-size cucumbers, finely chopped
1	small hot green pepper, seeded and finely chopped*
4 cups	(1 L) chilled tomato juice
½ tsp	(2 ml) Tabasco sauce
1 tbsp	(15 ml) olive oil
	salt and lemon pepper

Place finely chopped ingredients in a bowl. Add Tabasco sauce, tomato juice, olive oil, salt, and lemon pepper. Mix well.

Chill several hours.

Serve soup in chilled bowls and garnish with a thin slice of lemon.

* Hot peppers have a very strong essence which can irritate your eyes. It is therefore important to wash your hands thoroughly with soap and warm water after handling.

1 SERVING	94 CALORIES	15 g CARBOHYDRATE
4 g PROTEIN	2 g FAT	1.4 g FIBER

Fish Chowder *(serves 4)*

⅓ lb	(150 g) halibut
⅓ lb	(150 g) haddock filets
⅓ lb	(150 g) scallops
2 tbsp	(30 ml) butter
2	celery stalks, diced
1	carrot, pared and diced
1	small leek, diced
4 cups	(1 L) warm fish stock
2	dry shallots, finely chopped
1 tbsp	(15 ml) fresh chopped parsley
2 cups	(500 ml) warm water
1 cup	(250 ml) croutons
	salt and pepper

Melt butter in medium-size saucepan. Add diced vegetables and shallots. Cook, covered, 4 to 5 minutes.

Stir in fish stock and bring to a simmer. Gently lower halibut and haddock into saucepan. Poach fish, while stock is barely simmering, 5 minutes.

Gently lift fish from saucepan and transfer to a bowl.

Drop scallops into saucepan and poach gently 2 minutes. Transfer scallops to bowl.

Flake fish with fork and add a bit of cooking liquid to keep it warm.

Add water to saucepan. Simmer 15 to 20 minutes.

Return fish and scallops to saucepan. Stir gently and season. Garnish chowder with croutons and parsley. Serve at once.

1 SERVING	203 CALORIES	13 g CARBOHYDRATE
22 g PROTEIN	7 g FAT	0.5 g FIBER

TECHNIQUE: FISH CHOWDER

1 Melt butter in saucepan. Add vegetables and shallots. Cook, covered, 4 to 5 minutes.

2 Stir in fish stock and bring to a simmer.

3 Gently lower halibut and haddock into saucepan. Poach fish, while stock is barely simmering, 5 minutes.

4 Gently lift fish from saucepan and transfer to a bowl.

TECHNIQUE: EGG TIPS

1 Before cooking bring eggs to room temperature, especially before placing in boiling water as cold shells will crack when immersed.

2 In the cooking preparation of eggs, break egg into small bowl before adding to the pan. This method will allow you to check if the egg is bad before it is too late!

3 Avoid using eggs with large blood spots.

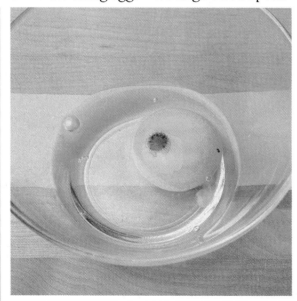

4 Butter and margarine are good fats for cooking eggs. The fat should be completely melted and foaming slightly before eggs are added.

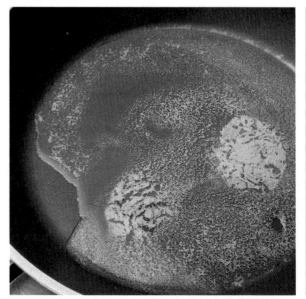

5 When using a fork to beat or mix eggs, tilt bowl towards you and keep wrist flat while moving fork in a large circular motion.

6 Though the yolk colour may differ, there is no nutritional difference between white and brown eggs.

7 One way to avoid confusion between raw and boiled eggs is to dent the shell of boiled egg. But if in doubt, spin the egg on a flat surface; if it rotates quickly, it has been boiled.

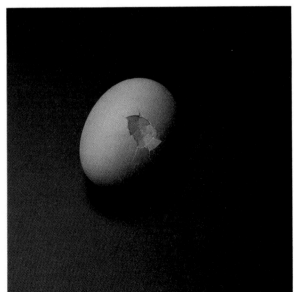

8 Perform the 'egg check' when you are uncertain of an egg's age. Simply place the egg in a glass of water and observe its position: the less the egg floats, the fresher it is.

TECHNIQUE: SCRAMBLED EGGS

1 If serving garnish with eggs, prepare in advance.

2 Break eggs into bowl and mix with whisk. Season with salt and pepper.

3 Heat butter or margarine in nonstick frying pan. Pour eggs into hot butter and cook over medium heat.

4 Start stirring rapidly with wooden utensil. Continue until they are scrambled. Continue to cook without stirring, but not too long, as they are best served soft and moist.

Scrambled Eggs with Vegetables *(serves 4)*

2 tbsp	(30 ml) butter
2 tbsp	(30 ml) chopped onion
½	celery stalk, diced small
1	small zucchini, diced small
¼ tsp	(1 ml) marjoram
1 tsp	(5 ml) curry powder
2	tomatoes, diced
8	eggs
¼ cup	(50 ml) 10% cream
	salt and pepper

Heat 1 tbsp (15 ml) butter in large frying pan.

When hot, add onion, celery and zucchini. Season and add spices; cook 3 minutes over medium heat.

Add tomatoes; continue cooking 3 to 4 minutes.

Meanwhile, break eggs into bowl and mix with whisk. Season well and pour in cream; mix again.

Heat remaining butter in large nonstick frying pan. When hot, pour in eggs and cook 1 minute over medium heat.

Stir eggs rapidly and cook 1 minute.

Add vegetables to eggs, mix and serve over toast.

1 SERVING	261 CALORIES	4 g CARBOHYDRATE
14 g PROTEIN	21 g FAT	0.8 g FIBER

Scrambled Eggs with Shrimp Sauce   *(serves 4)*

3 tbsp	(45 ml) butter
8	shrimp, shelled, deveined and cut in two
14 oz	(398 ml) can asparagus, drained and cut in two
8	beaten eggs, well seasoned
1 cup	(250 ml) shrimp sauce*, heated
	salt and pepper

Heat butter in large nonstick frying pan. When hot, add shrimp and season; cook 3 minutes over high heat.

Add asparagus, mix and pour in eggs. Stir rapidly and continue cooking 3 minutes over high heat.

Pour shrimp sauce into serving platter. Arrange eggs in sauce and serve with toasted French bread.

* See Shrimp Sauce, page 101.

1 SERVING	490 CALORIES	12 g CARBOHYDRATE
34 g PROTEIN	34 g FAT	0.5 g FIBER

TECHNIQUE: SHRIMP SAUCE

1 Add shrimp, shallot and parsley to hot butter; mix well, season and cook 4 minutes over medium heat.
Pour in wine and cook 2 minutes over high heat.

2 Add white sauce; season and add fennel and paprika. Stir and simmer 4 to 5 minutes over low heat.

Shrimp Sauce

1 tbsp	(15 ml) butter
½ lb	(250 g) shrimp, shelled, deveined and finely chopped
1	shallot, finely chopped
1 tsp	(5 ml) chopped parsley
¼ cup	(50 ml) dry white wine
1½ cups	(375 ml) quick white sauce*
¼ tsp	(1 ml) fennel
	dash paprika
	salt and pepper

Heat butter in small saucepan or frying pan. When hot, add shrimp, shallot and parsley; mix well.

Season with pepper and cook 4 minutes over medium heat.

Pour in wine and cook 2 minutes over high heat.

Add white sauce; season and add fennel and paprika. Stir and simmer 4 to 5 minutes over low heat.

This sauce serves well with many egg dishes.

*See Quick White Sauce, page 145.

1 SERVING	204 CALORIES	9 g CARBOHYDRATE
15 g PROTEIN	12 g FAT	0 g FIBER

Scrambled Eggs Cristoff   *(serves 4)*

4	frozen commercial vol-au-vent
2 tbsp	(30 ml) butter
¼ lb	(125 g) mushrooms. cleaned and diced
1	shallot, chopped
1 tsp	(5 ml) chopped chives
8	beaten eggs, well seasoned salt and pepper

Preheat oven 150°F (70°C).

Cook vol-au-vent as directed on package. Keep warm in oven until use.

Heat butter in nonstick frying pan. When hot, add mushrooms and shallot; season well. Cook 3 minutes over medium heat.

Add chives and pour in eggs; stir rapidly and continue cooking 3 minutes over high heat.

Fill vol-au-vent with egg mixture and garnish with parsley sprigs. Serve.

1 SERVING	394 CALORIES	16 g CARBOHYDRATE
15 g PROTEIN	30 g FAT	0.2 g FIBER

Scrambled Eggs with Crabmeat (serves 4)

2 tbsp	(30 ml) butter
5 oz	(142 g) can crabmeat, drained
1 tsp	(5 ml) chopped chives
½ cup	(125 ml) grated cheddar cheese
8	beaten eggs, well seasoned
	salt and pepper

Heat butter in nonstick frying pan. When hot, add crabmeat and chives; simmer 2 minutes over low heat. Season with salt and pepper.

Stir cheese into beaten eggs; pour over crabmeat in frying pan. Cook 3 minutes while stirring.

Serve.

1 SERVING	317 CALORIES	0 g CARBOHYDRATE
23 g PROTEIN	25 g FAT	0 g FIBER

Scrambled Eggs Archiduchesse (serves 4)

14 oz	(398ml) can asparagus, drained
2½ tbsp	(40 ml) butter
¼ cup	(50 ml) water
2	slices cooked ham, diced
¼ lb	(125 g) mushrooms, cleaned and diced
8	beaten eggs, well seasoned
	salt and pepper

Place asparagus in saucepan and add 1 tsp (5 ml) butter. Pour in water, cover and simmer over low heat until eggs are cooked.

Heat remaining butter in nonstick frying pan. When hot, add ham and mushrooms; season and cook 3 minutes.

Pour in eggs and continue cooking 1 minute over high heat.

Stir rapidly and continue cooking 1 minute.

Season and transfer eggs to serving platter. Garnish with asparagus and serve with toasted French bread.

1 SERVING	286 CALORIES	4 g CARBOHYDRATE
18 g PROTEIN	5 g FAT	0 g FIBER

Mexican Egg Brunch   *(serves 4)*

1 tbsp	(15 ml) olive oil
2	small hot peppers, seeded and chopped
1	onion, peeled and thinly sliced
3	large tomatoes, chopped
1 tsp	(5 ml) butter
8	beaten eggs, well seasoned
	salt and pepper

Heat oil in nonstick frying pan. When hot, add peppers and onion; cook 3 to 4 minutes over medium heat.

Add tomatoes, mix and season. Continue cooking 7 to 8 minutes over medium heat.

When mixture is cooked, remove from frying pan and keep hot in oven.

Clean pan, add butter and heat. When hot, pour in eggs. Scramble 2 to 3 minutes over medium heat.

Arrange eggs on serving platter and surround with tomato mixture.

1 SERVING	252 CALORIES	5 g CARBOHYDRATE
13 g PROTEIN	20 g FAT	1.2 g FIBER

Scrambled Eggs à la Moutarde   *(serves 4)*

8	eggs
¼ cup	(50 ml) grated Gruyère cheese
2 tbsp	(30 ml) French mustard
2 tbsp	(30 ml) butter
3	slices toasted white bread, cut into fingers
	salt and pepper
	chopped parsley or chives

Break eggs into bowl and mix with whisk. Season with salt and pepper.

Add cheese and mustard; mix again.

Heat butter in nonstick frying pan. When hot, pour in eggs. Stir rapidly and cook 3 to 4 minutes over high heat.

Serve eggs with bread fingers. Sprinkle with chopped parsley or chopped chives.

See Technique next page.

1 SERVING	307 CALORIES	9 g CARBOHYDRATE
16 g PROTEIN	23 g FAT	0 g FIBER

TECHNIQUE:

1 Break eggs into bowl.

2 Mix with whisk and season with salt and pepper. Add cheese and mustard; mix again.

3 Cook eggs in hot butter 3 to 4 minutes; stir rapidly.

4 Serve eggs with bread fingers. Sprinkle with chopped parsley or chives.

TECHNIQUE: OMELET

1 Break eggs into bowl and beat with fork. Season with salt and pepper. Heat butter in nonstick frying pan or omelet pan.

2 When butter is hot, pour in eggs and cook but do not stir.

3 When eggs have settled, stir rapidly with wooden utensil. Gently pat omelet back into place and continue cooking without stirring.

4 Add filling.

5 Roll omelet away from you while tilting pan.

6 Tip pan up against plate and allow omelet to slide out.

Plain Omelet   *(serves 2)*

5 to 6	eggs
1 tbsp	(15 ml) water or 10% cream*
1 tbsp	(15 ml) butter
	salt and pepper

Break eggs into bowl and beat with fork; season well. Add cream and mix.

Heat butter in nonstick frying pan or omelet pan.

When hot, pour in eggs and cook 1 minute over high heat.

Stir rapidly with wooden utensil. Roll omelet (see technique) and serve.

*If you use water, the omelet will be lighter than if cream is used.

1 SERVING	324 CALORIES	0 g CARBOHYDRATE
18 g PROTEIN	28 g FAT	0 g FIBER

Salsify Omelet *(serves 2)*

2 tbsp	(30 ml) butter
1	cooked carrot, diced
3	canned salsify, diced large
5	eggs
	salt and pepper

Heat 1 tbsp (15 ml) butter in small saucepan. When hot, add vegetables and season with pepper. Cover and simmer 3 minutes over low heat.

Break eggs into bowl and beat with fork; season well.

Heat remaining butter in nonstick frying pan. When hot, pour in eggs and cook 1 minute over high heat.

Stir eggs rapidly and continue cooking 1 minute.

Add half of filling. Roll omelet (see technique) and continue cooking 30 seconds.

Serve with remaining filling and, if desired, assorted vegetables.

1 SERVING	385 CALORIES	14 g CARBOHYDRATE
17 g PROTEIN	29 g FAT	0.5 g FIBER

Shrimp Omelet   *(serves 2)*

2 tbsp	(30 ml) butter
1 tbsp	(15 ml) chopped onion
¼ lb	(125 g) cooked shrimp, deveined and sliced in half
1 cup	(250 ml) chopped tomatoes (if canned, drain)
¼ tsp	(1 ml) fennel
5	eggs
	few drops Tabasco sauce
	lemon juice
	salt and pepper

Heat 1 tbsp (15 ml) butter in frying pan.

When hot, add onion and shrimp; season well. Cook 2 minutes over medium heat.

Add tomatoes, fennel, Tabasco sauce and lemon juice. Season, mix and simmer 5 minutes over low heat.

Break eggs into bowl and beat with fork; season well.

Heat remaining butter in nonstick frying pan.

When hot, pour in eggs and cook 1 minute over high heat.

Stir eggs rapidly and continue cooking 1 minute.

Add shrimp filling and fold omelet in half. Continue cooking 10 seconds and serve with cauliflower.

1 SERVING	298 CALORIES	6 g CARBOHYDRATE
28 g PROTEIN	18 g FAT	0.9 g FIBER

Omelet Lyonnaise *(serves 2)*

2 tbsp	(30 ml) butter
1	small onion, peeled and thinly sliced
¼	apple, cored, peeled and thinly sliced
5	eggs
½ tsp	(2 ml) chopped parsley
	salt and pepper

Heat 1 tbsp (15 ml) butter in nonstick frying pan.

When hot, add onion and season. Cook 4 minutes over medium heat.

Add apples, mix and continue cooking 2 minutes. Meanwhile, break eggs into bowl and beat with fork; season well.

Transfer onion filling to small bowl and set aside. Heat remaining butter in frying pan.

When hot, pour in eggs and cook 1 minute over high heat. Stir eggs rapidly and continue cooking 1 minute.

Add half of onion filling. Roll omelet (see technique) and continue cooking 30 seconds.

Place omelet on serving platter and garnish with remaining onion filling. Sprinkle with parsley and serve.

1 SERVING	353 CALORIES	7 g CARBOHYDRATE
16 g PROTEIN	29 g FAT	0.4 g FIBER

Quick Artichoke Omelet *(serves 2)*

2 tbsp	(30 ml) butter
4	canned artichoke hearts, cut in half
12	stuffed green olives
8	mushrooms, cleaned and cut in half
5	eggs
	salt and pepper

Heat 1 tbsp (15 ml) butter in frying pan.

When hot, add artichokes, olives and mushrooms. Cover and cook 3 minutes. Season to taste.

Break eggs into bowl and beat with fork; season well.

Heat remaining butter in nonstick frying pan or omelet pan. When hot, pour in eggs and cook 1 minute over high heat. Stir eggs rapidly and continue cooking 1 minute.

Add half of filling. Roll omelet (see technique) and continue cooking 30 seconds.

Place omelet on serving platter and garnish with remaining artichoke mixture.

1 SERVING	484 CALORIES	11 g CARBOHYDRATE
20 g PROTEIN	40 g FAT	1.0 g FIBER

Last Minute Omelet *(serves 2)*

2 tbsp	(30 ml) butter
1	onion, peeled and thinly sliced
¼	red pepper, thinly sliced
2	cherry tomatoes, chopped
5	eggs
	salt and pepper

Heat 1 tbsp (15 ml) butter in frying pan.

When hot, add onion and cook 3 minutes over high heat.

Add red pepper and tomatoes; season and cook 3 minutes over medium heat. Meanwhile break eggs into bowl and beat with fork; season well.

Heat remaining butter in nonstick frying pan. When hot, pour in eggs and cook 1 minute over high heat. Stir eggs rapidly and continue cooking 1 minute.

Add half of filling. Roll omelet (see technique) and continue cooking 30 seconds.

Serve with remaining filling and vegetables.

1 SERVING	349 CALORIES	5 g CARBOHYDRATE
17 g PROTEIN	29 g FAT	0.7 g FIBER

Ham Omelet and Maple Syrup   *(serves 2)*

2 tbsp	(30 ml) butter
1	small onion, peeled and chopped
½	slice cooked ham, diced large
½	apple, cored, peeled and cubed
1 tbsp	(15 ml) maple syrup
5	eggs
	salt and pepper

Heat 1 tbsp (15 ml) butter in nonstick frying pan.

When hot, add onion, ham and apple. Season and cook 3 to 4 minutes over medium heat.

Add maple syrup, mix and continue cooking 2 minutes. Set aside.

Break eggs into bowl and beat with fork; season well.

Heat remaining butter in nonstick frying pan or omelet pan.

When hot, pour in eggs and cook 1 minute over high heat.

Stir eggs rapidly and continue cooking 1 minute.

Add half of filling. Roll omelet (see technique) and continue cooking 30 seconds.

Serve with remaining filling and assorted vegetables.

1 SERVING	414 CALORIES	8 g CARBOHYDRATE
28 g PROTEIN	30 g FAT	0.2 g FIBER

Farmer's Omelet *(serves 2)*

2 tbsp	(30 ml) butter
1 tbsp	(15 ml) finely chopped onion
2	cooked sausages, diced
4	slices cooked bacon, diced
20	mushrooms, cleaned and diced
6	eggs
	chopped chives to taste
	salt and pepper

Heat 1 tbsp (15 ml) butter in frying pan.

When hot, add onion, sausages and bacon; cook 2 minutes.

Add mushrooms, chives and season; cook 3 minutes over medium heat. Set aside.

Heat remaining butter in nonstick frying pan. Meanwhile, break eggs into bowl and beat with fork; season well.

Pour eggs into pan and cook 1 minute over high heat.

Stir rapidly; continue to cook 1 minute.

Add filling and cook 1 minute.

Fold omelet (see technique) and serve.

1 SERVING	557 CALORIES	8 g CARBOHYDRATE
39 g PROTEIN	41 g FAT	1.3 g FIBER

Quick Cheese Omelet *(serves 2)*

5	eggs
1 tbsp	(15 ml) butter
¼ cup	(50 ml) grated cheddar cheese
	salt and pepper

Break eggs into bowl and beat with fork; season well.

Heat butter in nonstick frying pan or omelet pan.

When hot, pour in eggs and cook 1 minute over high heat. Meanwhile, set oven at grill (broil).

Stir eggs rapidly and add ¾ of cheese. Roll omelet (see technique) and continue cooking 1 minute.

Place omelet on ovenproof serving platter and sprinkle with remaining cheese. Broil 2 minutes

Serve with vegetables.

1 SERVING	324 CALORIES	0 g CARBOHYDRATE
18 g PROTEIN	28 g FAT	0 g FIBER

Omelet, Nouvelle Cuisine *(serves 4)*

1	large carrot, peeled and diced
½	zucchini, diced
1 cup	(250 ml) broccoli flowerets
½ cup	(125 ml) 10% cream
¼ tsp	(1 ml) nutmeg
1 tsp	(5 ml) cornstarch
2 tbsp	(30 ml) cold water
8	eggs
1 tbsp	(15 ml) butter
	pinch powdered clove
	few drops Tabasco sauce
	salt and pepper

Place carrot in saucepan containing 2 cups (500 ml) salted water. Cover and cook 4 minutes over medium heat.

Add zucchini; continue cooking 3 minutes.

Add broccoli and cook 3 minutes.

Drain vegetables well and replace in saucepan. Pour in cream, add spices and few drops Tabasco sauce. Cook 1 minute.

Mix cornstarch with water; stir into vegetables. Simmer several minutes.

Break eggs into bowl and beat with fork; season well.

Heat butter in large nonstick pan.

When hot, pour in eggs and cook 1 minute over high heat.

Stir eggs rapidly; continue cooking 1 to 2 minutes.

Add vegetable filling to omelet, fold in two and cook 1 minute.

1 SERVING	237 CALORIES	7 g CARBOHYDRATE
14 g PROTEIN	17 g FAT	0.9 g FIBER

Mushroom Omelet *(serves 2)*

3 tbsp	(45 ml) butter
1 tbsp	(15 ml) chopped onion
¼ lb	(125 g) fresh mushrooms, cleaned and sliced
1 tbsp	(15 ml) chopped red pimento
5	eggs
1 tbsp	(15 ml) chopped parsley
	salt and pepper

Heat 2 tbsp (30 ml) butter in nonstick frying pan.

When hot, add onion and mushrooms; season well. Cook 3 minutes over high heat.

Stir in pimento; continue cooking 1 minute. Set aside.

Break eggs into bowl and beat with fork; season well and add parsley.

Heat remaining butter in second nonstick frying pan or omelet pan. When hot, pour in eggs and cook 1 minute over high heat.

Stir eggs rapidly and add mushroom filling; cook 1 to 2 minutes.

Roll omelet (see technique) and serve on platter. Accompany with assorted vegetables.

1 SERVING	386 CALORIES	3 g CARBOHYDRATE
17 g PROTEIN	34 g FAT	0.5 g FIBER

Spanish Omelet   *(serves 4)*

1 tbsp	(15 ml) vegetable oil
2	onions, peeled and sliced
1	garlic clove, smashed and chopped
2	tomatoes, diced
1	red pepper, thinly sliced
1 tsp	(5 ml) chopped chives
8	eggs
1 tbsp	(15 ml) butter
	dash paprika
	salt and pepper

Heat oil in large nonstick frying pan.

When hot, add onions and cook 4 to 5 minutes over medium heat. Mix once during cooking process.

Add garlic, tomatoes and red pepper; season with paprika, salt and pepper. Continue cooking 5 minutes.

Sprinkle in chives and cook 1 minute; set aside and keep hot.

Break eggs into bowl and beat with fork; season well.

Heat butter in another large nonstick frying pan. When hot, pour in eggs and cook 1 minute over high heat.

Stir eggs rapidly and continue cooking 2 minutes.

Spread vegetables over omelet and broil 2 minutes. Serve.

1 SERVING	281 CALORIES	9 g CARBOHYDRATE
14 g PROTEIN	21 g FAT	1.5 g FIBER

Flat Zucchini Omelet   *(serves 2)*

2 tbsp	(30 ml) butter
½	zucchini, cut into julienne
1	small chile pepper, seeded and chopped
6	beaten eggs, well seasoned
	dash paprika
	salt and pepper

Heat 1 tbsp (15 ml) butter in nonstick frying pan. When hot, add zucchini and season. Sprinkle in dash paprika.

Add chile pepper and cook 3 minutes.

Remove frying pan from heat and transfer mixture to bowl containing beaten eggs.

Add remaining butter to pan. When hot, pour in egg mixture. Cook 2 minutes over medium heat. Do not stir!

Flip omelet over with spatula; continue to cook 2 minutes.

Serve.

See Technique next page.

1 SERVING	384 CALORIES	5 g CARBOHYDRATE
19 g PROTEIN	32 g FAT	0.6 g FIBER

TECHNIQUE: FLAT ZUCCHINI OMELET

1 Add zucchini to hot butter; season and sprinkle with paprika.
Add chile pepper and cook 3 minutes.

2 Transfer zucchini mixture to bowl containing beaten eggs.

3 Pour egg mixture into hot butter; cook 2 minutes over medium heat. Do not stir.
Flip omelet and finish cooking 2 minutes.

TECHNIQUE: OMELET MOUSSELINE

1 Place egg yolks in bowl.

2 Add 35% cream.

3 Mix very well with whisk.

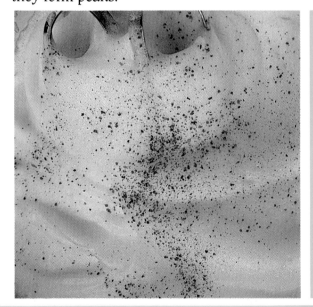

4 In separate bowl, beat egg whites until they form peaks.

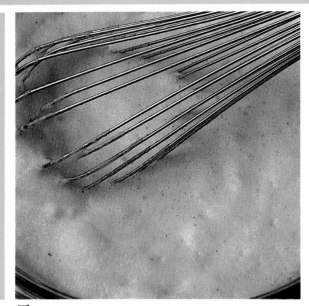

5 Fold egg whites into yolks.

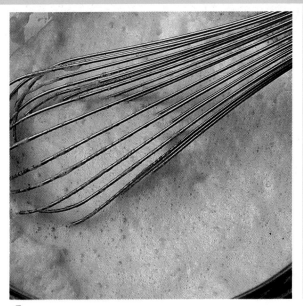

6 Mix very well with whisk.

7 The omelet mousseline after cooking.

Omelet Soufflé with Pears   *(serves 2)*

2 tbsp	(30 ml) butter
1 tbsp	(15 ml) granulated sugar
1	large ripe pear, peeled, cored and thinly sliced
4	egg yolks
2 tbsp	(30 ml) 10% cream
4	egg whites, beaten stiff
1 tbsp	(15 ml) icing sugar
	juice 1 orange

Heat 1 tbsp (15 ml) butter in small saucepan or frying pan. Add granulated sugar and cook over medium heat. Mix constantly until sugar turns golden brown. Add orange juice and continue mixing. Cook about 30 seconds or until golden brown.

Add pear, mix and cook 30 seconds. Remove pan from heat and set aside. Place egg yolks in bowl and add cream; mix well.

Fold in beaten egg whites; incorporate well.

Heat remaining butter in nonstick frying pan. When hot, pour in eggs and cook 2 to 3 minutes. Mix twice during cooking process.

When top of omelet is nearly cooked, flip omelet over. Spread pear mixture over eggs and fold in half. Continue cooking 10 seconds.

Transfer omelet to ovenproof platter and sprinkle with icing sugar. Grill (broil) 1 minute.

See Technique next page.

1 SERVING	398 CALORIES	28 g CARBOHYDRATE
13 g PROTEIN	26 g FAT	0.8 g FIBER

TECHNIQUE

1 Add granulated sugar to hot butter and cook over medium heat; mix constantly.

2 The sugar is beginning to turn golden brown.

3 Add orange juice and continue mixing.

4 Cook about 30 seconds or until golden brown.

Continued next page.

5 Add pear, stir and cook 30 seconds. Remove pan from heat and set aside.

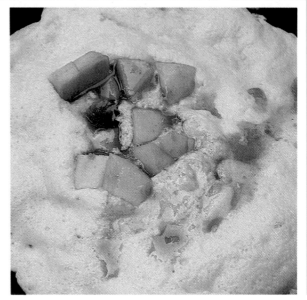

6 When top of omelet is nearly cooked, flip omelet over. Spread pear mixture over eggs. Fold, continue cooking 10 seconds and grill (broil).

Omelet Soufflé with Jam   *(serves 2)*

4	egg yolks
2 tbsp	(30 ml) 10% cream
4	egg whites, beaten stiff
1 tbsp	(15 ml) butter
2 tbsp	(30 ml) prepared jam
1 tbsp	(15 ml) icing sugar

Place egg yolks in bowl and add cream; mix well.

Fold in beaten egg whites; incorporate well.

Heat butter in nonstick frying pan. When hot, pour in eggs and cook 2 to 3 minutes. Mix twice during cooking process.

When top of omelet is nearly cooked, flip omelet over. Spread jam over eggs and fold in half. Continue cooking 10 seconds.

Transfer omelet to ovenproof platter and sprinkle with icing sugar. Grill (broil) 1 minute in oven or until lightly browned.

1 SERVING	309 CALORIES	18 g CARBOHYDRATE
12 g PROTEIN	21 g FAT	0 g FIBER

Weekend Omelet Soufflé   *(serves 2)*

½ cup	(125 ml) defrosted strawberries
2 tbsp	(30 ml) granulated sugar
1 tsp	(5 ml) chopped lemon rind
4	egg yolks
2 tbsp	(30 ml) 10% cream
4	egg whites, beaten stiff
1 tbsp	(15 ml) butter
1 tbsp	(15 ml) icing sugar

Place strawberries in small saucepan; add granulated sugar and lemon rind. Cook 3 to 4 minutes over medium heat.

Place egg yolks in bowl and add cream; mix well. Fold in beaten egg whites; incorporate well.

Heat butter in nonstick frying pan. When hot, pour in eggs and cook 2 to 3 minutes. Mix twice during cooking process.

When top of omelet is nearly cooked, flip omelet over. Spread half of strawberries over eggs and fold in half. Continue cooking 10 seconds.

Transfer omelet to ovenproof platter and sprinkle with icing sugar. Top with remaining strawberries and grill (broil) 1 minute in oven or until lightly browned.

1 SERVING	357 CALORIES	30 g CARBOHYDRATE
12 g PROTEIN	21 g FAT	0.4 g FIBER

Omelet Sandwich *(serves 4)*

3 tbsp	(45 ml) butter
1	onion, peeled and chopped
1 tsp	(5 ml) chopped parsley
½	zucchini, sliced
1	Chinese eggplant, sliced
1	garlic clove, smashed and chopped
2	tomatoes, coarsely chopped
¼ tsp	(1 ml) basil
¼ tsp	(1 ml) oregano
½ cup	(125 ml) grated parmesan cheese
2	slices toasted bread
6	beaten eggs, well seasoned
¼ cup	(50 ml) grated Gruyère cheese
	salt and pepper

Heat 1½ tbsp (25 ml) butter in frying pan. When hot, add onion and parsley. Cover and cook 3 minutes over low heat. Add zucchini, eggplant and garlic; season well. Cover and continue cooking 6 to 7 minutes.

Add tomatoes and spices; mix well. Continue cooking, uncovered, 6 to 7 minutes. Add half of parmesan cheese and cook 2 minutes.

Cut toasted bread into sticks.

Heat half of remaining butter in nonstick frying pan. When hot, pour in half of beaten eggs. Cook omelet 2 minutes each side.

Set omelet on ovenproof plate and arrange bread sticks around outside. Trim if necessary.

Place filling in centre of omelet. Sprinkle with remaining parmesan cheese. Use remaining butter and prepare second flat omelet.

Place omelet over filling and sprinkle top with Gruyère cheese. Grill (broil) 3 minutes in oven.

1 SERVING	340 CALORIES	14 g CARBOHYDRATE
17 g PROTEIN	24 g FAT	1.9 g FIBER

TECHNIQUE: OMELET SANDWICH

1 Add onion and parsley to hot butter. Cover and cook 3 minutes over low heat.

2 Add zucchini, eggplant and garlic; season well. Cover and continue cooking 6 to 7 minutes.

3 Add tomatoes and spices; mix well. Continue cooking, uncovered, 6 to 7 minutes.

4 Add half of parmesan cheese and cook 2 minutes.

Continued next page.

129

5 Cut toasted bread into sticks. Prepare flat omelet and arrange bread sticks around outside. Trim if necessary.

6 Place filling in centre of omelet. Sprinkle with remaining parmesan cheese.

7 Prepare second flat omelet and place over filling.

8 Sprinkle top with Gruyère cheese. Grill (broil) 3 minutes in oven.

TECHNIQUE: FRIED EGGS

1 Heat butter or margarine in nonstick pan. The butter must be hot before eggs are added.

2 Cook eggs over low heat to avoid burning the butter or margarine.

3 To cook the egg yolk without turning the egg over, baste with the hot butter. If it is difficult to collect the fat, melt some extra butter in a separate pan.

4 By covering the pan with a lid, the heat will be reflected towards the yolks and will cook them further.

Eggs in Vegetables   *(serves 4)*

1 tbsp	(15 ml) vegetable oil
1 tsp	(5 ml) butter
1	onion, peeled and finely chopped
1 tsp	(5 ml) chopped fresh parsley
2	garlic cloves, smashed and chopped
1	small eggplant, diced
28 oz	(796 ml) can tomatoes, drained and chopped
¼ tsp	(1 ml) oregano
¼ cup	(50 ml) grated Gruyère cheese
4	eggs
	salt and pepper
	dash crushed chillies

Preheat oven to 350°F (180°C).

Heat oil and butter in large frying pan.

When hot, add onion, parsley and garlic; cook 3 minutes over medium heat.

Stir in eggplant and season well; cook 4 to 5 minutes.

Cover and continue cooking eggplant 14 minutes over low heat.

Add tomatoes, herbs and spices and season. Continue cooking, uncovered, for 4 to 5 minutes.

Add cheese and mix well.

Break eggs into pan over vegetables. Cook 10 to 12 minutes in oven.

Serve with garlic bread.

1 SERVING	236 CALORIES	12 g CARBOHYDRATE
11 g PROTEIN	16 g FAT	1.4 g FIBER

TECHNIQUE: EGGS IN VEGETABLES

1 Add onion, parsley and garlic to hot fat; cook 3 minutes over medium heat.

2 Add eggplant and season well; cook 4 to 5 minutes.

3 Cover and continue cooking eggplant 14 minutes over low heat.

4 Add tomatoes, spices and season. Continue cooking, uncovered, for 4 to 5 minutes.

Continued next page.

5 Add cheese and mix well.

6 Break eggs into pan over vegetables. Cook 10 to 12 minutes in oven.

Fried Eggs and Garlic Bread   *(serves 4)*

4	slices French bread
1 tbsp	(15 ml) butter
4	large eggs
½ cup	(125 ml) grated Gruyère cheese
	garlic butter
	salt and pepper

Toast bread and spread slices with garlic butter to taste. Place on ovenproof plate and set aside.

Heat butter in nonstick frying pan. When hot, add eggs and cook 3 minutes over medium heat. For those who prefer yolk cooked, flip eggs and continue frying 1 minute.

Remove eggs and set on bread slices. Sprinkle with cheese and season generously. Grill (broil) 3 minutes.

Serve.

1 SERVING	272 CALORIES	11 g CARBOHYDRATE
12 g PROTEIN	20 g FAT	0 g FIBER

TECHNIQUE: EGGS IN COCOTTE

1 Place cocotte dishes or ramekins in pan containing water heated to the boiling point. Add butter to each dish.

2 Add eggs to melted butter and reduce heat so that water simmers. Pour in cream and finish cooking in oven.

Eggs in Cocotte, the Easy Way *(serves 4)*

2 tbsp	(30 ml) butter
4	eggs
⅓ cup	(75 ml) 35% cream
1 tbsp	(15 ml) chopped chives
	salt and pepper

Fill large pan with 1 in (2.5 cm) hot water and place on stove top.

Butter four ramekins and add eggs to dishes. Be careful not to break yolks. Season well and add cream.

Place ramekins in pan and cover. Bring water to boil and cook 2 to 3 minutes.

Sprinkle with chives and serve with toast.

1 SERVING	204 CALORIES	0 g CARBOHYDRATE
6 g PROTEIN	20 g FAT	0 g FIBER

TECHNIQUE: POACHED EGGS

1 Place water, a bit of white vinegar, and salt in large saucepan; bring to boil.

2 Break first egg into small bowl.

3 Reduce heat so that water simmers. Carefully slide eggs, one at a time, into the water. Cook over medium heat for 3 to 4 minutes. The vinegar should encourage the whites to curl up around the yolks.

4 To remove eggs use slotted spoon and then drain.

Poached Eggs Charron *(serves 4)*

2	English muffins, cut in two
4	slices cooked bacon, chopped
4	poached eggs
¾ cup	(175 ml) hollandaise sauce*
2 tbsp	(30 ml) warm tomato purée

Toast muffin halves and place on ovenproof plate.

Arrange bacon over muffins and add poached eggs.

Mix hollandaise sauce with tomato purée; pour over eggs. Grill (broil) 2 minutes in oven.

*See Hollandaise Sauce, below.

1 SERVING	571 CALORIES	15 g CARBOHYDRATE
16 g PROTEIN	51 g FAT	0 g FIBER

Hollandaise Sauce

¾ lb	(375 g) unsalted butter
2	egg yolks
1 tbsp	(15 ml) water
1 tsp	(5 ml) lemon juice
	salt and pepper

Place butter in bowl set over saucepan containing hot water. Melt over low heat. Skim off foam and discard sediment. Keep clarified butter hot until use.

Place egg yolks and water in bowl also set over saucepan of hot water. Mix 10 seconds with whisk over low heat.

Continue cooking 30 seconds over low heat to thicken egg yolks.

Add clarified butter *very slowly* while whisking constantly.

When sauce is thick, add lemon juice and season to taste.

It is best to serve immediately but if necessary the hollandaise will keep for about 1 hour. Cover sauce with sheet of wax paper (be sure that paper touches surface) and set heat to very low.

See Technique next page.

1 SERVING	234 CALORIES	0 g CARBOHYDRATE
0 g PROTEIN	26 g FAT	0 g FIBER

TECHNIQUE: HOLLANDAISE SAUCE

1 Place butter in bowl set over saucepan of hot water. Clarify over low heat. Keep hot until use.

2 Place egg yolks and water in bowl also set over saucepan containing hot water. Mix 10 seconds with whisk over low heat.

3 Add clarified butter *very slowly* while whisking constantly.

4 Sauce should be thick and smooth. It is best served immediately.

Eggs Benedict   *(serves 4)*

2	English muffins, sliced in two
4	slices cooked hot ham
4	poached eggs
¾ cup	(175 ml) hollandaise sauce*

Toast muffin halves and place on ovenproof plate.

Set ham slices over muffins and top with poached eggs.

Cover with hollandaise sauce. Grill (broil) 2 minutes in oven.

Serve for brunch.

* See Hollandaise Sauce, page 137.

See Technique next page.

1 SERVING	527 CALORIES	14 g CARBOHYDRATE
12 g PROTEIN	47 g FAT	0 g FIBER

TECHNIQUE: EGGS BENEDICT

1 Place toasted English muffin halves on ovenproof plate.

2 Set ham slices over muffins.

3 Top with poached eggs.

4 Cover with hollandaise sauce. Grill (broil) 2 minutes in oven.

Eggs with Cheddar Sauce *(serves 2)*

3 tbsp	(45 ml) butter
3 tbsp	(45 ml) flour
1½ cups	(375 ml) hot milk
¼ cup	(50 ml) grated cheddar cheese
2	poached eggs
½ tsp	(2 ml) chopped parsley
	salt and pepper

Heat butter in saucepan.

When hot, add flour and mix. Cook 1 minute over low heat.

Pour in hot milk, season and mix with whisk. Continue cooking 6 to 7 minutes over low heat.

Add half of cheese and mix; cook 2 minutes. The cheese should be completely melted and the sauce thick.

Place poached eggs in baking dish and cover with sauce. Broil 3 minutes in oven.

Remove dish and sprinkle with remaining cheese and parsley. Serve with sautéed mushrooms.

See Technique next page.

1 SERVING	446 CALORIES	18 g CARBOHYDRATE
17 g PROTEIN	34 g FAT	0 g FIBER

TECHNIQUE: EGGS WITH CHEDDAR SAUCE

1 Heat butter in saucepan. When hot, add flour and mix. Cook 1 minute over low heat.

2 Pour in hot milk, season and mix with whisk. Continue cooking 6 to 7 minutes over low heat.

3 Add half of cheese and mix; cook 2 minutes.

4 The cheese should be completely melted and the sauce thick.

Eggs Baked in Potatoes   *(serves 4)*

4	large baked potatoes
4	large eggs
2 tbsp	(30 ml) butter
1 tbsp	(15 ml) chopped onion
1 tbsp	(15 ml) chopped chives
	salt and pepper
	sour cream

Preheat oven to 400°F (200°C).

Set baked potatoes on cutting board and slice off tops. Scoop out ¾ of potato flesh and set aside.

Season potato skins and add eggs. Bake 10 minutes in oven or until egg whites are set.

While eggs are cooking, heat butter in nonstick frying pan. When hot, add onion and chives; cook 3 minutes over medium heat.

Add potato flesh and press flat with metal spatula. Season generously and cook 3 minutes each side.

Serve potato pancake as a garnish along with sour cream.

See Technique next page.

1 SERVING	307 CALORIES	33 g CARBOHYDRATE
10 g PROTEIN	15 g FAT	0.9 g FIBER

TECHNIQUE: EGGS BAKED IN POTATOES

1 Set baked potatoes on cutting board and slice off tops.

2 Scoop out ¾ of potato flesh and set aside.

3 Season potato skins and add eggs. Bake in oven.

4 After 10 minutes in oven, the egg whites are set.

Baked Eggs with Spinach *(serves 4)*

1 tbsp	(15 ml) butter
2 cups	(500 ml) cooked spinach, chopped
1 cup	(250 ml) heated quick white sauce*
¼ tsp	(1 ml) nutmeg
4	large eggs
	salt and pepper

Preheat oven to 400°F (200°C).

Butter a baking dish.

Place spinach in bowl; add white sauce and nutmeg. Mix well and season.

Pour spinach mixture into baking dish. Add eggs and stir slightly with fork but avoid breaking yolks.

Place dish in oven and bake 6 to 8 minutes.

Serve with buttered toast.

*See Quick White Sauce, page 145.

1 SERVING	224 CALORIES	9 g CARBOHYDRATE
11 g PROTEIN	16 g FAT	0.8 g FIBER

Quick White Sauce

4 tbsp	(60 ml) butter
4½ tbsp	(70 ml) flour
3 cups	(750 ml) hot milk
¼ tsp	(1 ml) nutmeg
¼ tsp	(1 ml) celery seed
	dash paprika
	salt and white pepper

Heat butter in small saucepan. When hot, add flour and mix with whisk. Cook 1 minute over low heat.

Pour in half of milk and mix well; add remaining milk, spices, salt and pepper. Stir.

Cook sauce 8 minutes over low heat. Stir 2 to 3 times during cooking process.

This sauce will keep in refrigerator for 2 weeks covered with wax paper.

1 RECIPE	976 CALORIES	63 g CARBOHYDRATE
28 g PROTEIN	68 g FAT	0 g FIBER

Baked Eggs   *(serves 2)*

2 tbsp	(30 ml) butter
4	eggs
½ cup	(125 ml) 35% cream
1 tbsp	(15 ml) chopped fresh parsley
	salt and pepper

Preheat oven to 375°F (190°C).

Divide butter between two individual egg or gratin dishes. Place dishes in oven for 3 minutes.

Meanwhile, break two eggs into small bowl; break remaining eggs into another bowl.

Remove dishes from oven; carefully pour two eggs into each dish.

Pour in cream and season generously with salt and pepper. Cook 8 to 10 minutes in oven.

Sprinkle with chopped parsley and serve.

1 SERVING	447 CALORIES	2 g CARBOHYDRATE
13 g PROTEIN	43 g FAT	0 g FIBER

Egg Ham Rolls *(serves 4)*

4	hard-boiled eggs, sliced
14 oz	(398 ml) can asparagus, drained and cut into ½ in (1.3 cm) pieces
1½ cups	(375 ml) heated quick white sauce*
1 tsp	(5 ml) chopped parsley
4	thin slices cooked ham
¼ cup	(50 ml) grated cheddar cheese
	salt and pepper
	dash paprika

Preheat oven to 375°F (190°C).

Place eggs and asparagus in bowl; toss.

Add half of white sauce and parsley; mix well and season.

Place 2 tbsp (30 ml) of egg mixture on each ham slice. Roll and place in lightly buttered baking dish.

Pour remaining white sauce over rolls and sprinkle with paprika. Add cheese and bake 8 minutes in oven.

Serve for brunch or lunch.

*See Quick White Sauce, page 145.

See Technique next page.

1 SERVING	279 CALORIES	11 g CARBOHYDRATE
16 g PROTEIN	19 g FAT	0.5 g FIBER

TECHNIQUE: EGG HAM ROLLS

1 Place eggs and asparagus in bowl; toss. Add half of white sauce and parsley; mix well and season.

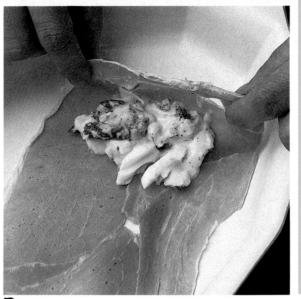

2 Place 2 tbsp (30 ml) of egg mixture on each ham slice.

3 Roll and place in lightly buttered baking dish.

4 Pour remaining white sauce over rolls and sprinkle with paprika. Add cheese and bake 8 minutes in oven.

Egg Croquette *(serves 4)*

3 tbsp	(45 ml) butter
1 tbsp	5 ml) chopped onion
1 tsp	(5 ml) chopped parsley
4 tbsp	(60 ml) flour
1 cup	(250 ml) hot milk
6	hard-boiled eggs, chopped
2	beaten eggs
1½ cups	(375 ml) breadcrumbs
	salt and pepper

Preheat peanut oil in deep-fryer to 350°F (180°C).

Heat butter in small saucepan. Add onion and parsley; cook 2 minutes.

Add flour and mix well.

Pour in hot milk, mix and season generously. Continue cooking 6 to 7 minutes over low heat. Stir often.

Remove pan from heat and cool. Place chopped eggs in large bowl and pour in sauce; mix until combined.

Form mixture into croquettes. Dip into beaten egg and then dredge with breadcrumbs.

Deep-fry 2 minutes. If desired, serve with tomato sauce.

See Technique next page.

1 SERVING	408 CALORIES	31 g CARBOHYDRATE
17 g PROTEIN	24 g FAT	0 g FIBER

TECHNIQUE: EGG CROQUETTE

1 Add onion and parsley to hot butter; cook 2 minutes.

2 Add flour and mix well.

3 Pour in hot milk, mix and season generously. Continue cooking 6 to 7 minutes over low heat.

4 Place eggs in large bowl and pour in cool sauce; mix until combined. Form mixture into croquettes.

5 Dip into beaten egg.

6 Dredge with breadcrumbs. Deep-fry 2 minutes.

Baked Eggs in Sauce *(serves 4)*

¼ cup	(50 ml) crumbled cheddar cheese
1 tsp	(5 ml) prepared mustard
1½ cups	(375 ml) heated quick white sauce*
4	large eggs
	dash paprika
	salt and pepper

Preheat oven to 375°F (190°C).

Add cheese and mustard to hot white sauce. Season generously and cook 3 minutes to melt cheese.

Pour half of sauce into baking dish; add eggs. Cover with remaining sauce and sprinkle with paprika. Bake 8 minutes.

Serve with sausages or bacon.

*See Quick White Sauce, page 145.

TECHNIQUE: BOILED EGGS

1 Have eggs at room temperature and using spoon, carefully ease one egg at a time into boiling water. Reduce heat so that water remains just below the boiling point.

2 This 4 minute egg can be used in various recipes but be careful when peeling as the white is only partly set.

3 This 10 minute egg is the traditional hardboiled egg. Eggs cooked longer than this time become rubbery and chemical reactions cause the yolks to change color.

4 When eggs are cooked to your preference, place in cold water to stop cooking process. Once they have cooled, they can be stored in the refrigerator for 2 to 3 days.

Baker's Eggs   *(serves 4)*

4	small individual fresh buns
3 tbsp	(45 ml) butter
2 tbsp	(30 ml) sliced onion
4 tbsp	(60 ml) flour
1½ cups	(375 ml) hot milk
¼ cup	(50 ml) grated Gruyère cheese
8	hard-boiled eggs, chopped
	dash paprika
	salt and pepper

Prepare buns using the technique following.

Heat butter in saucepan. When hot, add onion and cover; cook 4 minutes.

Mix in flour and continue cooking 1 minute.

Pour in milk and add dash paprika; mix well, season and cook 5 to 6 minutes over low heat.

Add cheese and mix until thoroughly incorporated. Simmer several minutes over low heat.

Place chopped eggs in buns and pour sauce over top. Grill (broil) 3 minutes in oven.

Serve and if desired decorate with sliced egg.

See Technique next page.

1 SERVING	457 CALORIES	28 g CARBOHYDRATE
21 g PROTEIN	29 g FAT	0 g FIBER

TECHNIQUE: BAKER'S EGGS

1 Cut thin top off buns and scoop out part of bread. Place on ovenproof platter.

2 Place buns in oven and toast until brown. Set aside.

3 Add onion to hot butter. Cover and cook 4 minutes.

4 Mix in flour and continue cooking 1 minute.

5 Pour in milk and add dash paprika; mix well, season and cook 5 to 6 minutes over low heat.

6 Add cheese and mix until thoroughly incorporated. Continue to simmer several minutes.

7 Place chopped eggs in buns.

8 Pour sauce over eggs. Grill (broil) 3 minutes in oven.

Eggs Surprise *(serves 2)*

1 tbsp	(15 ml) butter
½	small onion, peeled and chopped
1	small leek, white section sliced
6	mushrooms, cleaned and cut in half
2	hard-boiled eggs, diced large
2 tbsp	(30 ml) 35% cream
	dash paprika
	croutons
	salt and pepper

Heat butter in frying pan.

When hot, add onion and paprika. Season, cover and cook 3 minutes over medium heat.

Add leek and mushrooms; season well. Continue cooking, covered, 4 to 5 minutes.

Transfer mixture to baking dish and add hard-boiled eggs. Pour in cream and sprinkle with several croutons. Season with pepper and grill (broil) 5 minutes in oven.

Serve.

1 SERVING	242 CALORIES	10 g CARBOHYDRATE
10 g PROTEIN	18 g FAT	0.6 g FIBER

TECHNIQUE: EGGS SURPRISE

1 Add onion and paprika to hot butter. Season, cover and cook 3 minutes over medium heat.

2 Add leeks.

3 Add mushrooms and season well. Continue cooking, covered, 4 to 5 minutes.

4 Transfer mixture to baking dish and add hard-boiled eggs.
Add cream, croutons and pepper; grill (broil) 5 minutes in oven.

Breakfast Egg Treat   *(serves 4)*

4	slices toasted bread
2 tbsp	(30 ml) garlic butter
1 cup	(250 ml) peanut oil
4	large eggs
	salt and pepper

Arrange toasted bread on ovenproof platter and spread garlic butter over slices. Keep hot in oven at 150°F (70°C).

Pour oil into deep pan and heat. When hot, add first egg and quickly baste with spoon. Cook 30 to 40 seconds.

Remove cooked egg and drain. Repeat procedure for remaining eggs.

Set eggs on toasted garlic bread and season with salt and pepper. Serve.

1 SERVING	260 CALORIES	12 g CARBOHYDRATE
8 g PROTEIN	20 g FAT	0 g FIBER

Mushroom Duxelles

3 tbsp	(45 ml) butter
2	shallots, finely chopped
1 tbsp	(15 ml) chopped parsley
1 lb	(500 g) mushrooms, cleaned and finely chopped
¼ cup	(50 ml) 35% cream
	few drops Tabasco sauce
	salt and pepper

Heat butter in frying pan. When hot, add shallots and parsley; cook 3 minutes over low heat.

Add mushrooms and mix well. Add Tabasco sauce and season generously; continue cooking 8 to 10 minutes over low heat. Mix twice during cooking process.

Pour in cream and mix well. Continue cooking 3 to 4 minutes over low heat or until liquid evaporates.

When cooked, purée in mortar or blender.

1 RECIPE	648 CALORIES	22 g CARBOHYDRATE
14 g PROTEIN	56 g FAT	4.0 g FIBER

TECHNIQUE: MUSHROOM DUXELLES

1 Add shallots and parsley to hot butter. Cook 3 minutes over low heat.

2 Add mushrooms and mix well. Add Tabasco sauce and season generously; continue cooking 8 to 10 minutes. Mix twice during cooking process.

3 Pour in cream and mix well. Continue cooking 3 to 4 minutes or until liquid evaporates.

4 When cooked, purée in mortar or blender.

Eggs Stuffed with Mushroom Duxelles *(serves 4)*

8	hard-boiled eggs
2 tbsp	(30 ml) sour cream
1 cup	(250 ml) mushroom duxelles*
¼ cup	(50 ml) 35% cream
1 tbsp	(15 ml) chopped parsley
	salt and pepper

Preheat oven to 400°F (200°C).

Peel and slice eggs in half. Carefully remove yolks and force through sieve.

Add sour cream to egg yolks; mix well.

Add mushroom duxelles and season well; combine.

Fill egg whites with stuffing and place in baking dish. Pour in cream and cook 6 to 7 minutes in oven.

Sprinkle with parsley and serve.

*See Mushroom Duxelles, page 158.

1 SERVING	394 CALORIES	6 g CARBOHYDRATE
16 g PROTEIN	34 g FAT	1.0 g FIBER

1 Force egg yolks through sieve. Add sour cream and mix well.

2 Add mushroom duxelles and season well; combine.

3 Fill egg whites with stuffing and place in baking dish.

Quiche Dough

1 lb	(500 g) all-purpose flour
¼ tsp	(1 ml) salt
¼ lb	(125 g) butter
¼ lb	(125 g) shortening
4 to 5 tbsp	(60 to 75 ml) cold water

Sift flour and salt into large mixing bowl.

Add butter and shortening; incorporate with pastry blender. Continue to cut fat into flour until it resembles oatmeal.

Make a well in centre of flour and add water. Knead dough until smooth.

Form dough into ball and cover with clean cloth. Refrigerate 1 hour.

Dough must be brought to room temperature before using.

1 CRUST	1273 CALORIES	127 g CARBOHYDRATE
18 g PROTEIN	77 g FAT	0.5 g FIBER

Precooking Quiche Dough

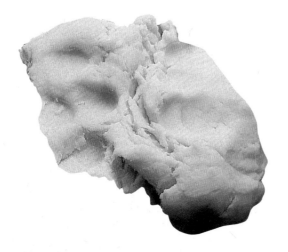

When using vegetables which have a high water content, such as tomatoes, it is preferable to precook the pie shell. Otherwise, the dough will absorb the excess water during the cooking process and will remain too moist.

Line selected mold with dough; prick bottom with fork. Set aside 20 to 30 minutes.

Preheat oven to 400°F (200°C).

Place sheet of wax paper on bottom of dough. Add 1½ cups (375 ml) baking weights to prevent dough from bubbling.

Precook 15 minutes.

TECHNIQUE: QUICHE DOUGH

1 Sift flour and salt into large mixing bowl. Add butter and shortening.

2 Incorporate with pastry blender. Continue to cut fat into flour until it resembles oatmeal.

3 Make a well in centre of flour and add water. Knead dough until smooth.

4 Form dough into ball. Cover with clean cloth and refrigerate 1 hour.

Tomato Quiche   *(serves 4)*

½ lb	(250 g) quiche dough*
2 tbsp	(30 ml) vegetable oil
1	garlic clove, peeled and cut in two
2	large tomatoes, peeled and cut in ¼ in (0.65 cm) slices
½ cup	(125 ml) grated Gruyère cheese
3	beaten eggs
1 cup	(250 ml) 35% cream
	pinch cayenne pepper
	chopped parsley to taste
	salt

1 oval quiche mold, 10½ × 7½ × 1½ in deep (27 × 19 × 4 cm).

Preheat oven to 375°F (190°C).

Line mold with dough and set aside 20 to 30 minutes. Precook shell.**

Heat oil in frying pan. When hot, add garlic and cook 2 minutes.

Remove and discard garlic. Add tomato slices to pan and season well. Cook 3 minutes each side over medium heat.

Place tomato slices in pie shell. Sprinkle with cheese.

Mix eggs with cream; add cayenne pepper, parsley and salt. Pour into pie shell.

Bake 45 minutes. Note that this quiche will remain quite moist when cooked.

* See Quiche Dough, page 162.
** See Precooking Dough, page 162.

1 SERVING	604 CALORIES	37 g CARBOHYDRATE
15 g PROTEIN	44 g FAT	0.6 g FIBER

Eggplant Quiche   *(serves 4)*

½ lb	(250 g) quiche dough*
2 tbsp	(30 ml) butter
1	small onion, peeled and finely chopped
1	garlic clove, smashed and chopped
1	small eggplant, cut into medium-size pieces
2 tbsp	(30 ml) tomato paste
¼ cup	(50 ml) grated Emmenthal cheese
2	beaten eggs
1 cup	(250 ml) 35% cream
	salt and pepper

1 round quiche mold, 9 × 1½ in deep (23 × 4 cm).

Preheat oven to 375°F (190°C).

Line mold with dough and set aside 20 to 30 minutes. Precook shell.**

Heat butter in frying pan. When hot, add onion and garlic; cover and cook 5 minutes over medium heat.

Stir in eggplant and season well; cover and cook 14 minutes over low heat. Mix several times during cooking process.

Add tomato paste and stir; continue cooking 6 minutes.

Place eggplant mixture in pie shell. Sprinkle with cheese.

Mix eggs with cream; pour into pie shell.

Bake 45 minutes.

* See Quiche Dough, page 162.
** See Precooking Dough, page 162.

1 SERVING	534 CALORIES	37 g CARBOHYDRATE
11 g PROTEIN	38 g FAT	0.3 g FIBER

Spinach Quiche   *(serves 4)*

½ lb	(250 g) quiche dough*
2 cups	(500 ml) cooked chopped spinach, sautéed in butter
¼ cup	(50 ml) grated Gruyère cheese
3	beaten eggs
1 cup	(250 ml) 35% cream
	dash nutmeg
	salt and pepper

1 round quiche mold, 9 × 1½ in deep (23 × 4 cm).

Preheat oven to 375°F (190°C).

Line mold with dough and set aside 20 to 30 minutes. Precook shell.**

Place spinach in pie shell; sprinkle with cheese.

Mix eggs with cream; add nutmeg and season well. Pour into pie shell.

Bake 45 minutes.

* See Quiche Dough, page 162.
** See Precooking Dough, page 162.

1 SERVING	533 CALORIES	36 g CARBOHYDRATE
14 g PROTEIN	37 g FAT	0.9 g FIBER

Onion Quiche   *(serves 4)*

½ lb	(250 g) quiche dough*
2 tbsp	(30 ml) butter
3	large onions, peeled and thinly sliced
2 tbsp	(30 ml) tomato paste
½ cup	(125 ml) grated Gruyère cheese
1 tbsp	(15 ml) chopped parsley
3	beaten eggs
1 cup	(250 ml) 35% cream
	pinch sugar
	few drops Tabasco sauce
	salt and pepper

1 round quiche mold, 9 × 1½ in deep (23 × 4 cm).

Preheat oven to 375°F (190°C).

Line mold with dough and set aside 20 to 30 minutes.

Heat butter in frying pan. When hot, add onions and season well. Cook 15 minutes over low heat. Stir occasionally. Stir in tomato paste and sugar; mix well. Continue cooking 5 minutes.

Place onions in pie shell and sprinkle with cheese. Season with Tabasco sauce, salt and pepper.

Mix parsley, eggs and cream together; season well. Pour into pie shell.

If desired, brush pie crust with a bit of beaten egg. This encourages the dough to brown during cooking.

Bake 45 minutes.

*See Quiche Dough, page 162.

1 SERVING	594 CALORIES	39 g CARBOHYDRATE
15 g PROTEIN	42 g FAT	0.7 g FIBER

TECHNIQUE: ONION QUICHE

1 Cook onions in hot butter over low heat. Season well.

2 The onions after 15 minutes of cooking.

3 Stir in tomato paste and sugar; mix well. Continue cooking 5 minutes.

4 Place onions in pie shell.

Continued next page.

5 Sprinkle with cheese.

6 Season with Tabasco sauce, salt and pepper.

7 Mix parsley, eggs and cream together; season well. Pour into pie shell.

8 If desired, brush pie crust with a bit of beaten egg. This encourages the dough to brown during cooking.

Peameal Bacon Quiche   *(serves 4)*

½ lb	(250 g) quiche dough*
5	slices cooked peameal bacon, cut into julienne
2	large slices Gruyère cheese, cut into julienne
3	beaten eggs
1	egg yolk
1 cup	(250 ml) 35% cream
1 tbsp	(15 ml) chopped chives
	pinch nutmeg
	freshly ground pepper

1 round quiche mold, 9 × 1½ in deep (23 × 4 cm).

Preheat oven to 375°F (190°C).

Line mold with dough and set aside 20 to 30 minutes.

Mix bacon and cheese together; place in pie shell.

Mix whole eggs, yolk and cream together; add chives, nutmeg and pepper. Pour into pie shell.

Bake 45 minutes.

*See Quiche Dough, page 162.

1 SERVING	578 CALORIES	33 g CARBOHYDRATE
17 g PROTEIN	42 g FAT	0 g FIBER

Hard-boiled Egg and Ham Quiche   *(serves 4)*

½ lb	(250 g) quiche dough*
3	hard-boiled eggs, sliced
3	slices cooked ham, cut into julienne
2 tbsp	(30 ml) grated mozzarella cheese
3	beaten eggs
1 cup	(250 ml) 35% cream
1 tbsp	(15 ml) chopped parsley
	pinch cayenne pepper
	pinch nutmeg
	salt

1 round quiche mold, 9 × 1½ in deep (23 × 4 cm).

Preheat oven to 375°F (190°C).

Line mold with dough and set aside 20 to 30 minutes.

Arrange sliced eggs in pie shell; add ham, cheese and cayenne pepper.

Mix beaten eggs with cream; add parsley, nutmeg and salt. Pour into pie shell.

Bake 45 minutes.

*See Quiche Dough, page 162.

1 SERVING	494 CALORIES	32 g CARBOHYDRATE
15 g PROTEIN	34 g FAT	0.1 g FIBER

Quiche Lorraine   *(serves 4)*

½ lb	(250 g) quiche dough*
3	slices bacon, diced large
⅓ cup	(75 ml) grated Gruyère cheese
3	beaten eggs
1 cup	(250 ml) 35% cream
1 tbsp	(15 ml) chopped parsley
	dash nutmeg
	salt and pepper

1 round quiche mold, 9 × 1½ in deep (23 × 4 cm).

Preheat oven to 375°F (190°C).

Line mold with dough and set aside 20 to 30 minutes.

Place bacon in saucepan filled with 2 cups (500 ml) boiling water. Cook 4 to 5 minutes.

Drain bacon and sauté 2 to 3 minutes in frying pan.

Using slotted spoon, place bacon in pie shell. Sprinkle with cheese; add nutmeg, parsley and season well.

Mix beaten eggs with cream; pour over bacon. Season well.

Bake 45 minutes.

*See Quiche Dough, page 162.

1 SERVING	551 CALORIES	33 g CARBOHYDRATE
17 g PROTEIN	39 g FAT	0.1 g FIBER

TECHNIQUE: QUICHE LORRAINE

1 If desired, prick dough with fork. This technique will keep bottom flat during cooking.

2 Place bacon in saucepan filled with 2 cups (500 ml) boiling water. Cook 4 to 5 minutes.

3 Drain bacon and sauté 2 to 3 minutes in frying pan.

4 Place bacon in pie shell.

Continued next page.

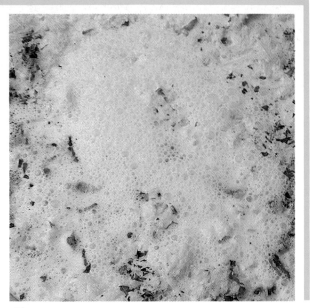

5 Sprinkle with cheese; add nutmeg, parsley and season well.

6 Pour eggs and cream into pie shell; season well.

Chicken and Mushroom Quiche *(serves 4)*

½ lb	(250 g) quiche dough*
3 tbsp	(45 ml) butter
½ lb	(250 g) mushrooms, cleaned and sliced
1	chicken breast, deboned, skinned and diced small
1 tbsp	(15 ml) chopped parsley
¼ cup	(50 ml) grated Emmenthal cheese
3	beaten eggs
1 cup	(250 ml) 35% cream
	salt and pepper

1 round quiche mold, 9 × 1½ in deep (23 × 4 cm).

Preheat oven to 375°F (190°C).

Line mold with dough and set aside 20 to 30 minutes.

Heat butter in frying pan. When hot, add mushrooms and season well. Cook 3 to 4 minutes over high heat.

Remove mushrooms and set aside.

Add chicken to pan and season well; cook 6 to 7 minutes over medium heat. Replace mushrooms in pan and add parsley; mix well. Place mixture in pie shell and sprinkle with cheese.

Mix beaten eggs with cream and season well. Pour into pie shell.

Bake 45 minutes.

* See Quiche Dough, page 162.

1 SERVING	603 CALORIES	34 g CARBOHYDRATE
20 g PROTEIN	43 g FAT	0.4 g FIBER

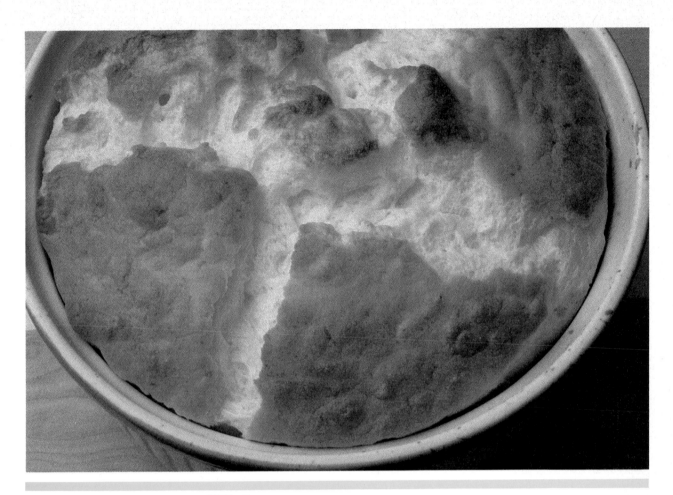

Gruyère Soufflé *(serves 4)*

4 tbsp	(60 ml) butter
1½ cups	(375 ml) grated Gruyère cheese
3 tbsp	(45 ml) flour
1½ cups	(375 ml) hot milk
4	extra-large egg yolks
5	extra-large egg whites, beaten very stiff*
	dash nutmeg
	salt and pepper

Preheat oven to 375°F (190°C).

Butter 6 cup (1.5 L) soufflé dish. Sprinkle some cheese on bottom and sides; set dish aside.

Heat remaining butter in saucepan. When hot, add flour and mix quickly. Cook 1 minute.

Pour in hot milk and add nutmeg; mix well with whisk. Season well and cook 8 minutes over low heat. Stir twice during cooking process.

Remove saucepan from heat and let cool slightly. Add egg yolks, one at a time, whisking between additions. The yolks must be well incorporated.

Transfer batter to bowl; stir in remaining cheese. Fold beaten egg whites into batter with spatula. Be careful not to overmix!

Pour batter into soufflé dish; it should reach about 1½ in (4 cm) from top. Bake 35 to 40 minutes in oven.

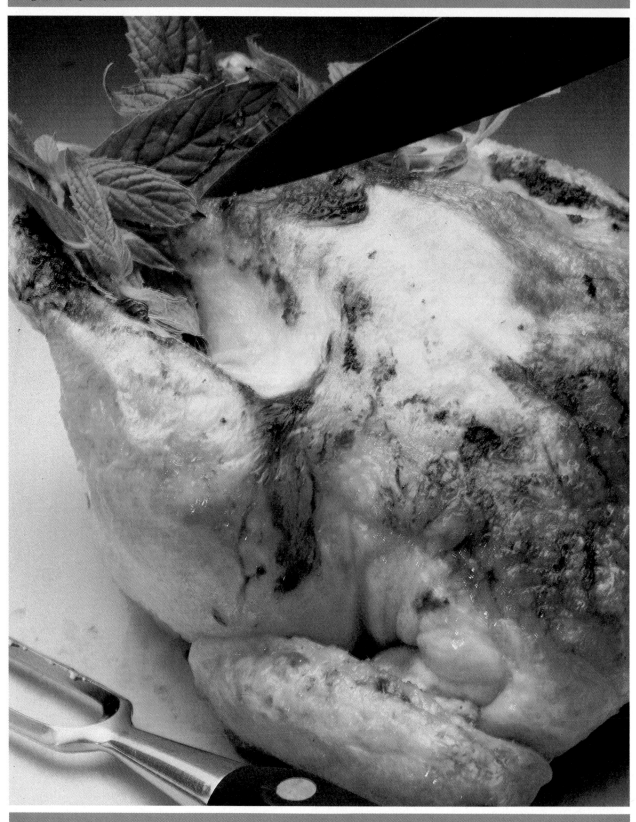

TECHNIQUE: DISJOINTING CHICKEN

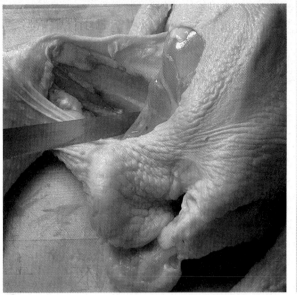

1 Cutting chicken into pieces is quite simple, but you will need a sharp knife and, ideally, a wooden cutting board.

2 Begin by placing bird, breast side up, on cutting board. Pull leg outwards and cut through skin, running knife along body.

3 Bend leg back and twist if necessary to disjoint. Cut with knife to sever ligaments and remove leg.

4 Repeat for other leg.

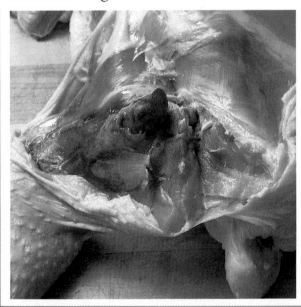

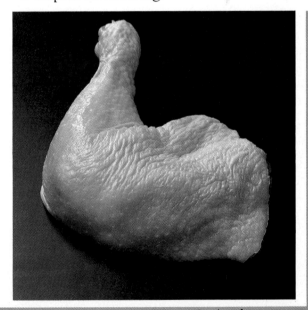

Continued next page.

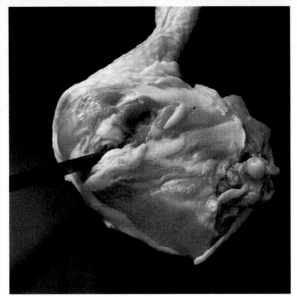

5 Place leg skin side down, and feel with knife for joint between thigh and drumstick; cut through.

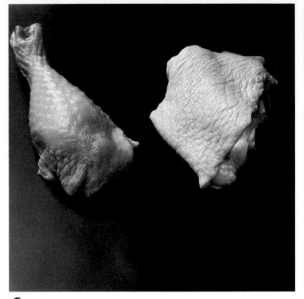

6 Repeat for other leg.

7 Cut through flesh and joints; remove both wings.
Cut carcass in half (as shown) and begin removing breast by cutting along rib cage.

8 Continue cutting toward front of bird and around wishbone.

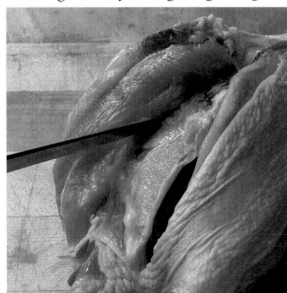

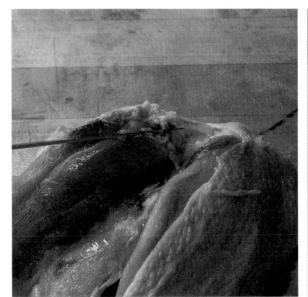

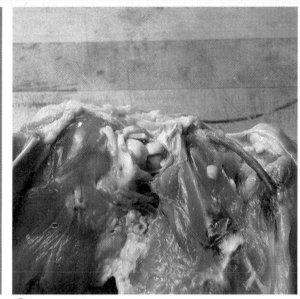

9 Force breast down and disjoint. Cut with knife to sever ligaments.

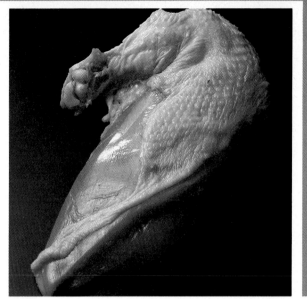

10 Repeat for other breast.
Note: Reserve carcass for making chicken stock.

11 Finish deboning breast by pushing back flesh as shown; tug on bone to remove.
Note: It is possible to remove this bone when wing is severed.

12 These are the pieces from half a chicken. Most recipes require a total of 6 to 10 pieces; to get the appropriate number of pieces for a given recipe, either leave breasts and legs whole or cut in two.

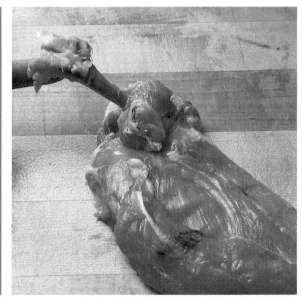

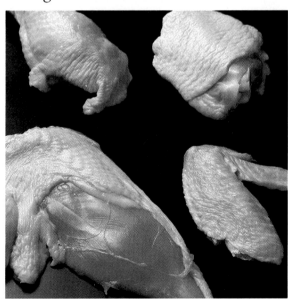

Steamed Rice *(serves 4)*

1 cup	(250 ml) long grain rice, rinsed and drained
5 cups	(1.2 L) boiling salted water

Drop rice into boiling water; stir. Cover saucepan and cook 12 minutes.

Drain rice and rinse with water; drain again.

Place rice in steamer; cover and steam 10 to 15 minutes.

Serve hot.

1 SERVING	108 CALORIES	25 g CARBOHYDRATE
2 g PROTEIN	0 g FAT	0.1 g FIBER

Horseradish White Sauce

4 tbsp	(60 ml) butter
2 tbsp	(30 ml) chopped onion
4 tbsp	(60 ml) flour
2 cups	(500 ml) hot milk
¼ tsp	(1 ml) nutmeg
2½ tbsp	(40 ml) horseradish
	pinch paprika
	salt and pepper

Heat butter in saucepan. When hot, add onion; cover and cook 3 minutes over low heat.

Add flour and mix; cook, uncovered, 1 minute.

Pour in half of milk and mix well. Add remaining milk, season and add spices.

Bring sauce to boil; continue cooking 8 to 10 minutes, uncovered, over medium-low heat. Stir frequently.

Mix in horseradish and simmer 2 minutes.

1 SERVING	211 CALORIES	14 g CARBOHYDRATE
5 g PROTEIN	15 g FAT	0.2 g FIBER

Chicken Leg Sauté   *(serves 4)*

2 tbsp	(30 ml) vegetable oil
4	large chicken legs, cut in two, skinned and cleaned
1	onion, peeled and sliced
1	small eggplant, sliced
2	garlic cloves, smashed and chopped
¼ tsp	(1 ml) oregano
⅓	English cucumber, sliced
2	ripe tomatoes, diced large
1	large carrot, pared and sliced
	salt and pepper

Heat oil in large sauté pan. When hot, add chicken and season generously. Cook 4 to 5 minutes each side over medium heat.

Add onion, eggplant and season; stir to mix.

Stir in garlic and oregano; cover and cook 10 minutes over low heat.

Add cucumber, tomatoes and carrot; correct seasoning. Cook 8 to 10 minutes, covered, over medium-low heat. Stir occasionally.

Serve.

Chicken Miranda *(serves 4)*

4 to 5 lb	(1.8 to 2.3 kg) capon, cut into 8 pieces*, skinned and cleaned
1 cup	(250 ml) seasoned flour
2 tbsp	(30 ml) vegetable oil
½	onion, peeled and finely chopped
1 tbsp	(15 ml) chopped fresh ginger
1	green pepper, thinly sliced
1	red pepper, thinly sliced
1 cup	(250 ml) blanched broccoli flowerets
1 tbsp	(15 ml) soya sauce
	some banana pepper, thinly sliced
	salt and pepper

Preheat oven to 375°F (190°C).

Debone chicken thighs and slash leg meat with knife. Dredge with flour.

Heat oil in large ovenproof pan. Add chicken pieces and cook 4 to 5 minutes over medium heat.

Season and turn pieces over; continue cooking 4 to 5 minutes.

Add onion to pan, stir and correct seasoning. Cover pan and cook 15 minutes in oven.

Remove white meat from pan and set aside. Continue cooking remaining chicken 10 minutes in oven.

Replace white meat and add ginger. Place on burner over medium heat and add all vegetables; cook 4 to 5 minutes.

Mix in soya sauce and simmer several minutes over low heat.

* See Disjointing Chicken, page 175.

1 SERVING	496 CALORIES	18 g CARBOHYDRATE
52 g PROTEIN	21 g FAT	1.2 g FIBER

Chicken Wings in Tomato Sauce   *(serves 4)*

2 tbsp	(30 ml) vegetable oil
2½ lb	(1.1 kg) chicken wings, cleaned
1	onion, peeled and chopped
½	eggplant, finely chopped
1	garlic clove, smashed and chopped
28 oz	(796 ml) can tomatoes, drained and chopped
½ cup	(125 ml) commercial brown sauce, heated
	salt and pepper

Heat oil in large sauté pan. When hot, add chicken and cook 3 minutes over medium heat.

Season well and turn wings over; continue cooking 3 minutes.

Add onion to pan and cook 2 minutes.

Stir in eggplant and garlic; cook 8 minutes, partially covered, over medium heat. Stir as required.

Mix in tomatoes and cook 3 to 4 minutes, uncovered, over medium heat. Correct seasoning.

Pour in brown sauce and season well. Cook 8 minutes, partially covered, over medium heat. Stir occasionally.

1 SERVING	322 CALORIES	12 g CARBOHYDRATE
28 g PROTEIN	18 g FAT	1.3 g FIBER

Sliced Chicken on Linguine *(serves 4)*

1	large whole chicken breast, deboned, skinned and cleaned
1 tbsp	(15 ml) butter
1 tbsp	(15 ml) vegetable oil
¼ cup	(50 ml) chopped sweet pimento
¼ lb	(125 g) mushrooms, sliced
2	green onions, sliced
1	green pepper, sliced
1	garlic clove, chopped
1 cup	(250 ml) commercial tomato sauce, heated
1 cup	(250 ml) commercial brown sauce, heated
1 cup	(250 ml) cooked broccoli
4	portions cooked linguine
	salt and pepper
	grated parmesan cheese

Slice chicken into long pieces ¼ in (0.65 cm) thick.

Heat butter and oil in sauté pan. When hot, add chicken and cook 3 minutes over medium heat.

Season and turn chicken pieces over; add pimento, mushrooms, onions, green pepper and garlic. Cook 3 to 4 minutes over medium heat.

Pour in both sauces and add broccoli. Mix well and simmer several minutes over medium-low heat.

Arrange cooked linguine on plates and pour chicken mixture on top; sprinkle with cheese to taste.

Serve.

1 SERVING	381 CALORIES	27 g CARBOHYDRATE
39 g PROTEIN	13 g FAT	1.9 g FIBER

Abigail's Chicken   *(serves 4)*

3 tbsp	(45 ml) butter
1 tbsp	(15 ml) lemon juice
⅓ cup	(75 ml) heated chicken stock
2	large whole chicken breasts, deboned, skinned, cleaned and diced large
½ lb	(250 g) mushrooms, cleaned and whole
1	green pepper, diced large
1	red pepper, diced large
½ cup	(125 ml) cooked pearl onions
½ cup	(125 ml) Madeira wine
2 cups	(500 ml) heavy cream
	salt and pepper
	few drops Tabasco and Worcestershire sauce
	pinch nutmeg

Heat 1 tbsp (15 ml) butter in large pan. When hot, stir in lemon juice and chicken stock.

Add chicken and season; cover and cook 8 to 10 minutes over low heat.

Pour chicken and sauce into bowl; set aside.

Replace pan on stove top and add remaining butter. When hot, add mushrooms, peppers and onions; cook 3 minutes, uncovered, over high heat.

Remove vegetables from pan and set aside in bowl.

Pour wine into pan and cook 3 minutes over high heat.

Add cream and spices; mix and continue cooking 6 to 7 minutes over high heat.

Replace chicken mixture and vegetables in pan. Mix, season and simmer 3 minutes to reheat.

1 SERVING	764 CALORIES	11 g CARBOHYDRATE
63 g PROTEIN	52 g FAT	2.0 g FIBER

Maryland Fried Chicken *(serves 4)*

2	large whole chicken breasts, deboned, skinned and cleaned
1 cup	(250 ml) seasoned flour
2	beaten eggs
1½ cups	(375 ml) breadcrumbs
2 tbsp	(30 ml) vegetable oil
4	bananas
4 tbsp	(60 ml) brown sugar
8	slices cooked bacon for garnish
	salt and pepper

Preheat oven to 375°F (190°C).

Dredge chicken with flour; dip into beaten eggs and coat with breadcrumbs.

Heat oil in frying pan. When hot, add chicken and cook 4 minutes over medium-high heat.

Turn breasts over; continue cooking 4 minutes. Season well.

Place chicken in baking dish and cook 10 to 12 minutes in oven.

Meanwhile, prepare bananas by cutting away part of skin as shown in picture. Sprinkle brown sugar over bananas and place on baking sheet.

Cook bananas 5 to 6 minutes in oven alongside chicken. Skins should become black.

184

1 SERVING	860 CALORIES	72 g CARBOHYDRATE
80 g PROTEIN	28 g FAT	0.6 g FIBER

Pineapple Chicken *(serves 4)*

2 tbsp	(30 ml) butter
2	large whole chicken breasts, deboned, skinned and cleaned
3	apples, cored, peeled and sliced
1 ½ cups	(375 ml) heated chicken stock
¼ cup	(50 ml) pineapple juice
	pineapple rings
	few drops lime juice
	salt and pepper

Heat butter in sauté pan. When hot, add chicken and sprinkle with lime juice. Cover and cook 4 minutes over medium-low heat.

Season chicken and turn over; continue cooking, covered, 4 minutes.

Turn chicken again; cover and cook 8 minutes over medium-low heat.

Add apples, chicken stock and pineapple juice to pan. Mix well and cover; cook 3 to 4 minutes.

Season well and add pineapple rings; cover and simmer 1 to 2 minutes over medium-low heat.

Serve.

Baked Chicken in Sauce   *(serves 4)*

2 tbsp	(30 ml) butter
2	large whole chicken breasts, deboned, skinned and cleaned
½ lb	(250 g) fresh mushrooms, cleaned and sliced
2 cups	(500 ml) commercial cheese sauce, heated
¼ cup	(50 ml) grated mozzarella cheese
	few drops lemon juice
	salt and pepper
	dash celery seed
	pinch basil

Preheat oven to 375°F (190°C).

Heat butter in large pan. When hot, add chicken and sprinkle with lemon juice. Cover and cook 2 minutes each side over medium-low heat. Season well.

Add mushrooms and herbs; cook, covered, 3 to 4 minutes.

Mix in cheese sauce and transfer to ovenproof dish. Sprinkle top with cheese and bake 6 to 7 minutes in oven.

1 SERVING	445 CALORIES	14 g CARBOHYDRATE
41 g PROTEIN	25 g FAT	0.6 g FIBER

Breaded Chicken Breasts with Cheese *(serves 4)*

2	large whole chicken breasts, deboned, skinned and cleaned
1 cup	(250 ml) seasoned flour
2	beaten eggs
1½ cups	(375 ml) breadcrumbs
2 tbsp	(30 ml) vegetable oil
4	slices Gruyère cheese
1 cup	(250 ml) your preferred tomato sauce, heated
	salt and pepper

Preheat oven to 400°F (200°C).

Dredge chicken with flour. Dip into beaten eggs and coat with breadcrumbs.

Heat oil in frying pan. When hot, add chicken and cook 4 minutes over medium-high heat.

Turn chicken over and cook 4 more minutes.

Place chicken in ovenproof dish and cook 5 minutes in oven.

Place cheese slices on each breast; continue to bake 5 minutes.

Season tomato sauce if necessary and serve with chicken.

1 SERVING	647 CALORIES	51 g CARBOHYDRATE
50 g PROTEIN	27 g FAT	0.4 g FIBER

Fried Chicken Breasts in Horseradish White Sauce *(serves 4)*

2	large whole chicken breasts, deboned, skinned and cleaned
1 cup	(250 ml) seasoned flour
2	beaten eggs
1½ cups	(375 ml) breadcrumbs
2 tbsp	(30 ml) vegetable oil
1½ cups	(375 ml) hot horseradish white sauce*
	salt and pepper

Preheat oven to 375°F (190°C).

Dredge chicken with flour. Dip into beaten eggs and coat with breadcrumbs.

Heat oil in frying pan. When hot, add chicken and cook 4 minutes over medium-high heat.

Turn chicken over; continue cooking 4 minutes. Season well.

Finish cooking chicken in oven 10 to 12 minutes.

Serve with *Horseradish White Sauce, page 178.

1 SERVING	742 CALORIES	47 g CARBOHYDRATE
71 g PROTEIN	30 g FAT	0.2 g FIBER

Chicken Breasts and Mushroom Cream Sauce

2	large whole chicken breasts, deboned, skinned and cleaned
1 tbsp	(15 ml) finely chopped parsley
4 cups	(1 L) cold chicken stock
½ lb	(250 g) mushrooms, cleaned and sliced
¼ tsp	(1 ml) lemon juice
4 tbsp	(60 ml) butter
3 tbsp	(45 ml) flour
¼ cup	(50 ml) heavy cream
1 tsp	(5 ml) finely chopped lemon rind
½ cup	(125 ml) cooked pearl onions
1	green pepper, thinly sliced
1 tsp	(5 ml) chopped chives
	salt and pepper
	pinch paprika

(serves 4)

Preheat oven to 150°F (70°C).

Place chicken breasts in sauté pan. Sprinkle with parsley and pour in chicken stock; bring to boil. Partly cover and cook 8 to 10 minutes over medium heat. Add mushrooms and lemon juice; continue cooking 3 minutes.

Remove chicken and mushrooms from pan; keep hot in oven and reserve 2 cups (500 ml) cooking liquid.

Heat 3 tbsp (45 ml) butter in saucepan. When hot, add flour and mix; cook 1 minute.

Add 2 cups (500 ml) reserved cooking liquid and season generously; cook 5 minutes over medium heat.

Pour in cream and lemon rind; season with paprika. Continue cooking sauce 2 minutes.

Meanwhile, quickly heat remaining butter in frying pan. When hot, sauté onions and green pepper about 3 to 4 minutes. Season well.

Arrange chicken on serving platter and pour sauce over top. Garnish.

1 SERVING	487 CALORIES	9 g CARBOHYDRATE
61 g PROTEIN	23 g FAT	1.3 g FIBER

Chicken Breasts in Tomatoes *(serves 4)*

1 tbsp	(15 ml) butter
1 tbsp	(15 ml) vegetable oil
2	large whole chicken breasts, deboned, skinned and cleaned
1	small onion, peeled and finely chopped
1 tsp	(5 ml) paprika
28 oz	(796 ml) can tomatoes, drained and chopped
¼ tsp	(1 ml) basil
¼ tsp	(1 ml) oregano
¼ cup	(50 ml) heavy cream
	salt and pepper
	chopped parsley to taste

Heat butter and oil in frying pan. When hot, add chicken and cook 3 to 4 minutes over medium heat.

Season well and turn chicken over; partially cover and continue cooking 4 minutes.

Add onion and paprika; mix well. Partially cover and cook 3 to 4 minutes over low heat.

Stir in tomatoes and spices; cover and cook 8 to 9 minutes over medium-low heat.

2 minutes before end of cooking, pour in cream; mix well.

Sprinkle with parsley and serve.

1 SERVING	446 CALORIES	11 g CARBOHYDRATE
60 g PROTEIN	18 g FAT	1.0 g FIBER

Harvest Chicken *(serves 4)*

2 tbsp	(30 ml) butter
2	large whole chicken breasts, deboned, skinned and cleaned
1	zucchini, cut in two lengthwise and sliced
½	English cucumber, cut in two lengthwise and sliced
½ cup	(125 ml) sweet pimento, sliced
½ tsp	(2 ml) tarragon
1½ cups	(375 ml) heated chicken stock
1 tbsp	(15 ml) cornstarch
2 tbsp	(30 ml) cold water
	salt and pepper
	dash celery seed
	few drops Tabasco sauce
	steamed rice*

Heat butter in sauté pan. When hot, add chicken and cover; cook 4 minutes over medium-low heat.

Turn chicken and cook another 4 minutes.

Season chicken breasts well; continue cooking, covered, 10 to 12 minutes.

Three minutes before end of cooking, add vegetables and spices to pan.

When cooked, transfer chicken and vegetables to serving platter. Add chicken stock to pan and bring to boil.

Meanwhile, mix cornstarch with water; stir into sauce. Cook several minutes over low heat to thicken.

Add few drops Tabasco and season well. Pour sauce over chicken and serve with rice.

* See Steamed Rice, page 178.

1 SERVING	360 CALORIES	5 g CARBOHYDRATE
58 g PROTEIN	12 g FAT	0.4 g FIBER

Chicken with Julienne Vegetables   *(serves 4)*

3 tbsp	(45 ml) butter
2	large whole chicken breasts, deboned, skinned and cleaned
1	large carrot, pared and cut into julienne
1	celery stalk, pared and cut into julienne
1	small zucchini, cut into julienne
	juice ½ lemon
	salt and pepper
	green onions for decoration.

Place 2 tbsp (30 ml) butter, chicken, lemon juice, salt and pepper in deep frying pan. Cover and cook 12 to 15 minutes over medium-low heat. Turn twice.

Before chicken is done, heat remaining butter in second frying pan. Add vegetables and cook 5 to 6 minutes over medium heat. Season well.

Decorate finished dish with green onions.

1 SERVING	383 CALORIES	4 g CARBOHYDRATE
58 g PROTEIN	15 g FAT	0.7 g FIBER

Chicken Curry Dish   *(serves 4)*

3 tbsp	(45 ml) butter
2	onions, peeled and thinly sliced
2 tbsp	(30 ml) curry powder
2	large whole chicken breasts, deboned, skinned, cleaned and cut into large pieces
2 cups	(500 ml) heated chicken stock
1 tbsp	(15 ml) cornstarch
2 tbsp	(30 ml) cold water
¼ cup	(50 ml) heavy cream
1 tbsp	(15 ml) chopped chives or parsley
	salt and pepper
	black olives

Heat butter in large frying pan. When hot, add onions; cook 5 to 6 minutes over medium heat. Stir occasionally.

Mix in curry powder and cook 3 to 4 minutes over low heat.

Add chicken and stir; season well. Cook 2 to 3 minutes over medium heat.

Pour in chicken stock and bring to boil. Continue cooking 9 to 10 minutes over medium-low heat.

Mix cornstarch with water; stir into sauce. Cook 1 minute.

Pour in cream and bring to boil; cook 2 to 3 minutes and season well.

Arrange chicken mixture in serving platter. Sprinkle with chives and decorate with olives.

1 SERVING	444 CALORIES	7 g CARBOHYDRATE
59 g PROTEIN	20 g FAT	0.3 g FIBER

Coq au Vin *(serves 4)*

5 to 6 lb	(2.3 to 2.7 kg) capon, cut into 8 pieces*, skinned and cleaned
1 cup	(250 ml) seasoned flour
2 tbsp	(30 ml) vegetable oil
1	onion, peeled and chopped
2	garlic cloves, smashed and chopped
2 cups	(500 ml) dry red wine
2 cups	(500 ml) commercial brown sauce, heated
1/4 tsp	(1 ml) chervil
1	bay leaf
1/2 lb	(250 g) mushroom caps, sautéed in butter
1/2 cup	(125 ml) cooked pearl onions
	pinch thyme
	salt and pepper

Preheat oven to 375°F (190°C).

Dredge chicken with flour; shake off excess.

Heat oil in sauté pan or deep frying pan. When hot, add chicken and sear 8 to 10 minutes over medium heat. Turn pieces occasionally.

Add chopped onion and garlic; cook 2 to 3 minutes over low heat.

Pour in wine and cook 5 to 6 minutes over high heat.

Stir mixture well and add brown sauce and herbs; mix again and bring to boil.

Cover and cook 35 minutes in oven.

Add mushrooms and pearl onions to pan; continue cooking coq au vin 10 minutes.

Serve with thick slices of toast.

1 SERVING	392 CALORIES	22 g CARBOHYDRATE
76 g PROTEIN	33 g FAT	1.3 g FIBER

Classic Boiled Chicken and Rice   *(serves 4)*

4 to 5 lb	(1.8 to 2.3 kg) capon, cut into 8 pieces*, skinned and cleaned
8 cups	(2 L) cold water
¼ tsp	(1 ml) chervil
¼ tsp	(1 ml) nutmeg
1 tsp	(5 ml) chopped parsley
1 tsp	(5 ml) chopped chives
1½ cups	(375 ml) long grain rice, rinsed and drained
3 tbsp	(45 ml) butter
4 tbsp	(60 ml) flour
	pinch ground ginger
	salt and pepper

Place chicken pieces in large saucepan. Pour in enough water to cover; bring to boil. Cook 4 to 5 minutes over medium heat.

Drain chicken and return to pan; add 8 cups (2 L) cold water, herbs and ginger; season well. Bring to boil and cook 35 to 40 minutes, partially covered, over low heat.

18 minutes before end of cooking, add rice.

Remove chicken and transfer to serving platter. Drain rice but reserve 2 cups (500 ml) cooking liquid.

Heat butter in saucepan. When hot, add flour and cook 1 minute over low heat. Stir as required to avoid burning.

Pour in 2 cups (500 ml) cooking liquid; continue cooking 3 to 4 minutes over medium heat. Stir frequently.

Pour sauce over chicken and rice. Serve.

*See Disjointing Chicken, page 175.

1 SERVING	577 CALORIES	45 g CARBOHYDRATE
52 g PROTEIN	21 g FAT	0.2 g FIBER

Chicken Pieces au Gratin   *(serves 4)*

4 to 5 lb	(1.8 to 2.3 kg) capon, cut into 6 pieces*, skinned and cleaned
3	parsley sprigs
1	bay leaf
½	onion, studded with clove
1 tsp	(5 ml) nutmeg
3 tbsp	(45 ml) butter
3½ tbsp	(55 ml) flour
½ cup	(125 ml) grated Emmenthal cheese
	heated chicken stock
	salt and pepper

Place chicken in large roasting pan. Pour in enough water to cover and bring to boil on stove top; cover with aluminium foil.

Drain chicken and replace liquid with enough hot chicken stock to cover.

Add parsley sprigs, bay leaf, onion and nutmeg; season well. Cover with foil and bring to boil. Cook 30 minutes over low heat.

Remove chicken from pan and transfer to serving platter. Reserve 2 cups (500 ml) cooking liquid; set aside.

Heat butter in saucepan. When hot, add flour and cook 1 minute over low heat.

Pour in 2 cups (500 ml) reserved cooking liquid; bring to boil. Season and cook 5 to 6 minutes over medium heat.

Add ¾ of cheese to sauce; mix well and continue cooking 1 minute.

Pour sauce and cheese over chicken.

*See Disjointing Chicken, page 175.

1 SERVING	461 CALORIES	6 g CARBOHYDRATE
53 g PROTEIN	25 g FAT	0 g FIBER

New Wave Curried Chicken *(serves 4)*

4 to 5 lb	(1.8 to 2.3 kg) capon, cut into 8 pieces*, skinned and cleaned
1 cup	(250 ml) seasoned flour
2 tbsp	(30 ml) vegetable oil
2 tbsp	(30 ml) butter
1	small onion, peeled and chopped
2 tbsp	(30 ml) curry powder
2	apples, cored, peeled and sliced
2 cups	(500 ml) heated chicken stock
20	blanched pea pods
1½ cups	(375 ml) bean sprouts
1 tbsp	(15 ml) soya sauce
1 tbsp	(15 ml) cornstarch
3 tbsp	(45 ml) cold water
	few crushed chillies
	pinch ground ginger
	salt and pepper

Dredge chicken pieces with flour.
Heat oil in sauté pan. When hot, add chicken and cook 4 to 5 minutes over medium heat. Turn chicken over. Cook 5 minutes.
Add 1 tbsp (15 ml) butter, onion and curry powder to pan. Mix well and cook 8 to 10 minutes, covered, over low heat.
Stir in apples; continue cooking, covered, 3 to 4 minutes.
Pour in chicken stock, add spices and season well. Partially cover and cook 15 minutes over low heat.
Meanwhile, heat remaining butter in frying pan. When hot, add pea pods and bean sprouts; sauté 3 minutes over medium heat.
Mix in soya sauce and continue cooking 2 minutes. When chicken is cooked, remove and place on serving platter. Leave sauté pan with cooking liquid on burner.
Mix cornstarch with cold water; stir into cooking liquid. Cook sauce 1 to 2 minutes over medium heat.
*See Disjointing Chicken, page 175.

1 SERVING	561 CALORIES	32 g CARBOHYDRATE
52 g PROTEIN	25 g FAT	0 g FIBER

Braised Chicken Mama Knox   *(serves 4)*

2 tbsp	(30 ml) vegetable oil
4 to 5 lb	(1.8 to 2.3 kg) capon, cut into 10 pieces*, skinned and cleaned
1	onion, peeled and coarsely diced
1 tbsp	(15 ml) butter
3 cups	(750 ml) heated beef stock
¼ tsp	(1 ml) thyme
¼ tsp	(1 ml) oregano
¼ tsp	(1 ml) marjoram
3 tbsp	(45 ml) tomato paste
2	carrots, cut into sticks
1 cup	(250 ml) Parisienne potatoes
½ lb	(250 g) small mushroom caps
	few crushed chillies
	pinch sage
	salt and pepper

Preheat oven to 375°F (190°C).

Heat oil in large ovenproof casserole. When hot, add chicken and cook 4 to 5 minutes over medium heat.

Turn pieces over; continue cooking 4 to 5 minutes.

Add onion and butter; cook 6 to 7 minutes.

Pour in beef stock and add herbs; bring to boil.

Mix in tomato paste and simmer 1 minute over low heat. Place casserole in oven and cook, covered, 20 minutes.

Add carrots and potatoes; continue cooking, covered, 15 minutes.

Add mushrooms and finish cooking 5 minutes.

Serve.

*See Disjointing Chicken, page 175.

1 SERVING	442 CALORIES	10 g CARBOHYDRATE
51 g PROTEIN	22 g FAT	0.9 g FIBER

TECHNIQUE: BRAISED CHICKEN MAMA KNOX

1 Sear chicken pieces 4 to 5 minutes on each side in hot oil.

2 Add onion and butter; cook 6 to 7 minutes.

3 Pour in beef stock and add herbs; bring to boil.

4 Mix in tomato paste and simmer 1 minute over low heat. Cover and cook 20 minutes in oven.

Continued next page.

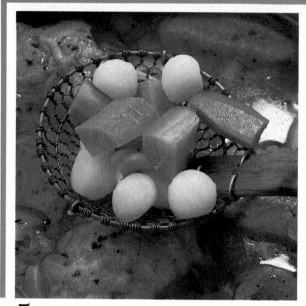

5 Add carrots and potatoes; continue cooking, covered, 15 minutes.

6 Add mushrooms and finish cooking 5 minutes.

Rice Stuffing

1 tbsp	(15 ml) butter
2	green onions, chopped
½	celery stalk, finely chopped
4	water chestnuts, thinly sliced
¼ cup	(50 ml) bamboo shoots, chopped
2 cups	(500 ml) cooked long grain and wild rice
5	slices white bread
1 tbsp	(15 ml) chopped parsley
¼ cup	(50 ml) heavy cream
	pinch thyme
	pinch ginger
	pinch allspice
	salt and pepper

Heat butter in frying pan. When hot, add vegetables and mix well; cook 2 minutes over medium heat. Season generously.

Stir in rice and herbs; mix very well. Remove pan from heat and cool.

Place bread, parsley and cream in large bowl. Mash bread and add rice; mix until combined.

Correct seasoning.

1 RECIPE	982 CALORIES	158 g CARBOHYDRATE
20 g PROTEIN	30 g FAT	1.8 g FIBER

Chicken Fricassée   *(serves 4 to 6)*

5 lb	(2.3 kg) capon, cut into 8 pieces*, skinned and cleaned
2	carrots, pared and cut into thick sticks
2	onions, peeled and cut into 4
1	celery stock, cut into thick sticks
1 tsp	(5 ml) chopped parsley
4	small potatoes, peeled and cut in ½ if necessary
3 tbsp	(45 ml) butter
3½ tbsp	(55 ml) flour
	generous pinch oregano
	pinch sage
	dash paprika
	few celery seed
	salt and pepper

Place chicken in large saucepan and pour in enough water to cover; bring to boil. Cook 5 to 6 minutes over low heat.

Drain chicken and replace in saucepan. Add vegetables, parsley and herbs. Cover with cold water and season well. Cover saucepan and bring to boil over high heat.

Cook chicken, covered, 30 minutes over low heat. Remove white meat and any cooked vegetables from saucepan; set aside.

Continue cooking remaining ingredients 10 to 15 minutes over low heat. When cooked, remove chicken and any remaining vegetables; set aside with others. Reserve 3 cups (750 ml) cooking liquid.

Heat butter in separate saucepan. When hot, add flour; mix and cook 1 minute.

Pour in 3 cups (750 ml) cooking liquid and season sauce well. Cook 8 minutes, uncovered. Add chicken and vegetables to sauce; simmer 3 to 4 minutes over low heat or until reheated.

*See Disjointing Chicken, page 175.

1 SERVING	338 CALORIES	17 g CARBOHYDRATE
36 g PROTEIN	14 g FAT	0.9 g FIBER

Roast Chicken with Rice Stuffing *(serves 4 to 6)*

5 to 5½ lb	(2.3 to 2.5 kg) chicken, cleaned and prepared for roasting
1	recipe rice suffing*
1 tbsp	(15 ml) butter
1 tbsp	(15 ml) vegetable oil
	salt and pepper

Preheat oven to 400°F (200°C).

Season chicken cavity with salt and pepper; fill with rice stuffing. Secure with kitchen string.

Place butter and oil in roasting pan and heat on burner. Place chicken on its back in pan and baste with fat; season well.

Cook chicken 45 minutes in oven; baste frequently.

Turn chicken on its side; continue cooking 15 minutes.

Reduce heat to 375°F (190°C) and replace chicken on its back. Finish cooking 35 to 40 minutes. Baste frequently.

*See Rice Stuffing, page 200.

1 SERVING	890 CALORIES	26 g CARBOHYDRATE
57 g PROTEIN	62 g FAT	0.3 g FIBER

Deep-Fried Wings *(serves 4)*

1 cup	(250 ml) seasoned flour
½ tsp	(2 ml) paprika
½ tsp	(2 ml) ginger
½ tsp	(2 ml) oregano
¼ tsp	(1 ml) thyme
¼ tsp	(1 ml) sage
½ tsp	(2 ml) celery seed
20	chicken wings, cleaned and cut in two
4	beaten eggs
3 cups	(750 ml) breadcrumbs

Preheat peanut oil in deep-fryer to 350°F (180°C).
Preheat oven to 400°F (200°C).

Mix flour and herbs together in large bowl. Add wings and mix until thoroughly coated.

Dip wings in beaten eggs and coat in breadcrumbs.

Deep-fry in several batches 5 to 6 minutes.

Remove and finish cooking 10 to 12 minutes in oven.

Serve.

1 SERVING 560 CALORIES 36 g CARBOHYDRATE
23 g PROTEIN 36 g FAT 0.2 g FIBER

Chicken Wrapped in Dough   *(serves 4)*

2	whole chicken breasts, deboned, skinned, cleaned and cut in half
1	beaten egg
	commercial flaky dough
	salt and pepper

Preheat oven to 425°F (220°C).

Grease and flour cookie sheet; set aside.

Roll out dough on floured surface until very thin.

Season chicken breasts and place one on portion of dough. Moisten inside of dough with a bit of water and fold over breast. Pinch edges shut and cut away unused dough.

Repeat procedure for remaining breasts.

Place wrapped chicken on cookie sheet and prick dough with fork. Brush with beaten egg. Cook 10 minutes in oven.

Reduce heat to 400°F (200°C) and continue cooking 15 minutes.

Serve with Mandarin Sauce, page 205.

1 SERVING	552 CALORIES	23 g CARBOHYDRATE
61 g PROTEIN	24 g FAT	0 g FIBER

Mandarin Sauce

1 tbsp	(15 ml) butter
¼ lb	(125 g) mushrooms, cleaned and diced
10 oz	(284 ml) can mandarin orange segments
¼ cup	(50 ml) mandarin juice
1¼ cups	(300 ml) hot chicken stock
1 tsp	(5 ml) chopped parsley
1 tbsp	(15 ml) cornstarch
2 tbsp	(30 ml) cold water
	salt and pepper

Heat butter in frying pan. When hot, add mushrooms and season; cook 3 to 4 minutes over medium heat.

Add mandarin segments and juice and chicken stock; stir well and continue cooking 2 to 3 minutes.

Sprinkle in parsley. Mix cornstarch with water; stir into sauce. Season and simmer 2 to 3 minutes before serving.

1 RECIPE	248 CALORIES	31 g CARBOHYDRATE
4 g PROTEIN	12 g FAT	2.7 g FIBER

Chicken Chow Mein *(serves 4)*

3 tbsp	(45 ml) vegetable oil
2	whole chicken breasts, deboned, skinned, cleaned and cut into bite-size pieces
2	green onions, chopped
¼ lb	(125 g) mushrooms sliced
1	celery stalk, sliced
½ cup	(125 ml) bamboo shoots
½ cup	(125 ml) water chestnuts, cut
1 cup	(250 ml) fresh bean sprouts
¼ cup	(50 ml) sweet pimento, chopped
1 cup	(250 ml) hot chicken stock
¼ tsp	(1 ml) ginger
1 tsp	(5 ml) cornstarch
2 tbsp	(30 ml) cold water
1 tbsp	(15 ml) soya sauce

Heat 2 tbsp (30 ml) oil in frying pan or wok. When hot, add chicken and stir-fry 6 minutes over medium heat.

Remove chicken and set aside.

Add remaining oil to pan. Stir-fry onions, mushrooms and celery 4 minutes; season well.

Add bamboo shoots, water chestnuts, bean sprouts and pimento; stir-fry 2 minutes.

Add chicken stock and ginger; bring to boil. Continue cooking 1 minute.

Replace chicken in pan. Mix cornstarch with water; stir into sauce. Stir in soya sauce and cook 1 minute to thicken.

Serve immediately.

1 SERVING	434 CALORIES	8 g CARBOHYDRATE
60 g PROTEIN	18 g FAT	1.2 g FIBER

Bag Chicken   *(serves 4)*

2 cups	(500 ml) flour
¼ tsp	(1 ml) thyme
¼ tsp	(1 ml) ground clove
¼ tsp	(1 ml) ginger
½ tsp	(2 ml) cinnamon
1 tsp	(5 ml) oregano
1 tsp	(5 ml) paprika
1 tsp	(5 ml) basil
4	whole chicken legs, cleaned
1 tsp	(5 ml) vegetable oil
	garlic salt and pepper

Place flour in bowl and mix in spices and herbs; set aside.

Parboil chicken legs 10 minutes. When cooled remove skin.

Place seasoned flour in brown paper bag. Add chicken legs, one at a time, and shake bag until thoroughly coated.

Heat oil in large frying pan. When hot, add chicken and cook, covered, 6 to 7 minutes over medium heat. Turn legs over once.

Remove cover and continue cooking 6 to 7 minutes or until done to taste.

Serve.

1 SERVING	279 CALORIES	12 g CARBOHYDRATE
33 g PROTEIN	11 g FAT	0 g FIBER

Chicken Liver Supreme   *(serves 4)*

2 tbsp	(30 ml) vegetable oil
1 lb	(500 g) chicken livers, fat removed and cleaned
1	garlic clove, smashed and chopped
3 tbsp	(45 ml) chopped onion
1	celery stalk, sliced
1	yellow pepper, cut in large pieces
2	tomatoes, cut in large pieces or wedges
1 tsp	(5 ml) chopped parsley
¼ tsp	(1 ml) Worcestershire sauce
1½ cups	(375 ml) hot chicken stock
1 tbsp	(15 ml) cornstarch
2 tbsp	(30 ml) cold water
	salt and pepper

Heat oil in frying pan. When hot, add chicken livers and season well. Stir and cook 2 minutes over medium heat.

Mix well and turn livers over; continue cooking 2 minutes.

Add garlic and onion; season and mix well. Cook 2 to 3 minutes over medium heat.

Add celery and yellow pepper; continue cooking 3 to 4 minutes.

Add tomatoes, parsley, Worcestershire sauce, salt and pepper. Mix and cook 3 minutes.

Pour in chicken stock and mix well; bring to boil. Continue cooking 4 to 5 minutes over low heat.

Mix cornstarch with water; stir into sauce. Simmer 1 to 2 minutes over low heat.

1 SERVING	248 CALORIES	9 g CARBOHYDRATE
26 g PROTEIN	12 g FAT	0.9 g FIBER

Cheese-Filled Chicken with Grape Sauce *(serves 4)*

2	whole chicken breasts, deboned, skinned and cleaned
4	small slices Gruyère cheese
1 cup	(250 ml) seasoned flour
3	beaten eggs
1 cup	(250 ml) coarse breadcrumbs
2 tbsp	(30 ml) butter
1 tbsp	(15 ml) vegetable oil
1 cup	(250 ml) seedless green grapes
1 tbsp	(15 ml) chopped parsley
2 to 3 tbsp	(30 to 45 ml) Port wine
½ cup	(125 ml) heavy cream
	few drops Tabasco sauce
	salt and pepper

Preheat oven to 350°F (180°C).

Make small incision in each chicken breast; place cheese inside. Dredge chicken with flour and dip into beaten eggs; lightly coat in breadcrumbs.

Heat butter and oil in large frying pan. When hot, add chicken and cook 5 to 6 minutes each side over medium heat.

Remove chicken from frying pan and place in baking dish. Finish cooking 8 to 10 minutes in oven.

Meanwhile, add grapes and parsley to frying pan; cook 1 to 2 minutes over medium heat.

Pour in wine and cook 2 minutes over high heat. Add cream, Tabasco sauce, salt and pepper; mix well. Continue cooking 3 to 4 minutes over medium heat.

Pour sauce over cooked chicken and serve. If desired, decorate with grapes dipped in sugar.

1 SERVING	670 CALORIES	22 g CARBOHYDRATE
69 g PROTEIN	34 g FAT	0.2 g FIBER

Bluegrass Bacon Chicken   *(serves 4)*

3	slices bacon, diced
4	whole chicken legs, skinned and cleaned
1 cup	(250 ml) seasoned flour
1	small onion, peeled and coarsely chopped
1	garlic clove, smashed and chopped
1 tsp	(5 ml) paprika
½ lb	(250 g) mushroom caps, cleaned
5 tbsp	(75 ml) sour cream
1 tsp	(5 ml) chopped fresh chives
	juice ¼ lemon
	salt and pepper

Place bacon in frying pan and heat; cook 4 to 5 minutes over medium heat.

Remove bacon and set aside; leave fat in pan.

Dredge chicken with flour and add legs to bacon fat. Cook 4 minutes each side over medium heat.

Add onion and garlic to pan; mix well and season with paprika. Cover and cook 12 minutes over low heat.

Add mushrooms and replace bacon in pan; cover and continue cooking 5 to 6 minutes over low heat depending on size of legs.

Remove pan from heat and mix in lemon juice.

Replace pan on stove top over very low heat. Add sour cream and chives; season generously. Mix until well blended.

1 SERVING	354 CALORIES	17 g CARBOHYDRATE
40 g PROTEIN	14 g FAT	1.1 g FIBER

Cornmeal Coated Chicken Legs *(serves 4)*

1 cup	(250 ml) cornmeal
1½ cups	(375 ml) breadcrumbs
¼ tsp	(1 ml) celery seed
¼ tsp	(1 ml) thyme
¼ tsp	(1 ml) nutmeg
4	whole chicken legs, cleaned
1 cup	(250 ml) flour
4	beaten eggs
	salt and pepper

Preheat peanut oil in deep-fryer to 350°F (180°C).

Mix cornmeal, breadcrumbs, herbs and spices in large bowl; set aside.

Place chicken in large pan and cover with water; season and bring to boil.

Skim water and continue cooking, partially covered, 20 to 22 minutes over low heat.

Remove chicken from saucepan and trim away skin.

Dredge chicken legs with flour and dip into beaten eggs; coat with cornmeal mixture.

Deep-fry 6 to 7 minutes. Be sure all sides are evenly browned.

Serve with Corn Fritters, page 211.

1 SERVING	723 CALORIES	65 g CARBOHYDRATE
46 g PROTEIN	31 g FAT	0.3 g FIBER

Sweet Chicken Wings   *(serves 4)*

2 tbsp	(30 ml) vegetable oil
2½ lb	(1.2 kg) chicken wings, cleaned
2	garlic cloves, smashed and chopped
2 tbsp	(30 ml) soya sauce
2 tbsp	(30 ml) maple syrup
	salt and pepper

Heat oil in large pan. When hot, add wings and season well; cook 2 to 3 minutes over medium heat.

Turn wings over and continue cooking 3 minutes.

Turn wings over again; cook 8 minutes over medium heat. Turn wings 3 to 4 times during cooking.

Remove chicken from pan and drain fat. Replace wings in pan and add garlic; mix well. Sprinkle with soya sauce and maple syrup; cover and cook 6 to 7 minutes over medium heat.

Correct seasoning and serve with your favourite sauce.

1 SERVING	298 CALORIES	7 g CARBOHYDRATE
27 g PROTEIN	18 g FAT	0 g FIBER

Corn Fritters   *(serves 6 to 8)*

3 tbsp	(45 ml) butter
3 tbsp	(45 ml) flour
1 cup	(250 ml) milk
2 cups	(500 ml) canned corn kernels, drained
1	egg yolk
	salt and pepper
	few drops Tabasco sauce
	for coating: flour, beaten egg and breadcrumbs

Heat butter in saucepan. When hot, add 3 tbsp (45 ml) flour and mix well; cook 1 minute over low heat.

Mix in milk and season; add Tabasco. Cook 5 minutes over low heat.

Add corn and egg yolk; mix until thoroughly combined. Cook 1 to 2 minutes over medium heat.

Transfer mixture to large dinner plate and cover with plastic wrap. Refrigerate 1 hour.

Form corn mixture into hamburger-like patties. Dredge with flour, dip into beaten eggs and coat in breadcrumbs.

Deep-fry or sauté in hot oil 4 minutes. Turn over once during cooking.

Serve with chicken.

1 SERVING	201 CALORIES	17 g CARBOHYDRATE
4 g PROTEIN	13 g FAT	0.4 g FIBER

Chicken Corn Croquettes *(serves 4)*

3 tbsp	(45 ml) butter
3 tbsp	(45 ml) flour
1 cup	(250 ml) hot milk
2 cups	(500 ml) canned corn kernels, drained
1	egg yolk
1½ cups	(375 ml) finely chopped cooked chicken
	salt and pepper
	for coating; flour, beaten eggs and breadcrumbs

Heat butter in saucepan. When hot, add 3 tbsp (45 ml) flour and mix well; cook 1 minute over low heat.

Mix in milk and season; cook 5 minutes over low heat.

Add corn, egg yolk and chicken; mix until thoroughly combined. Cook 1 to 2 minutes over medium heat.

Transfer mixture to large dinner plate and cover with plastic wrap; refrigerate 1 hour.

Form mixture into cylindrical rolls. Dredge with flour, dip into beaten eggs and coat in breadcrumbs.

Deep-fry or sauté in hot oil 4 minutes. Turn to brown all sides.

Serve with cocktail sauce.

212

1 SERVING	607 CALORIES	46 g CARBOHYDRATE
27 g PROTEIN	35 g FAT	0.8 g FIBER

Hearty Turkey Stew with Vegetables *(serves 4 to 6)*

2 tbsp	(30 ml) butter
2	onions, peeled and diced
1	celery stalk, cut into 1 in (2.5 cm) sticks
2	carrots, pared and cut into 1 in (2.5 cm) sticks
2	potatoes, peeled and cubed
3 tbsp	(45 ml) flour
3 cups	(750 ml) heated chicken stock
¼ tsp	(1 ml) marjoram
1	turkey breast, skinned and cubed
1	green pepper, diced
	several drops Tabasco sauce
	salt and pepper

Heat butter in sauté pan. When hot, add onions; cover and cook 3 minutes.

Add celery and carrots; mix well and season. Continue cooking 3 to 4 minutes.

Mix in potatoes and flour; cook 1 minute.

Stir in chicken stock, marjoram and Tabasco sauce. Stir and correct seasoning.

Add turkey and bring to boil. Cook stew 40 to 45 minutes over low heat.

Eight minutes before end of cooking, add green pepper. Serve.

1 SERVING	403 CALORIES	15 g CARBOHYDRATE
58 g PROTEIN	19 g FAT	1.5 g FIBER

Capon in Red Wine   *(serves 6 to 8)*

2	5 lb (2.3 kg) capons, cut into 8 pieces*, skinned and cleaned
1½ cups	(375 ml) seasoned flour
3 tbsp	(45 ml) vegetable oil
3 tbsp	(45 ml) butter
1	onion, peeled and diced
2	garlic cloves, chopped
1 tsp	(5 ml) tarragon
½ tsp	(2 ml) basil
3 tbsp	(45 ml) flour
4 cups	(1 L) dry red wine
2 tbsp	(30 ml) commercial beef extract
½ lb	(250 g) mushrooms, cleaned and diced
1 tbsp	(15 ml) chopped fresh parsley
	salt and pepper
	few drops Tabasco sauce

Preheat oven to 350°F (180°C).

Dredge chicken pieces with seasoned flour.

Heat half of oil in large sauté pan. When hot, add half of chicken; cook 3 to 4 minutes each side. Remove and set aside.

Repeat procedure for remaining chicken.

Heat half of butter in same pan. Add onion, garlic and all herbs; cook 6 to 7 minutes over low heat. Stir once or twice.

Mix in 3 tbsp (45 ml) flour and continue cooking 1 minute. Replace seared chicken pieces in sauté pan and season well. Stir in red wine and beef extract; bring to boil.

Cover pan and cook 1¼ hours in oven.

After 1 hour of cooking check if white meat is cooked. If so, remove and finish cooking dark meat. About 10 minutes before serving time, prepare garnish. Heat remaining butter in frying pan. When hot, sauté mushrooms 5 minutes over medium heat. Season well and serve with capon.

*See Disjointing Chicken, page 175.

1 SERVING	304 CALORIES	13 g CARBOHYDRATE
27 g PROTEIN	16 g FAT	0.7 g FIBER

Elegant Strawberry Chicken   *(serves 4)*

2 tbsp	(30 ml) butter
2	large whole chicken breasts, deboned, skinned and cleaned
½ cup	(125 ml) frozen strawberries, defrosted
4	pear halves
1 cup	(250 ml) heated chicken stock
1 tbsp	(15 ml) cornstarch
2 tbsp	(30 ml) cold water
	salt and pepper
	few drops lime juice

Heat butter in sauté pan. When hot, add chicken and sprinkle with lime juice. Cover and cook 4 minutes over medium-low heat.

Season chicken and turn over; continue cooking, covered, 4 minutes.

Turn chicken again; cover and cook 8 minutes over medium-low heat.

Add strawberries and pears to pan; continue cooking 3 to 4 minutes.

Remove chicken and pears from pan; set aside.

Add chicken stock to liquid remaining in pan; bring to boil. Cook sauce 2 to 3 minutes over medium heat.

Mix cornstarch with water; stir into sauce. Simmer 2 minutes over medium-low heat.

Correct seasoning and pour sauce over chicken and fruit.

1 SERVING	408 CALORIES	17 g CARBOHYDRATE
58 g PROTEIN	12 g FAT	0.5 g FIBER

Helpful Barbecue Hints

— Because there are so many types of barbecues on the market, please follow our cooking times as guidelines.

— Oil your barbecue grill before setting food on it, otherwise most foods will stick.

— Make a practice of preheating your barbecue in plenty of time. Consult your guide booklet for temperatures and suggestions.

— Because most meat is cooked quickly on a barbecue, it is necessary to turn the pieces often to avoid burning.

— You can use many of our marinades for other foods that you might like to barbecue.

— Timing an assortment of foods on the barbecue takes a little practice but with patience and perhaps a few helpers, it can be as easy as stove cooking.

Delicious B.B.Q. Chicken *(serves 4)*

1 tbsp	(15 ml) soya sauce
3 tbsp	(45 ml) catsup
2 tbsp	(30 ml) maple syrup
¼ tsp	(1 ml) Tabasco sauce
1 tbsp	(15 ml) lemon juice
1	garlic clove, smashed and chopped
½	chicken, cut into 4 pieces and cleaned
2 tbsp	(30 ml) vegetable oil
	salt and pepper

Preheat barbecue to medium.

Combine soya sauce, catsup, maple syrup and Tabasco sauce in bowl. Add lemon juice and garlic; mix well. Season and set aside.

Place chicken in roasting pan or large plate; baste generously with oil and season well.

Place chicken on barbecue grill; cover and cook 3 minutes.

Baste chicken with marinade and turn pieces over; cook, uncovered, 2 minutes.

Baste again; partially cover and continue cooking 3 minutes.

Transfer pieces to top grill; cover and cook 7 minutes. Open barbecue cover and continue cooking 20 to 25 minutes depending on size of pieces. Baste frequently.

Note: White meat will be cooked before dark meat.

If desired, serve with sweet and sour dipping sauce.

1 SERVING	268 CALORIES	9 g CARBOHYDRATE
31 g PROTEIN	12 g FAT	0 g FIBER

Vegetables and Sausages in Foil *(serves 4)*

12 oz	(340 g) baby carrots, washed
1	red onion, peeled and quartered
2	large slices garlic butter
1	zucchini, cut into sticks
1	green pepper, cut into large pieces
1	Polish sausage, sliced on the bias
	salt and pepper

Preheat barbecue to medium-high.

Take large sheet of aluminium foil and fold in half. Place flat on kitchen counter.

Add carrots, onion and garlic butter; shape foil with hands to form basket.

Cover with another sheet of foil and seal edges shut. Place on barbecue grill and cover; cook 30 minutes.

Remove top sheet of foil and add zucchini, green pepper and sausage; replace foil. Continue cooking on barbecue, covered, another 30 minutes.

Serve.

1 SERVING	677 CALORIES	15 g CARBOHYDRATE
26 g PROTEIN	57 g FAT	1.5 g FIBER

New York Steaks   *(serves 4)*

4	New York steaks, 1 in (2.5 cm) thick
1	recipe catsup marinade*
	salt and pepper

Preheat barbecue to high.

Brush steaks generously with marinade and place on barbecue grill. Observe the following cooking times for desired degree of doneness.

> Rare: 7 to 8 minutes
> Medium: 8 to 10 minutes
> Well done: 10 to 12 minutes

Turn steaks 2 to 3 times during cooking and season well.

If desired, serve with potatoes and other vegetables. For a treat top steaks with garlic butter.

*See Catsup Marinade, page 225.

1 SERVING	550 CALORIES	24 g CARBOHYDRATE
55 g PROTEIN	26 g FAT	0.3 g FIBER

Grilled Salmon Steaks *(serves 4)*

4 tbsp	(60 ml) clarified butter
1 tsp	(5 ml) chopped fresh parsley
1 tsp	(5 ml) oregano
½ tsp	(2 ml) basil
4	salmon steaks, ¾ in (2 cm) thick
	juice 2 limes
	salt and pepper

Preheat barbecue to medium.

Mix butter, parsley, herbs and lime juice together in small bowl.

Brush marinade over salmon and season with salt and pepper. Cook 4 minutes, uncovered, on barbecue grill.

Baste and turn salmon over; continue cooking, partially covered, 15 minutes. Baste and turn salmon frequently to avoid burning.

Serve with barbecued vegetables.

1 SERVING	329 CALORIES	0 g CARBOHYDRATE
35 g PROTEIN	21 g FAT	0 g FIBER

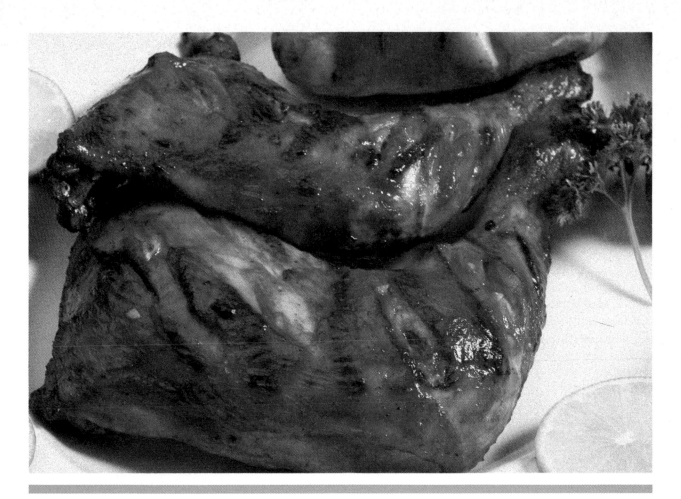

B.B.Q. Chicken Legs *(serves 4)*

½ cup	(125 ml) catsup
¼ cup	(50 ml) wine vinegar
3	garlic cloves, smashed and chopped
¼ tsp	(1 ml) cumin
¼ tsp	(1 ml) curry powder
½ cup	(125 ml) tomato clam juice
2 tbsp	(30 ml) oil
4	whole chicken legs, cleaned
	several drops Tabasco sauce
	pinch brown sugar
	salt and pepper

Preheat barbecue to medium.

Place catsup and vinegar in bowl; mix well.

Add garlic, spices and tomato clam juice; mix well. Stir in brown sugar.

Incorporate oil and correct seasoning.

Slash chicken legs and brush with marinade; season well.

Place chicken on barbecue grill; cover and cook 3 minutes.

Baste chicken and turn legs over; cook, uncovered, 2 minutes.

Baste again; partially cover and continue cooking 3 minutes.

Transfer legs to top grill; cover and cook 7 minutes.

Open barbecue cover and continue cooking 20 to 25 minutes or longer if necessary. Baste frequently.

Serve with baked potatoes.

1 SERVING	299 CALORIES	9 g CARBOHYDRATE
32 g PROTEIN	15 g FAT	0.3 g FIBER

Outdoor Half Chicken *(serves 4)*

2	garlic cloves, smashed and chopped
3 tbsp	(45 ml) olive oil
1 tbsp	(15 ml) soya sauce
1 tbsp	(15 ml) tomato paste
¼ cup	(50 ml) heated chicken stock
2	2¼ lb (1.3 kg) chickens, cleaned and split in half
	several drops Worcestershire sauce
	juice 1 lime
	dash paprika
	salt and pepper

Preheat barbecue to medium.

Mix all ingredients, except chickens, in bowl.

Place chickens on plate and brush with marinade; season well.

Set chickens on barbecue grill and cook 8 minutes.

Turn chickens over; brush with marinade and continue cooking 8 minutes.

Brush chickens again with marinade. Turn birds over and finish cooking 24 to 34 minutes, depending on size. Baste and turn chickens over during cooking.

When cooked, remove from grill and serve with salad.

1 SERVING	465 CALORIES	1 g CARBOHYDRATE
68 g PROTEIN	21 g FAT	0 g FIBER

Lamb Brochettes *(serves 4)*

3 lb	(1.4 kg) loin of lamb
1	recipe red wine marinade*
8	small new potatoes, cooked in jackets
1	red onion, peeled and cubed
2	zucchinis, sliced
	salt and pepper

Trim fat from lamb and cut meat into large cubes. Place on plate and cover with marinade; refrigerate 8 hours.

Preheat barbecue to medium-high.

Drain lamb and reserve marinade.

Alternate lamb, potato, onion and zucchini on skewers. Bruch with marinade and season well.

Place skewers on barbecue grill; cook, uncovered, 5 to 6 minutes. Baste frequently.

Turn skewers over and continue cooking 5 to 6 minutes; baste frequently.

Serve.

*See Red Wine Marinade, page 235.

1 SERVING	572 CALORIES	21 g CARBOHYDRATE
50 g PROTEIN	32 g FAT	1.0 g FIBER

223

B.B.Q. Pork Shish Kebabs   *(serves 4)*

1	pork tenderloin, trimmed and sliced
1	recipe soya sauce or catsup marinade*
2	apples, peeled and cut into wedges
1	Polish sausage, sliced
4	green onions, cut into sticks
1	green pepper, cubed
	salt and pepper

Place pork in dish and cover with marinade; refrigerate 2 hours. Turn pork slices over once while marinating.

Preheat barbecue to medium-high.

Drain pork and reserve marinade.

Alternate apple, sausage, green onion, pork and green pepper on skewers. Brush with marinade and season well.

Place skewers on barbecue grill; cook, uncovered, 6 to 7 minutes. Baste occasionally.

Turn skewers over and continue cooking 6 to 7 minutes; baste occasionally.

Serve with salad.

*See Catsup Marinade, page 225.

1 SERVING	627 CALORIES	37 g CARBOHYDRATE
32 g PROTEIN	39 g FAT	1.4 g FIBER

Catsup Marinade

3 tbsp	(45 ml) olive oil
½ cup	(125 ml) catsup
¼ cup	(50 ml) chili sauce
½ tsp	(2 ml) horseradish
¼ cup	(50 ml) wine vinegar
3 tbsp	(45 ml) liquid honey
1 tbsp	(15 ml) finely chopped chives
	several drops Tabasco sauce
	several drops soya sauce
	freshly ground pepper

Mix all ingredients together in bowl.

Refrigerate until use.

This marinade is particularly good with beef and chicken.

1 RECIPE	787 CALORIES	96 g CARBOHYDRATE
4 g PROTEIN	43 g FAT	1.2 g FIBER

Soya Sauce Marinade

¼ cup	(50 ml) soya sauce
2 tbsp	(30 ml) dry vermouth
1 tsp	(5 ml) sugar
¼	onion, finely chopped
1	thin slice fresh ginger, finely chopped

Place all ingredients in bowl and mix well.

Refrigerate until use.

1 RECIPE	72 CALORIES	12 g CARBOHYDRATE
6 g PROTEIN	0 g FAT	0.2 g FIBER

B.B.Q. Rabbit   *(serves 4)*

3½ to 4 lb	(1.6 to 1.8 kg) rabbit, cleaned
4 tbsp	(60 ml) soft butter
2 tbsp	(30 ml) Dijon mustard
¼ cup	(50 ml) dry white wine
	dash paprika
	salt and pepper

Preheat oven to 375°F (190°C).
Cooking time: 20 minutes per lb (500 g).

Place sheet of aluminium foil in bottom of roasting pan. Place rabbit on foil and season generously with salt and pepper. Sprinkle with paprika.

Mix butter with mustard; spread over rabbit. Pour in white wine. Cover roasting pan with another sheet of aluminium foil; seal well. Cook in oven.

Serve with Brussels sprouts and baked potatoes. Baste rabbit with cooking juice before serving.

1 SERVING	612 CALORIES	0 g CARBOHYDRATE
72 g PROTEIN	36 g FAT	0 g FIBER

B.B.Q. London Broil *(serves 4)*

3 tbsp	(45 ml) soya sauce
1 tbsp	(15 ml) honey
1	garlic clove, smashed and chopped
1 tbsp	(15 ml) vegetable oil
4	6 oz (170 g) London broil steaks
4	cooked potatoes with skin, cut in half
1	English cucumber, sliced in 2 in (5 cm) pieces
	juice ½ lemon
	salt and pepper

Preheat barbecue to medium

Combine soya sauce, honey, garlic, oil, lemon juice and pepper in bowl.

Place steaks and vegetables on plate; brush marinade over ingredients and season well.

Cook steaks on barbecue grill 10 to 12 minutes over medium heat. Baste frequently and turn meat over 4 times.

Before meat is fully cooked, add vegetables to grill. Cook 3 to 4 minutes on both sides; baste frequently.

Serve.

1 SERVING	361 CALORIES	22 g CARBOHYDRATE
39 g PROTEIN	13 g FAT	0.7 g FIBER

Butterfly Tenderloin Steaks   *(serves 4)*

2 tbsp	(30 ml) vegetable oil
1 tbsp	(15 ml) soya sauce
2	garlic cloves, smashed and chopped
½ cup	(125 ml) dry white wine
8	thick slices eggplant
4	8 oz (227 g) butterfly tenderloin steaks
	few drops Tabasco sauce
	salt and pepper

Preheat barbecue to medium-high.

Mix oil, soya sauce, garlic, wine and Tabasco sauce together.

Place eggplant slices in bowl and pour in marinade; refrigerate 15 minutes.

Generously baste meat with marinade. Cook eggplant and meat on grill 10 to 12 minutes, or to taste.

Baste frequently with marinade and turn items over at least 3 times; season well.

Serve with fresh corn, either boiled or barbecued.

1 SERVING	583 CALORIES	6 g CARBOHYDRATE
70 g PROTEIN	31 g FAT	0.9 g FIBER

Ginger Seasoned Wings   *(serves 4)*

2	garlic cloves, smashed and chopped
2 tbsp	(30 ml) chopped fresh ginger
2 tbsp	(30 ml) soya sauce
¼ cup	(50 ml) lemon juice
1 tsp	(5 ml) hot sauce or Tabasco
1 tbsp	(15 ml) wine vinegar
½ cup	(125 ml) olive oil
2 lb	(900 g) chicken wings, cleaned salt and freshly ground pepper

Preheat barbecue to medium.

Combine garlic, ginger, soya sauce, lemon juice, hot sauce, vinegar and oil together in large bowl; season with pepper.

Place wings in bowl and refrigerate 1 hour.

Place wings on barbecue grill and cook 12 to 15 minutes, depending on size.

Turn wings 4 to 5 times during cooking and baste occasionally. Season generously.

Serve with a light salad and pickles.

Scallops Wrapped in Bacon on Skewers

(serves 4)

1 lb	(500 g) fresh scallops
5	slices cooked bacon
1	apple, peeled and sliced
¼	cucumber, sliced
8	cherry tomatoes
3 tbsp	(45 ml) melted butter
1 tsp	(5 ml) Worcestershire sauce
1 tbsp	(15 ml) lemon juice
	salt and pepper

Preheat barbecue to medium.

Cut bacon into suitable pieces, depending on the size of scallops and wrap around scallops.

Alternate apple, wrapped scallop, cucumber and tomato on skewers. Try to end with a slice of apple.

Mix butter, Worcestershire sauce and lemon juice together; season with pepper.

Brush mixture over skewers and place on barbecue grill. Cook 5 to 6 minutes, depending on taste.

Be sure to rotate skewers and baste and season during cooking.

1 SERVING	294 CALORIES	15 g CARBOHYDRATE
27 g PROTEIN	14 g FAT	0.6 g FIBER

Vegetarian's Shish Kebabs *(serves 4)*

1	recipe soya sauce marinade*
8	cherry tomatoes
½	cucumber, sliced
½	green pepper, sliced
1	white onion, peeled and sliced
2	broccoli stalks, blanched and sliced
8	green onions, cut in 1 in (2.5 cm) pieces
	salt and pepper

Preheat barbecue to medium.

Alternate vegetables on skewers and brush with marinade.

Place skewers on barbecue grill and cook about 6 to 7 minutes, depending on taste. Baste occasionally and season very well.

Rotate skewers so that vegetables cook evenly.

Vegetables should still be crisp when served.

* See Soya Sauce Marinade, page 225.

1 SERVING	60 CALORIES	11 g CARBOHYDRATE
4 g PROTEIN	0 g FAT	1.4 g FIBER

Shrimp Kebabs   *(serves 4)*

1½ lb	(750 g) fresh or frozen shrimp, peeled and deveined
2 tbsp	(30 ml) lemon juice
2	garlic cloves, smashed and chopped
¼	English cucumber, sliced
12	cherry tomatoes
1	green pepper, sliced
	few drops commercial Mexican sauce
	dash celery seed
	salt and pepper

Place shrimp in bowl and add lemon juice and garlic; mix well.

Add Mexican sauce, celery seed and pepper; mix again. Refrigerate 1½ hours.

Preheat barbecue to high.

Alternate cucumber, tomato, shrimp and green pepper or skewers. Generously brush with marinade and season.

Place on barbecue grill and cook 7 to 8 minutes, or to taste. Turn 3 times during cooking and baste frequently.

Serve.

1 SERVING	190 CALORIES	7 g CARBOHYDRATE
36 g PROTEIN	2 g FAT	0.7 g FIBER

Sweet B.B.Q. Sausages *(serves 4)*

1 tbsp	(15 ml) soya sauce
¼ cup	(50 ml) catsup
1 tbsp	(15 ml) vegetable oil
8	knackwurst sausages
	salt and pepper

Combine soya sauce, catsup and vegetable oil together.

Score sausages with knife and baste with marinade. Place on barbecue grill and cook 8 to 10 minutes.

Turn sausages 3 to 4 times during cooking and baste frequently. Season well.

Serve with fresh corn.

1 SERVING	423 CALORIES	7 g CARBOHYDRATE
20 g PROTEIN	35 g FAT	0.1 g FIBER

Salmon Steaks in Wine Marinade *(serves 4)*

2 tbsp	(30 ml) vegetable oil
¼ cup	(50 ml) dry white wine or sake
1 tbsp	(15 ml) chopped fresh ginger
1 tsp	(5 ml) soya sauce
1 tsp	(5 ml) lemon juice
4	salmon steaks, about ¾ in (2 cm) thick
	few drops Tabasco sauce
	salt and pepper

Preheat barbecue to medium.

Combine oil, wine, ginger, soya sauce, lemon juice and Tabasco in large bowl; season with pepper.

Place salmon steaks in marinade and refrigerate 15 minutes.

Cook salmon on barbecue grill, covered, 12 to 14 minutes. Turn steaks over twice and baste occasionally; season.

Serve with Pepper Rice, page 235.

1 SERVING	370 CALORIES	0 g CARBOHYDRATE
52 g PROTEIN	18 g FAT	0 g FIBER

Red Wine Marinade

2 cups	(500 ml) dry red wine
¼ cup	(50 ml) wine vinegar
¼ cup	(50 ml) olive oil
2	garlic cloves, smashed and chopped
½	celery stalk, cut in strips
¼ tsp	(1 ml) chervil
2 tbsp	(30 ml) chopped chives
	pinch mint
	pinch nutmeg
	salt and freshly ground pepper

Place all ingredients in bowl and mix together with whisk.

Refrigerate until use.

Use this marinade for lamb, pork and beef.

1 RECIPE	504 CALORIES	0 g CARBOHYDRATE
0 g PROTEIN	56 g FAT	0 g FIBER

Pepper Rice *(serves 4)*

1 tbsp	(15 ml) vegetable oil
1	shallot, chopped
1	garlic clove, smashed and chopped
½	yellow or red pepper, diced
½	green pepper, diced
2	small tomatoes, diced
2 cups	(500 ml) cooked rice
1 tsp	(5 ml) chopped chives
	salt and pepper

Heat oil in large frying pan. When hot, add shallot and garlic; season.

Add vegetables and mix well. Cook 3 minutes over high heat.

Mix in rice and continue cooking 3 to 4 minutes. Stir to prevent sticking.

Sprinkle in chives and correct seasoning.

Serve with barbecued food.

1 SERVING	132 CALORIES	22 g CARBOHYDRATE
2 g PROTEIN	4 g FAT	0.7 g FIBER

Hot Chicken Strips *(serves 4)*

2	garlic cloves, smashed and chopped
2 tbsp	(30 ml) fresh chopped ginger
2 tbsp	(30 ml) soya sauce
¼ cup	(50 ml) lemon juice
1 tsp	(5 ml) hot sauce or Tabasco
1 tbsp	(15 ml) wine vinegar
¼ cup	(50 ml) olive oil
¼ tsp	(1 ml) ground pepper
2	whole chicken breasts, skinned and cut in strips

Preheat barbecue to medium.

Combine garlic, ginger, soya sauce, lemon juice, hot sauce, vinegar, oil and pepper in bowl.

Place chicken strips in marinade and refrigerate 15 minutes.

Place chicken on barbecue grill and cook 6 to 8 minutes, depending on size. Season during cooking and baste frequently. Turn chicken strips at least 3 times.

Serve with potatoes.

1 SERVING	212 CALORIES	0 g CARBOHYDRATE
26 g PROTEIN	12 g FAT	0 g FIBER

Lamb Steaks *(serves 4)*

¼ cup	(50 ml) olive oil
2 tbsp	(30 ml) wine vinegar
4	fresh mint leaves
½ cup	(125 ml) dry white wine
2	garlic cloves, smashed and chopped
4	lamb steaks with bone, ¾ in (2 cm) thick
	salt and pepper

Combine oil and vinegar in bowl. Add mint and season well.

Pour in wine and add garlic; mix.

Place lamb in deep plate and pour in marinade. Refrigerate 4 hours.

Preheat barbecue to medium-high.

Place lamb on barbecue grill. Cook 5 to 6 minutes each side. Season during cooking.

Serve with potatoes.

See Technique next page.

1 SERVING	238 CALORIES	0 g CARBOHYDRATE
28 g PROTEIN	14 g FAT	0 g FIBER

TECHNIQUE: LAMB STEAKS

1 Choose lamb steaks with bone.

2 Combine oil and vinegar in bowl. Add mint and season well. Pour in wine.

3 Add garlic and mix. Place lamb in deep plate and pour in marinade. Refrigerate 4 hours.

4 Place lamb on barbecue grill. Cook 5 to 6 minutes each side. Season during cooking.

Barbecued Bits and Bites *(serves 4)*

½ lb	(250 ml) lean ground beef
1	egg
1 tbsp	(15 ml) chopped fresh parsley
½ tsp	(2 ml) crushed chillies
¼ tsp	(1 ml) thyme
¼ tsp	(1 ml) basil
¼ tsp	(1 ml) ginger
2 tbsp	(30 ml) chopped onion, cooked
1	large Polish sausage, cut in ¾ in (2 cm) thick slices
4	chicken wings
2	pork chops, meat cubed
4	slices cooked bacon
1	whole chicken breast, cooked, skinned and sliced thick
	salt and pepper

Place ground beef in bowl and add egg; mix. Season well and mix again.

Add parsley, chillies, thyme, basil, ginger and onion; mix together well. Shape mixture into small meatballs.

Place meatballs in marinade. Add sausage slices, wings and pork; refrigerate 1 hour.

Preheat barbecue to medium-high.

Remove meat and chicken from marinade; transfer to plate.

Wrap pieces of cooked chicken breast in bacon; secure with toothpicks. Baste with marinade.

Cook bits and bites on barbecue grill until done to taste. Turn often to avoid burning and season generously.

Baste as needed and serve with dipping sauce.

See Technique next page.

1 SERVING	713 CALORIES	4 g CARBOHYDRATE
64 g PROTEIN	49 g FAT	0 g FIBER

TECHNIQUE:BARBECUED BITS AND BITS

1 Prepare your ingredients in advance.

2 Place ground beef in bowl and add egg; mix. Season well and mix again.

3 Add spices and onion; mix together well.

4 Shape mixture into small meatballs.

5 Pour oil and soya sauce into large bowl. Add garlic and catsup; mix together well. Finish marinade by adding lemon juice and Worcestershire to taste.

6 Place meatballs in marinade. Add sausage slices, wings and pork; refrigerate 1 hour.

Marinade

¼ cup	(50 ml) olive oil
3 tbsp	(45 ml) soya sauce
2	garlic cloves, smashed and chopped
¼ cup	(50 ml) catsup
	several drops lemon or lime juice
	Worcestershire sauce to taste

Pour oil and soya sauce into large bowl. Add garlic and catsup; mix together well.

Add lemon juice and Worcestershire sauce; mix and correct seasoning.

Salisbury Steak *(serves 4)*

2½ tbsp	(40 ml) vegetable oil
1	medium-size onion, peeled and finely chopped
2 lb	(900 g) lean ground beef
1	egg
2	onions, peeled and thinly sliced
1 tbsp	(15 ml) butter
1½ cups	(375 ml) commercial brown sauce, heated
	pinch sweet basil
	dash ground clove
	few crushed chillies
	salt and pepper

Preheat oven to 150°F (70°C).

Heat 1 tbsp (15 ml) oil in small frying pan. Add chopped onion and spices; cover and cook 4 minutes over low heat.

Place meat in large bowl and press down centre. Add egg to indentation and mix well with hands. Add cooked onion and mix until well incorporated. Correct seasoning.

Shape mixture into patties about ¾ in (2 cm) thick. Score with knife.

Heat remaining oil in large frying pan. When hot, add meat and cook 10 to 12 minutes over medium heat. Turn 3 to 4 times during cooking and once seared, season well.

Transfer meat to ovenproof platter and keep hot in oven.

Add sliced onions and butter to frying pan. Cook 6 to 7 minutes over medium heat.

Pour in brown sauce and season generously; mix well and continue cooking 3 minutes.

See Technique next page.

1 SERVING	517 CALORIES	11 g CARBOHYDRATE
62 g PROTEIN	25 g FAT	0.5 g FIBER

1 Place meat in large bowl and press down centre. Add egg to indentation.

2 Mix well with hands.

3 Add cooked onion and mix until well incorporated. Correct seasoning.

4 Shape mixture into patties about $\frac{3}{4}$ in (2 cm) thick. Score with knife. Cook meat as directed in recipe.

5 Add sliced onions and butter to frying pan. Cook 6 to 7 minutes over medium heat. Onions should brown but not burn, so stir as needed.

6 Pour in brown sauce and season generously; mix well and continue cooking 3 minutes.

New England Boiled Beef *(serves 4)*

4 lb	(1.8 kg) corned beef brisket
3	parsley sprigs
1	bay leaf
2	fresh mint sprigs
¼ tsp	(1 ml) thyme
5	large carrots, pared and cut in two
5	large potatoes, peeled and cut in two
4	small onions, peeled
1	butternut squash, cut in thick slices
	salt and pepper

Place meat in large saucepan and cover with cold water. Bring to gentle boil and skim.

Season well and add herbs. Partially cover and simmer over medium-low heat 2 hours.

Add carrots and potatoes to saucepan; continue cooking another hour.

Forty minutes before end of cooking, add remaining vegetables.

When cooked, remove beef and arrange on serving platter. Pour some juice on top and serve with vegetables. Have some mustard and pickles handy.

Beef Casserole *(serves 6 to 8)*

1 tbsp	(15 ml) vegetable oil
2	onions, peeled and finely chopped
2	garlic cloves, smashed and chopped
1 tbsp	(15 ml) chopped parsley
1¼ lb	(625 g) lean ground beef
1½ cups	(375 ml) chopped tomatoes
3 tbsp	(45 ml) tomato paste
4 cups	(1 L) hot mashed potatoes
	pinch thyme
	salt and pepper
	melted butter

Preheat oven to 375°F (190°C).

Heat oil in sauté pan. When hot, add onions, garlic and parsley; mix and cook 3 minutes over medium heat.

Add beef and thyme; mix well. Continue cooking 5 to 6 minutes over medium heat. Stir occasionally and season.

Add tomatoes and tomato paste; cook 4 to 5 minutes over low heat.

Spread half of mashed potatoes in bottom of large baking dish. Cover with beef mixture.

Spread remaining potatoes over beef and pour on some melted butter.

Cook 25 to 30 minutes in oven.

Serve hot and reheat any leftovers.

1 SERVING	290 CALORIES	29 g CARBOHYDRATE
21 g PROTEIN	10 g FAT	0.7 g FIBER

Cheese Burgers   *(serves 4)*

2 tbsp	(30 ml) vegetable oil
1	small onion, peeled and finely chopped
2 lb	(900 g) lean ground beef
1	egg
1 tbsp	(15 ml) chopped parsley
4	slices Roquefort cheese
	few drops Worcestershire sauce
	few drops Tabasco sauce
	salt and pepper

Heat 1 tbsp (15 ml) oil in small frying pan. Add onion; cover and cook 4 minutes over low heat.

Place beef in large bowl and press down centre. Add egg to indentation and mix well with hands.

Add cooked onion, parsley, Worcestershire and Tabasco sauces. Mix again until well incorporated.

Shape mixture into large patties and score with knife.

Heat remaining oil in large frying pan. When hot, add meat and cook 10 to 12 minutes over medium heat. Turn 4 times during cooking and once seared, season well.

When burgers are cooked, transfer to ovenproof dish. Add slices of cheese and broil 2 to 3 minutes in oven.

Serve with Green Onion Potatoes, page 264.

1 SERVING	380 CALORIES	2 g CARBOHYDRATE
57 g PROTEIN	16 g FAT	0.2 g FIBER

247

London Broil with Apples *(serves 4)*

2	apples, peeled and sliced thick
2 tbsp	(30 ml) vegetable oil
4	6 oz (170 g) London broil steaks
1 tbsp	(15 ml) butter
1 cup	(250 ml) sliced English cucumber
1	celery stalk, sliced
¼ tsp	(1 ml) celery seed
¼ tsp	(1 ml) thyme
1 cup	(250 ml) heated chicken stock
1 tbsp	(15 ml) cornstarch
2 tbsp	(30 ml) cold water
1 tbsp	(15 ml) soya sauce
	lemon juice
	salt and pepper

Preheat oven to 150°F (70°C).

Place sliced apples in bowl and add some lemon juice. This will prevent any discoloring.

Heat oil in large frying pan. When hot, add meat and cook 8 to 10 minutes over medium heat. Turn meat 3 to 4 times during cooking and once seared, season well.

Transfer meat to ovenproof platter and keep hot in oven.

Add butter to frying pan. When hot, add apples, cucumber and celery; mix in herbs and season well. Cook 4 to 5 minutes over medium heat.

Pour in chicken stock and cook 2 minutes over medium heat.

Mix cornstarch with water; stir into sauce. Add soya sauce and cook 2 minutes to thicken.

Pour sauce over meat and serve.

1 SERVING	428 CALORIES	16 g CARBOHYDRATE
46 g PROTEIN	20 g FAT	0.9 g FIBER

London Broil in Tomato and Mushroom Sauce   *(serves 4)*

2 tbsp	(30 ml) vegetable oil
4	6 oz (170 g) London broil steaks
1 tbsp	(15 ml) butter
2	green onions, sliced
½ lb	(250 g) mushrooms, cleaned and sliced
2 cups	(500 ml) canned tomatoes, drained and chopped
1	garlic clove, smashed and chopped
1½ cups	(375 ml) commercial brown sauce, heated
	salt and pepper

Preheat oven to 150°F (70°C).

Heat oil in large frying pan. When hot, add meat and cook 8 to 10 minutes over medium heat. Turn meat 3 to 4 times during cooking and once seared, season well.

Transfer meat to ovenproof platter and keep hot in oven.

Add butter to frying pan. When melted, add onions and mushrooms; season well. Cook 3 minutes over medium-high heat.

Add tomatoes and garlic; mix well. Continue cooking 3 minutes over medium heat.

Mix in brown sauce and cook 3 to 4 minutes; correct seasoning.

Pour sauce over meat and serve.

See Technique next page.

1 SERVING	437 CALORIES	13 g CARBOHYDRATE
49 g PROTEIN	21 g FAT	1.0 g FIBER

TECHNIQUE: LONDON BROIL

1 London broil steaks are an economical way of serving meat particularly for a large family. Your butcher probably carries London broil steaks on a regular basis.

2 Prepare meat as directed in recipe. Now, add butter to frying pan. When melted, add onions and mushrooms; season well. Cook 3 minutes over medium-high heat.

3 Add tomatoes and garlic; mix well. Continue cooking 3 minutes over medium heat.

4 Mix in brown sauce and cook 3 to 4 minutes; correct seasoning.

South of the Border London Broil *(serves 4)*

2 tbsp	(30 ml) vegetable oil
4	6 oz (170 g) London broil steaks
1 tbsp	(15 ml) butter
1	onion, peeled and finely chopped
2	garlic cloves, smashed and chopped
1 tbsp	(15 ml) chopped parsley
½ cup	(125 ml) dry white wine
28 oz	(796 ml) can tomatoes, drained and chopped
½ tsp	(2 ml) oregano
¼ tsp	(1 ml) ginger
	salt and pepper
	few crushed chillies

Preheat oven to 150°F (70°C).

Heat oil in large frying pan. When hot, add meat and cook 8 to 10 minutes over medium heat. Turn meat 3 to 4 times during cooking and once seared, season well.

Transfer meat to ovenproof platter and keep hot in oven.

Heat butter in separate frying pan. When hot, add onion, garlic and parsley; mix and cook 3 minutes over medium heat.

Pour in wine and cook 3 to 4 minutes over medium-high heat or until most of wine evaporates.

Mix in tomatoes and spices; cook 8 to 10 minutes over low heat. Stir occasionally. Pour sauce over meat and serve with green vegetables.

See Technique next page.

1 SERVING	412 CALORIES	11 g CARBOHYDRATE
47 g PROTEIN	20 g FAT	1.0 g FIBER

TECHNIQUE: SOUTH OF THE BORDER

1 Prepare meat as directed in recipe. To cook sauce, heat butter in separate frying pan. Add onion, garlic and parsley; mix and cook 3 minutes over medium heat.

2 Pour in wine and cook 3 to 4 minutes over medium-high heat.

3 It may be necessary to cook sauce longer as it is important that most of the wine evaporates.

4 Mix in tomatoes and spices; cook 8 to 10 minutes over low heat. Stir occasionally.

Curry Burgers *(serves 4)*

2 lb	(900 g) lean ground beef
1	egg
1	onion, peeled, finely chopped and cooked
1½ tbsp	(25 ml) vegetable oil
1 tbsp	(15 ml) butter
3 tbsp	(45 ml) chopped onion
2 tbsp	(30 ml) curry powder
2	apples, peeled, sliced and sprinkled with lemon juice
1½ cups	(375 ml) heated chicken stock
1½ tbsp	(25 ml) cornstarch
2 tbsp	(30 ml) cold water
¼ cup	(50 ml) sultana raisins
	salt and pepper

Preheat oven to 150°F (70°C).

Place meat in large bowl and press down centre. Add egg to indentation and mix well. Add cooked onion, salt and pepper; mix until well incorporated.

Shape mixture into patties and score with knife.

Heat oil in large frying pan. When hot, cook meat 10 to 12 minutes over medium heat. Turn over 4 times and season.

Transfer cooked burgers to ovenproof platter.

Add butter and remaining chopped onion to frying pan; mix in curry and cook 2 minutes.

Add apples, mix well and continue cooking 2 minutes over medium heat.

Pour in chicken stock and cook 5 to 6 minutes.

Mix cornstarch with water; stir into sauce. Cook 1 to 2 minutes.

Add raisins; simmer 1 to 2 minutes.

Serve with burgers.

1 SERVING	504 CALORIES	22 g CARBOHYDRATE
59 g PROTEIN	20 g FAT	0.7 g FIBER

Meatballs in Sour Cream Sauce   *(serves 4)*

2 lb	(900 g) lean ground beef
1	egg
1	onion, peeled, finely chopped and cooked
2 tbsp	(30 ml) vegetable oil
2 tbsp	(30 ml) chopped onions
½ lb	(250 g) mushrooms, cleaned and sliced thick
1 tbsp	(15 ml) chopped parsley
1½ cups	(375 ml) commercial brown sauce, heated
2 tbsp	(30 ml) sour cream
	salt and pepper
	celery seed to taste

Preheat oven to 150°F (70°C).

Place meat in large bowl and press down centre. Add egg to indentation and mix well.

Add cooked onion, salt and pepper; mix until well incorporated.

Shape mixture into large meatballs.

Heat oil in large frying pan. When hot, add meatballs and cook 6 to 7 minutes over medium heat. Turn often to sear all sides and season well.

Add onions and mix well; continue cooking 3 to 4 minutes, covered, over medium heat.

Remove meatballs and keep hot in oven.

Add mushrooms and parsley to frying pan. Stir and cook, uncovered, 3 to 4 minutes.

Pour in brown sauce and continue cooking 5 to 6 minutes. Correct seasoning.

Replace meatballs in sauce and remove pan from heat. Stir in sour cream and pour over hot pasta. Sprinkle with celery seed to taste.

1 SERVING	508 CALORIES	10 g CARBOHYDRATE
63 g PROTEIN	24 g FAT	0.7 g FIBER

Stuffed Burgers   *(serves 4)*

3 tbsp	(45 ml) butter
2 tbsp	(30 ml) finely chopped onion
1	garlic clove, smashed and chopped
1 tbsp	(15 ml) chopped parsley
½ lb	(250 g) mushrooms, cleaned and minced
½ cup	(125 ml) mashed potatoes
1½ lb	(750 g) lean ground beef, in patties*
1½ tbsp	(25 ml) vegetable oil
4	slices cheddar cheese
	salt and pepper

Heat half of butter in saucepan. When hot, add onion, garlic and parsley; cook 2 minutes over medium heat.

Add remaining butter and mix in mushrooms; season well. Continue cooking 6 to 7 minutes; stir occasionally.

Stir in potatoes and cook 2 to 3 minutes over high heat.

Remove saucepan from heat and stuff patties as shown in technique.

Heat oil in large frying pan. When hot, add meat and cook 12 to 15 minutes over medium heat. Turn 4 times during cooking and once seared, season well.

When burgers are cooked, transfer to ovenproof platter. Add slices of cheese and broil in oven until melted.

*See technique of Salisbury Steak, picture 1-4, for directions. This appears on page 244.

See Technique next page.

1 SERVING	509 CALORIES	8 g CARBOHYDRATE
54 g PROTEIN	29 g FAT	0.8 g FIBER

TECHNIQUE: STUFFED BURGERS

1 Cook onion, garlic and parsley in hot butter for 2 minutes.

2 Add remaining butter and mix in mushrooms; season well. Continue cooking 6 to 7 minutes over medium heat.

3 Stir in potatoes and cook 2 to 3 minutes over high heat.

4 To stuff patties, press down on centre of meat. Add several spoons of stuffing and tuck meat over until completely hidden.

Beef Hash and Potatoes *(serves 4)*

1½ tbsp	(25 ml) vegetable oil
1½ lb	(750 g) leftover cooked beef (roast beef, steak, etc.) chopped
3	boiled potatoes, chopped
1	small onion, peeled and chopped
½ tsp	(2 ml) oregano
	pinch ground clove
	dash ginger
	salt and pepper
	fried eggs (optional)

Heat oil in frying pan. When hot, add beef, potatoes and onion; mix together well.

Stir in all herbs and spices and correct seasoning. Cook 15 minutes over medium-high heat. Stir occasionally.

If desired, serve with fried eggs.

Beef Hash with Onions *(serves 4)*

2 tbsp	(30 ml) vegetable oil
2	red onions, peeled and sliced
1	garlic clove, smashed and chopped
1½ lb	(750 g) leftover cooked beef (roast beef, steak, etc.) chopped
2 tbsp	(30 ml) chopped parsley salt and pepper

Heat oil in frying pan. When hot, add onions; cook 5 to 6 minutes over high heat. Stir occasionally.

Mix in garlic and cook 3 to 4 minutes over medium-high heat.

Add beef and mix well; season and continue cooking 8 to 10 minutes over medium-high heat.

Sprinkle with parsley and serve with fresh vegetables.

1 SERVING	456 CALORIES	4 g CARBOHYDRATE
65 g PROTEIN	20 g FAT	0.3 g FIBER

Braised Short Ribs in Spicy Sauce *(serves 4 to 6)*

1½ tbsp	(25 ml) vegetable oil
4 lb	(1.8 kg) short ribs, fat trimmed
2	red onions, peeled and diced
2	garlic cloves, smashed and chopped
1½	28 oz (796 ml) cans tomatoes
½ cup	(125 ml) commercial brown sauce, heated
1	bay leaf
½ tsp	(2 ml) basil
½ tsp	(2 ml) oregano
¼ tsp	(1 ml) celery seed
3	carrots, pared and cut in large pieces
1	turnip, peeled and cut in large pieces
4	potatoes, peeled and cut in large pieces salt and pepper

Preheat oven to 350°F (180°C).

Heat oil in large ovenproof casserole. When hot, add meat and sear 6 to 7 minutes over medium-high heat.

Turn pieces over and season well; continue cooking 6 to 7 minutes.

Add onions and garlic; mix well. Cook another 5 to 6 minutes.

Pour in tomatoes with juice, brown sauce and herbs; season well. Bring to boil.

Cover casserole and cook 2 hours in oven.

Add vegetables to pan and finish cooking 1 hour in oven.

See Technique next page.

1 SERVING	590 CALORIES	23 g CARBOHYDRATE
66 g PROTEIN	26 g FAT	1.8 g FIBER

TECHNIQUE: BRAISED SHORT RIBS

1 Trim most of fat from short ribs.

2 Sear meat 6 to 7 minutes each side in hot oil; season well.

3 Add onions and garlic; mix well. Cook another 5 to 6 minutes.

4 Pour in tomatoes with juice, brown sauce and herbs; season well. Bring to boil and finish cooking in oven.

Marinated Short Ribs *(serves 4 to 6)*

3½ lb	(1.6 kg) marinated short ribs*
2 tbsp	(30 ml) vegetable oil
1	onion, peeled and coarsely chopped
3 tbsp	(45 ml) flour
4 cups	(1 L) heated beef stock
4 tbsp	(60 ml) tomato paste
3	potatoes, peeled and cut in large pieces
3	carrots, pared and cut in large pieces
4	small onions, peeled
	few drops Tabasco sauce
	dash Worcestershire sauce
	salt and pepper

Preheat oven to 350°F (180°C).

Drain meat and strain marinade; set aside.

Heat oil in large ovenproof casserole. When hot, add meat and sear 8 to 9 minutes over medium-high heat. Turn meat to brown all sides.

Add onion and mix well. Continue cooking 5 to 6 minutes; stir occasionally.

Mix in flour and cook 3 to 4 minutes over medium-high heat. Stir as needed. Flour and onion should brown and stick to bottom of pan.

Pour in strained marinade along with beef stock; mix well and bring to boil.

Add tomato paste, Tabasco and Worcestershire; season well. Bring to boil.

Cover casserole and cook 1 hour in oven.

Add vegetables to casserole and finish cooking 1½ hours in oven.

*See page 264.

1 SERVING	472 CALORIES	16 g CARBOHYDRATE
39 g PROTEIN	28 g FAT	0.7 g FIBER

TECHNIQUE: MARINATED SHORT RIBS

1 Marinate short ribs 12 to 24 hours in refrigerator.

2 Drain meat and strain marinade; set aside. Sear meat in hot oil 8 to 9 minutes over medium-high heat.

3 Add onion and mix well; continue cooking.

4 Mix in flour and cook 3 to 4 minutes over medium-high heat. Stir as needed.

5 Flour and onion should brown and stick to bottom of pan.

6 Pour in strained marinade.

7 Add beef stock, mix well and bring to boil.

8 After cooking 1 hour, add vegetables and finish cooking 1½ hours in oven.

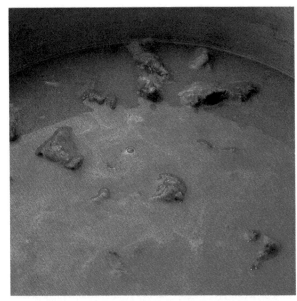

263

Marinade

3½ lb	(1.6 kg) boneless short ribs, cut in 1 in (2.5 cm) cubes
2 cups	(500 ml) dry red wine
1	bay leaf
1	garlic clove, peeled and split in two
4	onion slices
3	parsley sprigs
2 tbsp	(30 ml) oil
¼ tsp	(1 ml) thyme
	freshly ground pepper

Place meat and all remaining ingredients in large bowl. Cover with sheet of plastic wrap and refrigerate 12 to 24 hours.

Green Onion Potatoes   *(serves 4)*

1 tbsp	(15 ml) vegetable oil
3	potatoes, peeled, cut in half and sliced
1 tsp	(5 ml) butter
1	garlic clove, smashed and chopped
2	green onions, sliced
1 tbsp	(15 ml) chopped parsley
	dash paprika
	salt and pepper

Heat oil in large frying pan. When hot, add potatoes; cover and cook 6 to 7 minutes. Stir twice during cooking.

Season well and add butter. When melted, stir in garlic, onions and remaining ingredients. Cook 3 to 4 minutes, uncovered, over medium heat.

Serve immediately with burgers.

1 SERVING	105 CALORIES	13 g CARBOHYDRATE
2 g PROTEIN	5 g FAT	0.5 g FIBER

Rib Roast with Sauce *(serves 4 to 6)*

4 lb	(1.8 kg) rib roast, prepared for roasting
1	onion, cut in pieces
1	celery stalk, cut in large pieces
1	carrot, pared and cut in large chunks
½ tsp	(2 ml) thyme
½ tsp	(2 ml) basil
½ tsp	(2 ml) chervil
1 tbsp	(15 ml) chopped parsley
1	bay leaf
1½ cups	(375 ml) light beef stock, heated
	vegetable oil
	salt and pepper

Preheat oven to 400°F (200°C).

Place meat in roasting pan and brush with vegetable oil. Pepper generously and cook 30 minutes in oven.

Remove pan from oven and season meat well. Arrange vegetables around meat and sprinkle herbs on vegetables.

Replace pan in oven and continue cooking 30 minutes.

Reduce heat to 375°F (190°C) and finish cooking 20 minutes.

Remove roast from pan and set aside.

Place plan on stove top over high heat; cook 2 minutes.

Add beef stock and season; continue cooking 5 to 6 minutes.

Strain sauce through sieve and serve with roast.*

*If sauce is too thin for your liking, thicken with a bit of cornstarch mixed with cold water. Do this after adding beef stock.

See Technique next page.

1 SERVING	319 CALORIES	3 g CARBOHYDRATE
43 g PROTEIN	15 g FAT	0.3 g FIBER

TECHNIQUE: RIB ROAST WITH SAUCE

1 Place meat in roasting pan.

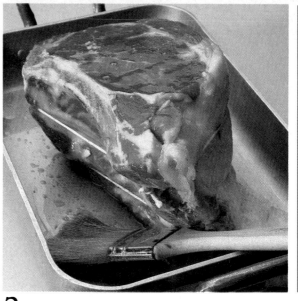

2 Brush with vegetable oil. Pepper generously and cook 30 minutes in oven.

3 Remove pan from oven and season meat well.

4 Arrange vegetables around meat.

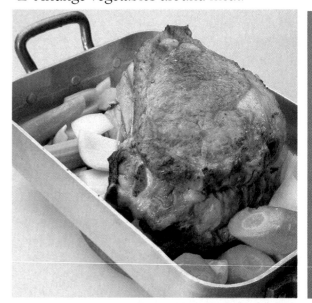

5 Sprinkle herbs on vegetables.

6 When roast is cooked, remove pan from oven. Set meat aside.

7 Place pan on stove top over high heat; cook 2 minutes.

8 Add beef stock and season; continue cooking 5 to 6 minutes.

Roast Eye-of-Round *(serves 4 to 6)*

1 tbsp	(15 ml) vegetable oil
3½ lb	(1.6 kg) eye-of-round roast, prepared for roasting
2 tbsp	(30 ml) melted butter
1	garlic clove, peeled and slivered
1	onion, peeled and chopped
½	celery stalk, chopped
1	bay leaf
¼ tsp	(1 ml) thyme
1¼ cups	(300 ml) heated beef stock
1 tsp	(5 ml) cornstarch
1 tsp	(5 ml) cold water
	salt and pepper

Preheat oven to 425°F (220°C).
Cooking time: 10 minutes per lb (500 g).

Heat oil in roasting pan on stove top. When hot, add meat and sear 4 to 6 minutes over high heat. Turn meat to brown all sides and season well.

Brush meat with melted butter and make several incisions in meat; insert garlic slivers. Cook about 30 minutes in oven or until done to taste.

Remove roasting pan from oven and set meat aside. Place vegetables and herbs in pan; cook 4 to 5 minutes over medium-high heat.

Add beef stock and continue cooking 4 to 5 minutes.

Mix cornstarch with water; stir into sauce. Strain through sieve and serve with roast.

1 SERVING	444 CALORIES	3 g CARBOHYDRATE
72 g PROTEIN	16 g FAT	0.2 g FIBER

Hearty Family Stew *(serves 4 to 6)*

1 tbsp	(15 ml) vegetable oil
3 lb	(1.4 kg) rib-eye steak, cubed
1	Spanish onion, peeled and diced large
1	garlic clove, smashed and chopped
1 tbsp	(15 ml) chopped parsley
2	celery stalks, diced large
1½ cups	(375 ml) commercial brown sauce, heated
1½ cups	(375 ml) heated beef stock
2	carrots, pared and diced large
3	potatoes, peeled and diced large
2	small turnips, peeled and diced large
½ tsp	(2 ml) thyme
½ tsp	(2 ml) basil
	salt and pepper

Preheat oven to 350°F (180°C).

Heat oil in large ovenproof casserole. When hot, add meat and sear 6 to 8 minutes over medium-high heat. Turn meat to brown all sides and season well.

Add onion, garlic and parsley; season well. Cook 6 to 7 minutes over medium-high heat.

Mix in celery and continue cooking 5 to 6 minutes.

Pour in brown sauce and beef stock; stir and bring to boil. Cover casserole and cook 1 hour in oven.

Add carrots, potatoes, turnips and herbs; cover casserole and finish cooking 1 hour in oven.

See Technique next page.

1 SERVING	541 CALORIES	18 g CARBOHYDRATE
43 g PROTEIN	33 g FAT	1.2 g FIBER

TECHNIQUE: HEARTY FAMILY STEW

1 Sear meat in large ovenproof casserole. Be sure to turn meat to brown all sides and season well.

2 Add onion, garlic and parsley; season well. Cook 6 to 7 minutes over medium-high heat.

3 Mix in celery and continue cooking 5 to 6 minutes.

4 Pour in brown sauce and beef stock; stir and bring to boil.

Roast Rib-Eye *(serves 4 to 6)*

1 tbsp	(15 ml) vegetable oil
4 lb	(1.8 kg) rib-eye roast, prepared for roasting
1	Spanish onion, peeled and diced
2	garlic cloves, peeled
¼ tsp	(1 ml) thyme
½ tsp	(2 ml) oregano
½ tsp	(2 ml) basil
1	bay leaf
1 tbsp	(15 ml) chopped parsley
1 cup	(250 ml) dry red wine
28 oz	(796 ml) can tomatoes and juice
3 tbsp	(45 ml) tomato paste
	salt and pepper
	few drops Tabasco sauce

Preheat oven to 350°F (180°C).

Heat oil in very large ovenproof casserole. Add meat and sear 7 to 8 minutes over high heat. Turn meat to brown all sides and season well.

Add onion, garlic and herbs; mix well. Cook 7 to 8 minutes over medium-high heat.

Pour in wine and continue cooking 3 to 4 minutes.

Pour in tomatoes with juice and mix again.

Season well and add tomato paste and Tabasco sauce. Bring to boil.

Cover casserole and cook 3 hours in oven.

See Technique next page.

1 SERVING	333 CALORIES	9 g CARBOHYDRATE
45 g PROTEIN	13 g FAT	0.8 g FIBER

TECHNIQUE: ROAST RIB-EYE

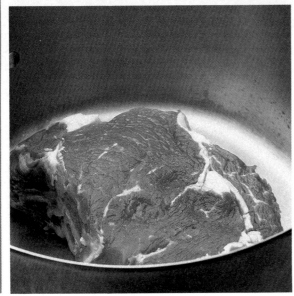

1 Sear meat in very large ovenproof casserole. Be sure to turn meat to brown all sides and season well.

2 Add onion, garlic and herbs; mix well. Cook 7 to 8 minutes over medium-high heat.

3 Pour in wine and continue cooking 3 to 4 minutes.

4 Pour in tomatoes with juice and mix again. Add remaining ingredients and finish cooking in oven.

Delicious Double Peppercorn Filet Mignon *(serves 4)*

1 tbsp	(15 ml) vegetable oil
4	8 oz (227 g) filet mignons
2 tbsp	(30 ml) butter
2	shallots, chopped
½ lb	(250 g) fresh mushrooms, cleaned and sliced
2 tbsp	(30 ml) green peppercorns
¼ cup	(50 ml) heavy cream
1 tbsp	(15 ml) black peppercorns, ground
1 tsp	(5 ml) chopped chives
1¼ cups	(300 ml) commercial brown sauce, heated
	salt and pepper

Preheat oven to 150°F (70°C).

Heat oil in large frying pan. When hot, add meat and cook 2 minutes over medium-high.

Turn meat over and season; continue cooking 6 minutes. Turn 3 times during cooking time.

Place meat on ovenproof platter and keep hot in oven.

Heat butter in frying pan. Add shallots and mushrooms; cook 3 to 4 minutes over medium heat. Stir occasionally.

Mash green peppercorns with cream; stir in ground black peppercorns. Add chives.

Pour pepper mixture and brown sauce into pan; cook 3 to 4 minutes over medium-high.

Season sauce to taste and continue cooking 2 minutes.

1 SERVING	535 CALORIES	9 g CARBOHYDRATE
46 g PROTEIN	35 g FAT	0.6 g FIBER

Filet Mignon Parisienne *(serves 4)*

3	large potatoes, peeled	
1	turnip, peeled	
2	large carrots, pared	
1 tbsp	(15 ml) vegetable oil	
4	8 oz (227 g) filet mignons	
2 tbsp	(30 ml) butter	
1	garlic clove, smashed and chopped	
	salt and pepper	
	garlic butter (optional)	

Use melon scoop to cut vegetables into balls. Cook 8 minutes in 1 ½ cups (375 ml) salted, boiling water.

Meanwhile, begin cooking meat. Heat oil in large frying pan. When hot, add meat and cook 2 minutes over medium-high heat.

Turn meat over and season well; continue cooking 6 minutes. Turn 3 times during cooking time.

Drain vegetables and pat dry. Heat butter in separate frying pan. Sauté vegetables with garlic 2 to 3 minutes. Season well.

Serve meat with garlic butter and surround with vegetables.

1 SERVING	522 CALORIES	18 g CARBOHYDRATE
45 g PROTEIN	30 g FAT	1.2 g FIBER

T-Bone Steaks au Cognac   *(serves 4)*

2 tbsp	(30 ml) vegetable oil
4	T-bone steaks, 1 in (2.5 cm) thick
1 tbsp	(15 ml) butter
1 lb	(500 g) fresh mushrooms, cleaned and sliced
2	shallots, chopped
1 tbsp	(15 ml) chopped fresh parsley
¼ cup	(50 ml) cognac
⅔ cup	(150 ml) heavy cream
	salt and pepper
	few drops Tabasco sauce
	few drops lemon juice

Preheat oven to 150°F (70°C).

Cook steaks in two batches using the following procedure. Heat half of oil in large frying pan. When hot, add meat and cook 4 to 5 minutes over high heat.

Turn meat over, season well and continue cooking 4 to 5 minutes. Remove meat from pan and keep steaks hot in oven.

Add butter, mushrooms, shallots and parsley to pan. Season well and cook 4 to 5 minutes over medium heat.

Pour in cognac and cook 3 minutes over high heat.

Add cream and Tabasco sauce; cook 5 to 6 minutes over high heat. Mix in lemon juice and serve with steaks.

See Technique next page.

1 SERVING	798 CALORIES	9 g CARBOHYDRATE
78 g PROTEIN	50 g FAT	1.1 g FIBER

TECHNIQUE: T-BONE STEAKS AU COGNAC

1 Ask your butcher for T-bone steaks about 1 in (2.5 cm) thick. Depending on the cut you may have to remove most of the fat.

2 Cook steaks in two batches in hot oil. Be sure to season after turning meat over.

3 To prepare sauce, add butter, mushrooms, shallots and parsley to pan. Season well and cook 4 to 5 minutes over medium heat.

4 Pour in cognac and cook 3 minutes over high heat. Add cream and Tabasco sauce; cook 5 to 6 minutes over high heat.

Pepper Steak   *(serves 4)*

4	boneless rib steaks, ¾ in (2 cm) thick
¼ cup	(50 ml) black peppercorns, crushed
1½ tbsp	(25 ml) vegetable oil
1 tbsp	(15 ml) butter
1 lb	(500 g) mushrooms, cleaned and sliced
1	shallot, chopped
1 tbsp	(15 ml) chopped parsley
2 tbsp	(30 ml) cognac
1 cup	(250 ml) heavy cream
	salt and pepper

Preheat oven to 150°F (70°C).

Cover both sides of steaks with crushed peppercorns. Press pepper into meat.

Cook steaks in two batches following this procedure. Heat half of oil in large frying pan. When hot, add meat and cook 3 to 4 minutes over high heat.

Turn meat over, season with salt and continue cooking 3 to 4 minutes. Remove meat from pan and keep steaks hot in oven.

Add butter, mushrooms, shallot and parsley to pan. Cook 3 to 4 minutes over medium heat.

Season and add cognac; cook 1 minute.

Add cream and season well; cook 3 to 4 minutes over medium-high heat.

Remove meat from oven and pour any juices into sauce. Replace steaks in oven.

Stir sauce and cook 2 minutes.

Pour sauce over steaks and serve.

1 SERVING	520 CALORIES	9 g CARBOHYDRATE
49 g PROTEIN	32 g FAT	1.1 g FIBER

277

Rib Steaks with Beer *(serves 4)*

1½ tbsp	(25 ml) vegetable oil
4	rib steaks, ¾ in (2 cm) thick
1	onion, peeled and chopped
¼ tsp	(1 ml) celery seed
¼ tsp	(1 ml) tarragon
¼ tsp	(1 ml) paprika
1 tsp	(5 ml) chopped parsley
1 cup	(250 ml) beer
1½ cups	(375 ml) commercial brown sauce, heated
	salt and pepper

Preheat oven to 150°F (70°C).

Cook steaks in two batches following this procedure. Heat half of oil in large frying pan. When hot, add meat and cook 3 to 4 minutes over high heat.

Turn meat over, season well and continue cooking 3 to 4 minutes. Remove meat from pan and keep steaks hot in oven.

Add onion to frying pan and cook 4 to 5 minutes over medium heat.

Sprinkle in herbs and cook 1 minute; mix well.

Add beer and cook 5 to 6 minutes over high heat. Liquid should be reduced by ⅔.

Stir in brown sauce and correct seasoning. Cook 2 to 3 minutes over medium heat.

Pour sauce over steaks and serve.

1 SERVING	499 CALORIES	9 g CARBOHYDRATE
46 g PROTEIN	31 g FAT	0.2 g FIBER

Marinated Beef on Skewers   *(serves 4)*

1	onion, peeled and chopped
3 tbsp	(45 ml) olive oil
1 tbsp	(15 ml) lemon juice
½ cup	(125 ml) Madeira wine
1½ lb	(750 g) top-round steak, cut in 1 in (2.5 cm) cubes
1	red onion, peeled and cut in 6 pieces
8	cherry tomatoes
16	fresh mint leaves
	salt and pepper
	few drops Tabasco sauce

Place onion and oil in large bowl; mix together.

Add lemon juice and wine; mix again. Season with salt, pepper and Tabasco sauce.

Place beef in marinade and cover with plastic wrap. Refrigerate 6 hours.

Drain meat and strain marinade; set aside.

Alternate meat, onion, tomato and mint on skewers. Brush with marinade and season.

Broil 4 minutes on both sides or until done to taste. Baste occasionally.

See Technique next page.

1 SERVING	410 CALORIES	6 g CARBOHYDRATE
56 g PROTEIN	18 g FAT	0.5 g FIBER

TECHNIQUE: MARINATED BEEF ON SKEWERS

1 Place onion and oil in large bowl; mix together.

2 Add lemon juice and wine; mix again. Season with salt, pepper and Tabasco sauce.

3 Place beef in marinade and cover with plastic wrap. Refrigerate 6 hours.

4 Alternate meat, onion, tomato and mint on skewers. Brush with marinade, season and broil.

Sautéed Beef Long Island   *(serves 4)*

2 tbsp	(30 ml) vegetable oil
1 ½ lb	(750 g) New York steak, sliced on the bias
1 tbsp	(15 ml) butter
⅓	English cucumber, thinly sliced
1	celery stalk, thinly sliced
1	green pepper, thinly sliced
½ lb	(250 g) fresh mushrooms, cleaned and sliced
½ cup	(125 ml) sweet pimento, sliced
1 ½ cups	(375 ml) commercial brown sauce, heated
2 tbsp	(30 ml) sour cream
	salt and pepper
	dash paprika

Heat oil in large frying pan. When hot add meat and sear 1 ½ minutes each side; season well.

When all meat is cooked, remove from pan and set aside.

Add butter, cucumber, celery and green pepper to pan; cook 2 to 3 minutes over medium heat.

Add mushrooms, pimento and paprika; mix well and cook 3 minutes.

Pour in brown sauce and season well; cook 2 minutes.

Replace meat in pan and simmer 2 minutes to reheat.

Remove pan from stove and mix in sour cream. Serve immediately.

See Technique next page.

1 SERVING	465 CALORIES	10 g CARBOHYDRATE
44 g PROTEIN	24 g FAT	1.1 g FIBER

TECHNIQUE: SAUTÉED BEEF LONG ISLAND

1 Sear meat 1½ minutes each side in hot oil. Depending on size of pan, you may have to do this in two batches.

2 When all meat is cooked, remove from pan and set aside.

3 Add butter, cucumber, celery and green pepper to pan; cook 2 to 3 minutes over medium heat.

4 Add mushrooms, pimento and paprika; mix well and cook 3 minutes.

New York Steaks in Green Peppercorn Sauce *(serves 4)*

1½ tbsp	(25 ml) vegetable oil
4	New York steaks, 1 in (2.5 cm) thick
1 tbsp	(15 ml) green peppercorns
2 tbsp	(30 ml) heavy cream
1 tbsp	(15 ml) butter
¾ lb	(375 g) mushrooms, cleaned and sliced in three
2	shallots, chopped
1 tbsp	(15 ml) chopped parsley
¼ cup	(50 ml) cognac
1 cup	(250 ml) heavy cream
	salt and pepper

Preheat oven to 150°F (70°C).

Cook steaks in two batches using the following procedure. Heat half of oil in large frying pan. When hot, add meat and cook 3 to 4 minutes over high heat.

Turn meat over, season well and continue cooking 3 to 4 minutes. Remove meat from pan and keep steaks hot in oven.

Place peppercorns in small bowl and add 2 tbsp (30 ml) cream. Mash together and set aside.

Add butter to pan and heat. Cook mushrooms, shallots and parsley 3 minutes. Season.

Add cognac and cook 3 minutes over high.

Mix in rest of cream and peppercorn mixture; cook 4 to 5 minutes over high.

See Technique next page.

1 SERVING	669 CALORIES	8 g CARBOHYDRATE
58 g PROTEIN	45 g FAT	0.9 g FIBER

TECHNIQUE: NEW YORK STEAKS

1 Ask your butcher for New York steaks about 1 in (2.5 cm) thick.

2 Cook steaks in two batches in hot oil. Be sure to season after turning meat over.

3 Green peppercorns (which are sold in cans) must be mashed before cooking.

4 Mash peppercorns with a bit of heavy cream. You can use a pestle or the back of a spoon.

5 Cook mushrooms, shallots and parsley in hot butter 3 minutes over medium heat. Season generously. Pour in cognac and cook 3 minutes over high heat.

6 Incorporate remaining cream and peppercorn mixture; mix well and continue cooking 4 to 5 minutes over high heat.

Beef Alfredo *(serves 4)*

2 tbsp	(30 ml) vegetable oil
1½ lb	(750 g) top-loin steak, cut in thin strips
4 tbsp	(60 ml) soft butter
1½ cups	(375 ml) heavy cream
¼ cup	(50 ml) fettuccini cooking liquid*
1¼ cups	(300 ml) grated parmesan cheese
1 lb	(500 g) cooked fettuccini noodles
	chopped chives
	chopped parsley
	salt and pepper

Preheat oven to 150°F (70°C).

Heat oil in large frying pan. When hot, add meat and cook 1½ minutes each side. Add some chopped chives and season well. Note: you may have to cook meat in two batches depending on the size of pan.

Remove cooked meat and keep hot in oven.

Heat butter in large saucepan. Pour in cream and mix together well; bring to boil.

Continue cooking 3 minutes over high heat.

Add fettuccini stock and half of cheese; incorporate well.

Stir in cooked noodles and correct seasoning. Add beef strips and mix again.

Serve with remaining cheese and herbs.

*Simply reserve some of the water in which the fettuccini was cooked.

Porterhouse Steaks with
Hot Olive Sauce   *(serves 4)*

4 tsp	(20 ml) vegetable oil
4	porterhouse steaks, 1½ in (4 cm) thick
1 tbsp	(15 ml) pine oil (or olive oil)
3	garlic cloves, smashed and chopped
½ cup	(125 ml) stuffed green olives, chopped
½ cup	(125 ml) pitted black olives, chopped
1½ cups	(375 ml) chopped tomatoes
2 tbsp	(30 ml) tomato paste
1 tsp	(5 ml) Worcestershire sauce
	salt and pepper
	crushed chillies to taste
	few drops lemon juice

Preheat oven to 400°F (200°C).

Cook steaks one at a time following this procedure. Heat 1 tsp (5 ml) vegetable oil in frying pan. When hot, add meat and sear 3 minutes each side; season well.

When steaks are seared, place on ovenproof platter and cook 8 to 10 minutes in oven.

While steaks are in oven prepare sauce. Heat pine oil (olive oil) in saucepan. When hot, add garlic and olives; cover and cook 3 minutes.

Add tomatoes and all spices; mix well. Cook 3 to 4 minutes, uncovered, over medium-high heat.

Add remaining ingredients and mix well. Cook 3 to 4 minutes, uncovered, over medium heat.

1 SERVING	774 CALORIES	6 g CARBOHYDRATE
75 g PROTEIN	50 g FAT	0.5 g FIBER

Porterhouse Steak   *(serves 4)*

2	shallots, chopped
1 tbsp	(15 ml) chopped parsley
½ lb	(250 g) soft butter
¼ tsp	(1 ml) paprika
¼ tsp	(1 ml) Tabasco sauce
1 tbsp	(15 ml) strong mustard
1 tsp	(5 ml) lemon juice
4 tsp	(20 ml) vegetable oil
4	porterhouse steaks, 1½ in (4 cm) thick
	salt and pepper

Preheat oven to 400°F (200°C).

To prepare shallot butter, place shallots and parsley in bowl.

Add butter and mash ingredients together with spoon.

Add paprika and Tabasco sauce. Mix in mustard and correct seasoning.

Add lemon juice and mix until thoroughly blended. Set aside until use.

Cook steaks one at a time following this procedure. Heat 1 tsp (5 ml) oil in frying pan. When hot, add meat and sear 3 minutes each side; season well.

When steaks are seared, place on ovenproof platter and cook 8 to 10 minutes in oven.

Remove steaks from oven and spread with shallot butter. Broil 2 minutes.

See Technique next page.

1 SERVING	1050 CALORIES	4 g CARBOHYDRATE
74 g PROTEIN	82 g FAT	0.1 g FIBER

TECHNIQUE: PORTERHOUSE STEAK

1 Porterhouse steaks are very large and usually need to be seared one at a time.

2 To prepare shallot butter, place shallots and parsley in bowl.

3 Add butter and mash ingredients together with spoon. Add paprika and Tabasco sauce.

4 Mix in mustard and correct seasoning. Add lemon juice and mix until thoroughly blended.

T-Bone Lyonnaise *(serves 4)*

3 tbsp	(45 ml) vegetable oil
3	onions, peeled and thinly sliced
1 tbsp	(15 ml) butter
1	garlic clove, smashed and chopped
1 tbsp	(15 ml) chopped parsley
2 tbsp	(30 ml) wine vinegar
¼ cup	(50 ml) dry red wine
1½ cups	(375 ml) commercial brown sauce, heated
¼ tsp	(1 ml) basil
¼ tsp	(1 ml) thyme
4	T-bone steaks, 1 in (2.5 cm) thick
	salt and pepper

Preheat oven to 150°F (70°C).

Begin by preparing sauce. Heat 1 tbsp (15 ml) oil in large frying pan. Add onions and cook 6 to 7 minutes over medium-high heat. Stir occasionally.

Stir in butter, garlic and parsley; cook 2 minutes over medium heat.

Pour in vinegar and wine; stir and cook 3 to 4 minutes over high heat.

Add brown sauce and herbs; continue cooking 2 to 3 minutes.

Keep sauce hot over low heat or in oven.

Cook steaks in two batches following this procedure. Heat 1 tbsp (15 ml) oil in large frying pan. When hot, add meat and cook 4 to 5 minutes over high heat.

Turn meat over, season well and continue cooking 4 to 5 minutes. Keep hot in oven until serving time. Pour sauce over steaks and serve.

See Technique next page.

1 SERVING	668 CALORIES	11 g CARBOHYDRATE
75 g PROTEIN	36 g FAT	0.5 g FIBER

TECHNIQUE: T-BONE LYONNAISE

1 Add butter, garlic and parsley to browning onions; cook 2 minutes over medium heat.

2 Pour in vinegar and wine; stir and cook 3 to 4 minutes over high heat.

3 Add brown sauce and herbs; continue cooking 2 to 3 minutes. Keep sauce hot while preparing meat.

Braised Rib-Eye Steaks *(serves 4)*

1 tbsp	(15 ml) vegetable oil
2	rib-eye steaks 1¼ lb (625 g) each, fat trimmed
1	large Spanish onion, peeled and diced large
1 tsp	(5 ml) oregano
1	garlic clove, smashed and chopped
2	celery stalks, diced large
3	tomatoes, cut in wedges
1 tbsp	(15 ml) chopped parsley
1 cup	(250 ml) tomato clam juice
2 cups	(500 ml) hot beef stock
1	medium-size turnip, peeled and cubed
	salt and pepper

Preheat oven to 350°F (180°C).

Heat oil in large sauté pan. When hot, add meat and sear 2 to 3 minutes each side. Season well.

Add onion and oregano; cook 5 to 6 minutes over medium heat.

Mix in garlic, celery and tomatoes. Turn meat over and add parsley, salt and pepper. Continue cooking 5 to 6 minutes.

Add tomato clam juice and beef stock. Season well and mix in turnip; bring to boil.

Cover pan and cook 2 hours in oven.

When cooked, remove and slice meat. Serve with vegetables.

See Technique next page.

1 SERVING	563 CALORIES	13 g CARBOHYDRATE
49 g PROTEIN	35 g FAT	1.3 g FIBER

TECHNIQUE: BRAISED RIB-EYE STEAKS

1 Sear meat 2 to 3 minutes each side in hot oil.

2 Add onion and oregano to pan; cook 5 to 6 minutes over medium heat.

3 Mix in garlic, celery and tomatoes. Turn meat over and add parsley, salt and pepper. Continue cooking 5 to 6 minutes.

4 Add tomato clam juice and beef stock. Add turnip and finish cooking in oven.

Beef and Vegetables   *(serves 4)*

1 tbsp	(15 ml) vegetable oil
1½ lb	(750 g) top-round steak, sliced in strips
1	green pepper, sliced
2	green onions, sliced
2	tomatoes, sliced
1	garlic clove, smashed and chopped
2 cups	(500 ml) commercial light brown sauce, heated
¼ tsp	(1 ml) oregano
4	portions cooked spaghetti
	salt and pepper

Heat oil in deep frying pan. Add beef and cook 2 minutes each side over high heat. Season well.

Remove meat from pan and set aside.

Add vegetables to pan; cook 3 to 4 minutes over high heat.

Add garlic, brown sauce and oregano; mix well and cook 2 to 3 minutes over low heat.

Replace meat in pan and mix. Simmer 1 minute to reheat.

Serve over spaghetti.

1 SERVING	528 CALORIES	44 g CARBOHYDRATE
61 g PROTEIN	12 g FAT	1.1 g FIBER

Boneless Marinated Rump Roast   *(serves 4 to 6)*

4 lb	(1.8 kg) marinated rump roast
1 tbsp	(15 ml) vegetable oil
1	celery stalk, diced
1	carrot, pared and diced
1	small onion, peeled and diced
3 tbsp	(45 ml) tomato paste
	salt and pepper

Preheat oven to 350°F (180°C).

Remove meat from pot and strain marinade; set aside.

Heat oil in large braising pot. Add meat and sear 5 to 6 minutes over medium-high heat. Turn meat to brown all sides and season well.

Add vegetables to pot; continue cooking 2 minutes.

Pour in strained marinade and mix in tomato paste. Bring to boil.

Cover pot and cook 2½ hours in oven.

Slice meat and serve.

See Technique next page.

1 SERVING	617 CALORIES	11 g CARBOHYDRATE
78 g PROTEIN	29 g FAT	0.4 g FIBER

Marinade

1 tsp	(5 ml) powdered mustard
2 cups	(500 ml) dry red wine
¼ cup	(50 ml) wine vinegar
1 tsp	(5 ml) chopped chives
4 lb	(1.8 kg) boneless rump roast
2	carrots, pared and sliced
1	large onion, peeled and sliced
1 cup	(250 ml) water
2 tbsp	(30 ml) brown sugar
1	bay leaf
¼ tsp	(1 ml) caraway seed
½ tsp	(2 ml) basil
1	clove
	pepper

Place mustard and wine in bowl; mix together well. Add vinegar and chives; mix again.

Place meat in large braising pot and pour in wine mixture. Add carrots, onion and water to pot.

Sprinkle meat with sugar, herbs and spices; pepper well.

Cover pot and refrigerate 12 hours.

TECHNIQUE

1 Place mustard and wine in bowl; mix together well. Add vinegar and chives; mix again.

2 Place meat in large braising pot and pour in wine mixture. Add carrots, onion and water to pot.

3 Sprinkle meat with sugar, herbs and spices; pepper well.

4 After meat has marinated 12 hours, begin recipe by searing roast in hot oil.

Steak Diane with Cognac   *(serves 4)*

2 tbsp	(30 ml) butter
1¾ lb	(800 g) beef tenderloin, thinly sliced
¼ cup	(50 ml) Courvoisier cognac
2	shallots, finely chopped
1 tbsp	(15 ml) chopped parsley
2 cups	(500 ml) commercial brown sauce, heated
1 tbsp	(15 ml) tomato paste
¼ tsp	(1 ml) Worcestershire sauce salt and pepper

Heat butter in large frying pan. When hot, add meat and cook 1½ minutes each side over medium-high heat. Season well and be careful not to allow butter to burn!

Pour in cognac and flambé.

Remove meat and set aside.

Add shallots and parsley to frying pan; cook 2 minutes.

Pour in brown sauce and tomato paste; mix well and season with Worcestershire sauce. Bring to boil and continue cooking 2 minutes.

Replace meat in pan and simmer several minutes.

Serve over pasta.

1 SERVING	456 CALORIES	28 g CARBOHYDRATE
23 g PROTEIN	11 g FAT	1.5 g FIBER

Rolled Beef with Horseradish Stuffing *(serves 4)*

3 tbsp	(45 ml) horseradish
1 tsp	(5 ml) chopped parsley
3 tbsp	(45 ml) breadcrumbs
1	egg
4	slices top-round steak, 2 in (5 cm) wide
2 tbsp	(30 ml) vegetable oil
1	large carrot, pared and diced
1	onion, peeled and diced
1	celery stalk, diced
¼ tsp	(1 ml) thyme
1½ cups	(375 ml) heated beef stock
¼ tsp	(1 ml) basil
1 tbsp	(15 ml) tomato paste
1 tbsp	(15 ml) cornstarch
2 tbsp	(30 ml) cold water
	salt and pepper

Preheat oven to 350°F (180°C).

Place horseradish and parsley in bowl. Add breadcrumbs and mix throughly; season well.

Add egg and mix until combined; set aside.

Pound meat slices with mallet. Lay flat on counter and spread some stuffing on each.

Roll meat slices and secure with toothpicks.

Heat oil in large ovenproof casserole. Add meat rolls and sear 4 to 5 minutes. Turn meat to brown all sides and season well.

Add vegetables and herbs to pan; brown 3 to 4 minutes.

Mix in beef stock and tomato paste; correct seasoning. Bring to boil.

Cover casserole and cook 1½ hours. Remove from oven and place beef on serving platter.

Place casserole over medium heat. Mix cornstarch with water and stir into sauce. Boil 1 minute. Pour sauce over beef and serve.

See Technique next page.

1 SERVING	456 CALORIES	28 g CARBOHYDRATE
23 g PROTEIN	11 g FAT	1.5 g FIBER

TECHNIQUE: ROLLED BEEF

1 Place horseradish and parsley in bowl. Add breadcrumbs and mix thoroughly; season well. Add egg and mix until combined; set stuffing aside.

2 Pound meat slices with mallet. Lay flat on counter and spread some stuffing on each.

3 Roll meat as shown in picture. Secure with toothpicks.

4 Sear meat in hot oil and season well.

Carbonado of Beef   *(serves 4)*

2 lb	(900 g) round steak, sliced and pounded
1 cup	(250 ml) seasoned flour
2 tbsp	(30 ml) vegetable oil
1	onion, peeled and finely chopped
2	garlic cloves, smashed and chopped
2 tbsp	(30 ml) wine vinegar
1 cup	(250 ml) beer
1½ cup	(375 ml) commercial brown sauce, heated
¼ tsp	(1 ml) nutmeg
	salt and pepper

Preheat oven to 350°F (180°C).

Dredge pounded meat slices with flour.

Heat oil in large frying pan. When hot, add meat and sear 2 to 3 minutes each side. Season well.

Remove meat and transfer to ovenproof casserole; set dish aside.

Add onion and garlic to frying pan; cook 3 minutes over medium heat.

Pour in vinegar and beer; cook 3 to 4 minutes over high heat.

Stir in brown sauce and nutmeg; cook 1 minute and correct seasoning.

Pour sauce over meat. Cover casserole and cook 1¼ hours in oven. See Technique next page.

1 SERVING	456 CALORIES	28 g CARBOHYDRATE
23 g PROTEIN	11 g FAT	1.5 g FIBER

TECHNIQUE: CARBONADO OF BEEF

1 Heat oil in large frying pan. When hot, add meat and sear 2 to 3 minutes each side. Season well.

2 Remove meat and transfer to ovenproof casserole. Add onion and garlic to frying pan; cook 3 minutes.

3 Pour in vinegar and beer; cook 3 to 4 minutes over high heat.

4 Stir in brown sauce and nutmeg; cook 1 minute and correct seasoning. Pour sauce over meat and finish cooking in oven

Beef Potato Cake   *(serves 4)*

4	large potatoes, peeled and cut in fine julienne
3 tbsp	(45 ml) vegetable oil
1½ lb	(750 g) top-round steak, thinly sliced
2 tbsp	(30 ml) chopped onion
½ lb	(250 g) mushrooms, cleaned and sliced
1½ cups	(375 ml) commercial brown sauce, heated
1 tbsp	(15 ml) finely chopped parsley salt and pepper

Preheat oven to 375°F (190°C).

Place potatoes in bowl with water to cover.

Heat 2 tbsp (30 ml) oil in frying pan. Add potatoes and season generously. Push potatoes flat with spatula and cook 3 to 4 minutes over medium heat.

Cover and continue cooking 8 minutes Remove cover and finish cooking 10 to 15 minutes in oven.

During this time prepare meat. Heat remaining oil in large frying pan. Add meat and cook 1 to 2 minutes each side; season well. Set aside.

Add onion, mushrooms, salt and pepper to pan. Cook 3 minutes over medium heat; stir.

Pour in brown sauce and parsley; continue cooking 2 minutes.

Replace meat in sauce and simmer several minutes to reheat.

See Technique next page.

1 SERVING	571 CALORIES	39 g CARBOHYDRATE
61 g PROTEIN	19 g FAT	1.2 g FIBER

TECHNIQUE: BEEF POTATO CAKE

1 Place potatoes in bowl with water to cover. Let stand about 1 hour. Drain and dry potatoes in lettuce dryer.

2 Add potatoes to hot oil and season generously. Push potatoes flat with spatula and cook 3 to 4 minutes over medium heat.

3 Cover and continue 8 minutes over medium-low heat.

4 Remove cover and finish cooking 10 to 15 minutes in oven to brown top.

Swiss Steak   *(serves 4)*

3½ lb	(1.6 kg) flank steak or top-round steak
1 cup	(250 ml) seasoned flour
3 tbsp	(45 ml) bacon fat or oil
1	onion, peeled and thinly sliced
1	garlic clove, smashed and chopped
28 oz	(796 ml) can tomatoes, drained and chopped
1 cup	(250 ml) commercial brown sauce, heated
¼ tsp	(1 ml) thyme
½ tsp	(2 ml) basil
1	bay leaf
	salt and pepper
	some chopped fresh mint
	chopped parsley

Preheat oven to 350°F (180°C).

Slice meat as shown in technique and pound with mallet; dredge with flour.

Heat 2 tbsp (30 ml) fat in large frying pan. Add meat and sear 2 to 3 minutes each side. Season well.

Transfer meat to ovenproof casserole and set dish aside.

If necessary add remaining fat to frying pan. Cook onion and garlic 8 to 10 minutes over medium heat. Stir occasionally.

Remove onion mixture from pan and spoon over meat.

Replace frying pan on stove top. Add tomatoes and season well. Cook 3 to 4 minutes over medium heat.

Pour in brown sauce and herbs; mix very well and cook 1 minute. Pour sauce over meat.

Cover casserole and cook 1½ hours in oven.

See Technique next page.

1 SERVING	835 CALORIES	34 g CARBOHYDRATE
114 g PROTEIN	27 g FAT	1.0 g FIBER

TECHNIQUE: SWISS STEAK

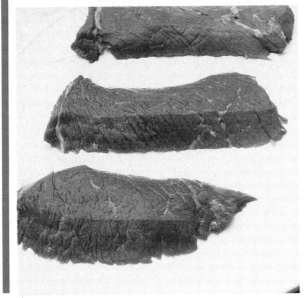

1 Slice meat on the bias into pieces.

2 Pound meat on both sides with mallet. You can do this directly on the counter or between two sheets of waxed paper.

3 Lightly coat meat with flour.

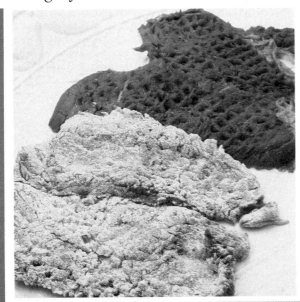

4 Sear meat and transfer to ovenproof casserole; set dish aside.

5 Cook onion and garlic together, then spoon over meat.

6 Cook tomatoes, brown sauce and herbs; pour sauce over meat.

Sirloin Roast with Yellow Squash *(serves 4)*

2 tbsp	(30 ml) vegetable oil
4 lb	(1.8 kg) boneless rolled sirloin roast, prepared
4 tbsp	(60 ml) butter
1½ lb	(750 g) yellow squash, cut in ½ in (1.2 cm) slices
1 cup	(250 ml) heated beef stock
1 tsp	(5 ml) cornstarch
2 tbsp	(30 ml) cold water
	salt and pepper

Preheat oven to 400°F (200°C).
Cooking time: 12 to 14 minutes per lb (500 g).

Heat oil in large roasting pan over high heat. Add meat and sear 6 to 7 minutes. Turn meat to brown all sides and season well.

Place pan in oven and cook 50 minutes or until done to taste. Baste occasionally.

30 minutes before roast is cooked, prepare squash. Heat butter in large frying pan. When hot, add squash and season well; cover and cook 25 to 30 minutes over medium heat. Stir occasionally.

When roast is cooked, remove from oven and transfer meat to serving platter.

Place pan on stove top and add beef stock; cook 2 to 3 minutes over medium-high heat.

Mix cornstarch with water; stir into sauce. Cook 2 minutes.

Slice roast and serve with sauce and squash.

French Boiled Beef   *(serves 4 to 6)*

4 lb	(1.8 kg) short ribs
1 lb	(500 g) veal bones
2 tsp	(10 ml) sea salt
3	parsley sprigs
2	bay leaves
2	mint sprigs
4	large carrots, pared
4	onions, peeled
4	large potatoes, peeled
4	leeks, cut in 4 lengthwise to within 1 in (2.5 cm) of base
¼ tsp	(1 ml) powdered clove
2	whole cloves
	few peppercorns
	freshly ground pepper

Place meat and bones in large stock pot. Cover with cold water and let stand 1 hour.

Drain and replace with fresh water. Bring to gentle boil over medium heat. Cook 1 hour and skim frequently.
Note: It is important that during this time, meat be covered with water. Therefore, change water several times and resume cooking process.

After 1 hour of cooking, water should be clean. If so, add remaining ingredients and season with pepper.
Cook 3 hours over low heat.
Therefore, add water several times and resume cooking process.

Serve meat with cooked vegetables and cooking liquid. If desired, sprinkle meat with a bit of oil and vinegar.

1 SERVING	509 CALORIES	8 g CARBOHYDRATE
45 g PROTEIN	33 g FAT	1.0 g FIBER

'Big Apple' Rib Steaks   *(serves 4)*

1½ tbsp	(25 ml) vegetable oil
4	rib steaks, ¾ in (2 cm) thick
1 tbsp	(15 ml) butter
3 tbsp	(45 ml) chopped onion
1 lb	(500 g) mushrooms, cleaned and sliced
1 tsp	(5 ml) chopped chives
3 tbsp	(45 ml) commercial steak sauce
1 tsp	(5 ml) chopped fresh parsley
	salt and pepper

Preheat oven to 150°F (70°C).

Cook steaks in two batches following this procedure. Heat half of oil in large frying pan. When hot, add meat and cook 3 to 4 minutes.

Turn meat over, season well and continue cooking 3 to 4 minutes. Remove meat from pan and keep steaks hot in oven.

Add butter to frying pan. When melted, add onion and cover; cook 2 minutes over medium heat.

Mix in mushrooms and chives; season generously. Continue cooking 3 to 4 minutes.

Stir in steak sauce and cook 1 minute.

Remove steaks from oven. Pour any juices into pan containing mushrooms; mix.

Pour sauce over steaks and serve with fresh parsley.

1 SERVING	509 CALORIES	8 g CARBOHYDRATE
45 g PROTEIN	33 g FAT	1.0 g FIBER

Steak Tartare *(serves 4)*

1 ½ lb	(750 g) lean ground tenderloin
¼ tsp	(1 ml) Tabasco sauce
1 tsp	(5 ml) Worcestershire sauce
1 tsp	(5 ml) olive oil
4	egg yolks
4 tbsp	(60 ml) chopped onion
4 tbsp	(60 ml) capers
4 tbsp	(60 ml) chopped fresh parsley
4	anchovy filets, chopped
	salt and pepper
	romaine lettuce leaves
	radicchio leaves
	alfalfa sprouts

Mix beef with Tabasco, Worcestershire, and olive oil. Season very generously.

Arrange individual plates as follows:

Place large patty of meat in centre of plate. Make indentation in middle and add egg yolk.

Arrange several lettuce leaves around edge of plate. Fill with onion and capers.

Decoratively arrange remaining ingredients.

Serve.

1 SERVING	392 CALORIES	1 g CARBOHYDRATE
43 g PROTEIN	24 g FAT	0 g FIBER

Marinated Beef Bourguignonne   *(serves 4 to 6)*

1½ tbsp	(25 ml) vegetable oil
3½ lb	(1.6 kg) marinated beef
2	garlic cloves, smashed and chopped
2	shallots, chopped
1 tbsp	(15 ml) chopped parsley
4 tbsp	(60 ml) flour
1 cup	(250 ml) dry red wine
2 tbsp	(30 ml) tomato paste
1 tbsp	(15 ml) butter
½ lb	(250 g) mushrooms, cleaned and quartered
1 cup	(250 ml) cooked pearl onions
	salt and pepper

Preheat oven to 350°F (180°C).
Remove meat, carrot and onion from marinade. Strain liquid and set aside.
Sear meat and vegetables in two batches following this procedure. Heat half of oil in large ovenproof casserole. Add meat and sear 8 minutes over medium-high heat. Turn to brown all sides and season well.
When all meat is seared, add garlic, shallots and parsley to casserole; cook 2 minutes. Add flour and mix very well. Cook 2 to 3 minutes over high heat.
Place strained marinade in separate pan and add wine; cook 5 to 6 minutes over medium heat. Pour marinade into casserole containing beef and mix in tomato paste; bring to boil. Cover casserole and cook 1½ hours in oven.
About 20 minutes before beef is cooked, prepare mushrooms. Heat butter in frying pan. Add mushrooms and onions; cook 3 to 4 minutes. Season well. Place mushrooms in casserole and resume cooking process.

1 SERVING	641 CALORIES	9 g CARBOHYDRATE
68 g PROTEIN	37 g FAT	0.5 g FIBER

TECHNIQUE

1 Place beef in large bowl. Add onion, carrot, peppercorns, bay leaf, garlic and wine. Sprinkle oil over meat but do not stir. Cover with sheet of plastic wrap and refrigerate 8 hours.

2 Sear meat and vegetables in hot oil. Turn meat to brown all sides and season well. When all meat is seared, add garlic, shallots and parsley to casserole; cook 2 minutes and mix.

3 Add flour and mix very well. Cook 2 to 3 minutes over high heat. Scrape bottom of pan with wooden spoon.

4 Place strained marinade in separate pan and add wine; cook 5 to 6 minutes over medium heat.

Continued next page.

5 Pour marinade into casserole containing beef and mix in tomato paste; bring to boil.

6 While beef is in oven, prepare mushrooms. Cook with onions in hot butter 3 to 4 minutes; add to beef about 15 minutes before it is done.

Marinade

3½ lb	(1.6 kg) boneless blade steak, cut in 1 in (2.5 cm) cubes
3 to 4	onion slices
½	carrot, pared and sliced
5	black peppercorns
1	bay leaf
1	garlic clove, peeled
1 cup	(250 ml) dry red wine
2 tbsp	(30 ml) vegetable oil

Place beef in large bowl. Add onion, carrot, peppercorns, bay leaf, garlic and wine.

Sprinkle oil over meat but do not stir. Cover with sheet of plastic wrap and refrigerate 8 hours.

Cream of Turnips with Horseradish *(serves 4 to 6)*

2 lb	(900 g) small turnips
3 tbsp	(45 ml) butter
½ cup	(125 ml) heavy cream, heated
3 tbsp	(45 ml) horseradish
1 tbsp	(15 ml) wine vinegar
1 tsp	(5 ml) strong mustard
½ cup	(125 ml) heavy cream, cold
	salt and pepper
	pinch sugar

Peel turnips and cook in saucepan filled with salted boiling water.

When cooked, drain and mash.

Mix in butter and hot cream; incorporate well. Set saucepan aside but keep hot.

Mix horseradish, vinegar and mustard together in small bowl.

Whip cold cream and incorporate this into horseradish mixture; add to turnips.

Sprinkle in sugar, correct seasoning and serve with beef.

1 SERVING	218 CALORIES	12 g CARBOHYDRATE
2 g PROTEIN	18 g FAT	1.5 g FIBER

Yorkshire Pudding *(serves 4 to 6)*

1¼ cups	(300 ml) flour
½ tsp	(2 ml) salt
2	extra-large eggs
¾ cup	(175 ml) milk
¾ cup	(175 ml) tepid water
2½ tbsp	(40 ml) beef drippings

Preheat oven to 400°F (200°C).

Sift flour and salt together in bowl.

Make well in centre and add eggs. Pour in half of milk and half of water; mix everything together.

Add remaining milk and water; mix until thoroughly combined.

Cover with wax paper and set aside 1 hour.

Heat beef drippings in small pan; pour into muffin pans and fill about half full with batter.

Cook 20 minutes in oven.

Serve with roast.

1 SERVING	216 CALORIES	28 g CARBOHYDRATE
8 g PROTEIN	8 g FAT	0.1 g FIBER

Beef Wellington *(serves 4 to 6)*

2 tbsp	(30 ml) vegetable oil
2 lb	(900 g) tenderloin roast, from top part
	salt and pepper
	flaky dough
	beaten egg
	Wellington sauce*

Preheat oven to 425°F (220°C).

Cooking time: 12 minutes per lb (500 g).

Heat half of oil in large pan. Add meat and sear 4 to 5 minutes over medium-high heat. Turn to brown all sides and season well. Remove meat from pan and set aside to cool. Grease roasting pan with remaining oil and set aside.

Roll out dough on floured surface. It must be large enough to encase meat and also be thin. Set meat in middle of rolled dough. Wet inside of dough with some water which will help it stick. Now fold over half of dough and press edges down on meat.

Wet dough again if needed and bring other half of dough over top. Tuck in corners and trim away excess dough.

Place wrapped meat, with seam side down, in roasting pan. Lightly score top.

Cook 25 minutes in oven.

*Serve with Wellington Sauce, see page 314.

1 SERVING	558 CALORIES	20 g CARBOHYDRATE
34 g PROTEIN	38 g FAT	0.4 g FIBER

TECHNIQUE: BEEF WELLINGTON

1 Have butcher cut tenderloin roast from the top part, which is wider.

2 Sear meat 4 to 5 minutes in hot oil over medium-high heat. Turn to brown all sides and season well.

3 Set meat in middle of rolled dough. Wet inside of dough with some water which will help it stick.

4 Now fold over half of dough and press edges down on meat.

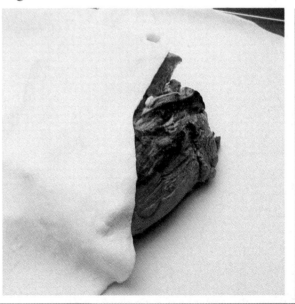

Continued next page.

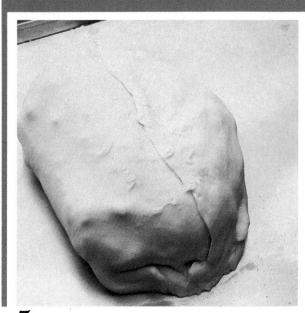

5 Wet dough again if needed and bring other half of dough over top. Tuck in corners and trim away excess dough.

6 Place wrapped meat, with seam side down, in roasting pan. Lightly score top. Brush with some beaten egg and insert chimney which will allow excess steam to escape during cooking.

Wellington Sauce

1 tbsp	(15 ml) butter
½ lb	(250 g) fresh mushrooms, cleaned and sliced
1	shallot, chopped
¼ cup	(50 ml) Madeira wine
1 tsp	(5 ml) chopped chives
1¼ cups	(300 ml) commercial brown sauce, heated
¼ cup	(50 ml) heavy cream
	salt and pepper
	few drops lemon juice

Heat butter in deep frying pan. When hot, add mushrooms and shallot; cook 3 minutes over medium heat.

Pour in wine and sprinkle with chives; mix well. Continue cooking 2 to 3 minutes over medium heat.

Add brown sauce and mix well; season and cook 3 to 4 minutes.

Incorporate cream and lemon juice; cook 2 to 3 minutes over medium heat.

1 SERVING	488 CALORIES	29 g CARBOHYDRATE
12 g PROTEIN	36 g FAT	2.1 g FIBER

TECHNIQUE: WELLINGTON SAUCE

1 Cook mushrooms and shallot in hot butter 3 minutes over medium heat.

2 Pour in wine and sprinkle with chives; mix well. Continue cooking 2 to 3 minutes over medium heat.

3 Add brown sauce and mix well; season and cook 3 to 4 minutes.

4 Incorporate cream and lemon juice; cook 2 to 3 minutes over medium heat.

Rib Roast and
Cream of Turnips with Horseradish *(serves 4 to 6)*

4 lb	(1.8 kg) rib roast, prepared for roasting
1½ cups	(375 ml) heated beef stock
1 tsp	(5 ml) chopped fresh herbs
1 tbsp	(15 ml) cornstarch
2 tbsp	(30 ml) cold water
	vegetable oil
	salt and pepper

Preheat oven to 400°F (200°C).

Place meat in roasting pan and brush with vegetable oil. Pepper generously and cook 30 minutes in oven.

Remove pan from oven and season meat again; baste with cooking juices. Replace pan in oven and continue cooking 30 minutes. Reduce heat to 375°F (190°C) and finish cooking 20 minutes.

Remove roast from pan and set aside.

Place pan on stove top and add beef stock; bring to boil. Continue cooking 4 to 5 minutes. Stir in herbs. Mix cornstarch with water; stir into sauce. Cook 1 minute to thicken.

Serve with Cream of Turnips, see page 311.

1 SERVING	284 CALORIES	1 g CARBOHYDRATE
43 g PROTEIN	12 g FAT	0 g FIBER

Pepper Sauce

1 tsp	(5 ml) vegetable oil
1	green pepper, sliced
½	red pepper, sliced
1½ cups	(375 ml) heated beef stock
1 tbsp	(15 ml) tomato paste
1 tbsp	(15 ml) cornstarch
2 tbsp	(30 ml) cold water
1 tsp	(5 ml) chopped chives
	salt and pepper

Heat oil in frying pan. When hot, add both peppers and season well. Cook 3 to 4 minutes over medium heat.

Pour in beef stock and bring to boil. Correct seasoning and cook 2 minutes over medium heat.

Add tomato paste and mix well; cook 1 minute.

Mix cornstarch with water; stir into sauce. Bring to boil and continue cooking 2 minutes over medium heat.

Stir in chives and serve.

This sauce is delicious with meatloaf and with burgers.

1 SERVING	37 CALORIES	6 g CARBOHYDRATE
1 g PROTEIN	1 g FAT	0.6 g FIBER

Quick Tostada Meal *(serves 4)*

1 tsp	(5 ml) vegetable oil
1	onion, peeled and chopped
½	green pepper, finely chopped
2	garlic cloves, chopped
1 tbsp	(15 ml) parsley
½	zucchini, finely chopped
½ tsp	(2 ml) chervil
¼ tsp	(1 ml) thyme
¼ tsp	(1 ml) ginger
1¼ lb	(625 g) lean ground beef
1 tsp	(5 ml) soya sauce
¼ tsp	(1 ml) Tabasco sauce
1 cup	(250 ml) canned tomatoes, chopped
1 tbsp	(15 ml) tomato paste
¼ cup	(50 ml) heated chicken stock
¾ cup	(175 ml) grated Swiss cheese tostada shells

Heat oil in large frying pan. When hot, add onion, green pepper, garlic, parsley, zucchini and spices. Cook 4 to 5 minutes.

Mix in beef and continue cooking 3 to 4 minutes. Season well. Mix in soya sauce and Tabasco sauce; correct seasoning.

Add tomatoes and tomato paste; mix well. Pour in chicken stock and cook 3 to 4 minutes over medium-high heat.

Add most of cheese and mix until incorporated. Remove pan from heat.

Spread meat mixture on tostada shells and cover with another shell. Top tostada sandwiches with remaining cheese and place in ovenproof pan. Broil 3 to 4 minutes in oven or until cheese melts.

1 SERVING	547 CALORIES	26 g CARBOHYDRATE
41 g PROTEIN	31 g FAT	0.7 g FIBER

Zesty Meat Spaghetti Sauce   *(serves 4)*

1 tbsp	(15 ml) vegetable oil
2	small onions, peeled and chopped
1	celery stalk, diced
2	garlic cloves, chopped
1 tbsp	(15 ml) chopped fresh ginger (optional)
1 tsp	(5 ml) oregano
½ tsp	(2 ml) basil
¼ tsp	(1 ml) thyme
1	small bay leaf
1¼ lb	(625 g) lean ground beef
28 oz	(796 ml) can tomatoes, drained and chopped
1 tsp	(5 ml) brown sugar
½ cup	(125 ml) heated chicken stock
5½ oz	(156 ml) can tomato paste
	salt and pepper

Heat oil in deep frying pan or saucepan. When hot, add onions, celery, garlic, herbs and bay leaf. Mix well and cook 4 to 6 minutes over low heat.

Add beef and continue cooking 4 minutes.

Mix in tomatoes and season well; sprinkle in brown sugar.

Pour in chicken stock and stir in tomato paste. Bring to boil. Cook sauce 2 hours over low heat. Do not cover.

Note: If necessary add more chicken stock during cooking.

1 SERVING	412 CALORIES	22 g CARBOHYDRATE
36 g PROTEIN	20 g FAT	1.4 g FIBER

Stuffed Tomatoes   *(serves 4)*

8	medium-size tomatoes
1 tsp	(5 ml) olive oil
1 tbsp	(15 ml) vegetable oil
1	onion, peeled and finely chopped
½	celery stalk, finely chopped
2	garlic cloves, smashed and chopped
½ lb	(250 g) lean ground beef
1 cup	(250 ml) chopped tomatoes
¾ cup	(175 ml) cooked rice
½ tsp	(2 ml) oregano
½ cup	(125 ml) grated Swiss cheese
	salt and pepper

Preheat oven to 350°F (180°C).

Core tomatoes and place upside down on cutting board. Use sharp knife and slice off tops, either decoratively or plain.

Scoop out most of flesh but leave solid shell; sprinkle insides with olive oil.

Heat vegetable oil in saucepan. When hot, add onion, celery and garlic; cook 3 to 4 minutes over medium heat.

Mix in meat and season well; continue cooking 3 to 4 minutes.

Add chopped tomatoes, rice, herbs and spices to saucepan. Mix very well and cook 6 to 7 minutes over medium heat.

Place tomato shells in greased baking dish and fill with meat mixture.

Sprinkle with cheese and cook 25 minutes.

1 SERVING	324 CALORIES	24 g CARBOHYDRATE
21 g PROTEIN	16 g FAT	1.8 g FIBER

Stuffed Green Peppers   *(serves 4)*

4	large green or yellow peppers
1 tbsp	(15 ml) vegetable oil
1	small red onion, peeled and finely chopped
1	celery stalk, finely chopped
10	mushrooms, cleaned and finely chopped
1	garlic clove, smashed and chopped
1 lb	(500 g) lean ground beef
¼ tsp	(1 ml) basil
1½ cups	(375 ml) chopped tomatoes
2 tbsp	(30 ml) tomato paste
¼ cup	(50 ml) grated parmesan cheese
1 cup	(250 ml) tomato juice
½ cup	(125 ml) commercial brown sauce
	pinch thyme

Preheat oven to 350°F (180°C).
Place peppers standing up on cutting board. Slice off top and remove all seeds and fibers. Blanch peppers in salted boiling water 5 to 6 minutes. Cool under cold running water.
Heat oil in large frying pan. When hot, add onion and celery; cover and cook 2 to 3 minutes over medium-high heat.
Add mushrooms, garlic, salt and pepper; mix well. Continue cooking 2 to 3 minutes, covered.
Mix in meat and spices; cook 3 to 4 minutes, uncovered, over medium-high heat.
Stir in tomatoes and cook 3 to 4 minutes, uncovered, over medium heat.
Add tomato paste and mix well; cook 2 to 3 minutes over medium heat.
Add cheese and correct seasoning; mix well. Season inside of peppers and fill with meat mixture. Place in baking dish and pour in tomato juice and brown sauce.
Cook 30 to 35 minutes in oven.

1 SERVING	400 CALORIES	20 g CARBOHYDRATE
35 g PROTEIN	20 g FAT	2.7 g FIBER

Beef Liver and Onions *(serves 4)*

4	slices beef liver
1 cup	(250 ml) seasoned flour
1 tbsp	(15 ml) vegetable oil
2 tbsp	(30 ml) butter
1	Spanish onion, peeled and thinly sliced
1 tbsp	(15 ml) brown sugar
¼ tsp	(1 ml) celery seed
1 tbsp	(15 ml) wine vinegar
1 tsp	(5 ml) soya sauce
1¼ cups	(300 ml) heated beef stock
1 tbsp	(15 ml) cornstarch
2 tbsp	(30 ml) cold water
	salt and pepper

Preheat oven to 150°F (70°C).

Dredge liver with flour.

Heat oil and 1 tbsp (15 ml) butter in large frying pan. When hot, add liver and cook 3 minutes over medium heat.

Turn liver over and season well; continue cooking 3 minutes. Do not overcook liver as it will continue cooking in oven. Remove and keep hot in oven.

Add remaining butter to frying pan. Add onion and cook 6 to 7 minutes over medium heat; stir occasionally.

Mix in sugar and celery seed; season. Cook 2 minutes and mix well.

Add vinegar and cook 2 minutes.

Stir in soya sauce and beef stock; bring to boil.

Mix cornstarch with water; stir into sauce. Continue cooking 2 minutes over medium heat. Correct seasoning and pour sauce over liver.

Serve with yellow beans.

Beef Liver and Apples *(serves 4)*

4	slices beef liver
1 cup	(250 ml) seasoned flour
1 tbsp	(15 ml) vegetable oil
1 tbsp	(15 ml) butter
2 tbsp	(30 ml) chopped red onion
2	cooking apples, peeled and sliced thick
1 tsp	(5 ml) chopped parsley
1 cup	(250 ml) chopped tomatoes
1½ cups	(375 ml) heated chicken stock
¼ tsp	(1 ml) chervil
1 tbsp	(15 ml) cornstarch
2 tbsp	(30 ml) cold water
	salt and pepper
	pinch thyme

Preheat oven to 150°F (70°C).

Dredge liver with flour.

Heat both fats in large frying pan. When hot, add liver and cook 3 minutes over medium heat.

Turn liver over and season well; continue cooking 3 minutes or longer, depending on taste. Remove from pan and keep hot in oven.

Add onion and apples to frying pan; sprinkle with parsley. Mix well and cook 3 to 4 minutes over medium heat.

Stir in tomatoes and season well. Add chicken stock and herbs; bring to boil. Continue cooking 3 to 4 minutes over medium heat.

Mix cornstarch with water; stir into sauce. Bring to boil and cook 1 minute.

1 SERVING	389 CALORIES	22 g CARBOHYDRATE
37 g PROTEIN	17 g FAT	0.8 g FIBER

Sliced Beef Parmesan   *(serves 4)*

1 tbsp	(15 ml) vegetable oil
1 tbsp	(15 ml) butter
8	¼ in (0.65 cm) slices beef tenderloin
½ cup	(125 ml) sliced mushrooms
1	yellow or red pepper, sliced
2	hearts of palm, sliced
¼ cup	(50 ml) dry white wine
1½ cups	(375 ml) heated beef stock
¼ tsp	(1 ml) oregano
1 tbsp	(15 ml) cornstarch
2 tbsp	(30 ml) cold water
3 tbsp	(45 ml) heavy cream
¼ cup	(50 ml) grated Parmesan cheese
	salt and pepper
	dash paprika

Heat oil and butter in large frying pan. When hot, add meat and cook 2 minutes over medium-high heat.

Turn slices over and season well; continue cooking 2 minutes. Remove from pan.

Add mushrooms, yellow pepper and hearts of palm to frying pan. Mix and cook 3 minutes over high heat.

Pour in wine and cook 2 minutes.

Mix in beef stock and spices; bring to boil. Continue cooking 2 minutes over medium heat.

Mix cornstarch with water; stir into sauce. Cook 1 minute. Stir in cream and cook 2 minutes; correct seasoning.

Sprinkle in cheese and mix well; finish cooking 1 minute.

Replace meat in sauce and simmer until reheated. Serve immediately.

Top-Loin Strips and Spaghetti (serves 4)

2 tbsp	(30 ml) vegetable oil
2 lb	(900 g) top-loin steak, cut in thin strips
1	onion, peeled and chopped
2	garlic cloves, smashed and chopped
¼ tsp	(1 ml) oregano
1	zucchini, cut in strips
16	cherry tomatoes, cut in half
1 cup	(250 ml) commercial brown sauce, heated
1½ cups	(375 ml) commercial tomato sauce, heated
½ cup	(125 ml) grated parmesan cheese
4	portions cooked spaghetti, hot salt and pepper

Heat oil in large frying pan. When hot, add meat and cook 1½ minutes each side; season well. Note: You may have to cook meat in two batches depending on the size of pan.

Remove meat and set aside.

Add onion and garlic to pan; cover and cook 2 minutes over medium heat.

Mix in oregano, zucchini and tomatoes; cook 3 to 4 minutes over medium heat.

Pour in brown and tomato sauces; mix well and season to taste. Continue cooking 3 to 4 minutes over medium-low heat.

Replace meat in frying pan and reheat several minutes.

Pour beef mixture into large serving platter. Sprinkle with half of cheese and add cooked spaghetti; toss together. Top with remaining cheese and serve immediately.

1 SERVING	687 CALORIES	46 g CARBOHYDRATE
56 g PROTEIN	31 g FAT	1.0 g FIBER

Rump Roast and Potatoes (serves 4 to 6)

2 tbsp	(30 ml) vegetable oil
4 lb	(1.8 kg) boneless rolled rump roast, prepared for roasting
8	small potatoes, peeled
1	garlic clove, peeled and split in two
1½ cups	(375 ml) heated beef stock
1 tbsp	(15 ml) cornstarch
2 tbsp	(30 ml) cold water
	salt and pepper

Preheat oven to 400°F (200°C). Cooking time: 12 to 15 minutes per lb (500 g).

Heat oil in large roasting pan over medium-high heat. When hot, add meat and sear 6 to 7 minutes. Turn meat to brown all sides and season well.

Place pan in oven and cook about 50 minutes or until done to taste. Baste occasionally.

About 10 minutes after roast has been cooking, add potatoes and garlic to pan. Resume cooking process.

When roast is cooked, transfer to serving platter and surround with potatoes. Reduce oven heat and keep meat hot.

Place roasting pan on stove top and add beef stock. Cook 2 to 3 minutes over high heat.

Mix cornstarch with water; stir into sauce. Continue cooking 2 minutes over medium heat.

Serve sauce with meat and potatoes.

1 SERVING	655 CALORIES	16 g CARBOHYDRATE
78 g PROTEIN	31 g FAT	0.4 g FIBER

Beef and Vegetable Mix in Sake *(serves 4)*

2 tbsp	(30 ml) vegetable oil
1½ lb	(750 g) beef tenderloin, sliced
1½ cups	(375 ml) fresh pea pods
¼ lb	(125 g) fresh mushrooms
1	small zucchini, cut in half and sliced
4	green onions, cut in short sticks
1	garlic clove, smashed and chopped
1 tbsp	(15 ml) chopped fresh ginger
¼ cup	(50 ml) sake
1 tbsp	(15 ml) soya sauce
1½ cups	(375 ml) heated beef stock
1 tbsp	(15 ml) cornstarch
2 tbsp	(30 ml) cold water
12	cherry tomatoes, cut in half

Heat oil in wok or large frying pan. When hot, meat add and cook 1½ minutes each side over high heat. Stir as needed and season well. Remove meat and set aside.

Add pea pods, mushrooms, zucchini, onions and garlic to wok. Season well and continue cooking 3 to 4 minutes over high heat.

Add ginger and sake; cook 2 minutes over high heat.

Mix in soya sauce and continue cooking 1 minute.

Pour in beef stock and cook another minute.

Mix cornstarch with water; stir into sauce. Cook 1 minute.

Add meat and tomatoes to mixture; stir and cook 1 minute.

Correct seasoning and serve.

Lemon Beef   *(serves 4)*

2 tbsp	(30 ml) vegetable oil
1½ lb	(750 g) top-round steak, cut in strips
2 tbsp	(30 ml) chopped shallots
¼ cup	(50 ml) lemon juice
1 tbsp	(15 ml) fresh chopped mint
¼ lb	(125 g) mushrooms caps, cleaned
¼	cucumber, sliced
1	red pepper, diced large
2 tbsp	(30 ml) chopped lemon rind
1¼ cups	(300 ml) hot beef stock
3 tbsp	(45 ml) plain yogurt
1 tbsp	(15 ml) cornstarch
2 tbsp	(30 ml) cold water
1½ cups	(375 ml) melon balls
	salt and pepper

Heat oil in large frying pan. When hot, add meat and cook 2 minutes over high heat.

Turn pieces over and season well; continue cooking 2 minutes. Remove meat and set aside.

Add shallots to frying pan and cook 1 minute.

Stir in lemon juice and cook 2 minutes over high heat.

Add mint, mushrooms, cucumber, red pepper and lemon rind; mix well. Cook 3 minutes over high heat; season well.

Pour in beef stock and bring to boil. Continue cooking 2 minutes.

Stir in yogurt and correct seasoning. Cook 2 to 3 minutes over medium heat.

Mix cornstarch with water; stir into sauce. Cook 1 minute.

Place melon balls and meat in frying pan. Cook 1 minute to reheat.

Mix well and serve.

1 SERVING	372 CALORIES	14 g CARBOHYDRATE
43 g PROTEIN	16 g FAT	1.3 g FIBER

Olive-Lover's Filet Mignon   *(serves 4)*

1 tbsp	(15 ml) vegetable oil
4	8 oz (227 g) filet mignons
½ cup	(125 ml) stuffed green olives, sliced
½ cup	(125 ml) pitted black olives, sliced
¼ cup	(50 ml) slivered almonds, blanched
¼ cup	(50 ml) dry white wine
1½ cups	(375 ml) heated beef stock
1 tbsp	(15 ml) cornstarch
2 tbsp	(30 ml) cold water
	salt and pepper
	dash Tabasco sauce
	dash Worcestershire sauce
	pinch ginger

Preheat oven to 150°F (70°C).

Heat oil in large frying pan. When hot, add meat and cook 2 minutes over medium-high heat.

Turn meat over and season well; continue cooking 6 minutes. Turn 3 times during cooking time.

Remove meat from pan and keep hot in oven. Add olives and almonds to frying pan; cook 2 minutes over medium heat.

Pour in wine and mix well; cook 2 minutes over medium-high heat.

Mix in beef stock, Tabasco, Worcestershire and spices; bring to boil.

Mix cornstarch with water; stir into sauce. Cook 2 minutes over medium heat.

Correct seasoning and pour sauce over meat. Serve with pea pods.

1 SERVING	563 CALORIES	8 g CARBOHYDRATE
45 g PROTEIN	39 g FAT	0.3 g FIBER

Basic Filet Mignon
with Anchovy Butter *(serves 4)*

1 tbsp	(15 ml) vegetable oil
4	8 oz (227 g) filet mignons
1	recipe anchovy butter*
	salt and pepper

Heat oil in large frying pan. When hot, add meat and cook 2 minutes over medium-high heat.

Turn meat over and season well; continue cooking 6 minutes. Turn 3 times during cooking time.

Spread anchovy butter over meat and broil 1 minute.

Serve with vegetables.

* See Anchovy Butter, page 330.

1 SERVING	851 CALORIES	0 g CARBOHYDRATE
44 g PROTEIN	75 g FAT	0 g FIBER

TECHNIQUE: ANCHOVY BUTTER

1 Drain anchovies and pat dry with paper towel. Place filets in mortar.

2 Mash with pestle.

3 Add butter and mix together well with spoon.
Place mixture in fine sieve and force through using pestle.

4 Add chives, lemon juice and pepper to taste. Mix thoroughly and refrigerate until use.

Anchovy Butter

4	anchovy filets
½ lb	(250 g) unsalted butter, soft
1 tst	(5 ml) chopped chives
¼ tsp	(1 ml) lemon juice
	freshly ground pepper

Drain anchovies and pat dry with paper towel. Place filets in mortar; mash with pestle.

Add butter and mix together well with spoon.

Place mixture in fine sieve and force through using pestle.

Add chives, lemon juice and pepper to taste. Mix thoroughly and refrigerate until use.

This butter is delicious on almost any steak.

1 SERVING	117 CALORIES	0 g CARBOHYDRATE
0 g PROTEIN	13 g FAT	0 g FIBER

Applesauce *(serves 4)*

2 lb	(900 g) cooking apples, peeled and sliced thick
2 tbsp	(30 ml) lemon juice
¼ cup	(50 ml) sugar
½ cup	(125 ml) water
¼ tsp	(1 ml) nutmeg
1 tsp	(5 ml) cinnamon
	pinch clove powder
	pinch ginger powder
	dash chopped lemon rind

Place apples, lemon juice, sugar and water in saucepan.

Add spices and lemon rind; mix very well. Cover and cook 8 to 10 minutes over medium heat. Stir occasionally.

Pour applesauce into food processor; blend until smooth.

Transfer to bowl and let cool.

Cover and refrigerate 2 to 3 hours before serving.

1 SERVING	189 CALORIES	45 g CARBOHYDRATE
0 g PROTEIN	1 g FAT	1.0 g FIBER

Rump Roast in Beer *(serves 4 to 6)*

2 tbsp	(30 ml) bacon fat
4 lb	(1.8 kg) rump roast, prepared
1	onion, peeled and diced
1	celery stalk, diced
1	carrot, peeled and diced
¼ tsp	(1 ml) thyme
½ tsp	(2 ml) chervil
½ tsp	(2 ml) basil
2 tbsp	(30 ml) flour
1¼ cups	(300 ml) beer
1 cup	(250 ml) heated beef stock
	few crushed chillies
	salt and pepper
	sprig fresh mint

Preheat oven to 350°F (180°C).

Heat 1 tbsp (15 ml) bacon fat in large braising pot. When hot, add meat and sear 6 to 7 minutes over medium-high heat. Turn meat to brown all sides and season well.

Remove meat and set aside.

Add remaining fat to pot and heat. Mix in onion, celery, carrot and spices; cook 6 to 7 minutes over medium heat. Stir occasionally.

Mix in flour and continue cooking 2 to 3 minutes over medium-high heat.

Pour in beer; cook 3 to 4 minutes over high heat.

Stir in beef stock and season well; bring to boil.

Replace meat in pot and add mint. Cover and cook 2½ hours in oven.

Slice meat and serve.

Beef Tournedos with Cucumbers *(serves 4)*

1 tbsp	(15 ml) vegetable oil
4	tournedos, about 1¼ in (3 cm) thick
2 tbsp	(30 ml) Courvoisier cognac
1	cucumber, peeled, seeded and sliced ½ in (1.2 cm) thick
½	red pepper, diced large
1	yellow pepper, diced large
2	green onions, sliced
½ cup	(125 ml) light brown sauce, heated
2 tbsp	(30 ml) plain yogurt
	salt and pepper

Heat oil in large frying pan. When hot, add tournedos and cook 3 minutes over medium-high heat.

Season well and turn beef over; continue cooking 3 minutes or longer to taste.

Pour in cognac and flambé. Continue cooking 1 minute over medium-high heat.

Remove beef from pan and set aside.

Add cucumber, both peppers and onions to pan. Season very generously and cook 2 to 3 minutes over high heat.

Mix in brown sauce and continue cooking 1 minute.

Stir in yogurt and replace beef in sauce; simmer 1 to 2 minutes over low heat.

Serve.

1 SERVING	353 CALORIES	5 g CARBOHYDRATE
45 g PROTEIN	17 g FAT	0.6 g FIBER

Meatloaf *(serves 4 to 6)*

1 tbsp	(15 ml) vegetable oil
1 cup	(250 ml) chopped onions
1	garlic clove, smashed and choped
1½ lb	(750 g) lean ground beef
1 tbsp	(15 ml) chopped parsley
4	slices white bread, crust trimmed and soaked in ¼ cup (50 ml) milk
½ tsp	(2 ml) basil
¼ tsp	(1 ml) thyme
¼ tsp	(1 ml) chervil
2	eggs
	pinch clove powder
	salt and pepper

Preheat oven to 350°F (180°C).

Heat oil in small frying pan. Cook onions and garlic 3 to 4 minutes over medium heat.

Remove onions and place in large bowl. Add meat and remaining ingredients; mix very well with hands.

Press mixture into 8 × 4 × 2 in (20 × 10 × 5 cm) loaf pan. Cook 1¼ hours in oven.

About 15 minutes before meatloaf is cooked, heat the following ingredients in small saucepan. Pour over meatloaf and resume cooking.

3 tbsp	(45 ml) catsup
1 tsp	(5 ml) brown sugar
½ tsp	(2 ml) dry mustard

Pork Chops with Sauce Roberto *(serves 4)*

1 tbsp	(15 ml) vegetable oil
4	deboned pork chops, about ¾ in (2 cm) thick and fat trimmed
	salt and pepper
	sauce Roberto*
	deep-fried carrots**

Preheat oven to 150°F (70°C).

Heat oil in frying pan. When hot, add pork and cook 3 minutes over medium heat.

Season well and turn pork over; continue cooking 3 minutes over medium heat.

Turn pork again; cook 1 minute over low heat or until done to taste. Keep hot in oven.

Prepare deep-fried carrots and serve with pork. If desired, accompany with broccoli. Top with sauce Roberto.

* See Sauce Roberto, page 336.
** See Deep-Fried Carrots, page 339.

1 SERVING	358 CALORIES	3 g CARBOHYDRATE
19 g PROTEIN	30 g FAT	0 g FIBER

Sauce Roberto

1 tbsp	(15 ml) butter
2	shallots, chopped
1	garlic clove, smashed and chopped
1 tbsp	(15 ml) chopped fresh parsley
½ tsp	(2 ml) tarragon
¼ cup	(50 ml) wine vinegar
½ cup	(125 ml) dry white wine
2 cups	(500 ml) hot brown sauce*
1	bay leaf
2	pickles, sliced
1 tbsp	(15 ml) Dijon mustard
	salt and pepper fresly ground

Heat butter in saucepan. When hot, add shallots and garlic; cook 2 minutes over medium heat.

Add parsley and tarragon; mix and continue cooking 1 minute.

Add vinegar and wine. Stir and cook 6 minutes over high heat.

Pour in brown sauce and season well. Drop in bay leaf and bring to boil. Simmer sauce 10 to 12 minutes over low heat.

Add pickles and mustard**; stir and serve.

* See Brown Sauce, page 355.
** If you plan to reheat this sauce, do not add mustard.

1 SERVING	66 CALORIES	3 g CARBOHYDRATE
0 g PROTEIN	6 g FAT	0 g FIBER

Hearty Sausages and Sauerkraut *(serves 4)*

1	slice side bacon, diced
1	small onion, peeled and diced
2	19 oz (540 ml) packages sauerkraut, drained
1	clove
¼ cup	(50 ml) dry white wine
1 cup	(250 ml) cold water
1	bay leaf
8	knackwurst sausages
	pepper

Preheat oven to 350°F (180°C).

Place bacon in ovenproof casserole; cook 2 to 3 minutes over low heat.

Stir in onion and continue cooking, covered, 6 minutes over low heat.

Add sauerkraut and mix well. Season well with pepper and add clove.

Add wine, water and bay leaf. Season and bring to boil. Cover and cook 2 hours in oven.

Slash sausage skins on the bias using sharp knife. This technique will prevent sausages from splitting during cooking.

8 minutes before end of cooking, add sausages to the casserole. Serve.

1 SERVING	405 CALORIES	6 g CARBOHYDRATE
21 g PROTEIN	33 g FAT	0.6 g FIBER

Pork Chops with Sauce Charcutière *(serves 4)*

1 tbsp	(15 ml) vegetable oil
4	deboned pork chops, about ¾ in (2 cm) thick with fat trimmed
	salt and pepper
	sauce charcutière*

Heat oil in frying pan. When hot, add pork and cook 3 minutes over medium heat.

Season well and turn pork over; continue cooking 3 minutes over medium heat.

Turn pork again; cook 1 minute over low heat or until done to taste.

Serve with sauce charcutière and vegetables.

*See Sauce Charcutière, page 339.

1 SERVING	463 CALORIES	3 g CARBOHYDRATE
25 g PROTEIN	39 g FAT	0.2 g FIBER

Sauce Charcutière

1 tbsp	(15 ml) butter
2	shallots, chopped
1 tbsp	(15 ml) chopped fresh parsley
¼ cup	(50 ml) wine vinegar
¼ cup	(50 ml) dry white wine
1 tsp	(5 ml) chopped tarragon
1½ cups	(375 ml) brown sauce*, heated
3	pickles, thinly sliced
	salt and pepper

Heat butter in saucepan. When hot, add shallots and cook 2 to 3 minutes over medium heat.

Add parsley and season. Pour in vinegar and wine; sprinkle with tarragon. Cook 6 to 7 minutes over high heat.

Add brown sauce and mix well; cook 8 to 9 minutes over very low heat.

About 2 minutes before end of cooking, stir in pickles.

* See Brown Sauce, page 355.

1 SERVING	61 CALORIES	3 g CARBOHYDRATE
1 g PROTEIN	5 g FAT	0.2 g FIBER

Deep-Fried Carrots *(serves 4)*

4	large carrots, pared and cut into 2 in (5 cm) sticks
2	beaten eggs
1 cup	(250 ml) breadcrumbs
	salt and pepper
	dash paprika

Preheat peanut oil in deep-fryer to 325°F (160°C).

Place carrots in beaten eggs and mix thoroughly. Season generously.

Remove carrots from eggs and place in breadcrumbs; coat well.

Deep-fry carrots 4 minutes or until golden brown.

Drain on paper towels and serve immediately.

1 SERVING	240 CALORIES	26 g CARBOHYDRATE
7 g PROTEIN	12 g FAT	1.1 g FIBER

Butterfly Pork Chops *(serves 4)*

1 tbsp	(15 ml) vegetable oil
4	butterfly pork chops
2 tbsp	(30 ml) butter
2	onions, peeled and thinly sliced
1 tbsp	(15 ml) chopped whole pimento
1 cup	(250 ml) plum sauce
	salt and pepper

Preheat oven to 150°F (70°C).

Brush oil over nonstick grill or frying pan. Place on stove top and when hot, add half of pork. Cook 3 minutes over medium heat.

Season well and turn pork over; continue cooking 3 minutes over medium heat.

Turn pork again; cook 2 to 3 minutes over low heat or until done to taste. Keep hot in oven. Repeat procedure for remaining pork, adding more oil if necessary.

Heat butter in frying pan. When hot, add onions and cook 7 to 9 minutes over medium heat. Stir occasionally.

Add chopped pimento and cook 1 minute. Season well and mix in plum sauce; continue cooking 2 minutes.

Serve onions with pork and garnish with French fries.

1 SERVING	564 CALORIES	26 g CARBOHYDRATE
25 g PROTEIN	40 g FAT	0.3 g FIBER

Pork and Vegetables on Skewers   *(serves 4)*

1½ lb	(750 g) loin of pork, cut into 1 in (2.5 cm) cubes
1½	green peppers, cut into large pieces
2	small onions, peeled and cut into pieces
8	spiced crab apples
12	mushroom caps
3 tbsp	(45 ml) melted garlic butter
2 tbsp	(30 ml) soya sauce
	salt and pepper

Alternate pork, vegetables and crab apples on 4 skewers.

Mix garlic butter with soya sauce; brush over skewers. Season generously.

Broil 10 minutes in oven 4 in (10 cm) from top element. Baste occasionally and rotate every 3 minutes.

Serve over rice.

1 SERVING	589 CALORIES	12 g CARBOHYDRATE
34 g PROTEIN	45 g FAT	1.3 g FIBER

341

Pork Fingers *(serves 4)*

2 lb	(900 g) loin of pork, cut into thick strips
1 cup	(250 ml) flour, seasoned
2	beaten eggs
1 tsp	(5 ml) vegetable oil
	plum sauce

Preheat peanut oil in deep-fryer to 350°F (180°C).

Dredge pork with flour.

Place beaten eggs in large bowl and add oil; mix. Add half of pork, coat and remove.

Add remaining pork to eggs, coat and remove.

Deep-fry pork 4 to 5 minutes or until browned. Meat should no longer appear pink when cooked.

Serve with plum sauce for dipping and, if desired, potatoes.

1 SERVING	827 CALORIES	21 g CARBOHYDRATE
44 g PROTEIN	63 g FAT	0 g FIBER

Thin White Sauce

4 tbsp	(60 ml) butter
4½ tbsp	(70 ml) flour
3 cups	(750 ml) hot milk
¼ cup	(50 ml) hot light cream
1	small onion, studded with clove
¼ tsp	(1 ml) nutmeg
	salt and white pepper

Heat butter in saucepan. When hot, add flour; mix and cook 1 minute over low heat. Do not let flour burn.

Pour in half of milk and stir. Add remaining milk and incorporate thoroughly.

Add cream and remaining ingredients. Season well and bring to boil.

Cook sauce 12 minutes over low heat. Stir occasionally.

This sauce will keep up to 1 week in refrigerator, covered with waxed paper.

1 SERVING	82 CALORIES	5 g CARBOHYDRATE
2 g PROTEIN	6 g FAT	0 g FIBER

Sweet Potato Purée *(serves 4)*

3	sweet potatoes
3	large carrots, pared
½ cup	(125 ml) light cream, heated
1 tbsp	(15 ml) butter
	pinch nutmeg
	salt and pepper

Preheat oven to 375°F (190°C).

Bake sweet potatoes in oven until fully cooked.

Meanwhile, cook carrots in boiling salted water.

Place hot potato flesh and carrots in food processor; purée.

Add cream and butter; mix until well combined and smooth.

Add nutmeg and season well; process for 5 seconds.

Serve as vegetable or garnish.

1 SERVING	216 CALORIES	33 g CARBOHYDRATE
3 g PROTEIN	8 g FAT	1.3 g FIBER

Traditional Pork Chops and Apples   *(serves 4)*

1 tbsp	(15 ml) vegetable oil
4	pork chops with bone, about 1 in (2.5 cm) thick and fat trimmed
2	apples, cored, peeled and sliced
1 tbsp	(15 ml) butter
1 tsp	(5 ml) chopped parsley
¼ cup	(50 ml) dry white wine
1 cup	(250 ml) brown sauce* heated
	salt and pepper
	several drops lemon juice

Preheat oven to 150°F (70°C).

Heat oil in frying pan. When hot, add pork and cook 3 minutes over medium heat.

Season well and turn pork over; continue cooking 3 minutes over medium heat.

Turn pork again; cook 2 to 3 minutes over low heat or until done to taste. Keep hot in oven.

Place apples in bowl and sprinkle with lemon juice. Heat butter in frying pan and add parsley.

Add apples and sauté 2 minutes over medium heat.

Pour in wine and cook 3 to 4 minutes over high heat.

Mix in brown sauce; cook 4 to 5 minutes over low heat. Season well.

Pour apples and sauce over pork. Serve with pearl onions and fiddleheads.

* See Brown Sauce, page 355.

1 SERVING	514 CALORIES	10 g CARBOHYDRATE
24 g PROTEIN	42 g FAT	0.8 g FIBER

TECHNIQUE: DEBONING LOIN OF PORK

1 Place loin of pork, fat side down, on cutting board.

2 Begin removing tenderloin by cutting along bone.

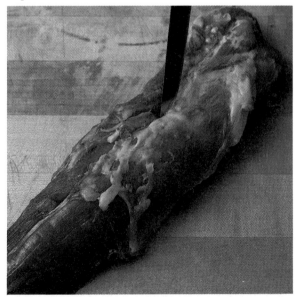

3 Continue cutting until tenderloin separates from bone.

4 When removed, trim fat from meat. Use this cut for roasting recipes.

Continued next page.

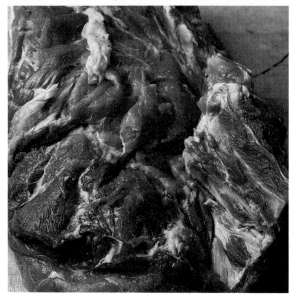

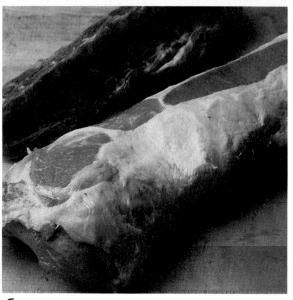

5 Cut loin in half. Use section where tenderloin was removed for various roasting recipes.

6 Debone other half and trim off most of fat.

7 Secure roast with kitchen string and reserve bone for cooking.

8 Use knife to begin separating chops then finish by chopping bone with cleaver. The size will depend on the original size of the loin.

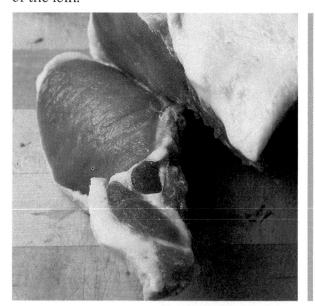

9 Cut 1¼ in (3 cm) slice of deboned loin. Divide into two but do not cut all the way through. When meat is opened, this cut is called butterfly pork chop.

10 Deboned pork chops are usually about ¾ in (2 cm) thick.

11 Pork cutlets are about ¼ in (0.65 cm) thick and should be trimmed of all fat.

12 Cutlets can be turned into scallopini. Place meat between two sheets of waxed paper. Pound with mallet until thin.

Continued next page.

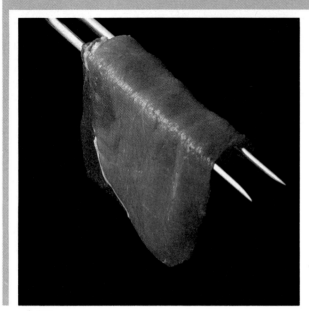

13 Pork scallopini is very thin so requires little cooking time.

14 Use almost any part of loin to prepare cubes of meat for skewers.

15 Pork cutlets are ideal for recipes requiring meat sliced on the bias, including sautéed dishes or stir-fry recipes.

16 All these cuts were from one loin of pork and with some practice can be prepared at home. If you prefer, you can ask your butcher to supply you with deboned and ready-to-cook cuts.

Pork Alfredo *(serves 4)*

3 tbsp	(45 ml) butter
1½ lb	(750 g) pork cutlets, sliced on the bias
1	shallot, chopped
½ lb	(250 g) mushrooms, cleaned and sliced
2½ cups	(625 ml) thin white sauce, heated
¼ tsp	(1 ml) nutmeg
4	small portions spinach fettuccine, cooked
4 tbsp	(60 ml) grated parmesan cheese
	salt and pepper
	chopped sweet pimento

Heat 2 tbsp (30 ml) butter in frying pan. When hot, add pork and cook 2 minutes over medium heat.

Season well and turn pork over; continue cooking 2 minutes. Remove and set aside.

Add remaining butter to frying pan. When hot, add shallot and mushrooms; cook 4 to 5 minutes over medium heat.

Pour in white sauce, stir and sprinkle with nutmeg; mix well. Cook 2 to 3 minutes over medium heat.

Add fettuccine to frying pan, stir and cook 2 to 3 minutes.

Replace pork in pan and simmer several minutes to reheat. Sprinkle with cheese and pimento and serve.

1 SERVING	840 CALORIES	32 g CARBOHYDRATE
43 g PROTEIN	60 g FAT	0.6 g FIBER

349

Sliced Pork Fiesta   *(serves 4)*

2 tbsp	(30 ml) vegetable oil
1½ lb	(750 g) pork loin, cut into 1 in (2.5 cm) strips, ¼ in (0.65 cm) thick
1	garlic clove, smashed and chopped
1 tbsp	(15 ml) butter
½ lb	(250 g) mushrooms, cleaned and sliced
2 cups	(500 ml) hot tomato sauce
½	green pepper, very thinly sliced salt and pepper

Heat oil in frying pan. When hot, add pork and cook 2 minutes over medium-high heat.

Season well and turn pork over; continue cooking 2 minutes.

Add garlic to pan and cook 1 minute. Remove pork and set aside.

Add butter to pan. When hot, add mushrooms, season and cook 4 to 5 minutes. Stir occasionally.

Pour in tomato sauce and add green pepper; bring to boil. Cook 2 minutes.

Replace pork in frying pan and simmer several minutes to reheat.

If desired, serve over pasta.

1 SERVING	579 CALORIES	13 g CARBOHYDRATE
35 g PROTEIN	43 g FAT	1.1 g FIBER

Sautéed Pork and Vegetables   *(serves 4)*

3 tbsp	(45 ml) vegetable oil
2 lb	(900 g) pork cutlets, sliced on the bias
2 tbsp	(30 ml) soya sauce
20	fresh mushrooms, cleaned and thinly sliced
20	cooked pearl onions
2 cups	(500 ml) blanched broccoli flowerets
½ cup	(125 ml) mandarin orange segments
2 cups	(500 ml) heated brown sauce*
3 tbsp	(45 ml) plum sauce
	salt and pepper

Heat 1 tbsp (15 ml) oil in frying pan. When hot, add half of pork and cook 2 minutes over medium-high heat.

Season well and turn pork over; sprinkle with half of soya sauce. Continue cooking 2 minutes; remove and set aside.

Repeat procedure for remaining pork.

Heat remaining oil in frying pan. When hot, add mushrooms, onions and broccoli; cook 3 minutes and stir occasionally.

Stir in mandarin segments and cook 1 minute.

Add brown sauce and plum sauce; mix well. Cook 3 minutes over low heat.

Replace pork in frying pan and simmer several minutes to reheat.

Serve over spaghetti.

*See Brown Sauce, page 355.

1 SERVING	604 CALORIES	19 g CARBOHYDRATE
43 g PROTEIN	64 g FAT	2 g FIBER

Sliced Pork Loin with Curry   *(serves 4)*

2 tbsp	(30 ml) vegetable oil
1½ lb	(750 g) pork loin, cut into 1 in (2.5 cm) strips, ¼ in (0.65 cm) thick
1	large onion, peeled and thinly sliced
1½ tbsp	(25 ml) curry powder
1½ cups	(375 ml) hot chicken stock
1 tbsp	(15 ml) cornstarch
2 tbsp	(30 ml) cold water
	salt and pepper

Heat oil in frying pan. When hot, add pork and cook 2 minutes over medium-high heat.

Season well and turn pork over; continue cooking 2 minutes. Remove and set aside.

If needed add extra oil to pan. Cook onion 4 to 5 minutes over medium heat. Stir occasionally.

Mix in curry powder and continue cooking 2 to 3 minutes; season to taste.

Pour in chicken stock and bring to boil. Season and cook 8 to 10 minutes over low heat.

Mix cornstarch with water; incorporate into sauce. Replace pork in pan and simmer several minutes to reheat.

Serve with Sweet Potato Purée, page 343.

1 SERVING	531 CALORIES	4 g CARBOHYDRATE
32 g PROTEIN	43 g FAT	0.2 g FIBER

Quick Breaded Cutlets *(serves 4)*

4	large pork cutlets
1 cup	(250 ml) flour
2	beaten eggs
1 cup	(250 ml) breadcrumbs
3 tbsp	(45 ml) vegetable oil
4	portions cooked spaghetti
¼ cup	(50 ml) grated parmesan cheese
	salt and pepper
	commercial spaghetti sauce, heated

Season pork and dredge with flour. Shake off excess.

Dip pork into beaten eggs and coat with breadcrumbs.

Heat half of oil in frying pan. When hot, add half of pork and cook 3 minutes over medium heat.

Turn pork over and continue cooking 3 minutes. Remove and set aside.

Repeat process for remaining cutlets.

Arrange cooked pork on serving platter with spaghetti; sprinkle with cheese and serve with spaghetti sauce.

1 SERVING	967 CALORIES	72 g CARBOHYDRATE
46 g PROTEIN	55 g FAT	0.7 g FIBER

Pork Cutlets Parisienne *(serves 4)*

5	large carrots, pared
4	large potatoes, peeled
¾ cup	(175 ml) pearl onions
2 tbsp	(30 ml) butter
1 tbsp	(15 ml) vegetable oil
8	pork cutlets, fat trimmed
½ lb	(250 g) mushrooms, cleaned and quartered
1 tsp	(5 ml) chopped chives
1 cup	(250 ml) heated brown sauce*
¼ tsp	(1 ml) basil
	salt and pepper

Preheat oven to 150°F (70°C).
Use melon scoop to cut carrots and potatoes into balls; bring salted water to boil in saucepan. Add carrots and cook 3 minutes; add potatoes and continue cooking 6 minutes; drop in onions and finish cooking 2 minutes; drain vegetables and set aside.

Heat half of butter and all oil in large frying pan. When hot, add pork and cook 3 to 4 minutes over medium heat.

Season well and turn pork over; continue cooking 3 to 4 minutes. Remove pork and keep hot in oven.

Add remaining butter to frying pan. When hot, add mushrooms and boiled vegetables; sprinkle with chives and season. Cook 3 minutes over medium heat.

Add brown sauce and basil; simmer several minutes over low heat. Serve with pork cutlets.

* See Brown Sauce, page 355.

1 SERVING	620 CALORIES	47 g CARBOHYDRATE
36 g PROTEIN	32 g FAT	1.9 g FIBER

Brown Sauce (for pork)

4 tbsp	(60 ml) pork drippings
1	small onion, peeled and diced
1	carrot, diced
¼ tsp	(1 ml) thyme
¼ tsp	(1 ml) rosemary
4½ tbsp	(70 ml) flour
3 cups	(750 ml) beef stock, heated
	salt and pepper

Heat drippings in saucepan. When hot, add onion, carrot and herbs; cook 5 to 6 minutes over low heat.

Mix in flour and cook 6 to 7 minutes over very low heat. Be careful that flour does not burn. Stir occasionally.

When flour has browned, remove saucepan from burner and cool several minutes.

Pour in beef stock and stir well; season generously. Return to burner and bring to boil.

Continue cooking 40 to 45 minutes over low heat.

Pass sauce through sieve when cooled.

1 SERVING	101 CALORIES	5 g CARBOHYDRATE
0 g PROTEIN	9 g FAT	0 g FIBER

Sweet Braised Ham *(serves 8 to 10)*

8 to 12 lb	(3.6 to 5.4 kg) fresh ham, prepared by butcher for cooking
3 cups	(750 ml) Madeira wine
3 tbsp	(45 ml) icing sugar

Place ham in very large stock pot; fill with cold water. Soak 12 hours.

Remove ham from pot and discard water; replace ham. Cover with fresh water and bring to boil on stove top. Cook 3½ to 4 hours, covered, over low heat.

Preheat oven to 350°F (180°C).

Remove ham from pot and cool; trim and remove fat. Replace in pot.

Pour in wine and cover. Cook 1 hour in oven; baste occasionally.

Remove ham from pot and transfer to roasting pan. Sprinkle icing sugar over ham and replace in oven.

Increase heat to 425°F (220°C) and cook until ham is glazed. Serve.

1 SERVING	403 CALORIES	3 g CARBOHYDRATE
55 g PROTEIN	19 g FAT	0 g FIBER

Veal Scallops in Sauce   *(serves 4)*

3 tbsp	(45 ml) butter
4	large veal scallops, flattened and floured
½ lb	(250 g) fresh mushrooms, cleaned and sliced
2	pickles, cut into julienne
1¼ cups	(300 ml) light white sauce, heated*
¼ cup	(50 ml) heavy cream
1 tsp	(5 ml) chopped fresh parsley
	dash paprika
	salt and pepper

Heat half of butter in nonstick frying pan. When hot, add veal and cook 3 minutes over high heat.

Season well and turn veal over; continue cooking 2 minutes. Remove and transfer to hot serving platter.

Heat remaining butter in frying pan. Add mushrooms, season and cook 4 minutes.

Add pickles and white sauce; stir well.

Add cream and parsley; season to taste. Cook 3 minutes over very high heat.

Replace veal in frying pan and remove from heat. Let stand 3 minutes before serving. Accompany with sautéed vegetables.

*See Light White Sauce, page 14.

1 SERVING	477 CALORIES	10 g CARBOHYDRATE
35 g PROTEIN	33 g FAT	0.8 g FIBER

Lemon Veal Scallops   *(serves 4)*

3 tbsp	(45 ml) butter
8	veal scallops, floured and seasoned
1 ½ cups	(375 ml) heated heavy cream
	juice 1 lemon
	chopped fresh parsley
	dash paprika
	salt and pepper

Preheat oven to 250°F (120°C).

Heat half of butter in nonstick frying pan. When hot, add half of veal; cook 2 minutes each side over high heat. Set aside.

Repeat procedure for remaining veal. Keep hot in oven.

Add lemon juice to frying pan; cook 1 minute over high heat.

Add cream and parsley; stir and continue cooking 3 to 4 minutes over high heat.

Replace veal in frying pan and sprinkle with paprika. Cook 1 minute to reheat veal.

Serve with assorted cooked vegetables.

1 SERVING	588 CALORIES	7 g CARBOHYDRATE
32 g PROTEIN	48 g FAT	0 g FIBER

Mushroom Cognac Stuffing

2 tbsp	(30 ml) butter
1	onion, peeled and finely chopped
¼ lb	(125 g) mushrooms, cleaned and finely chopped
1 tbsp	(15 ml) chopped parsley
1 tbsp	(15 ml) Courvoisier Cognac
¼ cup	(50 ml) breadcrumbs
1	small egg, beaten
	pinch thyme
	salt and pepper

Heat butter in saucepan. When hot, add onion and cook 3 minutes over low heat.

Add mushrooms, parsley, thyme, salt and pepper; mix well. Cook 3 minutes over high heat.

Add cognac and continue cooking 1 minute over high heat.

Remove saucepan from heat. Mix in breadcrumbs and add beaten egg; incorporate well.

Correct seasoning and set aside to cool before using.

1 RECIPE	481 CALORIES	32 g CARBOHYDRATE
14 g PROTEIN	33 g FAT	1.7 g FIBER

Veal Scallops in Tarragon Sauce *(serves 4)*

4	large thin veal scallops
½ cup	(125 ml) seasoned flour
2 tbsp	(30 ml) vegetable oil
½ cup	(125 ml) dry white wine
2 tbsp	(30 ml) fresh chopped tarragon
1 cup	(250 ml) hot chicken stock
2 tbsp	(30 ml) heavy cream
1 tsp	(5 ml) cornstarch
1 tbsp	(15 ml) cold water
¼ tsp	(1 ml) lemon juice
	salt and pepper

Preheat oven to 150°F (70°C).

Dredge veal with flour; shake off excess.

Heat oil in large frying pan. When hot, add veal and cook 2 to 3 minutes each side over medium heat. Season.

Remove veal and keep hot in oven.

Add wine to frying pan and cook 2 to 3 minutes over high heat.

Stir in tarragon, chicken stock and season well. Cook 3 minutes over medium heat.

Stir in cream and continue cooking 1 minute.

Mix cornstarch with water; stir mixture into sauce. Add lemon juice and bring to gentle boil. Continue cooking 2 minutes over medium-low heat.

Pour sauce over veal and serve.

1 SERVING	346 CALORIES	7 g CARBOHYDRATE
30 g PROTEIN	22 g FAT	0 g FIBER

Veal Parmesan *(serves 4)*

4	large veal scallops
½ cup	(125 ml) flour
2	beaten eggs
1 cup	(250 ml) fine breadcrumbs
2 tbsp	(30 ml) vegetable oil
1½ tbsp	(25 ml) butter
¼ lb	(125 g) mushrooms, cleaned and sliced
2	shallots, chopped
½ cup	(125 ml) grated parmesan cheese
	salt and pepper
	lemon juice to taste

Season and dredge veal with flour; shake off excess.

Dip veal in beaten eggs and coat with breadcrumbs.

Heat oil in large frying pan. When hot, add veal and cook 4 minutes each side over medium heat. Turn at least 3 times to prevent burning.

Heat butter in separate frying pan. Add mushrooms and shallots; cook 3 to 4 minutes over medium-high heat. Season well.

Meanwhile, place veal in large baking dish and top with grated cheese. Broil 3 to 4 minutes in oven.

Serve with lemon juice.

1 SERVING	535 CALORIES	23 g CARBOHYDRATE
41 g PROTEIN	31 g FAT	0.3 g FIBER

Veal Chops with Mixed Vegetables *(serves 4)*

4	loin chops, ½ in (1.2 cm) thick
½ cup	(125 ml) seasoned flour
1 tbsp	(15 ml) butter
1 tbsp	(15 ml) vegetable oil
¼ lb	(125 g) mushrooms, cleaned and diced
1	onion, peeled and diced
½	zucchini, diced
½ cup	(125 ml) black pitted olives
4	artichoke hearts, cut in 4
2	anchovy filets, chopped
1½ cups	(375 ml) commercial thin brown sauce, heated
2 tbsp	(30 ml) heavy cream
	salt and pepper

Preheat oven to 150°F (70°C).

Dredge chops with flour and shake off excess.

Heat butter and oil in large frying pan. When hot, add chops and cook 6 to 7 minutes over medium heat.

Turn veal over and season well; continue cooking 6 to 7 minutes.

Remove veal and keep hot in oven.

Add more butter to pan if necessary. Cook mushrooms, onion, zucchini, olives, artichoke hearts and anchovies 5 minutes over medium heat. Season generously.

Stir in brown sauce and cream; correct seasoning. Cook 3 to 4 minutes over low heat.

Pour sauce over veal and serve.

Veal Chops Tia Maria *(serves 4)*

4	loin chops, ½ in (1.2 cm) thick
½ cup	(125 ml) seasoned flour
1 tbsp	(15 ml) butter
1 tbsp	(15 ml) vegetable oil
½ lb	(250 g) mushroom caps, cleaned
½ cup	(125 ml) cooked pearl onions
1 cup	(250 ml) Parisienne potatoes blanched
3 tbsp	(45 ml) Tia Maria liqueur
1¼ cups	(300 ml) commercial thin brown sauce, heated
	salt and pepper

Preheat oven to 150°F (70°C).

Dredge chops with flour and shake off excess.

Heat butter and oil in large frying pan. When hot, add chops and cook 6 to 7 minutes over medium heat.

Turn veal over and season well; continue cooking 6 to 7 minutes.

Remove chops and keep hot in oven.

Add mushrooms, onions and potatoes; stir and cook 3 to 4 minutes over medium heat. Season well.

Stir in Tia Maria and cook 2 to 3 minutes over high heat.

Add brown sauce and correct seasoning; cook 2 minutes over medium heat.

Pour sauce over veal and serve.

1 SERVING	415 CALORIES	18 g CARBOHYDRATE
34 g PROTEIN	23 g FAT	0.8 g FIBER

Veal Cutlets, Prosciutto and Cheese   *(serves 4)*

8	small veal cutlets
½ cup	(125 ml) seasoned flour
3 tbsp	(45 ml) butter
¼ cup	(50 ml) Marsala or white wine
8	slices prosciutto
8	slices Gruyère cheese
	salt and pepper

Dredge veal with flour; shake off excess.

Heat butter in large frying pan. When hot, add veal (do not crowd) and cook 2 to 3 minutes each side over medium heat. Season well when cooking second side.

When all cutlets have been cooked, transfer to serving platter and set aside. There must be enough space for all cutlets to lie flat.

Add wine to frying pan and cook 2 minutes over high heat.

Pour reduced wine over veal. Layer cutlets with prosciutto and cheese. Season well.

Broil 2 to 3 minutes in oven or until cheese melts.

Serve immediately.

1 SERVING	499 CALORIES	5 g CARBOHYDRATE
41 g PROTEIN	35 g FAT	0 g FIBER

Stuffed Rolled Veal Scallops   *(serves 4)*

8	very thin veal scallops
1	recipe mushroom cognac stuffing*
3 tbsp	(45 ml) butter
2	shallots, finely chopped
2 tbsp	(30 ml) Marsala wine
1½ cups	(375 ml) hot chicken stock
1 tbsp	(15 ml) cornstarch
2 tbsp	(30 ml) cold water
	salt and pepper
	chopped chives to taste

Preheat oven to 375°F (190°C).
Lay veal scallops flat on cutting board. Spread stuffing on each and roll. Secure with thin kitchen string.
Cook veal rolls in two stages using the following procedure. Heat half of butter in large frying pan. When hot, add veal and sear 3 minutes; turn to brown all sides and season well.
When all veal rolls have been seared, place in large ovenproof dish. Set aside. Add shallots to frying pan and cook 2 minutes over medium heat. Pour in wine and cook 2 minutes over high heat.
Mix in chicken stock, correct seasoning and bring to boil.
Mix cornstarch with water; stir into sauce. Cook 1 minute over medium heat.
Pour sauce over veal rolls and sprinkle with chives. Cook 6 to 8 minutes in oven.
*See Mushroom Cognac Stuffing, page 359.

1 SERVING	433 CALORIES	10 g CARBOHYDRATE
33 g PROTEIN	29 g FAT	0.6 g FIBER

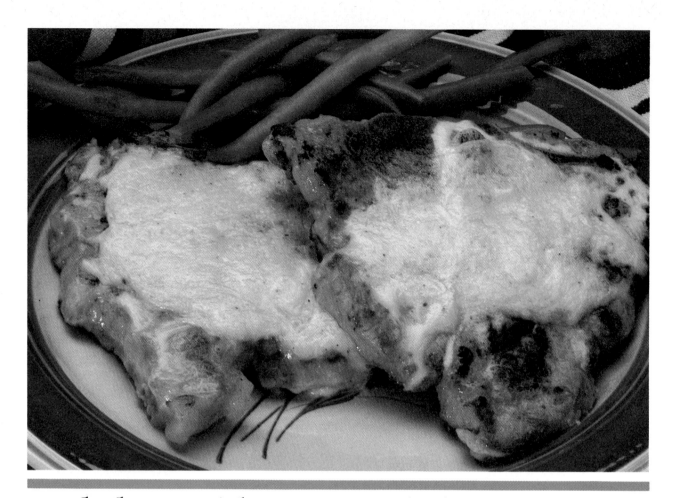

Veal Chops with Cream and Cheese *(serves 4)*

4	loin chops, ½ in (1.2 cm) thick
½ cup	(125 ml) seasoned flour
1 tbsp	(15 ml) butter
1 tbsp	(15 ml) vegetable oil
2 tbsp	(30 ml) heavy cream
½ cup	(125 ml) grated Gruyère cheese
	salt and pepper
	dash paprika
	dash cayenne pepper

Preheat oven to 400°F (200°C).

Dredge chops with flour and shake off excess.

Heat butter and oil in large frying pan. When hot, add chops and cook 6 to 7 minutes over medium heat.

Turn veal over and season well; continue cooking 6 to 7 minutes.

Transfer chops to large baking dish; set aside.

Mix cream, cheese, paprika and cayenne together; pour over veal.

Cook 4 to 5 minutes in oven.

Serve with fresh beans.

1 SERVING	421 CALORIES	5 g CARBOHYDRATE
35 g PROTEIN	29 g FAT	0 g FIBER

Veal on a Bun   *(serves 4)*

2 tbsp	(30 ml) butter
1 lb	(500 g) veal cutlets, sliced and pounded
4	large fresh buns
1 cup	(250 ml) hot chili or spaghetti sauce
	salt and pepper
	sliced tomatoes
	lettuce leaves

Heat butter in frying pan. When hot, add veal and cook 2 minutes each side over medium heat. Season well on second side.

Arrange veal on buns and cover with hot chili sauce. Top with tomato and lettuce. Close bun and serve immediately.

1 SERVING	427 CALORIES	36 g CARBOHYDRATE
28 g PROTEIN	19 g FAT	0.6 g FIBER

Delicious Veal Kidneys *(serves 4)*

2 tbsp	(30 ml) butter
2	small veal kidneys, fat trimmed and thinly sliced
1	shallot, chopped
¼ lb	(125 g) fresh mushrooms, cleaned and sliced
1 tbsp	(5 ml) chopped chives
2 tbsp	(30 ml) VSOP Courvoisier Cognac
½ cup	(125 ml) dry white wine
1½ cups	(375 ml) commercial brown sauce, heated
2 tbsp	(30 ml) heavy cream salt and pepper

Heat butter in large frying pan. When hot, add kidneys and cook 2 minutes over high heat.

Season well and add shallot; turn kidneys over. Continue cooking 2 minutes over high heat.

Remove kidneys and set aside.

Add mushrooms and chives to pan; cook 3 minutes over high heat.

Pour in cognac and cook 2 more minutes.

Add wine and cook 3 minutes over high heat; correct seasoning.

Stir in brown sauce and cook 2 to 3 minutes.

Stir in cream and replace kidneys in sauce; simmer 2 minutes to reheat.

Serve with peas and carrots.

1 SERVING	456 CALORIES	28 g CARBOHYDRATE
23 g PROTEIN	11 g FAT	1.5 g FIBER

Mint Veal Kebabs *(serves 4)*

1 ½ lb	(750 ml) top-loin veal, cubed
1 tbsp	(15 ml) lemon juice
2 tbsp	(30 ml) soya sauce
2 tbsp	(30 ml) vegetable oil
2 tbsp	(30 ml) fresh chopped ginger
32	fresh mint leaves
	salt and pepper

Place veal cubes in large bowl. Add remaining ingredients, except mint, and season well.

Mix well and refrigerate 30 minutes.

Place veal cube on skewer, followed by 2 mint leaves. Add another veal cube. Repeat and fill all skewers.

Brush skewers with marinade and broil 12 to 14 minutes in oven. Rotate skewers occasionally and baste as needed.

When cooked, serve veal kebabs with salad, potatoes or rice.

Quick Veal Sticks *(serves 4)*

1½ lb	(750 g) veal cutlets, cut in sticks
2 tbsp	(30 ml) lemon juice
¼ tsp	(1 ml) paprika
¼ tsp	(1 ml) Tabasco sauce
1 tbsp	(15 ml) vegetable oil
¼ tsp	(1 ml) Worcestershire sauce
1 cup	(250 ml) seasoned flour
3 tbsp	(45 ml) peanut oil
	few drops hot Mexican sauce
	salt and pepper
	fresh carrot, zucchini and green onion sticks

Place veal in large bowl. Sprinkle in lemon juice, paprika and Tabasco sauce.

Add vegetable oil, Worcestershire sauce, Mexican sauce, salt and pepper; mix and marinate 15 minutes.

Drain marinade. Lightly dredge veal sticks with flour; shake off excess.

Heat peanut oil in large frying pan. Cook veal 3 to 4 minutes each side over medium heat. Do not crowd in pan and add more oil if necessary.

Drain on paper towel and serve with vegetable sticks.

1 SERVING	472 CALORIES	10 g CARBOHYDRATE
36 g PROTEIN	32 g FAT	0 g FIBER

Breaded Veal Fingers   *(serves 4)*

1 cup	(250 ml) crushed soda crackers
½ cup	(125 ml) seasoned breadcrumbs
1 tbsp	(15 ml) sesame seeds
1½ lb	(750 g) veal cutlets, cut in strips
1 cup	(250 ml) seasoned flour
2	beaten eggs
3 tbsp	(45 ml) peanut oil
	salt and pepper

Preheat oven to 400°F (200°C).

Mix soda crackers, breadcrumbs and sesame seeds together in bowl; set aside.

Lightly dredge veal strips with flour; shake off excess.

Dip veal in beaten eggs and coat with soda cracker mixture.

Heat oil in large frying pan. Cook veal 2 to 3 minutes each side over medium heat. Do not crowd in pan and add more oil if necessary.

Drain on paper towel and transfer to baking dish. Finish cooking 6 to 8 minutes in oven.

Serve with green salad.

Veal and Mushroom Stew *(serves 4)*

1¼ lb	(625 g) veal leg or shoulder, cubed
1 cup	(250 ml) flour
2 tbsp	(30 ml) vegetable oil
3	shallots, chopped
½ cup	(125 ml) dry white wine
¼ tsp	(1 ml) thyme
¼ lb	(125 g) mushrooms, cleaned and sliced thick
¼ tsp	(1 ml) lemon juice
2 cups	(500 ml) hot chicken stock
1 tbsp	(15 ml) cornstarch
2 tbsp	(30 ml) cold water
3 tbsp	(45 ml) heavy cream
	salt and pepper
	dash paprika

Preheat oven to 350°F (180°C).

Dredge veal with flour.

Heat oil in large ovenproof casserole. When hot, add veal and sear 6 to 8 minutes over medium heat. Turn to brown all sides and season well.

Mix in shallots and continue cooking 2 minutes.

Pour in wine and thyme; cook 3 minutes over high heat.

Add mushrooms and lemon juice; mix well. Cook another 2 minutes over medium heat.

Pour in chicken stock and correct seasoning; bring to boil.

Mix cornstarch with water; stir into stew. Cook 1 minute over medium heat.

Stir in cream and paprika; correct seasoning. Cover casserole and cook 1½ hours in oven.

Serve with a side dish of vegetables.

370

1 SERVING	396 CALORIES	14 g CARBOHYDRATE
31 g PROTEIN	24 g FAT	0.3 g FIBER

Tomato Veal Stew   *(serves 4)*

1¼ lb	(625 g) veal leg or shoulder, cubed
1 cup	(250 ml) flour
2 tbsp	(30 ml) vegetable oil
2	garlic cloves, smashed and chopped
1	small onion, peeled and chopped
½ tsp	(2 ml) oregano
1 cup	(250 ml) dry white wine
3	tomatoes, diced large
2 tbsp	(30 ml) tomato paste
1 cup	(250 ml) commercial brown sauce, heated
	salt and pepper

Preheat oven to 350°F (180°C).

Dredge veal with flour.

Heat oil in large ovenproof casserole. When hot, add veal and sear 6 to 8 minutes over medium heat. Turn to brown all sides and season well.

Add garlic, onion and oregano; mix well. Continue cooking 5 minutes over medium heat.

Pour in wine and cook 3 to 4 minutes over high heat.

Mix in tomatoes and season well; cook 5 to 6 minutes over medium heat.

Stir in tomato paste and brown sauce; correct seasoning. Bring to gentle boil.

Cover casserole and cook 1½ hours in oven.

See Technique next page.

1 SERVING	414 CALORIES	21 g CARBOHYDRATE
33 g PROTEIN	22 g FAT	0.7 g FIBER

TECHNIQUE: TOMATO VEAL STEW

1 Sear veal 6 to 8 minutes in hot oil. Turn to brown all sides and season well.

2 Add garlic, onion and oregano; mix well. Continue cooking 5 minutes over medium heat. Pour in wine and cook 3 to 4 minutes over high heat.

3 Mix in tomatoes and season well; cook 5 to 6 minutes over medium heat.

4 Stir in tomato paste and brown sauce; correct seasoning. Bring to gentle boil. Cover casserole and finish cooking in oven.

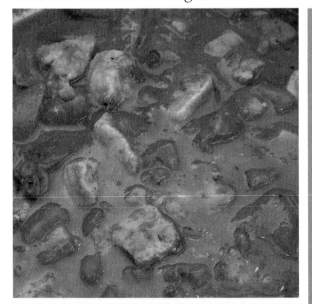

Veal Goulash *(serves 4 to 6)*

2 tbsp	(30 ml) vegetable oil
2 lb	(900 g) veal shoulder, cubed
1	large onion, peeled and finely chopped
2	garlic cloves, smashed and chopped
1 tbsp	(15 ml) paprika
½ tsp	(2 ml) oregano
3 tbsp	(45 ml) flour
3 cups	(750 ml) light chicken stock, heated
3 tbsp	(45 ml) tomato paste
3 tbsp	(45 ml) sour cream
	salt and pepper

Preheat oven to 350°F (180°C).

Heat oil in large ovenproof casserole. When hot, add veal and sear 3 to 4 minutes over medium heat. If necessary, seal veal in two batches. Turn to brown all sides and season well.

Add onion, garlic, paprika and oregano; mix well. Cook 4 to 5 minutes over medium-high heat.

Season and mix in flour; cook 2 minutes over medium heat.

Pour in chicken stock and add tomato paste; mix and season. Bring to boil.

Cover casserole and cook 1½ hours in oven.

Stir in sour cream just before serving. Accompany with noodles.

1 SERVING	311 CALORIES	6 g CARBOHYDRATE
29 g PROTEIN	19 g FAT	0.2 g FIBER

Blanquette of Veal *(serves 4)*

3 lb	(1.4 kg) stewing veal, cubed
1 tbsp	(15 ml) lemon juice
2	large carrots, pared and cut in 2
2	small onions, peeled and studded with clove
¼ tsp	(1 ml) thyme
1 tsp	(5 ml) tarragon
1	bay leaf
3 tbsp	(45 ml) butter
3 tbsp	(45 ml) flour
4 tbsp	(60 ml) heavy cream
1	egg yolk
	salt and pepper

Place veal in large saucepan; cover with cold water and add lemon juice. Place on stove top and bring to boil. Skim liquid and drain veal; rinse under cold water.

Replace veal in saucepan. Add carrots, onions and herbs; season well.

Pour in enough water to cover and cook 1½ hours over low heat or until veal is tender. When veal is cooked, drain and set aside. Reserve 3½ cups (875 ml) cooking liquid.

Now, heat butter in saucepan. Add flour and cook 1 minute over low heat; stir occasionally.

Pour in reserved cooking liquid and mix well; correct seasoning. Stir in 3 tbsp (45 ml) cream. Cook sauce 8 to 10 minutes over medium heat.

Place veal in sauce and simmer 5 to 6 minutes over low heat.

Mix remaining cream with egg yolk. Remove saucepan from heat and stir in the egg yolk mixture. Serve with boiled potatoes.

1 SERVING	672 CALORIES	5 g CARBOHYDRATE
64 g PROTEIN	44 g FAT	0 g FIBER

Osso Buco   *(serves 4)*

8	veal shanks, crosscut 1½ in (4 cm) thick
1 cup	(250 ml) seasoned flour
1½ tbsp	(25 ml) vegetable oil
1	onion, peeled and chopped
3	garlic cloves, chopped
1 cup	(250 ml) dry white wine
28 oz	(796 ml) can tomatoes, drained and chopped
2 tbsp	(30 ml) tomato paste
½ cup	(125 ml) commercial brown sauce, heated
½ tsp	(2 ml) oregano
1	bay leaf, chopped
¼ tsp	(1 ml) thyme
1 tsp	(5 ml) Worcestershire sauce
¼ tsp	(1 ml) Tabasco sauce
	pinch sugar

Preheat oven to 350°F (180°C).
Dredge veal with flour.
Heat oil in large ovenproof casserole. When hot, add half of veal; cook 3 to 4 minutes each side. Season when turning.
Repeat for remaining veal and add more oil if necessary. Set seared veal aside.
Add onion and garlic to casserole; mix and cook 3 to 4 minutes over medium heat.
Pour in wine and cook 4 minutes over high heat.
Mix in tomatoes, tomato paste and brown sauce; sprinkle in herbs and correct seasoning. Bring to boil.
Replace veal in casserole and cover; cook 2 hours in oven. When cooked, remove veal from casserole. Cook sauce 3 to 4 minutes over high heat.
Correct seasoning and pour sauce over veal.
If desired, serve with noodles or vegetables.

1 SERVING	429 CALORIES	22 g CARBOHYDRATE
38 g PROTEIN	21 g FAT	0.9 g FIBER

TECHNIQUE: OSSO BUCO

1 Dredge veal with flour.
Sear veal in two batches in hot oil.

2 Remove seared veal and add onion and garlic to casserole; mix and cook 3 to 4 minutes over medium heat.

3 Pour in wine and cook 4 minutes over high heat.
Add remaining ingredients. Bring to boil.

4 Replace veal in casserole and cover; cook 2 hours in oven.

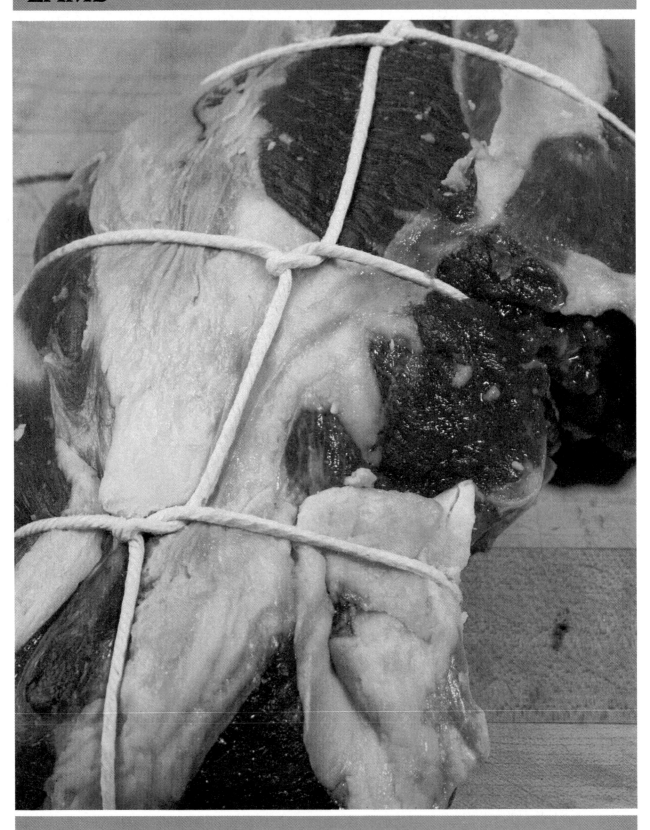

TECHNIQUE: DEBONING LEG OF LAMB

1 Place leg of lamb on cutting board. Remove most of fat.

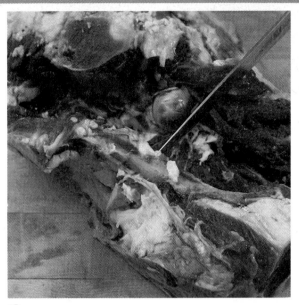

2 Find pelvic bone and slide knife between bone and flesh to remove.

3 Remove bottom portion of leg bone. Slide knife around joints to free bone.

4 Both bones have been removed from leg.

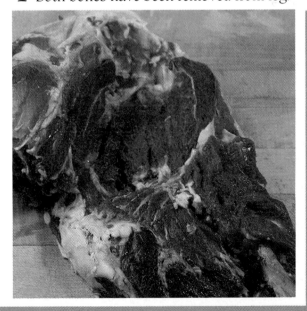

Continued next page.

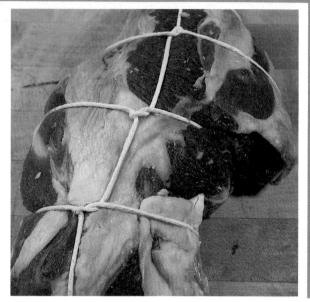

5 Remove enough flesh from top of leg bone to make a handle for easier carving. Discard the flesh.

6 If desired stuff leg before securing with string.

Stuffed Leg of Lamb *(serves 6 to 8)*

3 tbsp	(45 ml) butter
1	large onion, peeled and chopped
1	garlic clove, smashed and chopped
1 tbsp	(15 ml) chopped parsley
1 tsp	(5 ml) chopped chives
4 tbsp	(60 ml) breadcrumbs
½	beaten egg
5 to 6 lb	(2.3 to 2.7 kg) leg of lamb, prepared*
3 tbsp	(45 ml) melted butter
	salt and pepper

Preheat oven to 425°F (220°C). Cooking time: 15 to 18 minutes per lb (500 g).

Heat unmelted butter in small saucepan. When hot, add onion, garlic, parsley and chives; cook 3 minutes.

Mix in breadcrumbs and season. Remove saucepan from stove and add beaten egg; stir well.

Season lamb; stuff, roll and tie. Place in roasting pan and brush with melted butter. Cook 20 minutes in oven.

Reduce heat to 375°F (190°C) and finish cooking lamb. Baste 2 to 3 times during cooking process.

*Have butcher prepare lamb or see Deboning Leg of Lamb, page 377.

1 SERVING	655 CALORIES	2 g CARBOHYDRATE
47 g PROTEIN	51 g FAT	0 g FIBER

Spicy Stuffing

1 tbsp	(15 ml) bacon fat or oil
3	green onions, chopped
1	carrot, pared and finely chopped
½	green pepper, finely chopped
1	celery stalk, finely chopped
5	large mushrooms, cleaned and diced
1	garlic clove, smashed and chopped
¼ tsp	(1 ml) thyme
¼ tsp	(1 ml) basil
¼ tsp	(1 ml) allspice
¼ cup	(50 ml) heavy cream
2 tbsp	(30 ml) breadcrumbs

Heat bacon fat in frying pan. When hot, add onions, carrot, green pepper and celery; cook 6 to 7 minutes over medium heat.

Stir in mushrooms, garlic and spices; continue cooking 3 to 4 minutes.

Pour in cream and mix well; cook 3 to 4 minutes.

Add breadcrumbs and mix until combined. Cook 2 minutes over medium heat; stir occasionally.

When mixture has thickened, remove pan from heat and prepare to stuff meat.

1 RECIPE	467 CALORIES	31 g CARBOHYDRATE
7 g PROTEIN	35 g FAT	3.3 g FIBER

Braised White Beans *(serves 4 to 6)*

8 oz	(227 g) white beans
3 oz	(85 g) diced bacon, blanched
2	medium carrots, pared and diced
1	onion, peeled and diced
2	garlic cloves, smashed and chopped
1	bay leaf
3	parsley sprigs
¼ tsp	(1 ml) thyme
4 cups	(1 L) hot chicken stock
2 tbsp	(30 ml) tomato paste
	salt and pepper

Place beans in large bowl and pour in cold water to cover. Soak 8 hours.

Drain beans and transfer to large saucepan. Cover with water and bring to boil. Skim and cook 1 hour over low heat.

Preheat oven to 350°F (180°C).

Place bacon in ovenproof casserole; cook 4 minutes on stove top.

Add vegetables, garlic and all spices; cook 2 minutes.

Drain beans well and add to casserole; mix well.

Add chicken stock, stir and season. Mix in tomato paste and bring to boil.

Cover and cook 1½ hours in oven.

Serve beans with any leftover lamb.

1 SERVING	174 CALORIES	27 g CARBOHYDRATE
12 g PROTEIN	3 g FAT	2.0 g FIBER

Old-Fashioned Lamb Stew   *(serves 4)*

2	potatoes, peeled and cut in four
2	carrots, pared and cut into 1 in (2.5 cm) sticks
2	turnips, peeled and cut in four
3 tbsp	(45 ml) melted butter
3½ lb	(1.6 kg) lamb shoulder, cut into large cubes
2	small onions, peeled and diced
1	garlic clove, chopped
3 tbsp	(45 ml) flour
3 cups	(750 ml) hot chicken stock
1 cup	(250 ml) chopped tomatoes
2 tbsp	(30 ml) tomato paste
¼ tsp	(1 ml) thyme
¼ tsp	(1 ml) marjoram
1	bay leaf
	chopped parsley
	salt and pepper

Preheat oven to 350°F (180°C).

Place potatoes, carrots and turnips in bowl; cover with cold water. Set aside.

Heat butter in sauté pan. When hot, add lamb and sear 3 minutes each side over high heat.

Add onions and garlic; mix well. Season with salt and pepper; cook 3 to 4 minutes.

Mix in flour and continue cooking 2 minutes.

Pour in chicken stock and stir well. Add tomatoes, tomato paste, spices and vegetables; season to taste. Cover and cook 1½ hours in oven.

Sprinkle with chopped parsley before serving.

1 SERVING	540 CALORIES	26 g CARBOHYDRATE
46 g PROTEIN	28 g FAT	1.4 g FIBER

Onion Sauce for Roast Lamb

2	onions, peeled and diced large
1	garlic clove, smashed and chopped
1 tbsp	(15 ml) chopped parsley
1½ cups	(375 ml) hot chicken stock
1 tbsp	(15 ml) cornstarch
2 tbsp	(30 ml) cold water
	salt and pepper

Serve this sauce with roast lamb; prepare sauce while lamb is cooking.

Thirty minutes before lamb is cooked, add onions, garlic and parsley to roasting pan.

When lamb is cooked, remove it from pan and set aside.

Place roasting pan on stove top over medium heat. Remove ¾ of fat.

Add chicken stock to pan and bring to boil. Cook 5 to 6 minutes over high heat.

Mix cornstarch with water and stir the mixture into the stock. Cook 1 minute.

Strain sauce, season and serve with lamb.

1 SERVING	65 CALORIES	4 g CARBOHYDRATE
1 g PROTEIN	5 g FAT	0 g FIBER

Leg of Lamb with Parsley *(serves 6 to 8)*

5 to 6 lb	(2.3 to 2.7 kg) leg of lamb, prepared*
1	garlic clove, peeled and slivered
3 tbsp	(45 ml) melted butter
¼ lb	(125 g) butter
3	shallots, finely chopped
¼ cup	(50 ml) breadcrumbs
2 tbsp	(30 ml) chopped fresh parsley
	salt and pepper

Preheat oven to 425°F (220°C).
Cooking time: 15 to 18 minutes per lb (500 g).
Place prepared lamb in roasting pan and insert garlic slivers in flesh. Season generously.
Baste with melted butter and cook 20 minutes in oven.
Reduce heat to 375°F (190°C) and finish cooking lamb. Baste 2 to 3 times during cooking process.
Melt ¼ lb (125 g) butter in small sauté pan. When hot, add shallots; cook 2 to 3 minutes over low heat.
Add breadcrumbs and parsley; cook 2 to 3 minutes over low heat.
Ten minutes before lamb is cooked, spread breadcrumb mixture over leg.
When lamb is cooked, remove from oven and let stand several minutes before serving.

* Have butcher prepare lamb or see Deboning Leg of Lamb, page 377.

1 SERVING	619 CALORIES	2 g CARBOHYDRATE
47 g PROTEIN	47 g FAT	0 g FIBER

Friday Night Lamb Chop Dinner *(serves 4)*

2 tbsp	(30 ml) butter
8	small lamb chops
1 cup	(250 ml) hot hunter sauce*
	salt and pepper
	assorted cooked vegetables

Preheat oven to 150°F (70°C).

Heat 1 tbsp (15 ml) butter in frying pan. When hot, add half of lamb. Cook 3 to 4 minutes each side, depending on thickness. Season well and keep hot in oven.

Repeat procedure for remaining lamb.

Serve lamb with vegetables and hunter sauce.

*See Hunter Sauce, page 392.

1 SERVING	369 CALORIES	5 g CARBOHYDRATE
31 g PROTEIN	25 g FAT	0.3 g FIBER

Lamb Chops à la Béarnaise   *(serves 4)*

2 tbsp	(30 ml) butter
1	Chinese eggplant, sliced
1	green pepper, sliced
1	red pepper, sliced
1 tbsp	(15 ml) vegetable oil
8	lamb chops, 1 in (2.5 cm) thick
	dash paprika
	salt and pepper
	Béarnaise sauce*

Preheat oven to 350°F (180°C).

Heat butter in frying pan. When hot, add eggplant and season well. Cover and cook 5 minutes over medium heat.

Add green and red peppers; mix and season. Continue cooking 5 minutes over medium heat.

Transfer vegetables to baking dish. Cover with aluminium foil and place in oven 5 to 6 minutes.

Heat oil in same pan. When hot, add lamb chops and cook 3 minutes over high heat.

Turn lamb over and reduce heat slightly. Season generously and sprinkle with paprika; continue cooking 3 to 4 minutes.

Serve lamb chops with eggplant mixture and Béarnaise sauce.

* See Béarnaise Sauce, page 388.

1 SERVING	755 CALORIES	9 g CARBOHYDRATE
65 g PROTEIN	51 g FAT	1.6 g FIBER

Lamb Noisettes Sautéed with Cream Sauce   *(serves 4)*

4	large lamb noisettes, pounded*
1 cup	(250 ml) flour
3 tbsp	(45 ml) butter
½ cup	(125 ml) dry white wine
1 cup	(250 ml) 35% cream
1 tsp	(5 ml) chopped parsley
	salt and pepper
	juice ½ lemon

Preheat oven to 150°F (70°C).

Dredge lamb with flour and season well.

Heat butter in frying pan. When hot, add lamb; cook 2 to 3 minutes each side.

When lamb is cooked, remove and keep hot in oven.

Pour wine into frying pan; cook 2 minutes over high heat.

Add lemon juice, mix well and continue cooking 30 seconds.

Stir in cream and parsley; season well. Cook 2 to 3 minutes over high heat until sauce thickens.

Pour sauce over lamb and if desired, serve with pasta and sautéed mushrooms.

* Have butcher prepare noisettes or see Deboning Loin of Lamb, page 386.

1 SERVING	565 CALORIES	9 g CARBOHYDRATE
31 g PROTEIN	45 g FAT	0 g FIBER

TECHNIQUE: LAMB NOISETTES

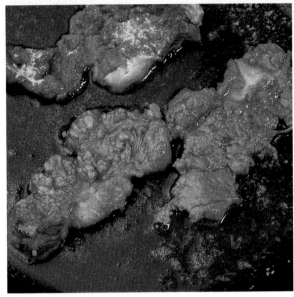

1 Add lamb to hot butter and cook 2 to 3 minutes each side.
When cooked, remove and keep hot in oven.

2 Pour wine into frying pan.

3 Cook wine 2 minutes over high heat, then add lemon juice; continue cooking 30 seconds.

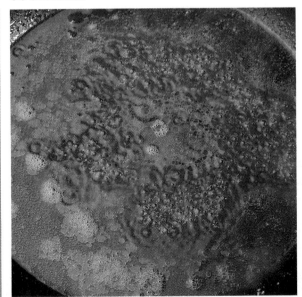

4 Add cream, stir and add parsley. Season well and continue cooking 2 to 3 minutes over high heat until sauce thickens.

TECHNIQUE: DEBONING LOIN OF LAMB

1 This is a double loin of lamb that has been split into two by the butcher. When deboned, loin of lamb can be roasted or cut into noisettes.

2 Place loin, fat side down, on cutting board. Remove filet by cutting along bone and reserve this cut for other uses.

3 Cut flank off loin, about 3 to 3½ in (8 to 9 cm) away from bone. This cut can also be reserved for other uses.

4 Turn loin over and remove fat, then cut along bone and remove loin. Loin can be stuffed for roasting or left plain. In either case, loin must be rolled and tied for cooking.

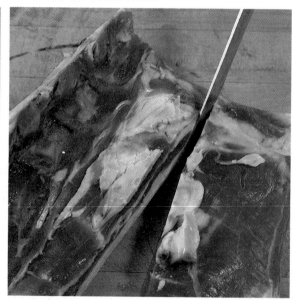

5 To cut loin into noisettes, slice on the bias into 1 in (2.5 cm) thick filets.

6 Depending on the recipe you may have to flatten noisettes. If so, place between waxed paper and pound with mallet.

Loin of Lamb with Béarnaise Sauce *(serves 4)*

4 lb	(1.8 kg) loin of Lamb, prepared*
2 tbsp	(30 ml) melted butter
½ tsp	(2 ml) dried mint leaves, crushed
1 cup	(250 ml) Béarnaise sauce**
	juice ¼ lemon
	salt and pepper

Preheat oven to 425°F (220°C).
Cooking time: 15 minutes per lb (500 g).

Place prepared lamb in roasting pan. Mix butter with lemon juice; brush over lamb.

Season generously and cook 20 minutes in oven.

Reduce heat to 350°F (180°C). Sprinkle mint over lamb and finish cooking. Baste 2 to 3 times during cooking process.

Serve lamb with Béarnaise sauce.

* Have butcher prepare lamb or see Deboning Loin of Lamb, page 386.
** See Béarnaise Sauce, page 479.

See Technique next page.

1 SERVING	1104 CALORIES	0 g CARBOHYDRATE
47 g PROTEIN	102 g FAT	0 g FIBER

TECHNIQUE: BÉARNAISE SAUCE

1 Place shallots, tarragon, vinegar and parsley in stainless steel bowl.
Place bowl on stove top over low heat. Cook until vinegar evaporates. Remove and cool.

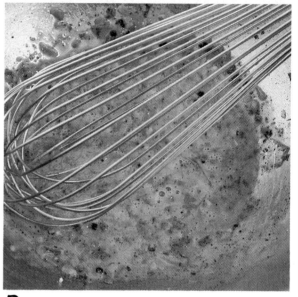

2 Add egg yolks and mix well with whisk.

3 Place bowl over saucepan containing hot water. Add clarified butter, drop by drop, while mixing constantly with whisk.

4 The finished sauce should be thick.

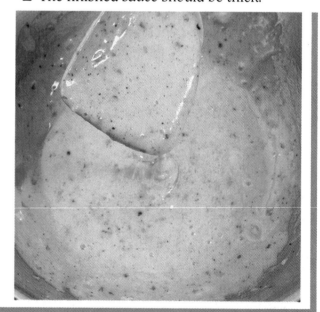

Curried Loin of Lamb   (serves 4)

4 lb	(1.8 kg) loin of Lamb, prepared*
4 tbsp	(60 ml) melted butter
2	large onions, peeled and finely chopped
2 tbsp	(30 ml) curry powder
1	garlic clove, smashed and chopped
4	potatoes, peeled and diced small
2 cups	(500 ml) hot chicken stock
1 tbsp	(15 ml) cornstarch
2 tbsp	(30 ml) cold water
1 tbsp	(15 ml) catsup
	salt and pepper

Preheat oven to 425°F (220°C).
Cooking time: 15 minutes per lb (500 g).

Place prepared lamb in roasting pan. Brush with melted butter and season well. Cook 20 minutes in oven.

Reduce heat to 350°F (180°C) and finish cooking lamb.

Twenty minutes before lamb is cooked, place onions in roasting pan.

About 5 minutes later, add curry powder, garlic and potatoes. Mix well.

When lamb is cooked, remove and set aside.

Place roasting pan on stove top and add chicken stock. Mix well.

Mix cornstarch with water; stir mixture into sauce. Cook 5 minutes over medium heat.

Stir in catsup and serve with lamb.

*Have butcher prepare lamb or see Deboning Loin of Lamb, page 386.

1 SERVING	820 CALORIES	29 g CARBOHYDRATE
50 g PROTEIN	56 g FAT	0.9 g FIBER

Loin of Lamb, Nouvelle Cuisine   (serves 4)

4 lb	(1.8 kg) loin of lamb, prepared
1	garlic clove, peeled and split in three
2 tbsp	(30 ml) melted butter
1	onion, peeled and diced
2	carrots, pared and thinly sliced on the bias
½	celery stalk, thinly sliced on the bias
½	zucchini, sliced on the bias
1 tbsp	(15 ml) butter
1¼ cups	(300 ml) hot chicken stock
1 tsp	(5 ml) cornstarch
2 tbsp	(30 ml) cold water
	salt and pepper

Preheat oven to 425°F (220°C).
Place prepared lamb in roasting pan and stud with garlic. Brush with melted butter and season generously. Cook 20 minutes in oven.
Reduce heat to 350°F (180°C) and finish cooking lamb. Baste 2 to 3 times during cooking process.
Ten minutes before lamb is cooked, add onion.
Meanwhile, place carrots and celery in saucepan containing 1½ cups (375 ml) boiling salted water. Cook 6 minutes.
Add zucchini and continue cooking 3 minutes.
Drain vegetables, add butter and toss. Set aside.
When lamb is cooked, remove and set aside.
Place roasting pan on stove top. Pour in chicken stock and mix well.
Mix cornstarch with water and stir into sauce; cook 1 minute over high heat.
Pass sauce through sieve and skim.
Serve lamb with vegetables and sauce.

1 SERVING	709 CALORIES	11 g CARBOHYDRATE
47 g PROTEIN	53 g FAT	0.9 g FIBER

Stuffed Loin of Lamb *(serves 4)*

4 lb	(1.8 kg) loin of lamb, prepared*
1	recipe cumin stuffing**
3 tbsp	(45 ml) melted butter
2	bananas
	salt and pepper

Preheat oven to 425°F (220°C).
Cooking time: 15 minutes per lb (500 g).
Place lamb flat on cutting board; season well.
Spread stuffing over lamb, roll and tie.
Place in roasting pan and brush with 1 tbsp (15 ml) melted butter. Cook 20 minutes in oven.
Reduce heat to 350°F (180°C) and finish cooking lamb. Baste 2 to 3 times during cooking process.
Just before lamb is cooked, peel bananas and slice in two. Heat remaining butter and sauté bananas several minutes.
Serve bananas with lamb.

* Have butcher prepare lamb or see Deboning Loin of Lamb, page 386.
** See Cumin Stuffing, page 403.

1 SERVING	595 CALORIES	27 g CARBOHYDRATE
52 g PROTEIN	31 g FAT	0.3 g FIBER

Loin of Lamb and Garden Vegetables *(serves 4)*

4 lb	(1.8 kg) loin of lamb, prepared*
3 tbsp	(45 ml) melted garlic butter
2	carrots, cut into julienne
1½ cups	(375 ml) Parisienne potatoes
1 cup	(250 ml) Parisienne turnips
1 tbsp	(15 ml) butter
16	cherry tomatoes
1 tbsp	(15 ml) chopped parsley
	salt and pepper

Preheat oven to 425°F (220°C).
Cooking time: 15 minutes per lb (500 g).

Place prepared lamb in roasting pan. Brush with melted garlic butter and season well. Cook 20 minutes in oven.

Reduce heat to 350°F (180°C) and finish cooking lamb. Baste 2 to 3 times during cooking process.

About 15 minutes before lamb is cooked, place vegetables, except tomatoes, in 2 cups (500 ml) boiling salted water. Cook 8 to 10 minutes.

Drain vegetables and season well.

Add butter, tomatoes and parsley; toss and serve with lamb.

* Have butcher prepare lamb or see Deboning Loin of Lamb, page 386.

1 SERVING	789 CALORIES	22 g CARBOHYDRATE
49 g PROTEIN	56 g FAT	1.4 g FIBER

Quick Lamb Noisettes   *(serves 4)*

8	lamb noisettes, 1 in (2.5 cm) thick*
1 cup	(250 ml) flour
3	beaten eggs
1½ cups	(375 ml) breadcrumbs
¼ cup	(50 ml) peanut oil
	salt and pepper
	Parmesan cheese to taste

Season lamb and place between waxed paper; pound until thin.

Dredge with flour and dip into eggs. Coat lamb with breadcrumbs. Refrigerate 15 minutes.

Heat oil in deep frying pan or sauté pan. When hot, add half of lamb and cook 2 minutes each side. Drain on paper towel.

Repeat procedure for remaining lamb.

Place lamb on serving platter and sprinkle with cheese. Serve with tomato sauce if desired.

* Have butcher prepare noisettes or see Deboning Loin of Lamb, page 386.

See Technique next page.

1 SERVING	770 CALORIES	30 g CARBOHYDRATE
41 g PROTEIN	54 g FAT	0 g FIBER

TECHNIQUE: QUICK LAMB NOISETTES

1 Prepare lamb noisettes and season.

2 Place between waxed paper and pound until thin.

Hunter Sauce

2 tbsp	(30 ml) butter
1	shallot, finely chopped
20	mushrooms, cleaned and diced
3 tbsp	(45 ml) dry white wine
¼ cup	(50 ml) chopped tomato
2 cups	(500 ml) heated brown sauce*
	chopped parsley to taste
	salt and pepper

Heat butter in saucepan. When hot, add shallot and cook 1 minute.

Add mushrooms and season; continue cooking 3 minutes over medium heat.

Pour in wine and cook 3 minutes.

Add tomato and mix. Pour in brown sauce and season well. Simmer 15 minutes over low heat.

Sprinkle with chopped parsley and serve.

This sauce will keep up to 2 weeks in refrigerator, covered with wax paper.

*See Brown Sauce, page 397.

1 SERVING	46 CALORIES	5 g CARBOHYDRATE
2 g PROTEIN	2 g FAT	0.3 g FIBER

Garlic Lamb Noisettes *(serves 4)*

2 tbsp	(30 ml) butter
8	lamb noisettes, 1 in (2.5 cm) thick*
½ lb	(250 g) mushrooms, cleaned and sliced
2 tbsp	(30 ml) garlic butter
	salt and pepper
	few drops lemon juice

Preheat oven to 150°F (70°C).

Heat butter in frying pan. When hot, add lamb and cook 3 to 4 minutes each side. Season well.

Remove lamb from pan and transfer to ovenproof platter. Keep hot in oven.

Add mushrooms to pan; season well. Cook 2 minutes over high heat.

Add garlic butter, stir and cover. Cook 5 minutes over medium heat.

Pour mushrooms over lamb and serve. Sprinkle with lemon juice.

*Have butcher prepare noisettes or see Deboning Loin of Lamb, page 386.

1 SERVING	509 CALORIES	3 g CARBOHYDRATE
32 g PROTEIN	41 g FAT	0.5 g FIBER

Lamb Noisettes Milanaise *(serves 4)*

4	slices cooked ham, cut into julienne
¼ lb	(125 g) mushrooms, cleaned and sliced
4 tbsp	(60 ml) butter
2 tbsp	(30 ml) Madeira wine
2 cups	(500 ml) tomato sauce*, heated
4	lamb noisettes, 1 in (2.5 cm) thick**
4	portions cooked spaghetti
	salt and pepper

Place ham, mushrooms and 2 tbsp (30 ml) butter in saucepan. Cover and simmer 4 to 5 minutes over low heat.

Add wine and cook, uncovered, 2 minutes.

Pour in tomato sauce, mix and simmer over low heat. Correct seasonings.

Meanwhile, heat remaining butter in frying pan. When hot, add lamb and cook 3 to 4 minutes each side. Season well.

Transfer lamb to serving platter and surround with spaghetti. Pour sauce over top and serve.

* See Tomato Sauce, page 399.
** Have butcher prepare noisettes or see Deboning Loin of Lamb, page 386.

1 SERVING	501 CALORIES	43 g CARBOHYDRATE
26 g PROTEIN	25 g FAT	0.9 g FIBER

Roast Leg of Lamb Jardinières   *(serves 6 to 8)*

5 to 6 lb	(2.3 to 2.7 kg) leg of lamb, prepared (reserve bones)
1	garlic clove, peeled and slivered
3 tbsp	(45 ml) melted butter
2	onions, peeled and diced large
2	carrots, pared and sliced on the bias
1	zucchini, sliced on the bias
½	celery stalk, sliced
1 tbsp	(15 ml) butter
1	garlic clove, smashed and chopped
1 tbsp	(15 ml) chopped parsley
1½ cups	(375 ml) hot chicken stock
1 tbsp	(15 ml) cornstarch
2 tbsp	(30 ml) cold water
	salt and pepper

Preheat oven to 425°F (220°C).

Cooking time: 15 to 18 minutes per 1 lb (500 g).

Insert garlic pieces in lamb, set in roasting pan and add bones. Baste with melted butter, season and cook 20 minutes.

Reduce heat to 375°F (190°C) and finish cooking; baste 2 to 3 times. 30 minutes before lamb is done, add onions.

Just before lamb is done, cook vegetables 8 minutes in 2 cups (500 ml) boiling eater. Drain, add butter and garlic; simmer until serving.

Remove cooked lamb from pan; discard bones. Add parsley to pan; cook 3 minutes on high.

Remove part of fat, add chicken stock and cook 3 to 4 minutes.

Mix cornstarch with water; stir in sauce, season and bring to boil. Cook 1 minute.

Pass sauce through sieve and serve with lamb.

394

1 SERVING	707 CALORIES	6 g CARBOHYDRATE
47 g PROTEIN	55 g FAT	0.5 g FIBER

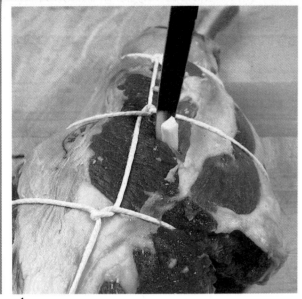

1 Place prepared leg of lamb on cutting board.
Insert garlic pieces in flesh.

2 Set lamb in roasting pan and add reserved bones. Baste with melted butter.

3 Season generously. Place lamb in oven and begin cooking process.

4 30 minutes before lamb is cooked, add onions to pan.
Just before lamb is cooked, prepare vegetables.

Continued next page.

5 When lamb is cooked, remove and set aside. Discard bones. Place roasting pan on stove top over high heat. Add parsley and cook 3 minutes.

6 Remove part of fat and pour in chicken stock; mix well and cook 3 to 4 minutes over low heat.

7 Add cornstarch mixture to sauce. Season and bring to boil; cook 1 minute.

8 Pass sauce through sieve.

Brown Sauce

4 tbsp	(60 ml) strained drippings
2 tbsp	(30 ml) chopped onion
½	carrot, diced small
2 tbsp	(30 ml) diced celery
5 tbsp	(75 ml) flour
2 tbsp	(30 ml) tomato paste
3 cups	(750 ml) beef stock, heated
1	bay leaf
	pinch thyme
	salt and pepper

Heat drippings in heavy saucepan. When hot, add vegetables and cook 2 minutes. Season well.

Add flour, reduce heat to low and cook until light brown. Stir frequently to avoid burning.

Remove saucepan from burner and cool.

Add tomato paste and mix well. Pour in beef stock, add spices and season. Stir well and bring to gentle boil.

Reduce heat to low and simmer sauce 1 hour or longer if possible. Skim often.

Pass sauce through sieve and refrigerate for up to 2 weeks, covered with waxed paper.

1 SERVING	20 CALORIES	4 g CARBOHYDRATE
1 g PROTEIN	0 g FAT	0.1 g FIBER

Potatoes Boulangère *(serves 4 to 6)*

2 tbsp	(30 ml) butter
1	large onion, peeled and thinly sliced
1 tbsp	(15 ml) chopped parsley
5	potatoes, peeled and thinly sliced
2 cups	(500 ml) hot chicken stock
1 tbsp	(15 ml) melted butter
	salt and pepper

Preheat oven to 400°F (200°C).

Heat 2 tbsp (30 ml) butter in frying pan. When hot, add onion and parsley; season well. Cook 6 to 7 minutes over medium-low heat.

Add potatoes (reserve 20 slices) season and mix well. Cook 2 minutes.

Arrange potatoes in ovenproof casserole. Top with reserved potato slices and pour in chicken stock to cover; season generously. Cook 20 minutes in oven.

Press potatoes down with spatula. Reduce heat to 350°F (180°C) and continue cooking until all liquid is absorbed and potatoes are very soft.

5 minutes before potatoes are cooked, brush with melted butter.

Garnish with parsley and serve with leg of lamb.

1 SERVING	142 CALORIES	19 g CARBOHYDRATE
3 g PROTEIN	6 g FAT	0.6 g FIBER

Tomato Sauce

4	bacon slices, diced large
2 tbsp	(30 ml) olive oil
1	onion, peeled and chopped
1	carrot, diced
½	celery stalk, diced
1 tsp	(5 ml) basil
½ tsp	(2 ml) oregano
½ tsp	(2 ml) sugar
1 tbsp	(15 ml) finely chopped parsley
12	large tomatoes, peeled, cut in two and seeded
1	chile pepper, seeded and sliced
5½ oz	(156 ml) can tomato paste
1 cup	(250 ml) chicken stock
	salt and pepper

Blanch bacon in saucepan containing simmering water. Drain and set aside.

Heat oil in large saucepan. When hot, add bacon and cook 3 to 4 minutes.

Add onion, carrot, celery, herbs and sugar to saucepan. Mix and continue cooking 6 to 7 minutes to brown vegetables.

Add remaining ingredients and season well. Cook 2 hours over low heat. Stir frequently.

Pass sauce through sieve using pestle or spoon. Serve or refrigerate until use. Cover with sheet of waxed paper.

See Technique next page.

1 SERVING	25 CALORIES	3 g CARBOHYDRATE
1 g PROTEIN	1 g FAT	0 g FIBER

TECHNIQUE: TOMATO SAUCE

1 Blanch bacon in saucepan containing simmering water.

2 Drain and set aside.

3 Heat oil in large saucepan and add bacon. Cook and add onion, carrot, celery and herbs. Mix and continue cooking to brown vegetables.

4 Add tomatoes.

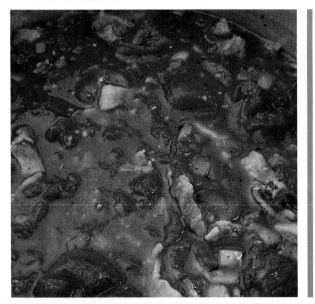

5 Add chile pepper.

6 Add tomato paste.

7 Pour in chicken stock. Finish cooking process 2 hours over low heat.

8 Pass sauce through sieve using pestle or spoon.

401

TECHNIQUE: CUMIN STUFFING

1 Heat butter in saucepan.

2 When hot, add onion and parsley; mix well. Cook 5 minutes over low heat.

3 Add cumin, mix and continue cooking 1 minute.

4 Mix in rice, season and cook 2 to 3 minutes over low heat.

5 Remove saucepan from stove and cool 1 minute. Add beaten egg to bind mixture; stir.

6 Stuff lamb.

Cumin Stuffing

2 tbsp	(30 ml) butter
1	large onion, peeled and finely chopped
1 tbsp	(15 ml) chopped parsley
2 tbsp	(30 ml) cumin
1½ cups	(375 ml) cooked rice
½	beaten egg
	salt and pepper

Heat butter in saucepan. When hot, add onion and parsley; mix well. Cook 5 minutes over low heat.

Add cumin, stir and continue cooking 1 minute.

Mix in rice, season and cook 2 to 3 minutes over low heat.

Remove saucepan from stove and cool 1 minute.

Add beaten egg to bind mixture. Stir and stuff lamb.

TECHNIQUE: BRAISING FISH

1 Cut an assortment of vegetables into julienne and place in ovenproof dish. Season and add some butter.

2 Pour in some wine or stock. Add various herbs and spices.

3 Place fish over vegetables and season again. Cook in preheated oven at 400°F (200°C) for 20 to 22 minutes, depending on size.

4 Turn fish over once during cooking and season other side.
Fish should flake when done.

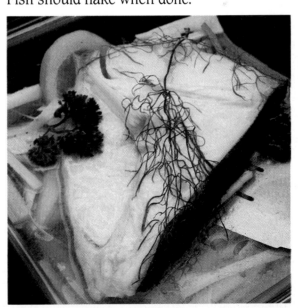

TECHNIQUE: STEAMING FISH

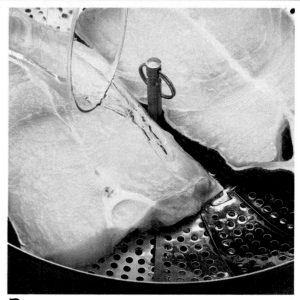

1 Use a steamer or use a steaming basket placed in a pan. Both will do the job equally well.

2 Arrange fish in steaming basket. The liquid (wine, water, etc.) should be poured through the basket into the pan.

3 Season fish and add some spices and herbs.
Cover and bring to boil.

4 Steam fish about 12 to 14 minutes, depending on size, over medium heat. Fish should flake when done.

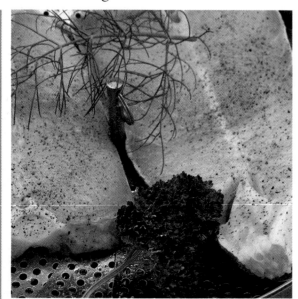

TECHNIQUE: POACHING FISH IN STOCK

1 Heat some butter in large poaching pan. Add a selection of vegetables and spices; sprinkle with lemon juice.

2 Cover and cook vegetables 3 to 4 minutes.
Add some liquid to pan and mix well.

3 Now set fish in vegetable stock. There should be enough liquid to cover fish.

4 Cover and bring to boil. Turn fish over and simmer over low heat to finish cooking. Fish should flake when done.

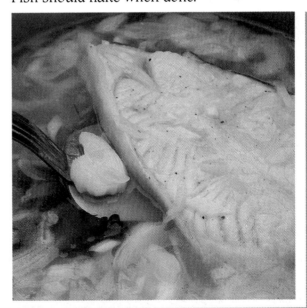

TECHNIQUE: PREPARING A WHOLE FISH

1 Have your fishmonger help you by removing scales, fins and tail. The inside should also be gutted.

2 If you are planning to barbecue, score flesh several times on both sides.

3 Slice from the tail toward the head as close to the bone as possible.

4 Once the filet has been completely removed, place flat on cutting board and remove skin.

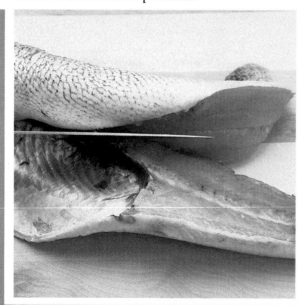

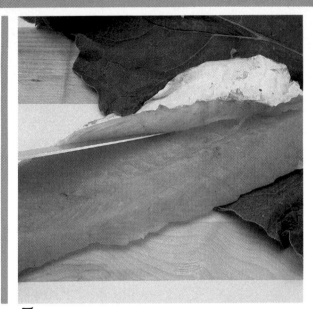

5 Find the section of flesh that contains the bones and remove.

6 Trim filets and prepare to cook.

Homemade White Stock

2¼ lb	(1 kg) chicken bones
16 cups	(4 L) cold water
1 tbsp	(15 ml) vegetable oil
1	carrot, coarsely chopped
1	onion, peeled and coarsely chopped
1	celery stalk, coarsely chopped
1	leek, cut in half
2	large tomatoes, cut in half
1	bay leaf
½ tsp	(2 ml) peppercorns
½ tsp	(2 ml) thyme
½ tsp	(2 ml) basil
1	garlic clove, peeled
	few parsley sprigs
	salt and pepper

Place bones in large stockpot. Pour in water and bring to boil. Skim and season well.

Heat oil in large frying pan. When hot, add all vegetables and spices. Cook 4 to 5 minutes.

Discard fat and transfer vegetables to stockpot containing bones. Cook 2 hours, uncovered, over very low heat.

Pass stock through sieve. Refrigerate or freeze until use.

1 SERVING	15 CALORIES	0 g CARBOHYDRATE
0 g PROTEIN	0 g FAT	0 g FIBER

Cold Halibut Salad *(serves 4)*

4	halibut steaks, poached
2 tbsp	(30 ml) finely chopped red onion
1 tbsp	(15 ml) chopped parsley
1/3	celery stalk, very finely chopped
2 tbsp	(30 ml) wine vinegar
3 tbsp	(45 ml) olive oil
2	hard-boiled eggs, chopped
	juice 1/4 lemon
	salt and pepper
	lettuce leaves
	tomato wedges

Flake fish with fork and place in serving bowl.

Add onion, parsley, celery and lemon juice; toss to combine.

Pour in vinegar and oil; season well. Add eggs and mix everything together.

Correct seasoning and serve with lettuce leaves and tomato wedges.

410

Pike Filets, Mushrooms and Shrimp   *(serves 4)*

4	pike filets
½ cup	(125 ml) flour
2 tbsp	(30 ml) butter
1 tbsp	(15 ml) vegetable oil
¼ lb	(125 g) mushrooms, cleaned and thinly sliced
16	cooked shrimp, peeled, deveined and sliced in half
1 tbsp	(15 ml) chopped chives
	salt and pepper
	juice ½ lemon

Preheat oven to 150°F (70°C).

Dredge pike with flour.

Heat oil and half of butter in large frying pan. When hot, add fish and cook 3 to 4 minutes each side over medium heat. Season well.

Remove fish from pan and keep hot in oven.

Add remaining butter to pan. When melted, cook mushrooms, shrimp and chives 3 to 4 minutes over medium-high heat.

Season well and mix in lemon juice.

Pour sauce over fish and serve with asparagus.

Sole Filets Rolls *(serves 4)*

2 tbsp	(30 ml) butter
½	celery stalk, finely chopped
½	onion, finely chopped
2	seafood sticks, finely chopped
½ cup	(125 ml) heavy cream
4	large sole filets
1 tbsp	(15 ml) finely chopped shallot
1 tbsp	(15 ml) finely chopped parsley
½ lb	(250 g) mushrooms, cleaned and thinly sliced
3 tbsp	(45 ml) Courvoisier cognac
1 tbsp	(15 ml) cornstarch
2 tbsp	(30 ml) cold water
	salt and pepper

Prepare stuffing by heating butter in frying pan. When hot, add celery, onion and chopped seafood; season well. Cover and cook 4 to 5 minutes over medium heat. Mix in 2 tbsp (30 ml) cream and continue cooking 1 minute. Spread stuffing over sole filets and roll. Place rolls in lightly greased pan and sprinkle with shallot and parsley.

Add mushrooms, cognac and 2 cups (500 ml) water. Cover pan with waxed paper and bring to boil.

Turn filets over and season; continue cooking 3 to 4 minutes over very low heat. Remove fish rolls and set aside.

Bring liquid in pan to boil; cook 4 to 5 minutes over high heat.

Add remaining cream and correct seasoning; cook 2 to 3 minutes over medium heat.

Mix cornstarch with water; stir into sauce. Bring to boil then pour over sole. Serve.

1 SERVING	326 CALORIES	8 g CARBOHYDRATE
33 g PROTEIN	18 g FAT	0.7 g FIBER

Filet of Sole au Gratin   *(serves 4)*

1 tsp	(5 ml) peanut oil
2 tbsp	(30 ml) chopped onion
1	garlic clove, smashed and chopped
3	tomatoes, diced large
¼ tsp	(1 ml) oregano
1 tsp	(5 ml) chopped parsley
1 tsp	(5 ml) butter
8	sole filets
1 cup	(250 ml) water
½ cup	(125 ml) grated Gruyère cheese
	salt and pepper
	juice 1 lemon

Heat oil in heavy saucepan. When hot, add onion and garlic; cover and cook 3 minutes over medium heat.

Add tomatoes, oregano and parsley; season generously. Continue cooking, covered, 12 minutes over low heat.

Spread butter in frying pan. Add sole and sprinkle fish with lemon juice; season well.

Pour in water and cover with sheet of waxed paper. Be sure that paper touches fish. Bring liquid to boiling point.

Remove frying pan from heat and turn fish over; let stand 3 minutes.

Transfer fish to ovenproof serving platter. Partially cover with tomatoes and sprinkle with cheese. Broil 2 minutes in oven.

Serve.

1 SERVING	228 CALORIES	7 g CARBOHYDRATE
32 g PROTEIN	8 g FAT	0.7 g FIBER

Pike Filets in Simple Caper Sauce *(serves 4)*

4	pike filets
¼ cup	(125 ml) flour
2 tbsp	(30 ml) butter
1 tbsp	(15 ml) vegetable oil
2 tbsp	(30 ml) slivered roasted almonds
2 tbsp	(30 ml) capers
1 tsp	(5 ml) chopped parsley
	salt and pepper
	juice ½ lemon

Preheat oven to 150°F (70°C).

Dredge pike with flour.

Heat oil and half of butter in large frying pan. When hot, add fish and cook 3 to 4 minutes each side over medium heat. Season well.

Remove fish from pan and keep hot in oven.

Add remaining butter to pan. When melted, cook almonds and capers 1 minute over medium heat.

Stir in parsley and lemon juice; correct seasoning. Continue cooking 1 minute.

Pour sauce over fish and serve with vegetables.

1 SERVING	285 CALORIES	12 g CARBOHYDRATE
30 g PROTEIN	13 g FAT	0.2 g FIBER

Bluefish with Tomatoes and Onions *(serves 4)*

1 tbsp	(15 ml) vegetable oil
1	onion, peeled and finely chopped
2	garlic cloves, smashed and chopped
½	celery stalk, diced
3	tomatoes, chopped
½ tsp	(2 ml) oregano
4	bluefish filets, 6 to 7 oz (170 to 198 g)
3	parsley sprigs
1 tsp	(5 ml) fennel seed
1	carrot, pared and sliced
½	white onion, sliced
	salt and pepper
	lemon juice

Heat oil in saucepan. When hot, add chopped onion and garlic; mix well. Cover and cook 3 minutes over medium heat.

Stir in celery and season; continue cooking, covered, 2 minutes.

Add tomatoes, oregano and lemon juice to taste; mix well and correct seasoning. Cover and cook 9 to 12 minutes over medium heat. Remove cover and finish cooking 3 minutes.

While tomatoes are cooking, prepare fish. Place remaining ingredients in poaching pan. Pour in enough cold water to cover and bring to boil.

Turn fish over; let stand 4 to 5 minutes in hot liquid over low heat.

Serve poached fish with tomato mixture.

1 SERVING	289 CALORIES	13 g CARBOHYDRATE
39 g PROTEIN	9 g FAT	1.2 g FIBER

Poached Bluefish with Peppers in Wine *(serves 4)*

4	bluefish filets, 6 to 7 oz (170 to 198 g)
1 tbsp	(15 ml) lemon juice
1	fennel sprig
1	carrot, pared and thinly sliced
½	red onion, sliced
1 tbsp	(15 ml) butter
½	red pepper, thinly sliced
½	green pepper, thinly sliced
½ lb	(250 g) fresh mushrooms, cleaned and sliced
¼ cup	(50 ml) dry white wine
1 tbsp	(15 ml) chopped fresh fennel
	salt and pepper

Place fish in poaching pan. Add lemon juice, fennel sprig, carrot, onion, salt and pepper.

Pour in enough cold water to cover and bring to boil over medium heat.

Turn fish over; let stand 4 to 5 minutes in hot liquid over low heat.

Meanwhile, heat butter in saucepan. When hot, add peppers and mushrooms; cook 2 minutes over medium heat.

Season and add wine and chopped fennel; mix well. Cook 3 minutes over high heat.

Remove fish from poaching liquid and serve with peppers in wine.

1 SERVING	241 CALORIES	3 g CARBOHYDRATE
37 g PROTEIN	9 g FAT	0.6 g FIBER

Broiled Bluefish with Cheese   *(serves 4)*

4	bluefish filets 6 to 7 oz (170 to 198 g)
1 tsp	(5 ml) chopped fresh tarragon
1	carrot, pared and sliced
½	onion, sliced
1	bay leaf
3	parsley sprigs
3 tbsp	(45 ml) butter
3 tbsp	(45 ml) flour
2 tbsp	(30 ml) heavy cream
½ cup	(125 ml) grated Swiss cheese
	salt and pepper
	dash paprika
	few drops Tabasco sauce

Place fish in poaching pan. Add tarragon, carrot, onion, bay leaf and parsley; season well. Pour in enough cold water to cover and bring to boil over medium heat.

Turn fish over; let stand 4 to 5 minutes in hot liquid over low heat.

Remove fish from pan and transfer to baking dish; set aside. Reserve poaching liquid.

Heat butter in saucepan. When hot, add flour and cook 1 to 2 minutes over low heat. Stir occasionally.

Strain 2 cups (500 ml) of poaching liquid and incorporate very slowly into flour mixture. Cook 8 to 10 minutes over low heat.

Stir in cream and mix well. Add half of cheese, paprika and Tabasco sauce; correct seasoning. Cook 1 minute.

Pour sauce over fish in baking dish and sprinkle with remaining cheese. Broil 5 to 6 minutes in oven. Serve.

1 SERVING	366 CALORIES	2 g CARBOHYDRATE
40 g PROTEIN	22 g FAT	0 g FIBER

Fried Bluefish with Shrimp *(serves 4)*

4	bluefish filets, 6 to 7 oz (170 to 198 g)
½ cup	(125 ml) flour
2 tbsp	(30 ml) butter
1 tbsp	(15 ml) vegetable oil
12	cooked shrimp, peeled and deveined
2 tbsp	(30 ml) slivered roasted almonds
1 tbsp	(15 ml) chopped fresh parsley
	salt and pepper
	juice ½ lemon

Preheat oven to 150°F (70°C).

Dredge fish with flour.

Heat 1 tbsp (15 ml) butter and oil in large frying pan. When hot, add fish and cook 3 minutes over medium heat.

Turn fish over and season well; continue cooking 3 to 4 minutes. Remove fish from pan and keep hot in oven.

Add remaining butter to frying pan. When melted, add shrimp, almonds and parsley. Cook 2 minutes over medium heat and season well.

Stir in lemon juice and simmer 1 minute; correct seasoning.

Pour over fish and serve with asparagus.

1 SERVING	398 CALORIES	12 g CARBOHYDRATE
47 g PROTEIN	18 g FAT	0.2 g FIBER

Poached Salmon Steaks New Cuisine *(serves 4)*

4	salmon steaks
1	bay leaf
1	carrot, pared and sliced
1	small leek, thinly sliced
1 tsp	(5 ml) lemon juice
1	parsley sprig
½	zucchini, cut in thick julienne
½	red pepper, cut in thick julienne
1	bunch fresh asparagus, tips only
¼ lb	(125 g) mushrooms, cleaned and sliced
1 tbsp	(15 ml) lemon juice
½ cup	(125 ml) dry white wine
1 tbsp	(15 ml) butter
	salt and pepper

Place fish in poaching pan. Add bay leaf, carrot, leek, 1 tsp (5 ml) lemon juice and parsley sprig; season.

Pour in enough cold water to cover and bring to boil over medium heat.

Turn fish over; let stand 4 to 5 minutes in hot liquid over low heat.

Meanwhile, place remaining vegetables, lemon juice, wine and butter in another pan. Cover and cook 3 minutes over medium heat.

Remove vegetables from wine liquid and set aside. Continue cooking liquid 2 to 3 minutes over high heat; correct seasoning.

Remove salmon steaks from poaching liquid and remove skin. Serve with julienne vegetables and with wine liquid.

1 SERVING	317 CALORIES	10 g CARBOHYDRATE
40 g PROTEIN	13 g FAT	1.3 g FIBER

Fried Salmon Steaks with Anchovies *(serves 4)*

4	salmon steaks
½ cup	(125 ml) flour
2 tbsp	(30 ml) vegetable oil
1 tbsp	(15 ml) butter
4	anchovy filets, chopped
½ lb	(250 g) mushrooms, cleaned and thinly sliced
1 tbsp	(15 ml) chopped parsley
	salt and pepper
	lemon juice to taste

Preheat oven to 150°F (70°C).

Dredge fish with flour.

Heat 1½ tbsp (25 ml) oil in large frying pan. When hot, add fish and cook 5 minutes over medium heat.

Turn fish over and season well; continue cooking 5 minutes, depending on size. Remove fish from pan and keep hot in oven.

Heat remaining oil and butter in same frying pan. Add anchovies and mushrooms; cook 3 to 4 minutes over medium-high heat.

Season well, add parsley and lemon juice to taste. Cook 1 minute and serve with salmon.

1 SERVING	409 CALORIES	14 g CARBOHYDRATE
41 g PROTEIN	21 g FAT	0.6 g FIBER

Fried Salmon, Olives and Mushrooms *(serves 4)*

4	salmon steaks
½ cup	(125 ml) flour
1 tbsp	(15 ml) vegetable oil
2 tbsp	(30 ml) butter
¼ lb	(125 g) mushrooms, cleaned and quartered
¼ cup	(50 ml) pitted black olives
1 cup	(250 ml) artichoke hearts
1	garlic clove, smashed and chopped
1 tbsp	(15 ml) chopped parsley
	salt and pepper
	lemon juice to taste

Preheat oven to 150°F (70°C).

Dredge fish with flour.

Heat oil and 1 tbsp (15 ml) butter in large frying pan. When hot, add fish and cook 5 minutes over medium heat.

Turn fish over and season well; continue cooking 5 minutes depending on size. Remove fish from pan and keep hot in oven.

Heat remaining butter in pan. Add mushrooms, olives, artichoke hearts, garlic and parsley; season. Cook 4 to 5 minutes over medium-high heat.

Sprinkle in lemon juice and continue cooking 30 seconds.

Remove salmon from oven and serve with vegetables.

Garnish dish with lemon slices.

1 SERVING	426 CALORIES	16 g CARBOHYDRATE
41 g PROTEIN	22 g FAT	1.0 g FIBER

Salmon Steaks with Tomatoes *(serves 4)*

4	salmon steaks
1	bay leaf
3	parsley sprigs
2	carrots, pared and sliced
1 tsp	(5 ml) wine vinegar
1 tsp	(5 ml) lemon juice
1 tsp	(5 ml) vegetable oil
2	shallots, chopped
1	garlic clove, smashed and chopped
1 tsp	(5 ml) chopped chives
2	tomatoes, peeled and finely chopped
3 tbsp	(45 ml) heavy cream
	salt and pepper
	few drops Tabasco sauce

Place fish in poaching pan. Add bay leaf, parsley, carrots, vinegar and lemon juice; season.

Pour in enough cold water to cover; bring to boil over medium heat.

Turn fish over; let stand 4 to 5 minutes in hot liquid over low heat.

Meanwhile, heat oil in saucepan. When hot, add all remaining ingredients, except cream. Cook 5 to 6 minutes over high heat.

Season well and stir in cream; continue cooking 2 to 3 minutes over medium heat.

Remove salmon steaks from poaching liquid and remove skin. Serve with tomatoes.

1 SERVING	324 CALORIES	6 g CARBOHYDRATE
39 g PROTEIN	16 g FAT	0.7 g FIBER

Trout Cooked in Foil   *(serves 4)*

4	trout, cleaned and washed
1	lemon, sliced
1 tbsp	(15 ml) chopped fresh parsley
½ tsp	(2 ml) fennel
½ tsp	(2 ml) dill seed
4 tbsp	(60 ml) butter
	juice 1½ lemons
	salt and pepper

Preheat oven to 400°F (200°C).

Line roasting pan with aluminium foil and add trout.

Add remaining ingredients; season well with salt and pepper.

Cover with aluminium foil and cook 20 to 25 minutes in oven, depending on size.

Serve with lemon juice.

Brook Trout with Almonds   *(serves 4)*

4	brook trout, cleaned and scaled
¼ cup	(50 ml) flour
1 tbsp	(15 ml) vegetable oil
3 tbsp	(45 ml) butter
¼ cup	(50 ml) slivered almonds
1 tbsp	(15 ml) chopped parsley
	salt and pepper
	juice ½ lemon

Preheat oven to 375°F (190°C).

Season trout and dredge with flour.

Heat oil and 1 tbsp (15 ml) butter in large frying pan. When hot, add trout and cook 3 minutes over medium heat.

Turn fish over; continue cooking 3 minutes. Remove from pan and finish cooking 8 to 10 minutes in oven.

Just before trout are cooked, heat remaining butter in frying pan. Add almonds and cook 3 minutes to brown.

Stir in parsley and lemon juice; cook 1 minute. Correct seasoning.

Pour almond sauce over trout and serve with vegetables and salad.

1 SERVING	352 CALORIES	7 g CARBOHYDRATE
36 g PROTEIN	20 g FAT	0.4 g FIBER

TECHNIQUE

1 Season trout and dredge with flour.

2 After 3 minutes of cooking, turn fish over. Continue cooking 3 minutes. Remove from pan and finish cooking in oven.

3 Just before trout are cooked, heat remaining butter in frying pan. Brown almonds 3 minutes.

4 Stir in parsley and lemon juice; cook 1 minute. Correct seasoning.

Brook Trout with Mushroom Stuffing *(serves 4)*

4	brook trout, cleaned and scaled
2 tbsp	(30 ml) butter
3	green onions, finely chopped
½	celery stalk, finely chopped
¼ lb	(125 g) mushrooms, cleaned and finely chopped
4 tbsp	(60 ml) breadcrumbs
3 tbsp	(45 ml) heavy cream
1 tbsp	(15 ml) chopped fresh fennel
1 tsp	(5 ml) chopped chives
½ cup	(125 ml) flour
	salt and pepper

Preheat oven to 375°F (190°C).

Have your fishmonger clean and scale trout. Be sure that fins are removed as well. Set fish aside.

Heat butter in frying pan. When hot, add onions and celery; cook 3 minutes over medium heat.

Stir in mushrooms and season well; continue cooking 3 minutes.

Add breadcrumbs and mix well. Add cream, fennel and chives; cook 3 minutes.

Remove pan from heat and stuff trout. Tie with string.

Dredge with flour and bake 12 to 15 minutes in oven.

1 SERVING	338 CALORIES	17 g CARBOHYDRATE
36 g PROTEIN	14 g FAT	0.3 g FIBER

TECHNIQUE

1 Have your fishmonger clean and scale trout. Be sure that fins are removed as well.

2 Heat butter in frying pan. Cook onions and celery 3 minutes over medium heat.

3 Stir in mushrooms and season well; continue cooking 3 minutes.

4 Add breadcrumbs and mix well.

Continued next page.

5 Add cream, fennel and chives; cook 3 minutes.

6 Remove pan from heat and stuff trout.

7 Tie trout with string.

8 Before baking dredge trout with flour.

Fancy Brook Trout *(serves 4)*

4	brook trout, cleaned and scaled
2 tbsp	(30 ml) butter
2	green onions, chopped
2	shallots, chopped
½	celery stalk, chopped
⅓ lb	(150 g) mushrooms, cleaned and chopped
3 tbsp	(45 ml) breadcrumbs
⅓ cup	(75 ml) heavy cream
	dash paprika
	chopped parsley to taste
	salt and pepper

Preheat oven to 375°F (190°C).

To remove backbone, place first trout on belly. Use sharp knife and cut from the back of the head to the beginning of the tail. Cut down far enough to reach backbone. Repeat long incision on other side.

Sever backbone near head and slice underneath bone to remove.

Repeat procedure for all trout.

To prepare stuffing, heat butter in frying pan. When hot, add onions, shallots and celery; cook 3 minutes over medium heat.

Add mushrooms and continue cooking 3 to 4 minutes. Season well and sprinkle in all spices.

Mix in breadcrumbs and add cream; cook another 2 minutes.

Spread stuffing in trout. Place in oiled roasting pan and cook 12 to 15 minutes in oven.

1 SERVING	317 CALORIES	6 g CARBOHYDRATE
35 g PROTEIN	17 g FAT	0.4 g FIBER

Delicious Rum Red Snapper   *(serves 4)*

4	red snapper, cleaned and scaled
8	fresh thyme sprigs
8	fresh fennel sprigs
5 tbsp	(75 ml) vegetable oil
¼ cup	(50 ml) Lamb's light rum
2 tbsp	(30 ml) wine vinegar
4 tbsp	(60 ml) chopped parsley
2	garlic cloves, smashed and chopped
	salt and pepper
	lime juice to taste

Have your fishmonger clean and scale snapper. Be sure that fins are removed as well.

Score flesh of each snapper several times on both sides. Place thyme and fennel sprigs inside cavity. Set snapper in roasting pan or large plate.

Mix oil, rum, vinegar, parsley, garlic, salt, pepper and lime juice together; pour over fish.

Marinate snapper 2 hours in refrigerator; turn fish over twice.

Preheat oven to 400°F (200°C).

Remove snapper from marinade and place on ovenproof platter. Set marinade aside.

Cook 15 to 20 minutes in oven, depending on size. Baste several times during cooking and turn over once.

Serve.

1 SERVING	311 CALORIES	0 g CARBOHYDRATE
35 g PROTEIN	19 g FAT	0 g FIBER

TECHNIQUE

1 Have your fishmonger clean and scale snapper. Be sure that fins are removed as well.

2 Score flesh of each snapper several times on both sides.

3 Place thyme and fennel sprigs inside cavity. Set snapper in roasting pan or large plate.

4 Pour marinade over snapper; refrigerate 2 hours before cooking.

TECHNIQUE: COOKING SHRIMP

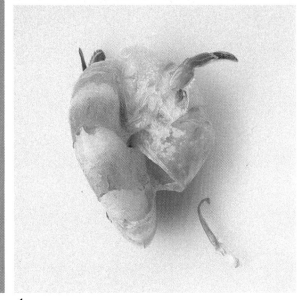

1 Depending on the recipe, shrimp may be cooked with or without the shells.

2 Place shrimp in cold water along with herbs and spices.

3 When water starts to boil, remove pan from heat and scoop out shrimp.

4 Cool shrimp in cold water.

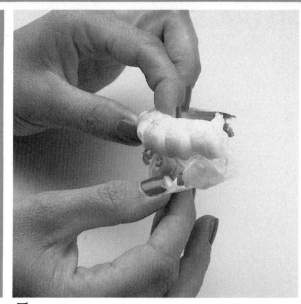

5 If using shrimp immediately, peel off shells with your fingers. Unpeeled cooked shrimp can be kept for 24 hours. Cover with plastic wrap and refrigerate.

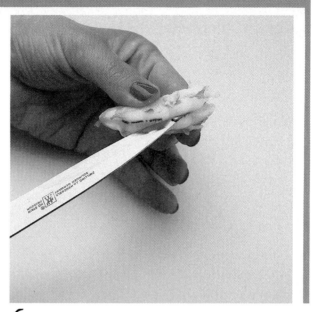

6 To devein shrimp, slit back and scoop out black vein with knife.

Pepper Shrimp *(serves 4)*

2 lb	(900 g) jumbo shrimp, peeled
2 tbsp	(30 ml) ground black pepper
1 tbsp	(15 ml) butter
2 cups	(500 ml) cold water
2 tbsp	(30 ml) paprika
	juice 1 lemon

Place shrimp, 1½ tbsp (25 ml) black pepper and lemon juice in saucepan.

Add butter, water and half of paprika. Stir and cover pan; bring to boil.

Remove saucepan from heat and turn shrimp over; let stand in hot liquid 3 to 4 minutes.

Drain shrimp and transfer to bowl; add remaining pepper and paprika. Mix well.

Traditionally this dish is served on newspaper.

1 SERVING	213 CALORIES	4 g CARBOHYDRATE
38 g PROTEIN	5 g FAT	0 g FIBER

Ginger Shrimp *(serves 4)*

1 tbsp	(15 ml) vegetable oil
1½ lb	(750 g) shrimp, peeled
1	red pepper, thinly sliced
1	celery stalk, thinly sliced
1	carrot, pared and thinly sliced
3	green onions, cut in short sticks
2 tbsp	(30 ml) chopped fresh ginger
1½ cups	(375 ml) heated chicken stock
1 tbsp	(15 ml) cornstarch
2 tbsp	(30 ml) cold water
	salt and pepper
	few drops commercial hot sauce

Heat oil in large frying pan. When hot, add shrimp and cook 4 to 6 minutes over high heat. Turn shrimp over once or twice during cooking and season well.

Remove shrimp from pan and set aside.

Add vegetables and ginger to frying pan; season well. Cook 3 to 4 minutes over high heat; stir occasionally.

Pour in chicken stock and bring to boil.

Mix cornstarch with water; stir into vegetables.

Replace shrimp in pan and stir well. Simmer 1 to 2 minutes over medium-low heat.

Serve.

1 SERVING	221 CALORIES	10 g CARBOHYDRATE
34 g PROTEIN	5 g FAT	0.7 g FIBER

Shrimp and Scallop Vol-au-Vent *(serves 4)*

1 tbsp	(15 ml) butter
½ lb	(250 g) mushrooms, cleaned and diced
16	shrimp, peeled
16	scallops
1 tbsp	(15 ml) chopped parsley
½ tsp	(2 ml) fennel seed
½ cup	(125 ml) dry white wine
½ cup	(125 ml) cold water
1½ cups	(375 ml) light cream, heated
1 tsp	(5 ml) lemon juice
1 tsp	(5 ml) cornstarch
2 tbsp	(30 ml) cold water
¼ tsp	(1 ml) Tabasco sauce
4	vol-au-vent shells, cooked
	salt and pepper

Grease large pan with butter. Add mushrooms, shrimp, scallops, parsley and fennel seed.

Pour in wine and water; season well. Cover pan and bring to boil.

Turn seafood over; simmer 3 to 4 minutes over very low heat.

Use slotted spoon and remove seafood; place in bowl.

Place pan containing cooking liquid over medium heat. Bring to boil.

Add cream and bring to boil again; season and stir in lemon juice.

Mix cornstarch with water; stir into sauce. Bring to boil and cook 1 minute.

Replace seafood in sauce and add Tabasco sauce; mix and simmer 2 minutes over very low heat.

Fill vol-au-vent shells and serve.

1 SERVING	616 CALORIES	28 g CARBOHYDRATE
36 g PROTEIN	40 g FAT	0.3 g FIBER

Seafood Stick Vol-au-Vent *(serves 4)*

2 tbsp	(30 ml) butter
½	onion, finely chopped
½	carrot, chopped
¼	celery stalk, chopped
2 tbsp	(30 ml) curry powder
3 tbsp	(45 ml) flour
1½ cups	(375 ml) heated chicken stock
¼ cup	(50 ml) heavy cream
1 tsp	(5 ml) chopped parsley
12	seafood sticks, diced
½ cup	(125 ml) canned mandarins, drained
4	vol-au-vent shells, cooked
	salt and pepper

Heat butter in frying pan. When hot, add onion, carrot and celery; cover and cook 3 to 4 minutes over medium heat.

Mix in curry powder and flour; mix again. Cook 1 minute, uncovered, over medium heat.

Pour in chicken stock and season well. Cook 8 to 10 minutes, uncovered, over medium heat.

Add cream and parsley; mix well. Continue cooking 3 to 4 minutes.

Stir in seafood sticks and mandarins; simmer 2 to 3 minutes over low heat. Fill vol-au-vent shells and serve.

1 SERVING	504 CALORIES	30 g CARBOHYDRATE
15 g PROTEIN	36 g FAT	0.4 g FIBER

Scallop Vol-au-Vent with Cheese *(serves 4)*

3 tbsp	(45 ml) butter
¼ lb	(125 g) fresh mushrooms, cleaned and diced
½	zucchini, diced
3 tbsp	(45 ml) flour
1½ cups	(375 ml) heated chicken stock
1 tbsp	(15 ml) chopped fresh fennel
2	mint leaves (fresh if available)
¼ cup	(50 ml) heavy cream
¾ lb	(375 g) shrimp, peeled
½ lb	(250 g) scallops
4	seafood sticks, diced
¾ cup	(175 ml) grated Swiss cheese
4	vol-au-vent shells, cooked
	salt and pepper
	lemon juice to taste

Heat butter in large deep pan. When hot, add mushrooms and zucchini; cook 3 minutes over medium-high heat.

Mix in flour and continue cooking 1 minute.

Pour in chicken stock and season well. Add fennel and mint; mix and cook 4 to 5 minutes over medium heat.

Pour in cream and cook 2 minutes over medium-high heat; correct seasoning.

Stir in shrimp and scallops; simmer 3 minutes over low heat.

Add seafood sticks, stir and simmer 2 more minutes.

Stir in half of cheese. Fill vol-au-vent shells and top with remaining cheese.

Broil 2 to 3 minutes in oven or until cheese melts. Serve immediately.

1 SERVING	642 CALORIES	27 g CARBOHYDRATE
39 g PROTEIN	42 g FAT	0.4 g FIBER

Coquille of Shrimp and Scallops   *(serves 4)*

3 tbsp	(45 ml) butter
8	tiger shrimp, peeled, deveined and cut in three
¾ lb	(375 g) scallops
1 tbsp	(15 ml) chopped parsley
1 cup	(250 ml) dry white wine
2 tbsp	(30 ml) flour
1¼ cups	(300 ml) light cream, heated
1 cup	(250 ml) grated Gruyère cheese
¼ tsp	(1 ml) nutmeg
	salt and pepper
	lemon juice to taste

Grease large pan with 1 tbsp (15 ml) butter. Add shrimp, scallops, half of parsley and wine. Season well; cover and bring to boil.

Turn seafood over; let stand 3 to 4 minutes over low heat.

Remove pan from heat and set seafood aside. Strain liquid into bowl; set aside as well. Heat remaining butter in saucepan. When hot, add flour and mix; cook 1 minute over low heat.

Place reserved poaching liquid in separate saucepan. Reduce by ½ over medium-high heat.

Stir reduced liquid into flour mixture. Add cream and remaining parsley; mix. Cook 8 to 10 minutes over very low heat.

Stir in half of cheese and nutmeg; cook 2 minutes over low heat.

Place seafood in sauce. Spoon mixture into individual scallop shells. Sprinkle with remaining cheese and broil 4 to 5 minutes in oven.

See Technique next page.

1 SERVING	489 CALORIES	11 g CARBOHYDRATE
37 g PROTEIN	33 g FAT	0 g FIBER

TECHNIQUE:

1 Grease large pan with 1 tbsp (15 ml) butter. Add shrimp, scallops and half of parsley.

2 Pour in wine and season well; cover and bring to boil.

3 Turn seafood over; let stand 3 to 4 minutes over low heat.

4 Remove pan from heat and set seafood aside. Strain liquid into bowl; set aside as well.

5 Heat remaining butter in saucepan. When hot, add flour and mix; cook 1 minute over low heat.
Pour reduced liquid into saucepan containing flour mixture.

6 Mix and add cream and remaining parsley; mix again. Cook sauce 8 to 10 minutes over very low heat.

7 Stir in half of cheese and nutmeg; cook 2 minutes over low heat.

8 Place seafood in sauce and remove pan from heat. Spoon mixture into individual scallop shells. Sprinkle with remaining cheese and broil 4 to 5 minutes in oven.

Famous Coquilles Saint-Jacques *(serves 4)*

3 tbsp	(45 ml) butter
1 lb	(500 g) fresh scallops
2 tbsp	(30 ml) chopped shallots
1 tbsp	(15 ml) chopped fresh parsley
2 tbsp	(30 ml) chopped fresh chives
½ cup	(125 ml) coarse breadcrumbs
	salt and pepper
	melted butter

Preheat oven to 400°F (200°C).

Heat 3 tbsp (45 ml) butter in frying pan. When hot, add scallops and cook 3 minutes over high heat.

Add shallots, parsley and chives; season well. Cook 2 minutes over medium heat.

Mix well and spoon into individual scallop shells. Sprinkle with breadcrumbs and moisten with melted butter.

Cook 3 minutes in oven.

Serve with lemon.

1 SERVING	249 CALORIES	12 g CARBOHYDRATE
21 g PROTEIN	13 g FAT	0.1 g FIBER

Rich and Creamy Coquilles Saint-Jacques *(serves 4)*

4 tbsp	(60 ml) butter
1 lb	(500 g) fresh scallops
¼ lb	(125 g) fresh mushrooms, cleaned and diced
1	shallot, chopped
1 tbsp	(15 ml) chopped chives
2 tbsp	(30 ml) dry vermouth
1½ cups	(375 ml) cold water
3 tbsp	(45 ml) flour
½ cup	(125 ml) heavy cream
	pinch fennel
	few drops lemon juice
	salt and pepper

With 1 tbsp (15 ml) butter, lightly grease deep pan. Add scallops, mushrooms, shallot, chives, fennel, vermouth, water, lemon juice, salt and pepper. Cover with waxed paper and bring to boil.

When boiling, remove pan from heat. Let stand 3 to 4 minutes. Use slotted spoon and remove scallops; set aside. Replace pan over high heat and boil 3 to 4 minutes.

Heat remaining butter in saucepan. Add flour and cook 2 minutes over low heat; stir constantly.

Pour cooking liquid into saucepan containing flour; incorporate with whisk. Add cream and mix well; continue cooking 3 to 4 minutes.

Replace scallops in sauce and correct seasoning. Mix well and sprinkle with lemon juice to taste. Serve immediately.

1 SERVING	274 CALORIES	7 g CARBOHYDRATE
21 g PROTEIN	18 g FAT	0.3 g FIBER

Halibut Casserole   *(serves 4)*

3 tbsp	(45 ml) butter
3 tbsp	(45 ml) flour
2 cups	(500 ml) hot milk
¼ tsp	(1 ml) nutmeg
¼ tsp	(1 ml) paprika
½ tsp	(2 ml) fennel seed
4	steamed halibut steaks*, flaked
½ cup	(125 ml) grated Gruyère cheese
1 tsp	(5 ml) chopped chives
	few drops lemon juice
	salt and pepper

Heat butter in saucepan. When hot, add flour and mix well. Cook 2 minutes over low heat.

Pour in hot milk and add spices; correct seasoning. Mix well with whisk and cook 10 minutes over low heat. Stir several times during cooking.

Remove saucepan from heat and carefully incorporate flaked fish and lemon juice.

Mix in half of cheese. Pour into baking dish and sprinkle with remaining cheese and chives. Broil 2 to 3 minutes in oven.

Serve with fresh corn.

*See Steaming Fish, page 406.

Broiled Maine Lobster *(serves 4)*

4	1½ lb (750 g) boiled Maine Lobsters*
4 tbsp	(60 ml) soft butter
1	shallot, finely chopped
1 tbsp	(15 ml) chopped parsley
1 tbsp	(15 ml) breadcrumbs
1 tsp	(5 ml) lemon juice
¼ tsp	(1 ml) Tabasco sauce
	dash paprika
	freshly ground pepper

*Do not boil lobsters longer than 12 minutes. Follow the technique for Boiling Live Lobsters on page 445.

Place lobster halves on ovenproof serving platter; set aside.

Mix remaining ingredients together in bowl; spread over lobster flesh.

Broil 8 minutes on top rack in oven.

Serve immediately.

1 SERVING	263 CALORIES	2 g CARBOHYDRATE
30 g PROTEIN	15 g FAT	0 g FIBER

TECHNIQUE: BOILING LIVE LOBSTERS

1 Purchase live lobsters of about 1 ½ lb (750 g). If necessary, live lobsters can be stored for 2 or 3 days, depending on their condition.
To store, wrap in newspaper and refrigerate.

2 Bring lots of water to boil. Plunge lobster in water. Leaving pegs in claws will retain juices. Cover pan, cook 14 to 18 minutes depending on size. Water should not boil to rapidly.

3 The shell of a cooked lobster will change color to red.

4 When cooked, remove from water and let cool. Cut lobster in half using strong knife.

Continued next page.

5 Clean the inside of the lobster by removing the small intestinal sac.

6 The tomalley (green liver) is very tasty and is usually eaten along with the roe (lobster coral).

7 If desired, crack claws and remove meat before serving.

8 The meat from the tail comes out quite easily and the empty shell can be used as decoration.

Lobster Newburg   *(serves 4)*

4	1½ lb (750 g) boiled Florida lobsters*
1	egg yolk
2 cups	(500 ml) heavy cream
2 tbsp	(30 ml) butter
2	shallots, finely chopped
½ lb	(250 g) fresh mushrooms, cleaned and sliced
¼ cup	(50 ml) Madeira wine
1 tsp	(5 ml) chopped parsley
	salt and pepper
	dash cayenne

*Follow the technique for Boiling Live Lobsters on page 445. Remove all lobster meat and dice; set aside.

Mix egg yolk with 2 tbsp (30 ml) cream; set aside.

Heat butter in large frying pan. When hot, add shallots and mushrooms; season well. Cook 3 minutes over medium-high heat.

Pour in wine and cook 3 minutes over high heat.

Mix in remaining cream, parsley and cayenne; correct seasoning. Cook 4 to 5 minutes over medium-high heat.

Add lobster meat and mix quickly. Reduce heat to low and stir in egg yolk; mix and cook 2 minutes over very low heat to thicken.

Mix gently and serve immediately. If desired, decorate dishes with lobster shells.

1 SERVING	672 CALORIES	7 g CARBOHYDRATE
35 g PROTEIN	56 g FAT	0.5 g FIBER

Scallops with Rice *(serves 4)*

1 tbsp	(15 ml) butter
2 tbsp	(30 ml) finely chopped onion
1	zucchini, diced
1 cup	(250 ml) long grain rice, rinsed and drained
1½ cups	(375 ml) heated chicken stock
1 tsp	(5 ml) fennel seed
1 tbsp	(15 ml) butter
½ lb	(250 g) fresh mushroom caps, cleaned
1 tbsp	(15 ml) chopped chives
¾ lb	(375 g) small scallops
2 tbsp	(30 ml) soya sauce
	salt and pepper

Preheat oven to 350°F (180°C).

Heat 1 tbsp (15 ml) butter in ovenproof saucepan. Add onion and mix well; cook 2 to 3 minutes over medium heat.

Add zucchini, salt and pepper; continue cooking 2 minutes.

Mix in rice and cook 2 minutes.

Add chicken stock and fennel seed; stir well and bring to boil. Season, cover and cook 18 minutes in oven.

Meanwhile, heat 1 tbsp (15 ml) butter in frying pan. Add mushrooms and chives; cook 3 minutes.

Stir in scallops and cook 2 minutes over high heat. Add soya sauce and mix ingredients well.

About 4 minutes before rice is cooked, stir in the scallop mixture. Finish cooking process and correct seasoning.

Decorate with chopped peppers and serve with chutney sauce.

1 SERVING	339 CALORIES	48 g CARBOHYDRATE
21 g PROTEIN	7 g FAT	1.0 g FIBER

TECHNIQUE: SCALLOPS WITH RICE

1 Add zucchini to onion and season with salt and pepper; continue cooking 2 minutes.

2 Mix in rice and cook 2 minutes.

3 Add chicken stock and fennel seed; stir well and bring to boil. Finish cooking in oven.

4 While rice is cooking, cook mushrooms in hot butter. Add scallops and add to rice. Finish cooking process in oven.

449

King Crab Legs Marinated in Rum   *(serves 4)*

8	frozen King crab legs, thawed and split in two
¼ cup	(50 ml) Lamb's white rum
½ lb	(250 g) soft unsalted butter
2 tbsp	(30 ml) finely chopped parsley
1	garlic clove, smashed and chopped
1	shallot, finely chopped
3 tbsp	(45 ml) breadcrumbs
	juice ½ lemon
	few drops Tabasco sauce
	freshly ground pepper

Preheat oven to 400°F (200°C).

Place crab legs in deep dish and pour in rum. Marinate 5 to 6 minutes.

Mix butter and remaining ingredients together; set aside.

Drain crab legs from marinade and place on ovenproof platter. Spread butter mixture over meat.

Place in oven and cook 5 to 6 minutes.

Serve with French fries.

| *1 SERVING* | 583 CALORIES | 4 g CARBOHYDRATE |
| 27 g PROTEIN | 51 g FAT | 0 g FIBER |

Silver Hake Steaks and Melted Butter *(serves 4)*

4	silver hake steaks
1	celery stalk, thinly sliced
1	small leek, washed and thinly sliced
3	carrots, pared and thinly sliced
2	fresh fennel sprigs
1 tbsp	(15 ml) vegetable oil
1	zucchini, thinly sliced
¼ cup	(50 ml) butter
1 tbsp	(15 ml) chopped parsley
	salt and pepper
	juice 1 lemon

Place fish in roasting pan. Add celery, leek, 1 carrot, fennel, salt, pepper and lemon juice. Pour in enough water to cover and bring to boil.

Remove pan from stove; turn fish over and let stand 8 to 10 minutes.

Meanwhile, heat oil in frying pan. When hot, add remaining carrots and zucchini; season and cook 5 to 6 minutes over medium heat.

Place butter and parsley in small saucepan; heat to melt.

Arrange fish on plates and pour melted butter overtop. Serve with the vegetables.

1 SERVING	288 CALORIES	10 g CARBOHYDRATE
26 g PROTEIN	16 g FAT	1.1 g FIBER

Broiled Scampi *(serves 4)*

20	scampi
½ lb	(250 g) soft butter
1 tbsp	(15 ml) chopped parsley
2	shallots, chopped
2	garlic cloves, smashed and chopped
1 tbsp	(15 ml) lemon juice
¼ tsp	(1 ml) Tabasco sauce
2 tbsp	(30 ml) breadcrumbs
	salt and pepper

Preheat oven to 400°F (200°C).

Prepare scampi as directed in the technique following.

Place butter, parsley, shallots, garlic, lemon juice, Tabasco sauce and breadcrumbs in bowl. Mix together and correct seasoning.

Spread mixture over scampi. Cook 6 to 8 minutes in oven, depending on size.

Serve with rice.

1 SERVING	513 CALORIES	4 g CARBOHYDRATE
14 g PROTEIN	49 g FAT	0 g FIBER

TECHNIQUE: BROILED SCAMPI

1 Try to purchase fresh scampi.

2 Cut shell lengthwise.

3 Do not cut all the way through, so that scampi can be butterflied.

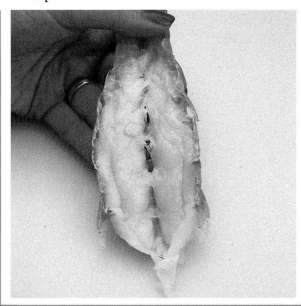

4 Place on ovenproof platter.

Continued next page.

5 Place butter and parsley in bowl.

6 Add shallots and garlic.

7 Add lemon juice, Tabasco sauce and breadcrumbs. Mix together and correct seasoning.

8 Spread mixture over scampi and cook in oven 6 to 8 minutes, depending on size.

Scampi, Mushrooms and Cheese *(serves 4)*

20	scampi
2 tbsp	(30 ml) butter
2	shallots, chopped
½ lb	(250 g) mushrooms, cleaned and sliced
1 tsp	(5 ml) chopped parsley
3 tbsp	(45 ml) Courvoisier cognac
1½ cups	(375 ml) light cream, heated
1 tsp	(5 ml) cornstarch
2 tbsp	(30 ml) cold water
½ cup	(125 ml) grated Swiss or Gruyère cheese
	salt and pepper

Prepare scampi as directed in the following technique.

Heat butter in large frying pan. When hot, add shallots and mushrooms; season and cook 3 minutes over medium-high heat. Sprinkle with parsley. Slice scampi in half and add to frying pan. Cook 2 minutes over medium heat and correct seasoning.

Pour in cognac; cook 2 minutes over medium-high heat.

Remove scampi from pan and set aside. Add cream to frying pan and cook 3 to 4 minutes over medium heat. Mix cornstarch with cold water; stir into sauce. Cook 1 minute.

Replace scampi in frying pan and add most of cheese; mix and cook 1 minute.

Spoon scampi over boiled rice and sprinkle with remaining cheese. Broil in oven to melt cheese. Serve.

See Technique next page.

1 SERVING	381 CALORIES	8 g CARBOHYDRATE
22 g PROTEIN	29 g FAT	0.2 g FIBER

TECHNIQUE

1 Snip along either side of shell to free membrane.

2 Pull membrane back to free scampi.

3 Set scampi aside and discard shells.

4 Cook shallots and mushrooms in hot butter 3 minutes over medium-high heat. Sprinkle with parsley.

5 Slice scampi in half and add to frying pan. Cook 2 minutes over medium heat and correct seasoning.

6 Pour in cognac; cook 2 minutes over medium-high heat.

7 Remove scampi from pan and set aside. Add cream and cook 3 to 4 minutes over medium heat.

8 After cooking cornstarch mixture 1 minute, replace scampi in pan and add most of cheese. Mix and cook 1 minute.

Flambéed Scampi *(serves 4)*

1 tbsp	(15 ml) vegetable oil
2 tbsp	(30 ml) butter
20	scampi, removed from shell
½ lb	(250 g) fresh mushrooms, cleaned and diced
4 tbsp	(60 ml) Courvoisier cognac
1 cup	(250 ml) plain yogurt
1 tbsp	(15 ml) chopped parsley
	few drops lemon juice
	dash paprika
	lemon wedges for decoration

Heat oil and half of butter in large frying pan. When hot, add scampi and season well; cook 2 to 3 minutes over high heat. Stir once.

Remove scampi from pan and set aside.

Add remaining butter to pan and heat. Add mushrooms, season and cook 3 minutes over medium-high heat.

Pour in cognac; flambé and cook 2 minutes over medium-high heat; mix well.

Add yogurt, parsley, lemon juice and paprika; mix well. Cook 2 to 3 minutes over medium heat.

Replace scampi in sauce and simmer 1 to 2 minutes.

Serve.

1 SERVING	208 CALORIES	7 g CARBOHYDRATE
18 g PROTEIN	12 g FAT	0.5 g FIBER

Steamed Cherrystone Clams *(serves 4)*

32	Cherrystone clams
1 tbsp	(15 ml) butter
	juice ½ lemon
	chopped parsley to taste

Prepare clams for steaming by rinsing under cold water. Scrub shells to remove all dirt and sand.

Place in deep pot; add butter and lemon juice. Cover with no more than 2 in (5 cm) water.

Cover and cook 8 to 10 minutes over medium heat. When shells are partly open, clams are cooked.

Remove clams from pot; be sure to pour liquid in shells back into pot.

Arrange clams on serving platter. Mix parsley into cooking liquid and pour over clams.

Serve immediately.

1 SERVING	148 CALORIES	10 g CARBOHYDRATE
18 g PROTEIN	4 g FAT	0 g FIBER

Littleneck Clams in Italian Sauce   *(serves 4)*

1 tbsp	(15 ml) butter
1 tbsp	(15 ml) chopped parsley
1 tbsp	(15 ml) chopped chives
2	garlic cloves, smashed and chopped
1	onion, peeled and chopped
1	celery stalk, finely chopped
48	Littleneck clams, steamed*
3	tomatoes, chopped
½ cup	(125 ml) grated parmesan cheese
	salt and pepper

Heat butter in saucepan. When hot, add parsley, chives, garlic and onion; mix and cook 3 to 4 minutes over medium heat.

Stir in celery; continue cooking 2 to 3 minutes over medium heat.

Remove steamed clams from shells and chop fine; set aside. Reserve shells.

Stir tomatoes into saucepan and season well; cook 4 to 5 minutes over high heat.

Add chopped clams and cook 2 more minutes.

Mix in half of cheese and correct seasoning. Spoon mixture into reserved shells and top with remaining cheese. Broil 2 to 3 minutes in oven.

Serve.

*See Steamed Cherrystone Clams, page 459.

1 SERVING	240 CALORIES	18 g CARBOHYDRATE
24 g PROTEIN	8 g FAT	0.8 g FIBER

Cherrystone Clams au Gratin *(serves 4)*

32	Cherrystone clams, steamed*
1 tbsp	(15 ml) butter
1	small onion, peeled and diced
1 tbsp	(15 ml) chopped parsley
1½ tbsp	(25 ml) chopped chives
1 cup	(250 ml) heavy cream
½ cup	(125 ml) grated Gruyère cheese
2 cups	(500 ml) chopped spinach, cooked
	salt and pepper
	few drops lime juice

*Prepare clams as directed in Steamed Cherrystone Clams on page 459. When cooked, remove clams from cooking liquid and open shells. Arrange clams in the half shell and set aside.

Heat butter in saucepan. When hot, add onion and cover; cook 2 minutes over medium heat.

Mix in parsley and chives; continue cooking 1 minute, covered, over low heat.

Pour in cream, season well and add half of cheese. Mix and cook 3 to 4 minutes, uncovered, over medium heat. Season with lime juice.

Arrange chopped spinach over clams in shells. Cover with sauce and top with remaining cheese. Broil 5 minutes in oven.

Serve.

1 SERVING	344 CALORIES	16 g CARBOHYDRATE
25 g PROTEIN	20 g FAT	0.7 g FIBER

Oyster Stew *(serves 4)*

32	oysters, shucked (reserve liquor)
1 tbsp	(15 ml) lemon juice
1½ cups	(375 ml) light cream
1 tbsp	(15 ml) butter
1 tbsp	(15 ml) chopped chives
	salt and pepper
	soda crackers

Place shucked oysters along with their liquor in saucepan. Add lemon juice and cover; cook 2 to 3 minutes over low heat.

Meanwhile pour cream into separate saucepan. Heat to boiling point.

Transfer cream to saucepan containing oysters. Mix in butter and chives; cook 1 to 2 minutes over low heat. Correct seasoning.

Serve in shallow bowls with soda crackers.

1 SERVING   295 CALORIES   8 g CARBOHYDRATE
14 g PROTEIN   23 g FAT   0 g FIBER

Oysters Rockefeller *(serves 4)*

24	oysters
1 tsp	(5 ml) lemon juice
4 tbsp	(60 ml) butter
½	celery stalk, minced
2	garlic cloves, smashed and chopped
1 tbsp	(15 ml) finely chopped parsley
1 cup	(250 ml) cooked spinach, finely chopped
3 tbsp	(45 ml) heavy cream
4 tbsp	(60 ml) breadcrumbs
	salt and freshly ground pepper

Shuck oysters and place in saucepan along with their liquor. Set shells aside.

Add lemon juice and 1 tbsp (15 ml) butter. Cover and cook 3 to 4 minutes over low heat. Season lightly. Drain oysters and set aside; reserve cooking liquid for other uses.

Heat remaining butter in separate saucepan. When hot, add celery, garlic and parsley; cover and cook 3 minutes over low heat.

Mix in spinach and season well; continue cooking, covered, 2 minutes over medium-high heat.

Add cream and 3 tbsp (45 ml) breadcrumbs; mix and cook 2 minutes, uncovered, over high heat.

Arrange oysters on the half shell. Spread spinach mixture on top and top with remaining breadcrumbs. Broil 3 to 4 minutes in oven. Serve.

Oysters in Sauce with Cheese *(serves 4)*

24	oysters
1 tsp	(5 ml) lemon juice
4 tbsp	(60 ml) butter
3 tbsp	(45 ml) flour
1½ cups	(375 ml) hot milk
¼ tsp	(1 ml) nutmeg
¼ tsp	ground clove
½ cup	(125 ml) grated Swiss cheese
	salt and pepper

Shuck oysters and place in saucepan along with their liquor. Set shells aside.

Add lemon juice and 1 tbsp (15 ml) butter. Cover and cook 3 to 4 minutes over low heat. Season lightly.

Drain oysters and set aside; reserve ½ cup (125 ml) cooking liquid.

Heat remaining butter in separate saucepan. When hot, add flour and mix; cook 1 minute over medium heat.

Pour in milk and whisk to incorporate; add ½ cup (125 ml) reserved oyster cooking liquid, spices and half of cheese. Cook 8 to 10 minutes over low heat.

Arrange oysters on the half shell. Spoon sauce on top and top with remaining cheese. Broil 3 to 4 minutes in oven.

Serve.

1 SERVING	437 CALORIES	10 g CARBOHYDRATE
16 g PROTEIN	37 g FAT	0 g FIBER

TECHNIQUE: COOKING FRESH MUSSELS

1 Before cooking, rinse mussels under cold running water. Scrub shells and remove beards with small knife.

2 If you find any open shells, discard and do not attempt to cook. Open shells often contain various bacteria that can be harmful if consumed.

3 Place cleaned mussels in large pan and add a bit of liquid (water or wine, for example).

4 Cover pan and bring to boil. Steam mussels until shells open.

Mussels Marinière *(serves 4)*

8½ lb	(4 kg) fresh mussels, scrubbed and bearded
2 tbsp	(30 ml) finely chopped shallots
½ cup	(125 ml) dry white wine
2 tbsp	(30 ml) chopped parsley
1 tbsp	(15 ml) lemon juice
3 tbsp	(45 ml) butter
½ cup	(125 ml) heavy cream
	freshly ground pepper

Place cleaned mussels in large pan. Add shallots, wine, 1 tbsp (15 ml) parsley, lemon juice and butter. Cover and bring to boil.

When shells are open, remove one at a time and pour liquid from shells back into pan. Set aside.

Strain liquid in pan through cheesecloth into saucepan. Mix in cream and season generously with pepper; cook 3 to 4 minutes over high heat.

Mix in remaining parsley and return mussels to sauce. Simmer 2 minutes over low heat.

Serve mussels in shells with plenty of sauce.

1 SERVING	328 CALORIES	6 g CARBOHYDRATE
22 g PROTEIN	24 g FAT	0 g FIBER

Italian Mussels   *(serves 4)*

8½ lb	(4 kg) fresh mussels, scrubbed and bearded
½ cup	(125 ml) water
2 tbsp	(30 ml) chopped parsley
3	garlic cloves, smashed and chopped
3 tbsp	(45 ml) butter
½ cup	(125 ml) dry white wine
28 oz	(796 ml) can tomatoes, drained and chopped
¼ tsp	(1 ml) oregano
	few crushed chillies
	freshly ground pepper
	juice ½ lemon

Place cleaned mussels and water in large pan. Add parsley, 1 chopped garlic clove, 2 tbsp (30 ml) butter and crushed chilies. Sprinkle in pepper and lemon juice; cover and bring to boil.

When shells are open, remove one at a time and pour liquid from shells back into pan. Set aside.

Strain liquid in pan through cheesecloth into bowl; reserve for other uses.

Heat remaining butter in frying pan. When hot, add remaining garlic and cook 2 minutes over medium heat.

Add wine and cook 2 minutes over high heat.

Mix in tomatoes and season with pepper; cook 1 minute.

Add oregano and finish cooking 7 to 8 minutes over high heat; stir occasionally.

Place mussels, on half shell, in tomato mixture. Cook 2 minutes to reheat. Serve.

1 SERVING	269 CALORIES	14 g CARBOHYDRATE
24 g PROTEIN	13 g FAT	0.8 g FIBER

Mussels in Vermouth *(serves 4)*

8½ lb	(4 kg) fresh mussels, scrubbed and bearded
2 tbsp	(30 ml) chopped onion
2 tbsp	(30 ml) chopped chives
3 tbsp	(45 ml) butter
½ cup	(125 ml) dry white wine
3 tbsp	(45 ml) dry vermouth
1 cup	(250 ml) heavy cream
	freshly ground pepper

Place cleaned mussels in large pan. Add onion 1 tbsp (15 ml) chives, butter, wine and pepper. Cover and bring to boil.

When shells are open, remove one at a time and pour liquid from shells back into pan. Set aside.

Strain liquid in pan through cheesecloth into saucepan. Pour in vermouth and cream; season with pepper. Cook 3 to 4 minutes over high heat.

Mix in remaining chives and simmer 2 minutes over medium-low heat.

Serve mussels in half shell and pour sauce on top.

1 SERVING	435 CALORIES	7 g CARBOHYDRATE
23 g PROTEIN	35 g FAT	0 g FIBER

Parmesan Seafood Crepes   *(serves 4)*

2 tbsp	(30 ml) butter
1	small zucchini, diced
¾ lb	(375 g) shrimp, peeled
¾ lb	(375 g) scallops, cut in half
1½ cups	(375 ml) heated white sauce
½ cup	(125 ml) grated parmesan cheese
8	crepes
	salt and pepper

Heat butter in large saucepan. When hot, add zucchini and season well; cover and cook 3 minutes over medium heat.

Add shrimp and scallops; mix and correct seasoning. Cover and cook 3 to 4 minutes over medium heat.

Pour in white sauce and half of cheese; cook 2 minutes, uncovered, over low heat.

Stuff crepes with most of seafood. Roll and arrange in baking dish. Pour remaining sauce over and top with cheese.

Broil in oven 1 minute then serve.

See Technique next page.

| *1 SERVING* | 523 CALORIES | 30 g CARBOHYDRATE |
| 40 g PROTEIN | 27 g FAT | 0.3 g FIBER |

1 Sift flour, salt and paprika into large bowl. Add eggs.

2 Add tonic water and tepid water.

3 Mix vigorously with whisk. Pour in milk and mix again until batter is smooth.

4 Add oil, mix again and pass batter through sieve. Refrigerate 15 minutes.

5 Butter cold crepe pan and place over medium heat. When hot, pour small ladle of batter in pan; cook 1 minute.

6 Turn crepe over and cook 1 more minute. Butter pan for each crepe.

7 Cooked crepes should be thin and light. Refrigerate or freeze until use.

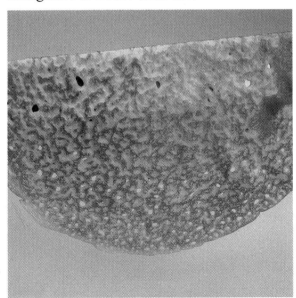

Ingredients

1½ cups	(375 ml) all-purpose flour
¼ tsp	(1 ml) salt
¼ tsp	(1 ml) paprika
3	large eggs
¼ cup	(50 ml) tonic water
2 cups	(500 ml) tepid water
1 cup	(250 ml) milk
3 tbsp	(45 ml) vegetable oil

Deep-Fried Tiger Shrimp *(serves 4)*

20	tiger shrimp, peeled
½ cup	(125 ml) flour
2	beaten eggs mixed with 1 tsp (5 ml) oil
1½ cups	(375 ml) seasoned breadcrumbs
	salt and pepper

Preheat peanut oil in deep-fryer to 350°F (180°C).

After peeling shrimp, slice along backs to open. Remove black vein.

Dredge shrimp with flour. Dip into beaten eggs and coat with breadcrumbs; season well.

Press breadcrumbs with your hands so that they will hold during cooking.

Deep-fry 3 to 4 minutes, depending on size.

Serve with Tartare Sauce, page 479.

1 SERVING	404 CALORIES	37 g CARBOHYDRATE
37 g PROTEIN	12 g FAT	0.2 g FIBER

TECHNIQUE: DEEP-FRIED TIGER SHRIMP

1 After peeling shrimp, slice along backs to open.

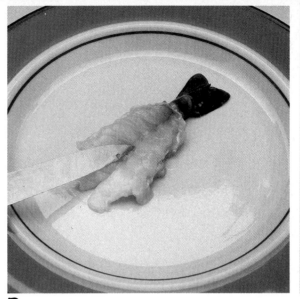

2 Remove black vein.

3 Dredge shrimp with flour.

4 Dip into beaten eggs.

Continued next page.

5 Coat with breadcrumbs and season well.

6 Press breadcrumbs with your hands so that they will hold during cooking.

Herb Mayonnaise

2	egg yolks
1 tsp	(5 ml) strong mustard
1¼ cups	(300 ml) oil
1 tbsp	(15 ml) chopped parsley
1 tsp	(5 ml) chopped chives
1 tsp	(5 ml) finely chopped fresh tarragon
	few drops lemon juice
	Tabasco sauce to taste
	salt and pepper

Mix egg yolks and mustard together in bowl.

Begin adding oil, drop by drop, while mixing with electric hand beater. Keep at low speed.

When mixture starts to thicken, increase flow of oil to stream. Mix at high speed.

When mixture becomes very thick, incorporate some lemon juice along with remaining oil.

Season mayonnaise well and fold in herbs; mix well.

Refrigerate until use.

1 SERVING	108 CALORIES	0 g CARBOHYDRATE
0 g PROTEIN	12 g FAT	0 g FIBER

Deep-Fried Scallops *(serves 4)*

1½ lb	(750 g) fresh scallops
¼ tsp	(1 ml) Tabasco sauce
¼ tsp	(1 ml) Worcestershire sauce
2 tbsp	(30 ml) lemon juice
½ cup	(125 ml) flour
2	beaten eggs mixed with 1 tsp (5 ml) oil
1 cup	(250 ml) breadcrumbs

Preheat peanut oil in deep-fryer to 350°F (180°C).

Place scallops in bowl. Add Tabasco sauce, Worcestershire sauce and lemon juice. Marinate 10 to 15 minutes.

Dredge scallops in flour. Dip in beaten eggs and coat with breadcrumbs.

Deep-fry 3 minutes or until done to taste.

Serve with baked sweet potatoes.

1 SERVING	384 CALORIES	33 g CARBOHYDRATE
36 g PROTEIN	12 g FAT	0.1 g FIBER

Fried Frog Legs   *(serves 4)*

24	frog legs
½ cup	(125 ml) flour
1 tbsp	(15 ml) butter
1 tbsp	(15 ml) vegetable oil
4 tbsp	(60 ml) garlic butter
½	zucchini, diced
¼ lb	(125 g) mushrooms, cleaned and diced
	salt and pepper

Preheat oven to 150°F (70°C).

Prepare frog legs by cutting off feet. Separate legs and wash thoroughly in cold water. Skin legs if not already done.

Make a slit in the flesh of one leg; insert other leg through hole. Legs should look as though they are crossed.

Dredge all frog legs with flour.

Heat butter and oil in large frying pan. When hot, add frog legs and cook 20 to 25 minutes over medium heat. Season well and turn at least 4 times during cooking.

When cooked, remove frog legs and keep hot in oven.

Heat garlic butter in separate frying pan. When hot, add vegetables and cook 4 minutes over medium heat. Season well.

Pour vegetables and garlic butter over frog legs and serve immediately.

1 SERVING	388 CALORIES	13 g CARBOHYDRATE
39 g PROTEIN	20 g FAT	0.5 g FIBER

Shrimp Cocktail *(serves 4)*

⅔ cup	(150 ml) catsup
⅓ cup	(75 ml) chili sauce
1 tbsp	(15 ml) horseradish
½ tsp	(2 ml) lemon juice
24	cooked shrimp, peeled and deveined
	commercial hot sauce to taste
	freshly ground pepper
	lettuce leaves

Place catsup, chili sauce and horseradish in small bowl. Mix thoroughly.

Add lemon juice, hot sauce and pepper; mix again and correct seasoning.

Line serving plates with lettuce leaves and arrange shrimp on top. Serve with sauce.

1 SERVING	157 CALORIES	17 g CARBOHYDRATE
20 g PROTEIN	1 g FAT	0.4 g FIBER

477

Aspic Trout   *(serves 4)*

1	carrot, pared and sliced
1	celery stalk, sliced
½ tsp	(2 ml) fennel seed
½	lemon, sliced
½ cup	(125 ml) dry white wine
4	parsley sprigs
4	trout, cleaned
	salt and pepper
	several blanched leek leaves
	unflavoured gelatine

Prepare gelatine following directions on package. You want about 2 cups (500 ml). Refrigerate until thick but not firm.

Place carrot and celery in roasting pan. Add fennel, lemon, wine and parsley.

Place trout in pan and pour in cold water to cover. Season with salt and pepper. Bring to boil on stove top then immediately remove from heat. Let trout stand in hot liquid 7 to 8 minutes. Remove trout from pan and set aside to cool.

Fit cake grill or rack on large plate. Carefully place trout on top.

Using small knife, remove skin from one side of each trout. Arrange leek leaves, cut into shapes, on each trout.

Using small ladle or spoon, pour some gelatine over trout. Refrigerate trout and gelatine. Repeat procedure every 10 minutes, 3 times. Serve on shredded lettuce and with mayonnaise.

1 SERVING	184 CALORIES	0 g CARBOHYDRATE
37 g PROTEIN	4 g FAT	0 g FIBER

Tartare Sauce

1 cup	(250 ml) mayonnaise
2	pickles, finely chopped
1 tbsp	(15 ml) finely chopped parsley
1 tsp	(5 ml) finely chopped chives
1 tsp	(5 ml) lemon juice
1 tsp	(5 ml) lime juice
	few drops Tabasco sauce
	freshly ground pepper

Place mayonnaise in bowl and add remaining ingredients.

Stir until well mixed and correct seasoning.

Refrigerate until use.

Serve with seafood.

1 SERVING	99 CALORIES	0 g CARBOHYDRATE
0 g PROTEIN	11 g FAT	0 g FIBER

Béarnaise Sauce

2	shallots, very finely chopped
1 tsp	(5 ml) tarragon
2 tbsp	(30 ml) wine vinegar
1 tsp	(5 ml) chopped parsley
3	egg yolks
¾ lb	(375 g) unsalted butter, clarified
	salt and freshly ground pepper

Place shallots, tarragon, vinegar and parsley in stainless steel bowl.

Place bowl on stove top over low heat. Cook until vinegar evaporates. Remove from heat and let cool.

Add egg yolks and mix well with whisk.

Place bowl over saucepan containing hot water. Add clarified butter, drop by drop, mixing constantly with whisk.

When sauce begins to thicken, continue to add butter but in a thin stream. Mix constantly with whisk.

Season sauce well and serve.

1 SERVING	476 CALORIES	1 g CARBOHYDRATE
1 g PROTEIN	52 g FAT	0 g FIBER

Quick Rice Pudding *(serves 4)*

1 cup	(500 ml) cooked rice
½ cup	(125 ml) sugar
¼ tsp	(1 ml) salt
2	large eggs
½ cup	(125 ml) sultana raisins
1 tsp	(5 ml) vanilla
1 tsp	(5 ml) cinnamon
1 tbsp	(15 ml) chopped lemon rind
¼ cup	(50 ml) shredded coconut
1 cup	(250 ml) whipped cream
1	10 oz (284 ml) can mandarin orange segments
2 tbsp	(30 ml) jelly or jam
1 tsp	(5 ml) cornstarch
2 tbsp	(30 ml) cold water

Preheat oven to 350°F (180°C).

Grease round or square mold; set aside.

Place rice, sugar, salt and eggs in bowl; mix together well.

Add raisins, vanilla, cinnamon and lemon rind; mix again.

Stir in coconut and fold in whipped cream. Pour pudding into mold and bake 35 to 40 minutes.

Just before serving, prepare sauce. Place mandarin segments along with juice in saucepan. Add jelly and mix; cook 3 to 4 minutes over medium heat.

Mix cornstarch with water; stir into sauce. Continue cooking 2 minutes over low heat.

Pour sauce over servings of rice pudding.

See Technique next page.

1 SERVING	401 CALORIES	66 g CARBOHYDRATE
5 g PROTEIN	13 g FAT	0.5 g FIBER

TECHNIQUE: QUICK RICE PUDDING

1 Place rice, sugar, salt and eggs in bowl; mix together well.

2 Add raisins, vanilla, cinnamon and lemon rind; mix again.

3 Stir in coconut.

4 Fold in whipped cream. Pour pudding into mold and bake in oven.

Cognac Fruit Pudding *(serves 4)*

3	ripe peaches, peeled and sliced
4	ripe plums, sliced
3 tbsp	(45 ml) sugar
3 tbsp	(45 ml) Courvoisier cognac
3 tbsp	(45 ml) soft butter
⅓ cup	(75 ml) sugar
2	large eggs
1 cup	(250 ml) all-purpose flour
1 tbsp	(15 ml) baking powder
½ cup	(125 ml) milk
2 tbsp	(30 ml) brown sugar

Preheat oven to 350°F (180°C).

Grease 9 in (23 cm) square mold; set aside.

Marinate peaches and plums 15 minutes in 3 tbsp (45 ml) sugar and 2 tbsp (30 ml) cognac.

Cream butter with remaining sugar. Incorporate eggs while mixing with electric hand beater.

Sift flour and baking powder together; incorporate into egg mixture with hand beater.

Beat in milk.

Spread fruit in greased mold. Using spatula, spread custard batter over top.

Bake 30 minutes in oven.

About 10 minutes before pudding is cooked, mix brown sugar with remaining cognac; sprinkle over pudding and resume cooking.

Serve warm.

1 SERVING	434 CALORIES	69 g CARBOHYDRATE
8 g PROTEIN	14 g FAT	0.7 g FIBER

French Bread Treat   *(serves 4)*

3	apples, peeled, cored and sliced
2 tbsp	(30 ml) lime juice
2 tbsp	(30 ml) golden seedless raisins
3 tbsp	(45 ml) slivered almonds
4 tbsp	(60 ml) butter
3 tbsp	(45 ml) raspberry jam
4	slices thick white bread
3	beaten eggs
	maple syrup to taste

Place apples in mixing bowl. Add lime juice, raisins and almonds; toss until combined.

Heat half of butter in nonstick frying pan. When hot, add apples and cook 7 to 8 minutes over medium-high heat. Stir often.

Add jam and mix until apples are evenly coated. Continue cooking 2 minutes over low heat.

Meanwhile dip bread in beaten eggs and heat remaining butter in separate nonstick frying pan.

Add bread to hot butter and cook 2 to 3 minutes on each side over medium-high heat.

Arrange French bread on serving platter, top with sautéed apples and serve with maple syrup.

1 SERVING   432 CALORIES   66 g CARBOHYDRATE
7 g PROTEIN   20 g FAT   1.3 g FIBER

1 Place strawberries, Tia Maria and sugar in saucepan. Cover and cook 8 to 10 minutes over medium heat.

2 Mix cornstarch with water; stir into mixture. Continue cooking 2 minutes.

Strawberry Sauce

4 cups	(1 L) strawberries, washed and hulled
2 tbsp	(30 ml) Tia Maria
½ cup	(125 ml) sugar
1 tbsp	(15 ml) cornstarch
2 tbsp	(30 ml) cold water

Place strawberries, Tia Maria and sugar in saucepan. Cover and cook 8 to 10 minutes over medium heat.

Mix cornstarch with water; stir into mixture. Continue cooking 2 minutes.

Remove saucepan from heat and set aside to cool.

Use as topping for cakes and with other dessert recipes.

Rich Chocolate Sauce

1 cup	(250 ml) icing sugar
2 oz	(60 g) mint flavored chocolate chips
3 tbsp	(45 ml) heavy cream
1 tbsp	(15 ml) unsalted butter

Place sugar, chocolate and cream in top portion of double boiler. Cook until mixture is completely melted; stir constantly.

Remove sauce and cool 1 minute.

Whisk in butter until completely incorporated. Let sauce cool slightly before using.

Basic Pie Dough

3 cups	(750 ml) all-purpose flour
¼ tsp	(1 ml) salt
4 oz	(124 g) shortening
3 oz	(90 g) butter
5 tbsp	(75 ml) very cold water

Place flour, salt, shortening and butter in large bowl. Mix together with pastry blender until texture resembles oatmeal.

Add water and knead dough until well incorporated. If dough is too stiff, add more water.

Form dough into ball, wrap in cloth and refrigerate 2 hours.

Bring dough to room temperature before using. Flour cutting board and cut dough in two. Place one half on board and shape with hands.

Roll out dough and flour as needed.

Turn dough over to roll out other side.

Line pie plate and roll edges with pin. Carefully remove excess dough.

Precook or fill as indicated in the particular recipe.

TECHNIQUE: BASIC PIE DOUGH

1 Place flour, salt, shortening and butter in large bowl.

2 Mix together with pastry blender until texture resembles oatmeal.

3 Add water and knead dough until well incorporated.

4 After dough has been refrigerated for 2 hours, bring to room temperature before using. Cut in two and shape with hands.

Continued next page.

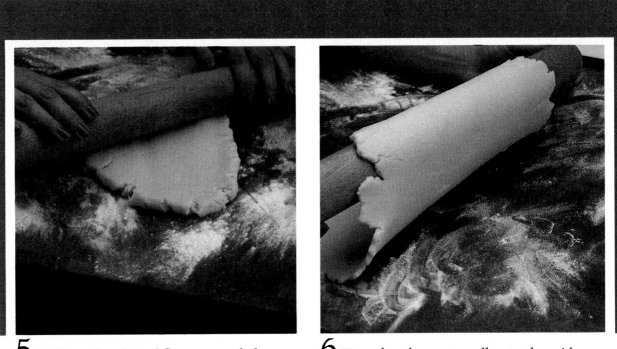

5 Roll out dough and flour as needed.

6 Turn dough over to roll out other side.

7 Line pie plate and roll edges with pin.

8 Carefully remove excess dough.

Apple Pie *(serves 6 to 8)*

5 cups	(1.2 L) cooking apples, peeled, cored and sliced
2 tbsp	(30 ml) lemon juice
½ cup	(125 ml) brown sugar
1 tsp	(5 ml) cinnamon
3 tbsp	(45 ml) flour
¼ tsp	(1 ml) nutmeg
1 tbsp	(15 ml) chopped lemon rind
	basic pie dough*
	eggwash

Preheat oven to 450°F (240°C).

Line 8 in (22 cm) pie plate with dough; set aside with remaining dough.

Place apples in large bowl and sprinkle with lemon juice; toss.

Add brown sugar, cinnamon, flour and nutmeg; mix well.

Add lemon rind; mix again.

Place apples in pie shell and wet edges of dough with water. Cover with upper crust; crimp edges.

Slash dough several times to allow steam to escape and brush with eggwash. If desired, sprinkle top with some granulated sugar.

Place pie on cookie sheet and bake 10 minutes in oven.

Reduce heat to 375°F (190°C) and finish baking 35 to 45 minutes.

Serve with cheese, ice cream or whipped cream.

*See Basic Pie Dough, page 486.

Sweet Peach Tart   *(serves 4 to 6)*

1 lb	(500 g) all-purpose flour
¼ tsp	(1 ml) salt
¼ lb	(125 g) butter
¼ lb	(125 g) shortening
4 to 5 tbsp	(60 to 75 ml) cold water

Sift flour and salt into large mixing bowl.

Add butter and shortening; incorporate with pastry blender. Continue to cut fat into flour until it resembles oatmeal.

Make a well in centre of flour and add water. Knead dough until smooth.

Form dough into ball and cover with clean cloth. Refrigerate 1 hour.

Bring dough to room temperature before using.

1 SERVING	756 CALORIES	89 g CARBOHYDRATE
10 g PROTEIN	40 g FAT	0.3 g FIBER

The filling

1	can sliced peaches, drained (reserve juice)
½ cup	(125 ml) plum jelly
1	beaten egg

Preheat oven to 400°F (200°C).

Line pie plate with dough; prick bottom with fork. Set aside 20 to 30 minutes.

Place sheet of waxed paper on bottom of dough. Add baking weights and precook 15 minutes.

Remove from oven and let cool. Remove waxed paper and baking weights.

Arrange peach slices evenly in bottom of pie shell. Set aside.

Place plum jelly in small saucepan. Add 3 tbsp (45 ml) of reserved peach juice; bring to boil and cook 2 minutes. Pour over peaches.

Brush pie crust with beaten egg. Bake 5 to 6 minutes in oven.

Cool slightly before serving.

Last Minute Blueberry Sauce

1 cup	(250 ml) fresh blueberries, washed
3 tbsp	(45 ml) sugar
1 tbsp	(15 ml) chopped lemon rind
2 tbsp	(30 ml) Lamb's navy rum
1 tsp	(5 ml) cornstarch
2 tbsp	(30 ml) cold water

Place berries, sugar, lemon rind and rum in saucepan. Cover and bring to boil.

Continue cooking 15 minutes over low heat; stir occasionally.

Mix cornstarch with water; stir into sauce. Finish cooking 1 minute over medium heat.

Cool sauce and serve with ice cream, puddings and cakes.

RECIPE	277 CALORIES	66 g CARBOHYDRATE
1 g PROTEIN	1 g FAT	2.1 g FIBER

Sweet Pie Dough

2½ cups	(625 ml) all-purpose flour
¼ cup	(50 ml) fine granulated sugar
1 cup	(250 ml) sweet butter, soft and in pieces
¼ tsp	(1 ml) salt
1	egg
1	egg yolk
2 tbsp	(30 ml) very cold water

Place flour, sugar, butter and salt in large bowl.

Beat whole egg with egg yolk; incorporate into flour. Mix together with pastry blender until texture resembles oatmeal.

Add water and pinch dough to incorporate.

Knead dough several times and form into ball. Wrap in cloth and refrigerate 2 hours.

Bring dough to room temperature before using.

See Technique next page.

RECIPE	2785 CALORIES	188 g CARBOHYDRATE
41 g PROTEIN	209 g FAT	0.5 g FIBER

TECHNIQUE: SWEET PIE DOUGH

1 Place flour, sugar, butter and salt in large bowl.

2 Incorporate beaten eggs into flour.

3 Mix together with pastry blender until texture resembles oatmeal.

4 Add water and pinch dough to incorporate.

Fancy Blueberry Tart *(serves 4 to 6)*

2½ cups	(625 ml) fresh blueberries, washed
¼ cup	(50 ml) Lamb's white rum
3 tbsp	(45 ml) sugar
1 tsp	(5 ml) cornstarch
2 tbsp	(30 ml) cold water
1	recipe chocolate sauce
2 cups	(500 ml) whipped cream
	puff pastry dough
	eggwash, well beaten

Preheat oven to 425°F (220°C).
Roll out dough on floured surface. Using pastry wheel, cut two lines, about 12 in (30 cm) long and about 4 in (10 cm) apart. Place strip of dough on cookie sheet.
Cut two more strips, the same length but only 1 in (2.5 cm) wide.

Brush some water on dough on cookie sheet and attach narrow strips on top to act as sides. Cut two more small strips for the ends and attach. Press all strips with fingers.
Brush dough with eggwash and prick bottom with fork. Cook in oven 16 to 18 minutes. When cooked, set aside to cool.
Meanwhile, marinate blueberries in rum and sugar for 10 minutes. Transfer berries and liquid to saucepan; cook 5 to 6 minutes over medium heat, stirring occasionally.
Mix cornstarch with water; stir into blueberries. Cook 1 minute then set saucepan aside to cool.
Spread layer of chocolate sauce in bottom of pastry shell; follow with layer of whipped cream. Add blueberries.
Top with more whipped cream, decorate with remaining chocolate; slice and serve.

See Technique next page.

1 SERVING   496 CALORIES   66 g CARBOHYDRATE
4 g PROTEIN   24 g FAT   0.9 g FIBER

TECHNIQUE: FANCY BLUEBERRY TART

1 Spread layer of chocolate sauce in bottom of pastry shell.

2 Add layer of whipped cream.

3 Add blueberries.

4 Top with more whipped cream and decorate with remaining chocolate sauce.

Individual Strawberry Tarts   *(serves 4 to 6)*

2 cups	(500 ml) all-purpose flour
½ cup	(125 ml) shortening
¾ cup	(75 ml) soft butter
1	egg
4 tbsp	(60 ml) cold water
1	recipe chocolate sauce*
	whipped cream
	ripe strawberries, hulled and cut in two
	pinch salt

Preheat oven to 400°F (200°C).

Sift flour and salt together into bowl. Add shortening and butter. Incorporate using pastry blender until mixture resembles oatmeal.

In separate bowl, beat egg and water together with fork.

Make well in middle of flour mixture and pour in liquid. Mix well until completely blended. Cover with cloth and refrigerate 1 hour.

Roll out dough on floured surface and line individual tart molds. Prick dough with fork and set aside 20 minutes.

Cook shells 15 minutes in oven.

Once shells have cooled, place about 1 tbsp (15 ml) chocolate sauce in bottom. Add some whipped cream and top with strawberries. Serve.

*See Chocolate Strawberry Treats, page 547.

See Technique next page.

1 SERVING	792 CALORIES	66 g CARBOHYDRATE
6 g PROTEIN	56 g FAT	0.4 g FIBER

1 After tart shells have been cooked and have cooled, place about 1 tbsp (15 ml) chocolate sauce in bottom.

2 Add some whipped cream and top with strawberries.

Cherry Pudding *(serves 4)*

1½ cups	(375 ml) milk
⅔ cup	(150 ml) graham crumbs
1 cup	(250 ml) cherries, pitted
¼ cup	(50 ml) sugar
1 tbsp	(15 ml) vanilla
1 tsp	(5 ml) white rum
2 tbsp	(30 ml) chopped lemon rind
3	medium-size eggs, beaten

Preheat oven to 350°F (180°C).

Grease and flour 8 in (20 cm) pie plate; set aside.

Heat milk and pour into bowl; incorporate graham crumbs. Cool 15 minutes.

Mix cherries, sugar, vanilla, rum and lemon rind with beaten eggs. Be sure mixture is well blended.

Incorporate cherry mixture to cooled milk; stir well.

Pour batter into pie plate. Bake 40 to 50 minutes.

Serve pudding warm with ice cream.

1 SERVING	339 CALORIES	49 g CARBOHYDRATE
11 g PROTEIN	11 g FAT	0.7 g FIBER

Individual Cherry Tarts *(serves 4)*

1 lb	(500 g) fresh cherries, pitted
3 tbsp	(45 ml) sugar
3 tbsp	(45 ml) water
¼ tsp	(1 ml) lemon juice
1 tsp	(5 ml) Tia Maria
½ tsp	(2 ml) cornstarch
2 tbsp	(30 ml) cold water
4	cooked tart shells
	whipped cream, optional

Place cherries, sugar, 3 tbsp (45 ml) water, lemon juice and Tia Maria in saucepan; bring to boil.

Mix well and continue cooking 2 minutes over medium heat.

Mix cornstarch with water; stir into cherries. Cook 1 more minute then set aside to cool.

Fill tart shells with cherry mixture and garnish with whipped cream.

Serve.

Individual Blueberry Tarts   *(serves 4)*

4	cooked tart shells
1 cup	(250 ml) blueberries, washed
2 tbsp	(30 ml) sugar
1 tsp	(5 ml) chopped lemon rind
1 tsp	(5 ml) cornstarch
4 tbsp	(60 ml) water
	pastry cream of your choice
	whipped cream for topping

Place tart shells on serving platter and set aside.

Cook blueberries, sugar, lemon rind and 2 tbsp (30 ml) water in saucepan. Mix ingredients well and cover; cook 5 to 6 minutes over medium heat; stir occasionally.

Mix cornstarch with 2 tbsp (30 ml) water; stir into blueberries. Continue cooking 1 to 2 minutes.

Remove pan from heat and set aside to cool.

Spoon some pastry cream in bottom of tart shells. Add blueberries and top with whipped cream.

Serve.

1 SERVING   491 CALORIES   47 g CARBOHYDRATE
6 g PROTEIN   31 g FAT   0.5 g FIBER

Individual Peach Tarts   *(serves 4)*

4	cooked tart shells
3	ripe peaches, peeled and sliced
3 tbsp	(45 ml) jelly or jam
1 tbsp	(15 ml) water
	pastry cream of your choice

Arrange tart shells on serving platter and fill with pastry cream.

Set sliced peaches decoratively on top; set aside.

Place jelly and water in small saucepan; bring to boil. Cook 1 minute and mix well.

When mixture has cooled, brush over peaches.

Refrigerate tarts 30 minutes before serving.

Tia Maria Caramel Custard   *(serves 4)*

½ cup	(125 ml) sugar
2 tbsp	(30 ml) water
4	large eggs
1	large egg yolk
2 cups	(500 ml) milk
3 tbsp	(45 ml) Tia Maria
⅓ cup	(75 ml) sugar
1 tsp	(5 ml) vanilla

Preheat oven to 350°F (180°C).

Place ½ cup (125 ml) sugar and water in small saucepan; cook over medium heat. Do not stir and keep mixture bubbling.

When sugar caramelizes (it will turn golden brown) and before its burns, remove saucepan from heat. Immediately plunge pan in bowl of cold water.

Replace pan on stove top and pour in ½ cup (125 ml) water; cook until melted and stir constantly!

Quickly pour caramel into custard dishes; it should coat bottom and part of sides.

Set custard dishes aside.

Break whole eggs and egg yolk into large bowl; set aside.

Place milk, Tia Maria, sugar and vanilla in saucepan. Bring to boiling point; mix occasionally.

Pour liquid over eggs; incorporate very well.

Pour mixture into custard dishes; place in roasting pan with about 1 in (2.5 cm) warm water. Bake 50 to 60 minutes in oven.

When custard is cooked, remove from oven and let cool. To serve, run knife around inside of dish; place plate against dish and unmold caramel custard upside-down.

TECHNIQUE:TIA MARIA CARAMEL CUSTARD

1 Place sugar and water in small saucepan.
Cook over medium heat and keep mixture bubbling; do not stir.

2 When sugar caramelizes, plunge pan in cold water.

3 Replace pan on stove top and pour in ½ cup (125 ml) water.

4 Cook until melted and stir constantly.

Continued next page.

5 Pour caramel into custard dishes.

6 Break all eggs into bowl.

7 Pour hot milk mixture over eggs; incorporate very well.

8 Pour into custard dishes and set in roasting pan with water.

Orange Rind Sauce for Caramel Custard

2 tbsp	(30 ml) sugar
2 tbsp	(30 ml) Lamb's light rum
½ cup	(125 ml) orange juice
½ tsp	(2 ml) cornstarch
2 tbsp	(30 ml) cold water
	grated rind of 1½ oranges
	grated rind of ½ lemon

Place sugar, rum, orange juice, orange and lemon rind in saucepan. Cover and cook 4 to 5 minutes over medium heat.

Mix cornstarch with water; stir into sauce. Continue cooking 1 to 2 minutes and mix very well.

Pour sauce over caramel custards and serve.

Toasted Almond Cream

1 cup	(250 ml) icing sugar
½ cup	(125 ml) slivered almonds
1	recipe Rum Pastry Cream

Place sugar and almonds in saucepan. Cook mixture over medium heat to brown; stir frequently.

When browned, transfer mixture to oiled roasting pan or cookie sheet; set aside to cool.

Place almonds in food processor and grind until smooth.

Now, fold into rum pastry cream.

For variation of this recipe, do not grind almonds and serve over ice cream or as a candy treat.

Rum Pastry Cream

6	egg yolks
⅔ cup	(150 ml) sugar
1 tsp	(5 ml) pure vanilla extract
2 tbsp	(30 ml) Lamb's light rum
½ cup	(125 ml) all-purpose flour
2 cups	(500 ml) milk
1 tbsp	(15 ml) butter

Place egg yolks and sugar in large bowl. Mix together with electric hand beater until thick. Add vanilla and rum; mix until incorporated. Add flour and mix again until incorporated. Pour milk into large, heavy saucepan. Bring to boiling point.
Remove saucepan from stove and pour half of milk into bowl containing egg mixture. Again use electric beater and mix until combined. Replace saucepan on stove top and bring remaining milk to boiling point. Very slowly add mixture in bowl to hot milk; whisk constantly!
Continue cooking and whisking cream until very thick. Do not allow a full boil.
When sauce becomes very thick, remove from heat. Immediately transfer to clean bowl. Stir in butter and whisk until completely dissolved. Set cream aside to cool, then cover with wax paper. Be sure that the paper touches surface. Refrigerate cream until use.

TECHNIQUE : RUM PASTRY CREAM

1 Place egg yolks and sugar in large bowl.

2 Mix together with electric hand beater until thick.
Add vanilla and rum; mix again.

3 Add flour and mix again until incorporated.

4 Pour half of hot milk into bowl. Again use electric beater and mix until combined.

Blueberries in Cream *(serves 4)*

1 cup	(250 ml) heavy cream
1 tsp	(5 ml) vanilla
2 tbsp	(30 ml) icing sugar
2 cups	(500 ml) blueberries, washed and drained
3 tbsp	(45 ml) brown sugar
2 tbsp	(30 ml) Lamb's light rum
	strawberries for decoration

Beat cream and vanilla together until firm.

Incorporate icing sugar and beat 30 seconds; set aside in refrigerator.

Place blueberries, brown sugar and rum in attractive bowl; toss. Let stand 7 to 8 minutes.

Incorporate whipped cream into blueberries by folding gently. Serve on dishes and decorate with strawberries.

1 SERVING	345 CALORIES	28 g CARBOHYDRATE
2 g PROTEIN	23 g FAT	1.1 g FIBER

Custard Cream

4	large egg yolks
½ cup	(125 ml) sugar
1¼ cups	(300 ml) hot milk
1 tsp	(5 ml) Lamb's navy rum
¼ tsp	(1 ml) cinnamon
2 tbsp	(30 ml) heavy cream

Beat egg yolks and sugar together until creamy.

Incorporate half of hot milk; whisk constantly.

Place remaining milk in saucepan. Add egg mixture, cinnamon and rum. Cook over medium heat while whisking constantly until it thickens.

Place heavy cream in bowl and incorporate cooked custard cream; whisk constantly. The cream should be thick enough to coat spoon.

Let cool then cover with wax paper. Refrigerate until use.

RECIPE	978 CALORIES	128 g CARBOHYDRATE
22 g PROTEIN	42 g FAT	0 g FIBER

TECHNIQUE: CUSTARD CREAM

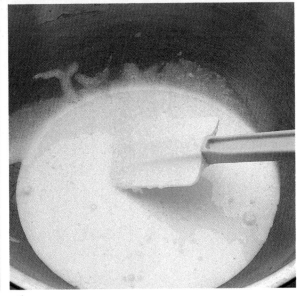

1 Beat egg yolks and sugar together until creamy.

2 Incorporate half of hot milk; whisk constantly.

3 Pour mixture along with cinnamon and rum into saucepan containing remaining hot milk. Cook over medium heat while whisking constantly until it thickens.

4 Place heavy cream in bowl and incorporate cooked custard cream. It should be thick enough to coat spoon. Be sure to whisk while incorporating.

Caramel-Coated Cream Puffs   *(serves 4 to 6)*

½ cup	(125 ml) sugar
2 tbsp	(30 ml) water
1	recipe cream puff dough*
1	recipe rum pastry cream**
1 cup	(250 ml) heavy cream, whipped

Place sugar and water in small saucepan; cook over medium heat. Do not stir and keep mixture bubbling.

When sugar caramelizes (it will turn golden brown) and before it burns, remove saucepan from heat. Immediately plunge pan in bowl filled with cold water.

Replace saucepan on stove top and pour in ½ cup (125 ml) water; cook until melted and stir constantly! Dip tops of cream puffs into caramel and set aside on tray.

Mix half of pastry cream with whipped cream. Reserve remaining pastry cream for other uses.

Spoon mixed creams into pastry bag fitted with star nozzle. Press nozzle into bottom of cream puffs and force mixture inside. Serve.

* See Cheese Cream Puffs, page 509.
** See Rum Pastry Cream, page 504.

1 SERVING	654 CALORIES	65 g CARBOHYDRATE
13 g PROTEIN	338 g FAT	0.1 g FIBER

Cheese Cream Puffs *(serves 4)*

1 cup	(250 ml) water
4 tbsp	(60 ml) sweet butter, cut into small pieces
¼ tsp	(1 ml) salt
1 cup	(250 ml) all-purpose flour
4	large eggs

Preheat oven to 375°F (190°C).
Butter and lightly flour two cookie sheets.

Place water, butter and salt in saucepan; bring to boil. When butter is completely melted, remove saucepan from heat. Add all flour and mix rapidly with wooden spoon.

Replace saucepan over low heat. Dry dough 5 to 6 minutes, stirring constantly with wooden spoon. (The dough should not adhere to your fingers when pinched.)

Transfer dough to bowl and let cool 6 to 7 minutes. Add eggs, one at a time, mixing well between additions. The dough *must* recover its original texture before next egg is added!

Spoon dough into pastry bag fitted with plain tip. Squeeze out walnut-size pieces onto cookie sheets. Brush tops with beaten egg. Using fork, gently smooth tails; set aside 20 minutes.

Cook 35 minutes in oven. Turn off oven heat; set door ajar. Let dry 1 hour before using.

1 SERVING	670 CALORIES	29 g CARBOHYDRATE
17 g PROTEIN	54 g FAT	0.1 g FIBER

Cheese Cream Puff Filling

¾ lb	(375 g) goat cheese
2 tbsp	(30 ml) sour cream
1 tbsp	(15 ml) honey
	several drops Worcestershire sauce
	several drops Tabasco sauce

Place ingredients in mixer or blender; incorporate well.

Spoon mixture into pastry bag fitted with star nozzle and fill cream puffs.

If desired, brush with melted honey before serving.

1 SERVING	670 CALORIES	29 g CARBOHYDRATE
17 g PROTEIN	54 g FAT	0.1 g FIBER

Tia Maria Cream Puffs   *(serves 4 to 6)*

1½ cups	(375 ml) 35% cream, cold
1 tsp	(5 ml) vanilla
2 tsp	(10 ml) Tia Maria
¼ cup	(50 ml) icing sugar
1	recipe cream puff dough*
1 tbsp	(15 ml) sweet cocoa mixed with some icing sugar

Pour cream into mixing bowl; add vanilla and Tia Maria. Whip cream with electric hand mixer until it peaks.

Incorporate icing sugar and continue beating 30 seconds.

Spoon cream into pastry bag fitted with star nozzle. Fill cream puffs.

Sprinkle cocoa mixture over cream puffs and serve.

* See Cheese Cream Puffs, page 509.

1 SERVING	443 CALORIES	24 g CARBOHYDRATE
8 g PROTEIN	35 g FAT	0.1 g FIBER

Tia Maria Chocolate Cream Puffs   *(serves 4)*

6	egg yolks
⅔ cup	(150 ml) sugar
1 tsp	(5 ml) vanilla
2 tbsp	(30 ml) Tia Maria
½ cup	(125 ml) all-purpose flour
2 cups	(500 ml) milk
1 tbsp	(15 ml) butter
1	recipe chocolate sauce*
½ cup	(125 ml) sugar
2 tbsp	(30 ml) water
8	cream puffs

Mix egg yolks and ⅔ cup (150 ml) sugar with electric hand beater. When thick, add vanilla and Tia Maria; mix again.

Mix in flour until well incorporated.

Pour milk into large, heavy saucepan; bring to boiling point. Remove from stove and pour half in bowl containing egg mixture. Mix until combined.

Replace pan on burner; bring rest of milk to boiling point. Very slowly add egg mixture; whisk constantly! Cook and whisk until cream is very thick; do not boil.

Remove from heat and pour into clean bowl. Whisk in butter until completely dissolved, then let cool.

Fold in chocolate sauce and set cream aside.

Place ½ cup (125 ml) sugar and water in saucepan; cook over medium heat. Do not stir and keep mixture bubbling.

When sugar turns golden brown and before it burns, plunge saucepan into bowl filled with cold water. Remove and set aside.

Spoon chocolate cream into pastry bag fitted with star nozzle. Stuff cream puffs from bottom and arrange on plates.

Replace saucepan of caramel on stove top. Pour in ½ cup (125 ml) water; cook until melted, stirring constantly! Pour caramel in thin stream over cream puffs and serve.

* See Chocolate Strawberry Treats, page 547.

1 SERVING	944 CALORIES	140 g CARBOHYDRATE
15 g PROTEIN	36 g FAT	0.1 g FIBER

Blueberry Sandwich *(serves 4)*

2 cups	(500 ml) blueberries, washed
3 tbsp	(45 ml) Lamb's navy rum
5 tbsp	(75 ml) sugar
1½ cups	(375 ml) whipped cream
	puff pastry dough
	eggwash, well beaten

Preheat oven to 425°F (220°C).

Roll out dough on floured surface. Cut 8 small circles and place them on cookie sheet. Brush with eggwash and prick with fork; cook about 15 minutes in oven.

Remove pastry circles and set aside to cool.

Meanwhile, place blueberries, rum and 2 tbsp (30 ml) sugar in bowl; marinate 15 to 20 minutes.

Drain berries and reserve marinade.

Transfer berries to another bowl and fold in whipped cream.

To prepare sandwiches, place circle of pastry on serving plate. Add berry mixture and cover with another circle of pastry.

Heat marinade in small saucepan with remaining sugar. Cook until light caramel in color.

Pour syrup over sandwiches and serve.

Chocolate Pears (serves 4)

4	pears, peeled
2 tbsp	(30 ml) lemon juice
2 oz	(60 g) semi-sweet chocolate
1 cup	(250 ml) icing sugar
2 tbsp	(30 ml) heavy cream
1 tbsp	(15 ml) white rum
	slivered almonds

Core pears and place on plate; sprinkle with lemon juice and refrigerate until serving.

Place chocolate, sugar, cream and rum in top portion of double boiler. Heat over medium-low heat to melt; stir constantly.

When sauce has thickened, remove and let cool.

Spoon chocolate over pears and if desired, sprinkle with slivered almonds.

Refrigerate until chocolate has set, then serve.

See Technique next page.

1 SERVING	431 CALORIES	90 g CARBOHYDRATE
2 g PROTEIN	7 g FAT	1.2 g FIBER

1 Core pears and place on plate.

2 Sprinkle with lemon juice and refrigerate until using.

3 Place chocolate, sugar, cream and rum in top portion of double boiler. Heat over medium-low to melt; stir constantly.

4 Spoon thickened chocolate over pears and refrigerate.

Floating Island   *(serves 4 to 6)*

4	egg yolks
¾ cup	(175 ml) sugar
1 cup	(250 ml) hot milk
1 tsp	(5 ml) vanilla
2 tbsp	(30 ml) Tia Maria
4	egg whites

Place egg yolks in bowl; add ¼ cup (50 ml) sugar and mix 2 minutes with electric hand beater. Incorporate milk and add vanilla and Tia Maria; mix well.

Place bowl over saucepan of hot water. Cook sauce until it thickens enough to coat the back of a spoon. Stir constantly!

Remove bowl and set sauce aside to cool.

Place egg whites in stainless steel bowl; beat with electric hand beater until stiff.

Add ¼ cup (50 ml) sugar; beat 30 seconds. Incorporate remaining sugar with spatula.

Fill large pan with water and heat until simmering. Using ice cream scoop, place small quantities of beaten egg whites in water.

Poach 1 to 1½ minutes each side. Use slotted spoon to remove and drain on paper towel.

When ready to serve, pour sauce in small plates and top with poached egg whites.

If desired, decorate with caramel.

See Technique next page.

1 SERVING	186 CALORIES	28 g CARBOHYDRATE
5 g PROTEIN	6 g FAT	0 g FIBER

TECHNIQUE: FLOATING ISLAND

1 Place egg yolks in bowl. Add ¼ cup (50 ml) sugar.

2 Mix 2 minutes with electric hand beater.

3 Incorporate milk and add vanilla and Tia Maria; mix well. Cook sauce.

4 Beat egg whites with electric hand beater until stiff. Add sugar.

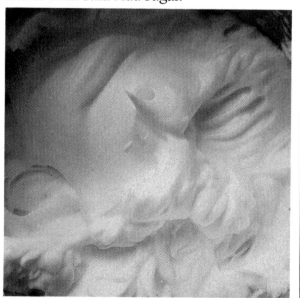

5 Using ice cream scoop, place small quantities of beaten egg whites in simmering water. Poach 1 to 1½ minutes each side.

6 Use slotted spoon to remove and drain on paper towel.

Meringues

6	egg whites, room temperature
1 cup	(250 ml) super fine sugar
½ tsp	(2 ml) Tia Maria
	pinch salt
	whipped cream

Preheat oven to 175°F (80°C).

Butter and flour cookie sheets; set aside. Beat egg whites until foamy. Add Tia Maria; continue beating until stiff.

Slowly incorporate ¾ cup (175 ml) sugar and salt. Beat at high speed about 1½ minutes. Add all remaining sugar; beat 30 seconds more.

Spoon meringue paste into pastry bag fitted with plain nozzle. Form various shapes and sizes on cookie sheets.

Bake 3 hours in oven.

Open oven door and set ajar; let meringues stand 5 to 10 minutes before removing.

When meringues have cooled, spoon whipped cream into pastry bag fitted with plain nozzle.

Crush bottom of one meringue; squeeze layer of whipped cream in indentation. Take another meringue and press the two together. If they do not hold, add whipped cream.

For a special treat, dip meringues in chocolate.

Rhubarb Cake   *(serves 6)*

1½ cups	(375 ml) all-purpose flour
1½ tbsp	(25 ml) baking powder
½ tsp	(2 ml) baking soda
1 tbsp	(15 ml) cinnamon
1 cup	(250 ml) vegetable oil
1½ cups	(375 ml) sugar
3	extra large eggs
1 cup	(250 ml) stewed rhubarb
½ cup	(125 ml) chopped walnuts
	pinch salt

Preheat oven to 350°F (180°C).

Butter and flour 8 in (20 cm) springform cake pan. Set aside.

Sift flour, baking powder, soda, cinnamon and salt into large bowl. Set aside.

Pour oil into second large bowl. Add sugar and cream together with electric beater.

Add eggs, one at a time, mixing 1 minute between additions.

Stir flour into oil mixture with spatula.

Add rhubarb and walnuts; incorporate well.

Pour batter into cake pan. Bake 1½ hours on middle rack of oven.

When cake is cooked*, remove from oven and let cool. Unmold and if desired spread with icing.

* The easiest way to check if cake is cooked is to prick the centre with a toothpick. If when removed the toothpick is clean, cake is done.

1 SERVING	764 CALORIES	74 g CARBOHYDRATE
9 g PROTEIN	48 g FAT	0.6 g FIBER

Banana Loaf *(serves 6 to 8)*

¾ cup	(175 ml) brown sugar
¼ cup	(50 ml) granulated sugar
½ cup	(125 ml) soft butter
4	small bananas, puréed
¼ cup	(50 ml) heavy cream
1 tsp	(5 ml) vanilla
2	extra-large eggs
2 cups	(500 ml) all-purpose flour
1 tsp	(5 ml) baking soda
½ tsp	(2 ml) cinnamon
½ tsp	(2 ml) salt
½ cup	(125 ml) chopped walnuts
½ cup	(125 ml) sultana raisins

Preheat oven to 350°F (180°C).

Grease 9 × 5 in (23 × 13 cm) loaf pan; set aside.

Place brown and granulated sugars in large bowl; mix together.

Add butter and mix until well combined.

Incorporate bananas, cream and vanilla with spatula.

Incorporate eggs, one at a time, beating well between additions.

Sift flour, baking soda, cinnamon and salt into second bowl. Mix into egg mixture using beater or blender.

Fold in walnuts and raisins. Pour batter into loaf pan and bake 65 to 70 minutes or until wooden pick inserted in centre of cake emerges clean.

Cool before serving.

TECHNIQUE: BANANA LOAF

1 Place brown and granulated sugars in large bowl; mix together.

2 Add butter.

3 Cream together.

4 Incorporate bananas, cream and vanilla with spatula.

Continued next page.

5 Incorporate eggs, one at a time, beating well between additions.

6 Sift flour, baking soda, cinnamon and salt into second bowl.

7 Mix flour into egg mixture, using beater or blender.

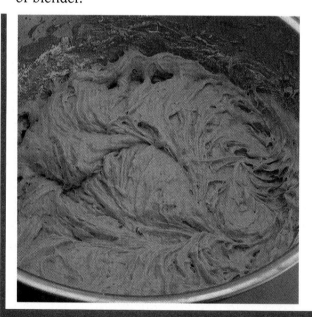

8 Fold in walnuts and raisins.

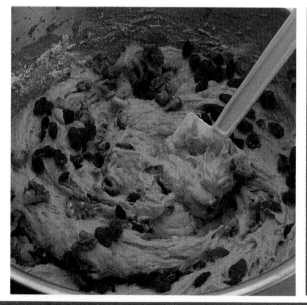

Carrot Coconut Cake *(serves 6 to 8)*

1¼ cups	(300 ml) vegetable oil
2 cups	(500 ml) granulated sugar
4	extra-large eggs
2¼ cups	(550 ml) all-purpose flour
2 tsp	(10 ml) baking powder
1 tsp	(5 ml) cinnamon
¼ tsp	(1 ml) nutmeg
1 tsp	(5 ml) baking soda
1 tsp	(5 ml) salt
3 tbsp	(45 ml) white rum
½ cup	(125 ml) shredded coconut
2 cups	(500 ml) grated carrots

Preheat oven to 350°F (180°C).

Grease and flour 10 in (25 cm) springform cake pan; set aside.

Place oil and sugar in bowl; mix together well.

Add two eggs, beating well between additions.

Sift all dry ingredients together. Beat half into wet batter.

Add remaining two eggs, beating well between additions.

Incorporate remaining dry ingredients until well blended. Fold in rum and coconut.

Fold in carrots and pour batter into mold. Bake 60 to 70 minutes or until wooden pick inserted in centre of cake emerges clean.

Cool before serving and if desired, ice.

See Technique next page.

1 Place oil and sugar in bowl.

2 Mix together well.

3 Add two eggs, beating well between additions.

4 Sift all dry ingredients together.

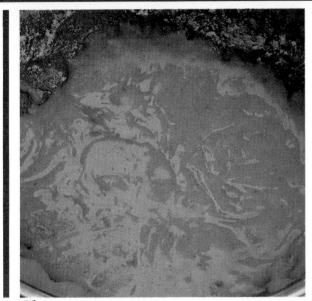

5 Beat half into wet batter.

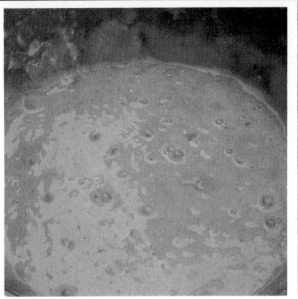

6 Add remaining two eggs, beating well between additions.

7 Incorporate remaining dry ingredients until well blended. Fold in rum and coconut.

8 Fold in carrots.

Apple Cake *(serves 6 to 8)*

1 cup	(250 ml) vegetable oil
1 cup	(250 ml) brown sugar
1 cup	(250 ml) granulated sugar
3	extra-large eggs
2½ cups	(625 ml) all-purpose flour
2 tsp	(10 ml) baking powder
1 tsp	(5 ml) baking soda
1 tsp	(5 ml) salt
1 tsp	(5 ml) cinnamon
3 tbsp	(45 ml) Tia Maria
3½ cups	(875 ml) chopped cooking apples
½ cup	(125 ml) chopped walnuts

Preheat oven to 325°F (160°C).

Grease and flour 10 in (25 cm) springform cake pan; set aside.

Put oil, brown and granulated sugars in bowl; mix with electric hand beater 2 to 3 seconds.

Incorporate eggs, one at a time, beating well between additions.

Sift flour, baking powder, baking soda, salt and cinnamon into separate bowl. Incorporate into egg mixture until well blended.

Fold in Tia Maria, apples and walnuts with spatula. Pour batter into mold and bake 1½ hours or until wooden pick inserted in centre of cake emerges clean.

1 SERVING	721 CALORIES	89 g CARBOHYDRATE
8 g PROTEIN	37 g FAT	1.2 g FIBER

Exotic Fruit Salad *(serves 4 to 6)*

2	green apples, sliced
1	orange, peeled and sliced in rings
2	peaches, peeled and sliced
½ cup	(125 ml) seedless green grapes
4	plums, sliced
1	mango, peeled and sliced
¼	Santa Claus melon, in small slices*
¼	Casaba melon, in small slices*
3 tbsp	(45 ml) sugar
¼ cup	(50 ml) white rum

Place fruit in large bowl. Sprinkle in sugar and rum; toss well.

Marinate 30 minutes before serving.

*If these exotic melons are not available, by all means substitute any melon that is.

Fruit Salad with Yogurt *(serves 4)*

2	bananas, peeled and sliced
2	apples, sliced with skin
3	oranges, peeled and sectioned
1	grapefruit, peeled and sectioned
¼ cup	(50 ml) chopped walnuts
3 tbsp	(45 ml) honey
4 tbsp	(60 ml) plain yogurt

Place fruit in serving bowl and toss.

Add walnuts and honey; toss again. Marinate 10 minutes.

Before serving top with yogurt.

1 SERVING	278 CALORIES	53 g CARBOHYDRATE
3 g PROTEIN	6 g FAT	2.0 g FIBER

Elegant Fruit Salad *(serves 4)*

1	mango, peeled and thinly sliced
2 cups	(500 ml) raspberries, washed
6	apricots, washed and thinly sliced
2 tbsp	(30 ml) sugar
2 tbsp	(30 ml) Lamb's navy rum
	juice 1 orange
	whipped cream

Place fruit in bowl and sprinkle in sugar; toss.

Add orange juice and rum; toss gently and marinate 15 minutes.

Serve with whipped cream.

1 Cut papayas in half as shown, then remove seeds.

2 Follow recipe and before serving decorate with whipped cream.

Delicious Papaya *(serves 4)*

2	ripe papayas
½ cup	(125 ml) orange juice
2 tbsp	(30 ml) brown sugar
1	small envelope unflavoured gelatine
	whipped cream for decoration

Cut papayas in half and remove seeds.

Remove most of flesh leaving border around shell. Place flesh in food processor or blender; set shells aside.

Blend flesh 1 minute; set aside.

Pour orange juice into small saucepan. Add brown sugar and bring to boil.

Sprinkle in gelatine and mix well. Remove saucepan from heat.

Mix puréed papaya flesh with orange juice; incorporate well.

Pour mixture into papaya shells and refrigerate 6 to 8 hours.

Decorate with whipped cream just before serving.

1 SERVING	118 CALORIES	24 g CARBOHYDRATE
1 g PROTEIN	2 g FAT	1.4 g FIBER

Cognac Cherry Dessert *(serves 4)*

2 tbsp	(30 ml) butter
2 tbsp	(30 ml) sugar
3 tbsp	(45 ml) cognac
2 lb	(900 g) cherries, washed and pitted
1 tsp	(5 ml) cornstarch
2 tbsp	(30 ml) cold water
	juice of 2 oranges
	vanilla ice cream

Heat butter and sugar together in frying pan. Continue cooking until golden brown; stir constantly.

Pour in orange juice; mix well and continue cooking 3 minutes over medium heat.

Add cognac and flambé.

Mix in cherries and cook 1 more minute.

Mix cornstarch with water; stir into sauce. Cook 1 minute to thicken.

Spoon over ice cream and serve.

Plums in Syrup *(serves 4)*

2 tbsp	(30 ml) butter
2 tbsp	(30 ml) sugar
½ cup	(125 ml) orange juice
8	plums, washed and pitted
3 tbsp	(45 ml) cognac
1 tsp	(5 ml) cornstarch
2 tbsp	(30 ml) cold water
	whipped cream
	blanched orange rind

Place butter and sugar in frying pan; cook over medium heat to thicken. Stir with fork.

Add orange juice and cook 2 to 3 minutes; stir constantly.

Place plums in sauce; cover and cook 4 to 5 minutes over medium-low heat.

Pour in cognac and mix well; continue cooking 2 minutes over medium-high heat.

Mix cornstarch with water; stir into sauce. Cook 1 to 2 minutes over medium heat.

Serve plums in syrup with whipped cream. Decorate with orange rind.

TECHNIQUE: PLUMS IN SYRUP

1 Place butter and sugar in frying pan; cook over medium heat to thicken. Stir with fork.

2 Add orange juice and cook 2 to 3 minutes; stir constantly.

3 Place plums in sauce; cover and cook 4 to 5 minutes over medium-low heat.

4 Pour in cognac, mix well and cook 2 minutes over medium-high heat. Thicken sauce with cornstarch.

Banana Flambé *(serves 4)*

4	bananas (not too ripe), peeled and cut in 1 in (2.5 cm) slices
2 tbsp	(30 ml) brown sugar
2 tbsp	(30 ml) cognac
2 tbsp	(30 ml) butter
2 tbsp	(30 ml) granulated sugar
2 tbsp	(30 ml) Tia Maria
	juice 1 lemon
	juice 2 oranges
	rind 1 lemon, thinly sliced
	whipped cream to taste
	dash cinnamon

Place bananas, brown sugar, cognac and lemon juice in bowl; marinate 15 minutes.

Meanwhile, heat butter and granulated sugar together. Cook until mixture caramelizes.

When mixture is golden brown, pour in orange juice and mix very well. Continue cooking 2 to 3 minutes over medium heat; stir constantly.

Add bananas along with marinade to orange mixture. Mix in lemon rind and cook 1 minute.

Pour in Tia Maria and flambé. Continue cooking 1 minute over high heat.

Garnish servings of banana flambé with whipped cream and cinnamon.

Crepes Suzettes   *(serves 4)*

8	sugar cubes
2	large oranges
1	lemon
2 tbsp	(30 ml) butter
12	crepes, folded in four
¼ cup	(50 ml) cognac
	rind 1 orange, in julienne

Rub the sugar cubes over the skin of whole oranges and lemon.

Place sugar in frying pan and melt over medium heat; stir with fork. Continue cooking 1 to 2 minutes.

Mix in butter and continue cooking 1 minute; stir constantly.

Cut oranges and lemon in half; add juice to frying pan. Mix and cook 3 to 4 minutes over medium heat; stir constantly.

Place crepes in frying pan. Cook 1 minute in sauce then turn crepes over.

Pour in cognac and add orange rind; bring to boil and flambé.

Remove crepes from pan and place on serving platter; set aside.

Continue cooking sauce 2 minutes over high heat.

Pour over crepes and serve immediately.

1 SERVING	275 CALORIES	35 g CARBOHYDRATE
9 g PROTEIN	11 g FAT	0 g FIBER

Crepes and Berries *(serves 4)*

1½ cups	(375 ml) fresh raspberries, washed
¼ cup	(50 ml) brown sugar
¼ cup	(50 ml) Tia Maria
1½ cups	(375 ml) heavy cream, whipped
8	crepes

Place most of raspberries (reserve some for decoration) in large bowl. Add sugar and Tia Maria; marinate about 15 to 20 minutes.

Incorporate half of whipped cream into marinated raspberries. Spread over flat crepes and roll.

Decorate stuffed crepes with remaining berries and whipped cream. Serve.

1 SERVING   505 CALORIES   39 g CARBOHYDRATE
9 g PROTEIN   34 g FAT   1.4 g FIBER

Cold Soufflé Dessert *(serves 4 to 6)*

5	large eggs, separated
¾ cup	(175 ml) sugar
¾ cup	(175 ml) chopped walnuts
3 tbsp	(45 ml) Tia Maria
2 cups	(500 ml) heavy cream, whipped
2 tbsp	(30 ml) slivered almonds

Choose 8 in (20 cm) soufflé dish that is 3 in (8 cm) deep. Butter and dust with sugar; set aside.

Place egg yolks and sugar in bowl; mix 3 to 4 minutes with electric beater.

Add walnuts and Tia Maria; incorporate with spatula.

Add whipped cream; fold in with spatula about 1 to 2 minutes or until well incorporated.

Beat egg whites until they peak; stir into batter.

Form a collar from double sheet of foil; it should be about 3 in (8 cm) high. Tape collar around inside of soufflé dish at the top.

Pour batter in and sprinkle with almonds. Refrigerate 8 hours. Remove collar before serving.

Sponge Cake   *(serves 6 to 8)*

6	extra-large eggs
¾ cup	(175 ml) fine sugar
1 cup	(250 ml) all-purpose flour
4 tbsp	(60 ml) clarified butter
	Tia Maria
	frosting of your choice

Preheat oven to 350°F (180°C).

Butter and flour 9 in (23 cm) springform cake pan; set aside.

Place eggs and sugar in large bowl set over hot water. Mix with electric hand beater until thick and foamy.

Remove bowl from hot water. Fold in flour and mix well with whisk.

Incorporate butter very slowly while mixing with spatula.

Pour batter into cake pan. Bake 40 to 45 minutes or until wooden pick inserted in centre of cake emerges clean.

Remove cake from oven and let stand in pan 10 minutes. Cool cake on wire rack.

Carefully slice cake into 2 layers. Sprinkle both with Tia Maria to taste.

Ice bottom layer, replace second layer and finish icing top and sides.

If desired decorate cake further before serving.

1 SERVING (WITHOUT ICING)   13 g FAT   0 g FIBER
7 g PROTEIN   261 CALORIES   29 g CARBOHYDRATE

1 Place eggs and sugar in large bowl set over hot water.

2 Mix with electric hand beater until thick and foamy.

3 Remove bowl from hot water. Fold in flour and mix well with whisk.

4 Incorporate butter very slowly while mixing with spatula.

Continued next page.

5 Pour batter into cake pan and bake.

6 Cool cake on wire rack.

7 Carefully slice cake into 2 layers; sprinkle with Tia Maria.

8 Ice bottom layer.

9 Replace top layer.

10 Finish icing top and sides. You can enhance the appearance of your cake by using different frostings.

Easy Afternoon Cake *(serves 4 to 6)*

½ cup	(125 ml) apricot jam
¾ cup	(175 ml) icing sugar
3 tbsp	(45 ml) water
	frozen puff pastry dough
	well beaten eggwash

Preheat oven to 425°F (220°C).

Sprinkle cookie sheet with cold water; set aside.

Roll out dough on floured surface. Cut out rectangular piece about 4 in (10 cm) wide; set on cookie sheet.

Roll out more dough making it a bit thicker; cut out another rectangular piece the same size as the first.

Spread jam over first piece of dough; place second layer on top. Press edges together.

Brush with beaten egg and prick with fork. Cook 15 minutes in oven.

Reduce heat to 375°F (190°C) and continue cooking 15 minutes.

Combine icing sugar with water to make icing. When cake has been removed from oven spread icing on top.

Slice and serve.

Baked Cheesecake *(serves 4 to 6)*

1 lb	(500 g) cream cheese, soft
3	egg yolks
⅓ cup	(75 ml) sugar
⅔ cup	(150 ml) heavy cream
1 tbsp	(15 ml) grated lemon rind
1 tbsp	(15 ml) Tia Maria
3	egg whites
	graham cracker crumb crust, cooked in 8½ in (22 cm) pie plate

Preheat oven to 300°F (150°C).

Mix cheese, egg yolks, sugar, cream, lemon rind and Tia Maria in food processor for 3 minutes.

Beat egg whites until firm; fold into cheese mixture and incorporate well.

Spoon mixture into pie crust. Bake 1¼ to 1½ hours in oven.

Remove cheesecake from oven and cool. Serve plain or with Strawberry Sauce, page 485.

1 SERVING	631 CALORIES	32 g CARBOHYDRATE
11 g PROTEIN	51 g FAT	0.2 g FIBER

1 Mix cheese, egg yolks, sugar, cream, lemon rind and Tia Maria in food processor for 3 minutes. Texture should be smooth and consistent.

2 Beat egg whites until firm; fold into cheese mixture and incorporate well.

Baked Apples   *(serves 4)*

4	cooking apples, cored
4 tbsp	(60 ml) brown sugar
4 tsp	(20 ml) apricot jam
4 tsp	(20 ml) butter
1 tbsp	(15 ml) cinnamon
1 cup	(250 ml) water
1 tsp	(5 ml) cornstarch
2 tbsp	(30 ml) cold water
	juice 1 lemon

Preheat oven to 375°F (190°C).

Using small knife, slit apple skins around middle. This technique will prevent skins from cracking during cooking.

Set apples in roasting pan. Fill cavities with brown sugar, jam, butter and cinnamon; sprinkle with lemon juice.

Pour water into pan and bake 45 minutes in oven.

When apples are cooked, remove pan and transfer apples to serving platter.

Place roasting pan on stove top over high heat. Bring to boil.

Mix cornstarch with 2 tbsp (30 ml) water; stir into sauce. Cook 2 minutes.

Pour sauce over apples and if desired, decorate with slivered almonds. Serve.

1 SERVING   213 CALORIES   42 g CARBOHYDRATE
0 g PROTEIN   5 g FAT   1.5 g FIBER

Fancy Dessert Treats *(serves 4)*

4	peaches, peeled and sliced
2 tbsp	(30 ml) Tia Maria
2 tbsp	(30 ml) sugar
1 ½ cups	(375 ml) whipped cream
	puff pastry dough
	eggwash
	strawberries for decoration

Preheat oven to 425°F (220°C).

Roll out dough on floured surface. Cut 8 small circles and place them on cookie sheet. Brush with eggwash and prick with fork; cook about 15 minutes in oven.

Remove pastry circles and set aside to cool.

Place peaches, Tia Maria and sugar in bowl; marinate 15 minutes.

Place 4 pastry circles on serving platter. Arrange peaches on top and add dollop of whipped cream.

Replace pastry tops and garnish with more whipped cream. Decorate with strawberries.

Serve.

Raspberries on Cream   *(serves 4)*

2 cups	(500 ml) fresh raspberries, washed
2 tbsp	(30 ml) cognac
1 ½ cups	(375 ml) rum pastry cream*
¾ cup	(175 ml) heavy cream, whipped
2 tbsp	(30 ml) brown sugar

Place raspberries in bowl and add cognac; marinate 8 to 10 minutes.

Mix pastry cream with whipped cream; spoon onto dessert plates.

Arrange raspberries over mixed cream and sprinkle with brown sugar.

Serve.

*See Rum Pastry Cream, page 504.

Elegant Strawberry Mousse   *(serves 6 to 8)*

2 cups	(500 ml) milk
⅓ cup	(75 ml) cold water
2 tbsp	(30 ml) unflavored gelatine
5	egg yolks
1 tbsp	(15 ml) vanilla
½ cup	(125 ml) sugar
1½ cups	(375 ml) puréed strawberries
1 cup	(250 ml) whipped cream
	walnut oil

Grease well 6 cup (1.5 L) fancy bundt mold with walnut oil. Set aside until use.

Heat milk until hot but not boiling; set aside. Pour water into small bowl and sprinkle in gelatine. Do not stir and also set aside.

Place egg yolks and vanilla in stainless steel bowl. Add sugar and mix with electric hand beater until batter forms ribbons.

Pour in hot milk and incorporate with whisk. Cook mixture in bowl over hot water. Stir constantly and remove bowl when mixture is thick enough to coat a spoon.

Mix gelatine into cooked mixture. Refrigerate 35 minutes and stir 2 to 3 times.

Incorporate strawberries and replace bowl in refrigerator. Remove when mixture is partially set.

Fold in whipped cream and transfer mixture to bundt mold. Refrigerate 12 hours. Unmold and decorate as desired.

1 SERVING	173 CALORIES	19 g CARBOHYDRATE
4 g PROTEIN	9 g FAT	0.5 g FIBER

Chocolate Strawberry Treats   *(serves 4)*

1 cup	(250 ml) icing sugar
2 oz	(60 g) bitter chocolate
1 tsp	(5 ml) vanilla
3 tbsp	(45 ml) milk
1	egg yolk
32	large ripe strawberries
8	large marshmallows

Place sugar, chocolate, vanilla and milk in top portion of double boiler. Melt chocolate and mix well.

Remove from heat and mix in egg yolk; let mixture stand several minutes.

Dip strawberries and marshmallows in chocolate. Serve.

Note: If you wish to increase the number of servings, double the ingredients with the exception of the vanilla.

A Look Into Microwaves At Work

Microwaves are invisible light waves much like television or radiowaves. Those used for cooking are produced by a magnetron tube which simply converts household electricity into microwaves. As they bounce off the metal walls of the oven, they pass through nonmetal utensils and are absorbed by the food.

Because microwaves only penetrate about 1 in (2.5 cm) into food (top, bottom and sides), the rest of the cooking is done by heat conduction. For this reason it is often necessary to turn the container a ¼ or ½ turn during the cooking process to ensure even cooking.

Please read your manufacturer's guide for detailed information on your particular model.

Microwave Power Settings

Please have a look at this chart before trying any of our recipes.

POWER SETTING	PERCENTAGE OF HIGH SETTING	WATTS
HIGH	100%	650
MEDIUM-HIGH	75%	485
MEDIUM	50%	325
LOW	25%	160

We recommend that you read your manufacturer's guide thoroughly if you have not already done so. Please consult the guide booklet for information on defrosting or thawing.

At the beginning of each recipe, we have listed the Power, Cooking Time and Utensil required. Unless a change is indicated in the recipe use the power that is listed!

Microwave Utensils

The following utensils are suitable for microwave cooking. You will probably already have many of these in your kitchen. To test a utensil for microwave cooking, fill the item with about 1 cup (250 ml) cold water. Microwave 1 minute at HIGH. If the water is hot and the utensil stays cool, it can be used for microwave cooking. If the opposite occurs do not use this particular utensil in the microwave.

Use nonmetal utensils such as: glassware, ceramic, paper, some plastic products, china, stoneware and pottery.

Many utensils are stamped on the bottom to indicate they are suitable for microwave use. If you are unsure of suitability, perform the microwave test.

More Microwave Tips

— To soften butter or margarine, microwave at LOW until softened.

— To boil water microwave at HIGH.

— To soften 8 oz (227 g) cream cheese, microwave about 1 minute at MEDIUM or until softened. Cheese should be removed from package and placed in bowl.

— To prevent exploding, pierce foods such as egg yolks and some vegetables.

— To ensure even cooking, stir foods from the outside toward the middle.

— Arrange foods with the thickest part toward the outside of the dish.

— Do not attempt to cook whole eggs in their shells as they can burst during microwaving.

TECHNIQUE: BROWNING ALMONDS

1 Place 1 cup (250 ml) slivered almonds in microwave bowl. Add 1 tbsp (15 ml) butter.

2 Microwave on HIGH for 3 minutes.

TECHNIQUE: SOFTENING BROWN SUGAR

1 Place brown sugar in bowl and microwave about 1 minute at HIGH.

2 Check sugar occasionally with fork.

Scrambling Eggs

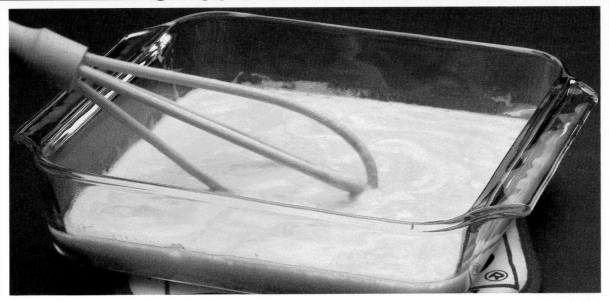

Simply pour beaten eggs along with a bit of butter and seasonings into an appropriate utensil. Eggs are usually microwaved on HIGH.

You will have to stir the eggs often so that they are evenly cooked.

As you can see in this picture, scrambled eggs turn out very well. Notice how moist and appetizing they are. Best of all, they take only minutes.

Cooking Bacon

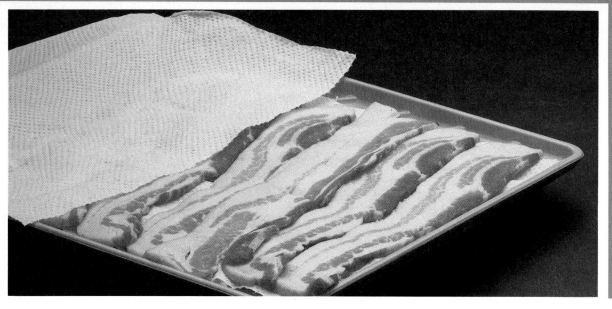

Cooking bacon is best done by placing slices between two sheets of paper towel. Not only will the paper towel prevent the fat from spattering on microwave walls, it will absorb most of the fat from the bacon.

Use as a guideline about ¾ minute for each bacon slice. This will vary depending on the thickness of the slices. The microwave should be set at HIGH.

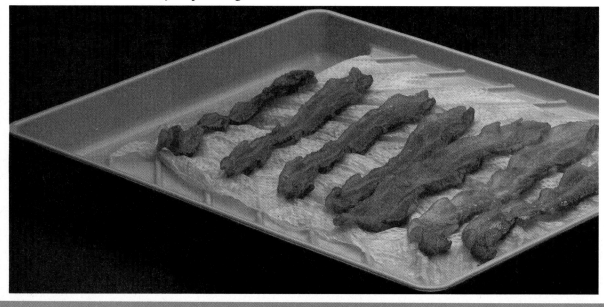

Covering Food

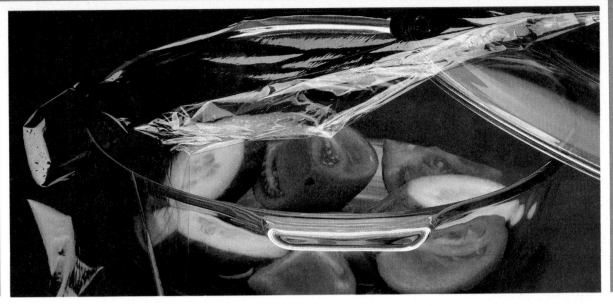

As with conventional cooking, it is often necessary to cover food during cooking.

Depending on the recipe, you may need to use a tight fitting lid or a sheet of plastic wrap. Be sure to have both on hand.

Covering Food with Plastic Wrap

When covering food with plastic wrap it is important to provide an escape for steam.

Either pierce the wrap with a knife or turn up one corner.

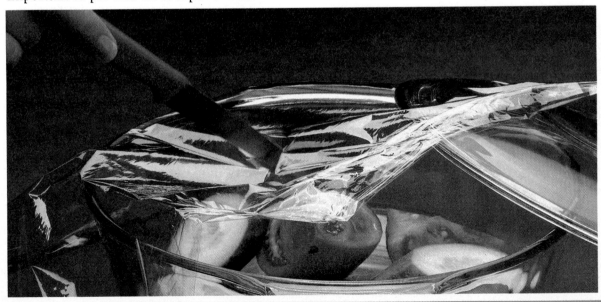

Cooking Vegetables

Vegetables are one of the foods that are most successfully prepared in your microwave. As you can see in this picture cooked broccoli loses very little of its original colour.

Microwaved vegetables are not only attractive to serve but also retain a great deal of flavour.

How To Arrange Food

With large or unevenly shaped foods, always place the thickest portion towards the outside of the dish.

This technique is particularly important when cooking poultry and whole vegetables.

Light Onion Soup *(serves 4)*

SETTING: *HIGH*
COOKING TIME: *24 minutes*
UTENSIL: *2 QT (2 L) round casserole
                dish with cover*

1	large Spanish onion, peeled and thinly sliced
1 tbsp	(15 ml) butter
2 tbsp	(30 ml) soya sauce
1 tbsp	(15 ml) chopped parsley
3½ cups	(875 ml) heated chicken stock
¼ cup	(50 ml) grated Swiss cheese salt and pepper

Place onion, butter and soya sauce in casserole; season well. Cover and microwave 5 minutes.

Stir well; continue microwaving 5 minutes.

Add parsley and chicken stock; mix well and correct seasoning. Microwave 10 minutes uncovered.

Add cheese and microwave 4 minutes uncovered.

Serve in soup bowls, topped with extra cheese if desired.

See Technique next page.

1 SERVING	77 CALORIES	5 g CARBOHYDRATE
3 g PROTEIN	5 g FAT	0.3 g FIBER

TECHNIQUE: LIGHT ONION SOUP

1 Place onion, butter and soya sauce in casserole; season well. Cover and microwave 5 minutes.

2 Add parsley and chicken stock; mix well and correct seasoning. Microwave 10 minutes uncovered.

3 When onion is cooked, add cheese and finish microwaving 4 minutes. Do not cover.

4 Serve in soup bowls, topped with extra cheese if desired.

TECHNIQUE: BROCCOLI AND CHEESE SAUCE

1 Microwave melted butter and flour 2 minutes uncovered.

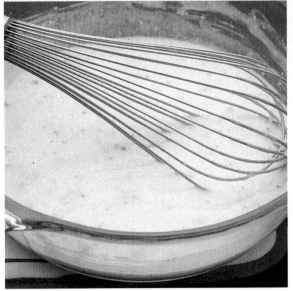

2 Incorporate milk with whisk. Continue microwaving 6 minutes uncovered. Stir every 2 minutes.

3 At some point during cooking, add nutmeg, parsley, salt and pepper.

4 Mix half of cheese into sauce.

Continued next page.

5 Pour sauce over cooked broccoli; top with remaining cheese.

6 Microwave 2 minutes to melt cheese and serve.

Broccoli and Cheese Sauce *(serves 4)*

SETTING: *HIGH*
COOKING TIME: *10 minutes*
UTENSIL: *2 QT (2 L) round casserole dish*
2 QT (2 L) rectangular dish

3 tbsp	(45 ml) melted butter
3½ tbsp	(55 ml) flour
1½ cups	(375 ml) hot milk
½ cup	(125 ml) grated cheddar cheese
2	heads broccoli, cooked and in flowerets with stalks
	pinch nutmeg
	chopped parsley to taste
	salt and pepper

Place melted butter and flour in round casserole. Mix together well and microwave 2 minutes uncovered.

Incorporate milk with whisk; continue microwaving 6 minutes uncovered. Stir every 2 minutes.

At some point during cooking, add nutmeg, parsley, salt and pepper.

Mix half of cheese into sauce. Place cooked broccoli in greased rectangular dish; pour sauce over top.

Top with remaining cheese and microwave 2 minutes uncovered.

1 SERVING	273 CALORIES	18 g CARBOHYDRATE
12 g PROTEIN	17 g FAT	1.9 g FIBER

Chinese Soup *(serves 4)*

SETTING: *HIGH*
COOKING TIME: *16 minutes*
UTENSIL: *2 QT (2 L) round casserole dish with cover*

1 tbsp	(15 ml) butter
2	large carrots, pared and thinly sliced
1	celery stalk, sliced
1	zucchini, sliced
1	green pepper, sliced
¼ tsp	(1 ml) thyme
2	parsley sprigs
4 cups	(1 L) heated chicken stock
2 tbsp	(30 ml) soya sauce
	fresh basil (if available)
	salt and pepper

Melt butter in casserole 1 minute.

Add carrots and celery; continue microwaving, covered, 3 minutes.

Add zucchini, green pepper, thyme, parsley and basil; cover and microwave 3 minutes.

Pour in chicken stock and soya sauce; mix well and correct seasoning. Microwave 9 minutes uncovered.

Serve with crackers or Chinese noodles.

See Technique next page.

1 SERVING	71 CALORIES	9 g CARBOHYDRATE
2 g PROTEIN	3 g FAT	1.2 g FIBER

TECHNIQUE: CHINESE SOUP

1 Microwave carrots and celery 3 minutes in hot butter. Be sure to cover casserole.

2 Now add zucchini, green pepper, thyme, parsley and basil; cover and microwave 3 minutes.

Everyday Vegetable Soup   *(serves 4)*

SETTING: *HIGH*
COOKING TIME: *10 minutes*
UTENSIL: *2 QT (2 L) round casserole dish with cover*

1 tbsp	(15 ml) butter
2	broccoli stalks, diced
1 tbsp	(15 ml) chopped fresh parsley
2	green onions, diced
½	green pepper, diced
½	cucumber, peeled, seeded and diced
2	large tomatoes, diced
1	thyme sprig
3½ cups	(875 ml) heated chicken stock salt and pepper

Place butter, broccoli and parsley in casserole. Cover and microwave 5 minutes.

Add remaining vegetables and thyme; season generously. Continue microwaving covered 3 minutes.

Pour in chicken stock and mix well. Finish microwaving 2 minutes uncovered.

Serve hot.

1 SERVING	75 CALORIES	9 g CARBOHYDRATE
3 g PROTEIN	3 g FAT	1.5 g FIBER

TECHNIQUE: EVERYDAY VEGETABLE SOUP

1 Microwave butter, broccoli and parsley 5 minutes.

2 Add remaining vegetables and thyme; season generously. Continue microwaving 3 minutes.

3 Add chicken stock; finish microwaving 2 minutes uncovered.

4 Vegetables should be crisp when done.

561

Cream of Chicken *(serves 4)*

SETTING: *HIGH*
COOKING TIME: *16 minutes*
UTENSIL: *2 QT (2 L) round casserole dish with cover*

3	chicken breast halves, skinned and deboned
½	celery stalk, diced
2	carrots, pared and finely diced
½	onion, peeled and diced
2 cups	(500 ml) hot water
1	parsley sprig
¼ tsp	(1 ml) thyme
4 tbsp	(60 ml) butter
4½ tbsp	(70 ml) flour
2¼ cups	(625 ml) hot milk
	salt and pepper
	pinch nutmeg, paprika, ginger

Arrange chicken in casserole. Add celery, carrots, onion, water, parsley, thyme, salt and pepper. Cover and microwave 8 minutes.

Remove chicken and dice; set aside with vegetables. Strain cooking liquid and set aside.

Wipe casserole clean; wash if necessary. Add butter and microwave 1 minute.

Mix in flour until paste-like; cover and microwave 1 minute.

Stir in strained cooking liquid; mix very well with whisk. Cover and microwave 3 minutes.

Mix well again; add milk and season with nutmeg, paprika, ginger, salt and pepper.

Mix thoroughly and replace chicken and vegetables in casserole. Microwave 3 minutes uncovered.

Serve.

1 SERVING	482 CALORIES	18 g CARBOHYDRATE
53 g PROTEIN	22 g FAT	0.5 g FIBER

TECHNIQUE: CREAM OF CHICKEN

1 Microwave chicken and vegetables 8 minutes.

2 After sauce has been microwaved, return diced chicken and vegetables to casserole.

Easy Tomato Rice   *(serves 4)*

SETTING: *HIGH*
COOKING TIME: *24 minutes*
UTENSIL: *2 QT (2 L) round casserole dish with cover*

1 tsp	(5 ml) vegetable oil
3 tbsp	(45 ml) chopped onion
1	garlic clove, smashed and chopped
½	28 oz (796 ml) can tomatoes, drained and chopped
1 tbsp	(15 ml) chopped parsley
1 cup	(250 ml) long grain rice, rinsed and drained
1½ cups	(375 ml) heated chicken stock salt and pepper

Place oil, onion, garlic, tomatoes and parsley in casserole; season well. Cover and microwave 4 minutes.

Mix in rice and chicken stock; correct seasoning. Continue microwaving 10 minutes covered.

Mix rice well with fork; finish microwaving 10 minutes covered.

Let rice stand in casserole 7 to 8 minutes before serving.

1 SERVING	248 CALORIES	48 g CARBOHYDRATE
5 g PROTEIN	4 g FAT	0.9 g FIBER

TECHNIQUE: QUICK GARLIC BREAD

1 Spread garlic butter evenly over toasted bread; place slices on plate.
Add parsley, tomato sauce, pepper and cheese.

2 Microwave 3 minutes uncovered.

Quick Garlic Bread   *(serves 4)*

SETTING: *HIGH*
COOKING TIME: *3 minutes*
UTENSIL: *large plate*

½ lb	(250 g) garlic butter
6 to 8	slices thick French or Italian bread, toasted
½ cup	(125 ml) coarsely grated Gruyère cheese
	chopped parsley to taste
	thick tomato sauce or sliced tomatoes
	freshly ground pepper

Spread garlic butter evenly over toasted bread. Place slices on plate.

Sprinkle chopped parsley over bread and add tomato sauce to taste; season well with pepper.

Add cheese and season again. Microwave 3 minutes uncovered.

Serve.

1 SERVING	632 CALORIES	24 g CARBOHYDRATE
8 g PROTEIN	56 g FAT	0 g FIBER

Knackwurst Sausages (serves 4)

SETTING: *HIGH*
COOKING TIME: *4 minutes*
UTENSIL: *plate*

4	knackwurst sausages

Slash sausages on all sides with knife. Place on plate and microwave 4 minutes; turn once during cooking.

These are perfect for snacks or delicious served with potato salad for lunch.

1 SERVING	192 CALORIES	2 g CARBOHYDRATE
10 g PROTEIN	16 g FAT	0 g FIBER

Scalloped Potatoes *(serves 4)*

SETTING: *HIGH*
COOKING TIME: *19 minutes*
UTENSIL: *2 QT (2 L) round casserole dish*

4	large potatoes, peeled and sliced very thinly
3 tbsp	(45 ml) butter
2 tbsp	(30 ml) chopped parsley
1	onion, chopped and partly cooked
1 cup	(250 ml) heavy cream, hot
1 cup	(250 ml) hot milk
½ cup	(125 ml) grated cheddar cheese
	dash paprika
	salt and pepper

Grease casserole. Layer with potatoes, butter, paprika, parsley, salt and pepper.

Sprinkle onion on last layer.

Pour in cream and milk. Microwave 16 minutes uncovered.

Sprinkle with cheese and finish microwaving 3 minutes uncovered.

Serve.

1 SERVING	533 CALORIES	39 g CARBOHYDRATE
11 g PROTEIN	37 g FAT	1.0 g FIBER

TECHNIQUE: SCALLOPED POTATOES

1 Layer potatoes, butter, paprika, parsley, salt and pepper in greased casserole. Repeat until all ingredients are used; sprinkle onion on last layer.

2 Pour in cream and milk. Microwave 16 minutes uncovered.

Baked Potatoes   *(serves 2)*

SETTING: *HIGH*
COOKING TIME: *15 minutes*
UTENSIL: *None*

2	baking potatoes
	chopped cooked bacon
	sour cream or butter

Unwrap potatoes and prick all over with knife or fork.

Set in oven and microwave 15 minutes. Turn potatoes over once during cooking (about half way through).

Cut potatoes open and dress as desired.

1 SERVING	103 CALORIES	17 g CARBOHYDRATE
2 g PROTEIN	3 g FAT	3.5 g FIBER

TECHNIQUE: MIXED BEANS

1 Place beans in casserole and pour in water; season with salt.
Cover and microwave 15 minutes.

2 Drain beans and serve.

Mixed Beans   *(serves 4)*

SETTING: *HIGH*
COOKING TIME: *15 minutes*
UTENSIL: *2 QT (2 L) round casserole dish with cover*

1 lb	(500 g) mixed fresh beans, pared
2 cups	(500 ml) hot water
	salt

Place beans in casserole and pour in water; season with salt.

Cover and microwave 15 minutes.

Drain and serve.

| *1 SERVING* | 40 CALORIES | 8 g CARBOHYDRATE |
| 2 g PROTEIN | 0 g FAT | 1.3 g FIBER |

Vegetarian's Dinner   *(serves 4)*

SETTING: *HIGH*
COOKING TIME: *18 minutes*
UTENSIL: *2 QT (2 L) rectangular dish*

1	large eggplant, sliced lengthwise into 8 pieces about ¼ in (0.65 cm) thick
3	ripe tomatoes, sliced
1½ cups	(375 ml) spaghetti sauce
½ cup	(125 ml) grated mozzarella cheese
	salt and pepper

Arrange 4 eggplant slices in rectangular dish.

Top with sliced tomatoes and season generously. Cover with remaining eggplant slices.

Pour spaghetti sauce over and cover with plastic wrap; microwave 15 minutes.

Add cheese and finish microwaving 3 minutes uncovered.

Serve.

See Technique next page.

1 SERVING	188 CALORIES	22 g CARBOHYDRATE
7 g PROTEIN	8 g FAT	2.6 g FIBER

TECHNIQUE: VEGETARIAN'S DINNER

1 Arrange eggplant slices in rectangular dish; top with sliced tomatoes and season generously.

2 Cover with remaining eggplant slices.

3 Pour spaghetti sauce over and cover with plastic wrap; microwave 15 minutes.

4 Add cheese and finish microwaving 3 minutes uncovered.

Braised Zucchini   *(serves 4)*

SETTING: *HIGH*
COOKING TIME: *16 minutes*
UTENSIL: *2 QT (2 L) round casserole*
with cover

3	large zucchini, peeled and sliced
½	onion, chopped
¼ tsp	(1 ml) basil
1 cup	(250 ml) light chicken stock
2 tbsp	(30 ml) butter
2½ tbsp	(40 ml) flour
½ cup	(125 ml) hot milk
⅓ cup	(75 ml) finely grated parmesan
	salt and pepper
	dash paprika

Arrange zucchini in casserole and season generously. Add onion, basil and chicken stock; cover and microwave 9 minutes.

Strain vegetables; set aside with liquid.

Microwave butter in casserole 1 minute.

Mix in flour; microwave 1 minute uncovered.

Pour strained liquid into casserole and incorporate with whisk. Microwave 2 minutes uncovered.

Stir mixture well and mix in reserved vegetables; season with paprika.

Pour in milk and mix in cheese; microwave 3 minutes uncovered.

Serve.

See Technique next page.

1 SERVING	155 CALORIES	16 g CARBOHYDRATE
7 g PROTEIN	9 g FAT	0 g FIBER

TECHNIQUE: BRAISED ZUCCHINI

1 After zucchini have microwaved 9 minutes, remove and strain vegetables; set aside with liquid.

2 Stir mixture well and mix in reserved vegetables; season with paprika.

TECHNIQUE: ZUCCHINI RATATOUILLE

1 Add eggplant and zucchini to onion mixture. Sprinkle in spices. Cover and microwave 15 minutes.

2 Mix in tomatoes and tomato paste; finish microwaving 8 minutes covered.

Zucchini Ratatouille *(serves 4)*

SETTING:	*HIGH*
COOKING TIME:	*26 minutes*
UTENSIL:	*2 QT (2 L) round casserole dish with cover*

1 tbsp	(15 ml) butter
1	onion, peeled and sliced
1 tbsp	(15 ml) soya sauce
1	small eggplant, sliced
3	zucchini, peeled and sliced ¼ in (0.65 cm) thick
2	garlic cloves, smashed and chopped
1 tbsp	(15 ml) chopped parsley
¼ tsp	(1 ml) thyme
3	tomatoes, diced large
2 tbsp	(30 ml) tomato paste
	salt and pepper
	pinch paprika

Place butter, onion and soya sauce in casserole; cover and microwave 3 minutes.

Add eggplant and zucchini; sprinkle in garlic, parsley, thyme, salt, pepper and paprika. Cover and microwave 15 minutes.

Mix in tomatoes and tomato paste; finish microwaving 8 minutes covered.

1 SERVING	136 CALORIES	20 g CARBOHYDRATE
5 g PROTEIN	4 g FAT	2.4 g FIBER

TECHNIQUE: EGGPLANT SURPRISE

1 Mix beef with cooked onion and season well. Cover and microwave 4 minutes.

2 Stir mixture well and incorporate tomatoes; correct seasoning.

3 Spoon portion of meat mixture over eggplant slices.

4 Cover with remaining eggplant slices and pour tomato sauce over. Cover dish with plastic wrap; microwave 15 minutes.

5 Add cheese and finish microwaving 1 minute uncovered.

6 Serve one eggplant surprise per person.

Eggplant Surprise   *(serves 4)*

SETTING: *HIGH*
COOKING TIME: *22 minutes*
UTENSIL: *2 QT (2 L) round casserole dish with cover*
2 QT (2 L) rectangular dish

1 tbsp	(15 ml) vegetable oil
1	onion, peeled and chopped
1	garlic clove, chopped
¾ lb	(375 g) lean ground beef
2 cups	(500 ml) canned tomatoes, drained and chopped
2 tbsp	(30 ml) tomato paste
¼ tsp	(1 ml) Tabasco sauce
¼ tsp	(1 ml) Worcestershire sauce
1	large eggplant, sliced lengthwise into 8 pieces about ¼ in (0.65 cm) thick
1½ cups	(375 ml) tomato sauce
½ cup	(125 ml) grated mozzarella cheese

Place oil, onion and garlic in casserole; cover and microwave 2 minutes.

Mix in beef and season well. Cover and microwave 4 minutes.

Stir mixture well (meat will not be fully cooked) and incorporate tomatoes; correct seasoning.

Mix in tomato paste, Tabasco and Worcestershire; set casserole aside.

Arrange 4 eggplant slices in rectangular dish. Spoon portion of meat mixture over each; top with remaining eggplant slices.

Pour tomato sauce over and cover with plastic wrap; microwave 15 minutes.

Add cheese and finish microwaving 1 minute uncovered.

Serve.

1 SERVING	357 CALORIES	24 g CARBOHYDRATE
27 g PROTEIN	17 g FAT	2.3 g FIBER

Stewed Tomatoes *(serves 4)*

SETTING: *HIGH*
COOKING TIME: *15 minutes*
UTENSIL: *2 QT (2 L) round casserole*
                 dish with cover

1 tbsp	(15 ml) vegetable oil
2	garlic cloves, smashed and chopped
½	celery stalk, diced
1	onion, peeled and chopped
6	tomatoes, diced large
¼ tsp	(1 ml) oregano
2 tbsp	(30 ml) tomato paste
	pinch sugar
	salt and pepper

Microwave oil, garlic, celery and onion 3 minutes covered.

Stir in tomatoes, oregano, tomato paste and sugar; season well. Cover and continue microwaving 12 minutes.

Serve in small bowls or purée in blender for use in other recipes.

1 SERVING	108 CALORIES	14 g CARBOHYDRATE
4 g PROTEIN	4 g FAT	1.5 g FIBER

Chicken in Sauce   *(serves 4)*

SETTING: *HIGH*
COOKING TIME: *13 minutes*
UTENSIL: *2 QT (2 L) round casserole dish with cover serving dish*

2	whole chicken breasts, skinned, boned and split
1 tsp	(5 ml) lemon juice
¼ cup	(50 ml) hot chicken stock
1 tbsp	(15 ml) liquid honey
¼ lb	(125 g) mushrooms, cleaned and sliced
1	recipe stewed tomatoes*, puréed in blender
3 tbsp	(45 ml) finely grated parmesan cheese
	salt and pepper

Arrange split breasts in casserole. Sprinkle with lemon juice; add chicken stock, honey, salt and pepper. Cover and microwave 4 minutes.

Turn breasts over; continue microwaving 4 minutes.

Add mushrooms; cover and microwave 2 minutes.

Transfer chicken to serving dish; cover with mushrooms and discard cooking liquid.

Pour puréed stewed tomatoes over mushrooms and top with cheese. Microwave 3 minutes uncovered.

Remove from microwave and serve immediately.

*See Stewed Tomatoes, page 576.

1 SERVING	444 CALORIES	20 g CARBOHYDRATE
64 g PROTEIN	12 g FAT	1.7 g FIBER

TECHNIQUE: CHICKEN IN SAUCE

1 Transfer cooked chicken and mushrooms to serving dish. Discard cooking liquid.

2 Pour puréed tomatoes over mushrooms and top with cheese. Microwave 3 minutes uncovered.

Chicken and Vegetable Casserole *(serves 4)*

SETTING: *HIGH*
COOKING TIME: *27 minutes*
UTENSIL: *2 QT (2 L) rectangular dish*
2 QT (2 L) round casserole dish with cover

2	whole chicken breasts, skinned, deboned and split
3	potatoes, peeled and cubed
1	celery stalk, diced large
1	thyme sprig
1½ cups	(375 ml) water
½	green pepper, in large pieces
½	red pepper, in large pieces
1	yellow pepper, in large pieces
3 tbsp	(45 ml) butter
3½ tbsp	(55 ml) flour
2 cups	(500 ml) hot milk
	paprika to taste
	salt and pepper

Lay split breasts flat in rectangular dish; cover with potatoes and celery.
Sprinkle in paprika, add thyme and water. Cover with plastic wrap and microwave 12 minutes.
Turn breasts over and add peppers; season well. Cover again and microwave 5 minutes.
Drain chicken and vegetables; either replace in dish or transfer to microwave serving dish. Discard liquid.
To prepare sauce, place butter in round casserole; microwave 1 minute.
Mix in flour with whisk; microwave 2 minutes uncovered.
Incorporate milk well and season with salt, pepper and paprika; microwave 4 minutes uncovered.
Pour sauce over chicken and vegetables; microwave 3 minutes uncovered.
Serve.

See technique next page.

1 SERVING	564 CALORIES	31 g CARBOHYDRATE
65 g PROTEIN	20 g FAT	1.2 g FIBER

TECHNIQUE

1 Lay breasts flat in rectangular dish; cover with potatoes and celery. Sprinkle in paprika, add thyme and water. Cover with plastic wrap and microwave 12 minutes.

2 Turn breasts over and add peppers; season well. Cover again and microwave 5 minutes.

3 Drain chicken and vegetables; either replace in dish or transfer to microwave serving dish. Discard liquid.

4 Once sauce is made, pour over chicken and vegetables; microwave 3 minutes uncovered.

Leftover Chicken and Vegetables *(serves 4)*

SETTING: *HIGH*
COOKING TIME: *14 minutes*
UTENSIL: *2 QT (2 L) round casserole dish with cover*

3 tbsp	(45 ml) butter
½ lb	(250 g) fresh mushrooms, cleaned and quartered
1 tsp	(5 ml) lemon juice
1	red pepper, sliced in strips
1½ cups	(375 ml) hot milk
2	whole chicken breasts, cooked and sliced
¼ lb	(125 g) blanched yellow beans, cut in two
3 tbsp	(45 ml) flour
	salt and pepper
	dash paprika

Place 1 tbsp (15 ml) butter, mushrooms, lemon juice and red pepper in casserole. Cover and microwave 3 minutes.

Stir in milk, chicken, and beans; season with paprika. Microwave 3 minutes uncovered.

Strain and set both aside.

Microwave remaining butter 1 minute in casserole.

Add flour and mix very well; microwave 3 minutes uncovered.

Stir strained cooking liquid into flour mixture in casserole. Mix well and microwave 3 minutes uncovered.

Stir in chicken and vegetables; microwave 1 minute uncovered. Correct seasoning.

Serve hot on toast.

1 SERVING	495 CALORIES	17 g CARBOHYDRATE
64 g PROTEIN	19 g FAT	1.2 g FIBER

TECHNIQUE

1 Begin by placing 1 tbsp (15 ml) butter, mushrooms, lemon juice and red pepper in casserole. Cover and microwave 3 minutes.

2 Stir in milk, chicken, and beans; season with paprika. Microwave 3 minutes uncovered.

Veal Chops with Apple Garnish   *(serves 2)*

SETTING: *HIGH*
COOKING TIME: *5 minutes in microwave*
UTENSIL: *2 QT (2 L) round casserole dish with cover*

2	large veal chops
½ cup	(125 ml) flour
1 tbsp	(15 ml) vegetable oil
2 tbsp	(30 ml) chopped green onion
1	apple, peeled, cored and sliced
¼	celery stalk, sliced
1 tsp	(5 ml) butter
	salt and pepper

Dredge veal lightly with flour. Heat oil in frying pan on conventional stove top. Sear chops 1 minute each side over medium heat; season well.

Transfer veal to casserole; add green onion, apple, celery and butter. Season, cover and microwave 4 minutes.

Rotate casserole ¼ turn; continue microwaving 1 minute.

Serve.

1 SERVING	307 CALORIES	21 g CARBOHYDRATE
31 g PROTEIN	11 g FAT	0.8 g FIBER

Veal Liver Dinner   *(serves 4)*

SETTING: *HIGH*
COOKING TIME: *10 to 12 minutes in microwave*
UTENSIL: *2 QT (2 L) round casserole dish with cover*

1 tbsp	(15 ml) olive oil
1	onion, peeled and chopped
1	green pepper, thinly sliced
3	tomatoes, peeled, seeded and chopped
1	garlic clove, smashed and chopped
1 tbsp	(15 ml) chopped parsley
1 tsp	(5 ml) soya sauce
4	slices veal liver, cut in strips
¼ cup	(50 ml) flour
3 tbsp	(45 ml) butter
	salt and pepper

Microwave oil 1 minute in casserole.

Add onion, green pepper, tomatoes, garlic and parsley; season well. Cover and microwave 8 to 10 minutes.

Mix in soya sauce and set casserole aside.

Season liver strips and dredge with flour. Heat butter in large frying pan on conventional stove top. Sear liver 1 minute each side over high heat.

When all liver has been seared, add it to tomato mixture in casserole. Mix well and microwave 1 minute uncovered.

If desired, serve with noodles or rice.

1 SERVING	409 CALORIES	16 g CARBOHYDRATE
30 g PROTEIN	25 g FAT	-- g FIBER

Mock Pork Stir-Fry   *(serves 4)*

SETTING: *HIGH*
COOKING TIME: *6 minutes in microwave*
UTENSIL: *2 QT (2 L) casserole dish with cover*

1 tbsp	(15 ml) vegetable oil
1 lb	(500 g) pork loin, cut in strips
1	red onion, peeled and sliced in rings
1 tsp	(5 ml) soya sauce
1	red pepper, sliced in rings
¼ lb	(125 g) fresh snow peas
1 cup	(250 ml) bean sprouts
1 cup	(250 ml) heated brown sauce
	salt and pepper
	extra soya sauce and oil

Heat 1 tbsp (15 ml) oil in frying pan on conventional stove top. Sear pork 2 minutes each side over high heat. Season well and set aside.

Place onion and soya sauce in casserose. Cover and microwave 2 minutes.

Stir in red pepper, snow peas and bean sprouts; sprinkle with a bit of soya sauce and oil for flavour. Season, cover and microwave 3 minutes.

Mix in brown sauce and pork; microwave 1 minute uncovered.

Serve.

1 SERVING	389 CALORIES	9 g CARBOHYDRATE
23 g PROTEIN	29 g FAT	0.8 g FIBER

Potato Salad   *(serves 4)*

SETTING: *HIGH*
COOKING TIME: *2 minutes*
UTENSIL: *large bowl*

3 to 4	large potatoes, boiled, peeled and cubed
1	green onion, chopped
1 tbsp	(15 ml) chopped parsley
2 tbsp	(30 ml) wine vinegar
2 tbsp	(30 ml) olive oil
	salt and pepper

Place potatoes in bowl.

Add onion, parsley, salt and pepper; toss gently.

Sprinkle in vinegar and oil. Microwave 2 minutes uncovered.

Toss gently and serve warm.

1 SERVING	171 CALORIES	24 g CARBOHYDRATE
3 g PROTEIN	7 g FAT	0.7 g FIBER

TECHNIQUE: SALMON BROCCOLI CASSEROLE

1 Place salmon, parsley, lemon slices, green onion, carrot, white onion, lemon juice and water in rectangular dish. Season well. Microwave.

2 Remove bones.

3 Remove skin and flake salmon.

4 Mix flaked salmon and broccoli together in round casserole.

5 Pour in white sauce, season and top with cheese. Microwave 4 minutes uncovered.

6 Serve with the vegetable of your choice.

Salmon Broccoli Casserole *(serves 4)*

SETTING: *HIGH*
COOKING TIME: *13 minutes*
UTENSIL: *2 QT (2 L) round casserole dish*

4	salmon steaks
2 tbsp	(30 ml) chopped parsley
4	lemon slices
1	green onion, coarsely chopped
1	carrot, pared and sliced
¼	white onion, peeled and sliced
1 tbsp	(15 ml) lemon juice
½ cup	(125 ml) hot water
1	head broccoli, cooked and in flowerets
1	recipe white sauce*
½ cup	(125 ml) grated cheddar cheese
	salt and pepper

Place salmon, parsley, lemon slices, green onion, carrot, white onion, lemon juice and water in rectangular dish. Season well.

Cover with plastic wrap and microwave 6 minutes.

Turn salmon over; continue microwaving 3 minutes covered.

Remove bones and skin from salmon. Discard vegetables and cooking liquid.

Place salmon in round casserole and flake with fork. Incorporate broccoli flowerets and mix together.

Pour in white sauce, season and top with cheese. Microwave 4 minutes uncovered.

*See White Sauce, page 598.

1 SERVING	596 CALORIES	15 g CARBOHYDRATE
62 g PROTEIN	32 g FAT	1.0 g FIBER

Scallops and Tomatoes *(serves 2)*

SETTING:	*HIGH & MEDIUM*
COOKING TIME:	*13 minutes*
UTENSIL:	*2 QT (2 L) round casserole dish with cover; individual serving dishes*

½ lb	(250 g) fresh scallops
1	green onion, chopped
¼ lb	(125 g) mushrooms, quartered
1 tsp	(5 ml) lemon juice
¼ cup	(50 ml) water
2 cups	(500 ml) canned tomatoes, drained and chopped
1 tbsp	(15 ml) chopped parsley
1	garlic clove, smashed and chopped
1 tbsp	(15 ml) tomato paste
¼ cup	(50 ml) grated cheese
	salt and pepper

Place scallops, onion, mushrooms and lemon juice in casserole. Pour in water and cover; microwave 2 minutes at HIGH.

Stir mixture; continue microwaving 2 minutes.

Drain mixture and set aside; discard liquid.

Place tomatoes in casserole; cover and microwave 3 minutes at HIGH.

Mix in parsley, garlic, salt, pepper and tomato paste; microwave 2 minutes uncovered.

Stir in drained scallop mixture. Spoon into serving dishes and top with cheese; season well. Finish microwaving 4 minutes uncovered at MEDIUM.

1 SERVING	221 CALORIES	17 g CARBOHYDRATE
27 g PROTEIN	5 g FAT	1.3 g FIBER

TECHNIQUE: SCALLOPS AND TOMATOES

1 Place scallops, onion, mushrooms and lemon juice in casserole. Pour in water and cover; microwave 2 minutes at HIGH.

2 Stir drained scallop mixture into cooked tomatoes. Finish microwaving in serving dishes topped with cheese.

Scallops and Cheese   *(serves 2)*

SETTING: *HIGH & MEDIUM*
COOKING TIME: *12 minutes in microwave*
UTENSIL: *2 QT (2 L) round casserole dish with cover; individual serving dishes*

½ lb	(250 g) fresh scallops
¼ lb	(125 g) mushrooms, quartered
1 tbsp	(15 ml) chopped chives
¼ cup	(50 ml) dry white wine
½ cup	(125 ml) water
2 tbsp	(30 ml) butter
2½ tbsp	(40 ml) flour
1 cup	(250 ml) hot milk
3 tbsp	(45 ml) hot milk
¼ cup	(50 ml) grated Gruyère cheese
	Tabasco sauce to taste
	salt, pepper and paprika

Place scallops, mushrooms and chives in casserole. Add wine, water and season well with pepper. Cover and microwave 2 minutes at HIGH. Stir mixture well; continue microwaving 2 minutes.

Drain liquid into small saucepan. Remove scallops and mushrooms; set aside on plate. Place saucepan on conventional stove top; reduce liquid by half over medium-high heat. Set aside. Wash and dry casserole. Add butter and microwave 1 minute at HIGH. Mix in flour with whisk; microwave 1 minute uncovered. Incorporate reduced liquid to cooked flour; now mix in 1 cup (250 ml) milk; microwave 3 minutes uncovered. Stir twice.

Mix in remaining milk, drained scallops and mushrooms.

Season to taste with Tabasco, salt, pepper and paprika. Spoon mixture into serving dishes and top with cheese. Microwave 3 minutes uncovered at MEDIUM. Serve immediately.

See Technique next page.

1 SERVING	406 CALORIES	22 g CARBOHYDRATE
30 g PROTEIN	22 g FAT	0.5 g FIBER

TECHNIQUE: SCALLOPS AND CHEESE

1 Place scallops, mushrooms and chives in casserole.

2 When incorporating the reduced liquid to cooked flour, you must mix very well.

3 The scallops and mushrooms must be well drained.

4 Finish microwaving in individual serving dishes.

Flounder with Egg Sauce   *(serves 2)*

SETTING: *HIGH*
COOKING TIME: *12 to 13 minutes*
UTENSIL: *2 QT (2 L) rectangular dish*
                 2 QT (2 L) round casserole
                 dish
                 serving dish (optional)

4	flounder filets
1	green onion, chopped
1 tsp	(5 ml) chopped chives
2	lemon slices
½ cup	(125 ml) water
2 tbsp	(30 ml) butter
2½ tbsp	(40 ml) flour
1 cup	(250 ml) hot milk
2	hard-boiled eggs, chopped
	salt and pepper
	dash paprika

Place flounder in rectangular dish. Add onion, chives, lemon and pepper.

Pour in water and cover with plastic wrap; microwave 3 minutes.

Drain fish; either replace in dish or transfer to serving dish. Reserve ½ cup (125 ml) cooking liquid.

Place butter in round casserole and microwave 1 minute.

Mix in flour with whisk; microwave 2 minutes uncovered.

Incorporate reserved cooking liquid and milk; season well and add paprika to taste.

Microwave 4 to 5 minutes uncovered. Stir twice.

Fold in chopped eggs and pour sauce over flounder. Microwave 2 minutes uncovered.

Serve immediately.

See Technique next page.

1 SERVING	264 CALORIES	7 g CARBOHYDRATE
32 g PROTEIN	12 g FAT	0 g FIBER

TECHNIQUE: FLOUNDER WITH EGG SAUCE

1 Place flounder in rectangular dish. Add onion, chives, lemon and pepper.
Pour in water and cover with plastic wrap; microwave 3 minutes.

2 Flounder will turn white and flake when cooked.

Beef and Vegetable Stew *(serves 4)*

SETTING: *HIGH*
COOKING TIME: *1 hour 13 minutes*
UTENSIL: *3 QT (3 L) round casserole dish with cover*

1½ lb	(750 g) beef flank, cubed
3 tbsp	(45 ml) soya sauce
1	onion, peeled and cubed
1 tsp	(5 ml) oil
2 tbsp	(30 ml) tomato paste
2½ cups	(625 ml) heated beef stock
1	bay leaf
3 tbsp	(45 ml) cornstarch
4 tbsp	(60 ml) cold water
½	turnip, peeled and cubed
2	potatoes, peeled and cubed
3	carrots, pared and cubed
3 tbsp	(45 ml) sour cream
	pinch oregano, pinch thyme

Place beef in bowl and pour in soya sauce; mix well. Season with pepper and marinate 30 minutes.

Place onion, oil, thyme and oregano in casserole. Cover and microwave 3 minutes.

Add marinated beef, tomato paste and beef stock; mix well. Drop in bay leaf and season well; cover and microwave 50 minutes.

Mix cornstarch with water; stir into stew. Stir in turnip, potatoes and carrots; cover and continue microwaving 20 minutes.

Let stew stand in casserole 6 to 7 minutes before serving, then mix in sour cream.

1 SERVING	432 CALORIES	28 g CARBOHYDRATE
44 g PROTEIN	16 g FAT	1.2 g FIBER

Cod Filets with Parsley Sauce   *(serves 4)*

SETTING: *HIGH*
COOKING TIME: *11 minutes*
UTENSIL: *2 QT (2 L) rectangular dish*
                 small bowl

2 lb	(900 g) cod filets
1	celery stalk, thinly sliced
2	large tomatoes, sliced
1	fennel sprig
2 cups	(500 ml) water
4 tbsp	(60 ml) butter
2 tbsp	(30 ml) chopped parsley
1 tsp	(5 ml) lemon juice
	salt and pepper
	dash paprika

Grease rectangular dish and add cod; season well and add paprika.

Cover with celery and tomatoes; drop in fennel. Pour in water and cover; microwave 5 minutes.

Turn fish over; continue microwaving 4 minutes covered.

Remove dish from microwave and let cod stand in hot liquid 4 minutes.

Meanwhile, place butter, parsley and lemon juice in the bowl. Microwave 2 minutes uncovered.

Serve sauce with cod and vegetables.

See Technique next page.

1 SERVING	301 CALORIES	5 g CARBOHYDRATE
41 g PROTEIN	13 g FAT	0.6 g FIBER

TECHNIQUE: FILETS WITH PARSLEY SAUCE

1 Grease rectangular dish and add cod; season well and add paprika.

2 Cover with celery and tomatoes.

3 Drop in fennel and pour in water; cover and microwave 5 minutes.
Turn fish over; finish microwaving 4 minutes.

4 Check if fish is cooked by flaking with fork.

Trout for One   *(serves 1)*

SETTING: *MEDIUM-HIGH*
COOKING TIME: *6 minutes*
UTENSIL: *1.5 QT (1.5 L) square dish*

1	10 oz (284 g) brook trout, cleaned and fins removed
1 tsp	(5 ml) chopped parsley
1 tbsp	(15 ml) butter
	lemon juice
	salt and pepper

Place all ingredients in dish. Cover with plastic wrap and microwave 3 minutes.

Turn fish over; continue microwaving 3 minutes covered.

Serve with fries.

1 SERVING	296 CALORIES	0 g CARBOHYDRATE
38 g PROTEIN	16 g FAT	0 g FIBER

Basic White Rice   *(serves 4)*

SETTING: *HIGH*
COOKING TIME: *18 minutes*
UTENSIL: *2 QT (2 L) round casserole dish with cover*

1 cup	(250 ml) long grain rice, rinsed and drained
2 cups	(500 ml) cold water
½	bay leaf
1½ tbsp	(25 ml) butter or margarine salt and white pepper

Place rice, water, bay leaf, salt and pepper in casserole; mix with fork. Cover and microwave 8 minutes.

Mix rice well; continue microwaving 10 minutes covered.

When cooked, let rice stand in casserole 7 to 8 minutes.

Remove and stir in butter. Serve immediately.

1 SERVING	139 CALORIES	26 g CARBOHYDRATE
2 g PROTEIN	3 g FAT	0.1 g FIBER

Rice with Vegetables   *(serves 4)*

SETTING: *HIGH*
COOKING TIME: *23 minutes*
UTENSIL: *2 QT (2 L) round casserole dish with cover*

1 tbsp	(15 ml) butter
3 tbsp	(45 ml) chopped celery
1 cup	(250 ml) long grain rice, rinsed and drained
2 cups	(500 ml) heated chicken stock
½	red pepper, in large pieces
1	head broccoli, in flowerets
8	mushrooms, quartered
1	large tomato, cubed
1	garlic clove, chopped
	salt and pepper
	dash paprika
	pinch oregano, pinch basil

Place butter and celery in casserole; cover and microwave 3 minutes.

Add rice, salt, pepper and paprika; mix well with fork. Pour in chicken stock; cover and microwave 10 minutes. Stir occasionally.

Add red pepper and broccoli; mix. Continue microwaving 5 minutes covered.

Mix in mushrooms, tomato, garlic and herbs; correct seasoning. Cover and finish microwaving 5 minutes.

Stir with fork and serve.

1 SERVING	256 CALORIES	48 g CARBOHYDRATE
7 g PROTEIN	4 g FAT	1.7 g FIBER

Pasta in Tomato Sauce *(serves 2)*

SETTING:	*HIGH & MEDIUM*
COOKING TIME:	*35 minutes*
UTENSIL:	*two — 2 QT (2 L) round casserole dishes with covers*

1½ tbsp	(25 ml) vegetable oil
½	onion, chopped
2	green onions, chopped
1 tbsp	(15 ml) chopped parsley
1 tsp	(5 ml) chopped fresh oregano
1 tsp	(5 ml) chopped fresh thyme
1 tsp	(5 ml) chopped fresh basil
3	garlic cloves, chopped
2	28 oz (796 ml) cans tomatoes, drained and chopped
5½ oz	(156 ml) can tomato paste
¼ tsp	(1 ml) sugar
2 cups	(500 ml) tubular pasta
4 cups	(1 L) hot water
1 tsp	(5 ml) white vinegar

Place 1 tbsp (15 ml) oil, both onions, parsley, fresh herbs and garlic in casserole. Cover and microwave 3 minutes at HIGH. Mix in tomatoes, paste and sugar; microwave 14 minutes uncovered at HIGH.

Remove casserole, stir and set aside.

Place pasta, water, vinegar, dash salt and rest of oil in other casserole. Cover and microwave 5 minutes at HIGH.

Stir pasta; cover and continue microwaving 12 minutes at MEDIUM. Stir frequently. When cooked, drain well and rinse. Spoon portions on plates.

Reheat tomato sauce 1 minute in microwave. Serve with pasta and add cheese if desired.

See Technique next page.

1 SERVING	456 CALORIES	28 g CARBOHYDRATE
23 g PROTEIN	11 g FAT	1.5 g FIBER

TECHNIQUE: PASTA IN TOMATO SAUCE

1 Place 1 tbsp (15 ml) oil, onions, parsley, fresh herbs and garlic in round casserole. Cover and microwave 3 minutes at HIGH.

2 The tomato sauce should be fairly thick after being microwaved 14 minutes.

3 Microwave pasta in water with vinegar, salt and oil. Stir frequently.

4 Pasta in best served 'al dente'.

Rigatoni and Leftover Pork   *(serves 4)*

SETTING: *HIGH*
COOKING TIME: *16 minutes*
UTENSIL: *2 QT (2 L) round casserole dish with cover*

1 tsp	(5 ml) olive oil
1	onion, peeled and chopped
½ lb	(250 g) mushrooms, chopped
1 tbsp	(15 ml) chopped parsley
2 cups	(500 ml) tomato juice
1 cup	(250 ml) brown sauce
2 tbsp	(30 ml) tomato paste
1 lb	(500 g) leftover cooked pork (loin, chops, etc.), diced
½ cup	(125 ml) grated parmesan cheese
3 cups	(750 ml) cooked rigatoni

Place oil and onion in casserole; cover and microwave 2 minutes.

Add mushrooms and parsley; continue microwaving 1 minute.

Stir in tomato juice, brown sauce and tomato paste; season generously. Stir well and microwave 10 minutes uncovered.

Incorporate pork and cheese; microwave 3 minutes uncovered. Spoon over cooked rigatoni and serve.

1 SERVING	512 CALORIES	43 g CARBOHYDRATE
49 g PROTEIN	16 g FAT	1.1 g FIBER

Hot Mexican Macaroni   *(serves 4)*

SETTING: *HIGH*
COOKING TIME: *10 minutes in microwave*
UTENSIL: *3 QT (3 L) casserole dish with cover*

2 cups	(500 ml) elbow macaroni
1 tsp	(5 ml) oil
2 tbsp	(30 ml) chopped onion
1	marinated pepper, chopped
28 oz	(796 ml) can tomatoes, drained and chopped
6 oz	(170 ml) can tomato juice
3 tbsp	(45 ml) tomato paste
3 tbsp	(45 ml) crushed chillies
3	small pepperoni sausages, sliced
	pinch sugar
	salt and pepper
	few drops Tabasco sauce

Cook pasta as directed on package. Rinse, drain and set aside.

Place oil, onion and chopped pepper in casserole. Cover and microwave 3 minutes.

Stir in tomatoes, tomato juice and paste, crushed chillies and sugar; season and add Tabasco sauce. Microwave 4 minutes uncovered.

Mix in pasta and pepperoni; finish microwaving 3 minutes uncovered.

1 SERVING	398 CALORIES	54 g CARBOHYDRATE
14 g PROTEIN	14 g FAT	1.1 g FIBER

White Sauce

SETTING: *HIGH*
COOKING TIME: *9½ minutes*
UTENSIL: *2 QT (2 L) round casserole dish*

3 tbsp	(45 ml) butter
3½ tbsp	(55 ml) flour
2 cups	(500 ml) hot milk
1 tsp	(5 ml) chopped parsley
	salt and pepper

Microwave butter in casserole 1½ minutes.

Whisk in flour until well incorporated. Microwave 2 minutes uncovered.

Whisk in milk, parsley, salt and pepper. Microwave 6 minutes uncovered. Stir three times during cooking.

This sauce can be used in many recipes.

1 SERVING	181 CALORIES	11 g CARBOHYDRATE
5 g PROTEIN	13 g FAT	0 g FIBER

Heavenly Chocolate Pudding (serves 4 to 6)

SETTING: *HIGH*
COOKING TIME: *2 minutes 30 seconds*
UTENSIL: *2 QT (2 L) round casserole dish*

4 oz	(125 g) semi-sweet chocolate
4 tbsp	(60 ml) soft butter
9 tbsp	(135 ml) fine granulated sugar
5	egg yolks
5	egg whites

Place chocolate, butter and 5 tbsp (75 ml) sugar in casserole. Microwave 2 minutes uncovered.

Add egg yolks and mix well; continue microwaving 30 seconds. Set casserole aside.

Beat egg whites with electric beater until stiff. Incorporate remaining sugar and continue beating 1 minute.

Fold egg whites into chocolate mixture. Do not overmix.

Spoon pudding into dessert dishes and serve.

1 SERVING	340 CALORIES	24 g CARBOHYDRATE
7 g PROTEIN	24 g FAT	0 g FIBER

Plain Cheesecake (serves 6 to 8)

SETTING: *HIGH & MEDIUM & LOW*
COOKING TIME: *35 minutes*
UTENSIL: *1.5 QT (1.5 L) to 2 QT (2 L) pie plate (preferably of glass)*

1½ cups	(375 ml) graham crumbs
1½ cups	(375 ml) granulated sugar
⅓ cup	(75 ml) soft butter
2	8 oz (220 g) packages cream cheese
3	large egg yolks
3 tbsp	(45 ml) Tia Maria
3	large egg whites, beaten stiff
1 cup	(250 ml) heavy cream, whipped
1 tsp	(5 ml) cinnamon

Place graham crumbs, ½ cup (125 ml) sugar and butter in bowl; mix well.
Place in pie plate and press lightly with fingers. Try to obtain an even surface.
Microware 1¾ minutes at HIGH. Do not cover. Remove from microwave and set aside to cool.
Meanwhile, prepare cheese filling by placing cheese, egg yolks and Tia Maria in bowl; mix well. Add remaining sugar; mix well with electric beater. Fold in stiff-beaten egg whites until well blended. Fold in whipped cream and add cinnamon.
Pour into pie plate. Microwave 10 minutes at MEDIUM. Do not cover.
Rotate ¼ turn; continue microwaving 20 minutes at LOW; rotate ¼ turn; finish microwaving 5 minutes at MEDIUM.
Remove cheesecake from microwave and set aside to cool for 15 minutes. Refrigerate 45 minutes before serving.

See Technique next page.

1 SERVING	699 CALORIES	59 g CARBOHYDRATE
10 g PROTEIN	47 g FAT	0.6 g FIBER

TECHNIQUE: PLAIN CHEESECAKE

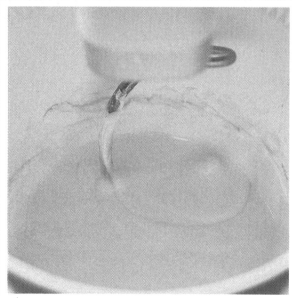

1 Prepare filling by placing cheese, egg yolks and Tia Maria in bowl; mix well. Add remaining sugar.

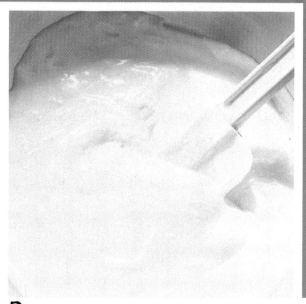

2 Fold in stiff-beaten egg whites until well blended.

3 Fold in whipped cream and add cinnamon.

Strawberry Delight   (serves 4)

SETTING: *HIGH*
COOKING TIME: *9 minutes*
UTENSIL: *2 QT (2 L) round casserole dish*

4 cups	(1 L) fresh strawberries, washed and hulled
2 tbsp	(30 ml) Lamb's White rum
5 tbsp	(75 ml) sugar
2 tbsp	(30 ml) cornstarch
4 tbsp	(60 ml) cold water
4	large scoops ice cream (vanilla or strawberry)
4	extra strawberries for decoration
	few drops lemon juice

Place strawberries in casserole; sprinkle with rum, sugar and lemon juice. Cover with plastic wrap and microwave 4½ minutes.

Purée strawberries in food processor or blender; replace in casserole.

Mix cornstarch with water; stir into strawberries. Microwave 4½ minutes uncovered. Stir each minute!

Cool mixture in refrigerator. To serve, place 3 tbsp (45 ml) of strawberry mixture in bottom of each dessert glass.

Add ice cream and top with remaining strawberry mixture. Decorate with extra strawberries.

1 SERVING	276 CALORIES	48 g CARBOHYDRATE
3 g PROTEIN	8 g FAT	2.0 g FIBER

After School Banana Cake   (serves 6)

SETTING: *MEDIUM*
COOKING TIME: *18 minutes*
UTENSIL: *9½ × 3¼ in (23 × 8 cm) bundt pan*

½ cup	(125 ml) oil
1 cup	(250 ml) sugar
2	eggs
3	bananas, puréed
1⅔ cups	(400 ml) flour
1 tbsp	(15 ml) baking powder
2 tbsp	(30 ml) Lamb's Light rum
½ cup	(125 ml) seedless golden raisins
2	egg whites, beaten firm
	pinch salt

Place oil and sugar in large bowl. Beat in eggs one at a time, using an electric beater at medium speed.

Fold in puréed bananas with spatula.

Sift flour, baking powder and salt together; fold into batter. Be sure dry ingredients are well incorporated.

Mix in rum, raisins and beaten egg whites. Pour batter into bundt pan and microwave 18 minutes. Do not cover and rotate ¼ turn several times.

Cool before unmolding.

1 SERVING	525 CALORIES	77 g CARBOHYDRATE
7 g PROTEIN	21 g FAT	0.5 g FIBER

INDEX

A

Abigail's chicken, 183
Aiolli with fresh vegetables, 53
  technique, 54
Almonds
  brook trout with, 425
  toasted almond cream, 504
Anchovy(ies)
  basic filet mignon and anchovy butter, 328
  butter, 330
  technique, 329
  fried salmon steaks with, 420
Apple(s)
  baked, 543
  beef liver and, 322
  cake, 526
  cauliflower and apple soup, 75
  London broil with, 248
  pie, 489
  traditional pork chops and, 344
Applesauce, 330
Artichoke(s)
  and vinaigrette, 18
    technique, 19
  quick artichoke omelet, 112
Asparagus
  au Parmesan, 16
  cream of, 68
  with butter, 15
Aspic trout, 478

B

Bacon
  bluegrass bacon chicken, 209
  peameal bacon quiche, 169
  scallops wrapped in bacon on skewers, 230
Bag chicken, 206
Baked apples, 543
Baked cheesecake, 542
  technique, 542
Baked chicken in sauce, 186
Baked eggs, 146
  in sauce, 151
  with spinach, 145
Baked leeks, 12
  technique, 13
Baked okra, 11
Baked potato skins, 29
Baker's eggs, 153
  technique, 154
Banana
  flambé, 534
  loaf, 520
  technique, 521
Barbecue(d)
  bits and bites, 239
    technique, 240
  butterfly tenderloin steaks, 228
  chicken legs, 221
  delicious B.B.Q. chicken, 217
  ginger seasoned wings, 229
  grilled salmon steaks, 220
  helpful hints, 216
  hot chicken strips, 236
  lamb brochettes, 223

lamb steaks, 237
London broil, 227
New York steaks, 219
outdoor half chicken, 222
porks shish kebabs, 224
rabbit, 226
salmon steaks in wine marinade, 234
scallops wrapped in bacon on skewers, 230
shrimp kebabs, 232
sweet B.B.Q. sausages, 233
vegetables and sausages in foil, 218
vegetarian's shish kebabs, 231
Basic pie dough, 486
  technique, 487
Batter
  special crepe, 470
Beans
  braised white, 379
  fava beans and zucchini, 24
  lemon beans and mushrooms, 8
Béarnaise sauce, 479
  loin of lamb with, 387
  technique, 388
Beef
  Alfredo, 285
  and vegetables, 293
  and vegetables mix in sake, 325
  basic filet mignon with anchovy butter, 328
  "big apple" rib steaks, 306
  boiled beef salad, 56
  boneless marinated rump roast, 294
  braised rib-eye steaks, 291
  braised short ribs in spicy sauce, 259
  carbonado of, 299
  casserole, 246
  cheese burgers, 247
  curry burgers, 253
  delicious double peppercorn filet mignon, 273
  filet mignon Parisienne, 274
  French boiled, 306
  hash and onions, 258
  hash and potatoes, 257
  hearty family stew, 269
  lemon, 326
  liver and apples, 322
  liver and onions, 321
  London boil in tomato and mushroom sauce, 249
  London broil with apples, 248
  marinated beef Bourguignonne, 308
  marinated beef on skewers, 279
  marinated short ribs, 261
  meatballs in sour cream sauce, 254
  meatloaf, 333
  New England boiled, 245
  New York steaks in green peppercorn sauce, 283
  olive lover's filet mignon, 327

pepper steak, 277
porterhouse steak, 287
porterhouse steaks with hot olive sauce, 286
potato cake, 301
  technique, 302
quick tostada meal, 317
rib roast and cream of turnips with horseradish, 316
rib roast with sauce, 265
rib steak with beer, 278
roast eye-of-round, 268
roast rib-eye, 271
rolled beef with horseradish stuffing, 297
rump roast and potatoes, 324
rump roast in beer, 331
Salisbury steak, 243
sautéed beef Long Island, 281
sirloin roast with yellow squash, 305
sliced beef Parmesan, 323
south of the border London broil, 251
steak Diane with cognac, 296
steak Tartare, 307
stuffed burgers, 255
stuffed green peppers, 320
stuffed tomatoes, 319
Swiss steak, 303
T-bone Lyonnaise, 289
T-bone steaks au cognac, 275
top-loin strips and spaghetti, 324
tournedos with cucumbers, 332
Wellington, 312
  technique, 313
zesty meat spaghetti sauce, 318
Beer
  rib steak with, 278
  rump roast in, 331
Berries
  crepes and, 537
Blanquette of veal, 373
Blueberry
  fancy blueperry tart, 493
  individual blueberry tarts, 498
  last minute blueberry sauce, 491
  sandwich, 512
Bluefish
  broiled bluefish with cheese, 417
  fried bluefish with shrimps, 418
  poached bluefish with peppers in wine, 416
  with tomatoes and onions, 415
Bluegrass bacon chicken, 209
"Big apple" rib steaks, 306
Bits and bites
  barbecued, 239
Boiled beef salad, 56
Boiled eggs, technique, 152
Boiling live lobsters, 445
Boneless marinated rump roast, 294
  technique, 295

Braised chicken mama Knox, 198
  technique, 199
Braised fennel roots in chicken stocks, 38
Braised rib-eye steaks, 291
  technique, 292
Braised short ribs in spicy sauce, 259
  technique, 260
Braised white beans, 379
Braising fish, 405
Bread
  French bread treat, 484
  fried eggs and garlic, 134
Breaded veal fingers, 369
Breakfast egg treat, 158
Breasts, chicken
  and mushroom cream sauce, 189
  breaded chicken breasts with cheese, 187
  fried chicken breasts in horseradish white sauce, 188
  in tomatoes, 190
Broccoli
  au gratin, 33
  with garlic, 40
Brochettes
  lamb, 223
Broiled bluefish with cheese, 417
Broiled Maine lobster, 444
Broiled scampi, 452
  technique, 453
Brook trout
  fancy, 429
  with almonds, 424
    technique, 425
  with mushrooms stuffing, 426
    technique, 427
Broth
  chicken broth and rice, 84
Brown sauce, 397
  for pork, 355
Brunch
  Mexican egg, 104
Bun
  veal on a, 365
Burgers
  cheese, 247
  curry, 253
  stuffed, 255
Butter
  asparagus with, 15
  basic filet mignon with anchovy, 328
  silver hake steaks with melted, 451
Butterfly pork chops, 340
Butterfly tenderloin steaks, 228

C

Cabbage
  Chinese, 38
  cold cabbage salad, 41
Ceasar salad, 60
  technique, 61
Cake
  apple, 526
  beef potato, 301
  carrot coconut, 523
  easy afternoon, 541
  rhubarb, 519
  sponge, 538

California vegetable salad, 51
Caper
  pike filets in simple caper sauce, 414
Capon in red wine, 214
Caramel
  coated cream puffs, 508
  orange rind sauce for caramel custard, 503
  Tia Maria caramel custard, 500
Carbonado of beef, 299
  technique, 300
Carrot(s)
  coconut cake, 523
    technique, 524
  deep-fried, 339
  soup, 85
Casserole
  beef, 246
  halibut, 443
Castle potatoes, 25
  tomatoes stuffed with, 36
Catsup marinade, 225
Cauliflower
  and apple soup, 75
  leftover cauliflower and zesty tomato sauce, 39
  special cauliflower and cheese sauce, 27
Cheddar
  eggs with cheddar cheese sauce, 141
Cheese
  breaded chicken breasts with, 187
  broiled bluefish with, 417
  burgers, 247
  cream puffs, 509
  cream puffs filling, 509
  eggs with cheddar cheese sauce, 141
  filled chicken with grape sauce, 208
  oysters in sauce with, 464
  quick cheese omelet, 116
  scallops vol-au-vent with cheese, 438
  scampi, mushrooms and, 455
  special cauliflower and cheese sauce, 27
  spicy cheese dip and vegetables, 48
  spinach with cream and melted, 21
  veal chops with cream and cheese, 364
  veal cutlets, prosciutto and, 363
  white sauce, 20
Cheesecake
  baked, 542
Cherry
  cognac cherry dessert, 531
  individual cherry tarts, 497
  pudding, 496
Cherrystone clams
  au gratin, 461
  steamed, 459
Chicken
  Abigail's, 183
  and mushroom quiche, 172
  and rice soup, 79
  bag, 206
  baked chicken in sauce, 186

B.B.Q. chicken legs, 221
bluegrass bacon, 209
braised chicken mama
  Knox, 198
braised fennel roots in
  chicken stock, 38
breaded chicken breasts
  with cheese, 187
breasts and mushroom
  cream sauce, 189
breasts in tomatoes, 190
broth and rice, 84
cheese filled chicken with
  grape sauce, 208
chow mein, 205
classic boiled chicken and
  rice, 195
coq au vin, 194
corn croquettes, 212
cornmeal coated chicken
  legs, 209
curry dish, 193
deep fried wings, 203
delicious B.B.Q., 217
disjointing, technique, 175
elegant strawberry, 215
fricassée, 201
fried chicken breasts in
  horseradish white
  sauce, 188
ginger seasoned
  wings, 229
harvest, 190
hot chicken strips, 235
leg sauté, 179
liver supreme, 207
Maryland fried, 184
miranda, 180
new wave curried, 197
old time favourite chicken
  noodle soup, 78
outdoor half, 222
pieces au gratin, 196
pineapple, 185
quick chicken soup, 80
rice stuffing, 200
roast chicken with rice
  stuffing, 202
sliced chicken on
  linguine, 182
sweet chicken wings, 211
vegetable chicken
  salad, 55
wings in tomato
  sauce, 181
with julienne
  vegetables, 192
wrapped in dough, 204
Chilled Mexican soup, 93
Chinese cabbage, 38
Chocolate
  pears, 513
    technique, 514
  rich chocolate sauce, 486
  strawberry treats, 547
  Tia maria chocolate cream
    puffs 511
Chop(s)
  butterfly pork chops, 340
  pork chops with sauce
    charcutière, 338
  pork chops with sauce
    Roberto, 335
  traditional pork chops and
    apples, 344
  veal chops Tia Maria, 362
  veal chops with cream and
    cheese, 364

veal chops with mixed
  vegetables, 361
Chop, lamb
  à la béarnaise, 383
  friday night lamb chops
    dinner, 382
Chowder
  fish, 94
Clams
  cherrystone clams au
    gratin, 461
  littleneck clams in Italian
    sauce, 460
  steamed cherrystone, 459
Classic boiled chicken and
  rice, 195
Club salad, 59
Cocktail
  shrimp, 477
Coconut
  carrot coconut cake, 523
Cognac
  cherry dessert, 531
  fruit pudding, 483
  mushroom cognac
    stuffing, 359
  steak Diane with, 296
  T-bone steaks au
    cognac, 275
Cold cabbage salad, 41
Cold halibut salad, 410
Cold soufflé dessert, 537
Cold vegetable loaf, 64
Cooking fresh mussels, 465
Cooking shrimps, 432
Coq au vin, 194
Coquille(s)
  famous coquilles
    Saint-Jacques, 442
  of shrimp and scallop, 439
    technique, 440
  rich and creamy coquilles
    Saint-Jacques, 442
Corn
  chicken corn
    croquettes, 212
  fritters, 211
  soup, 73
  cornmeal coated chicken
    legs, 210
Crab
  king crab legs marinated
    in rum, 450
Crabmeat
  scrambled eggs with, 103
Cream
  caramel coated cream
    puffs, 508
  cheese cream puffs, 509
  cheese cream puffs
    filling, 496
  chicken breasts and
    mushroom cream
    sauce, 189
  custard, 506
  lamb noisettes sautéed
    with cream sauce, 384
  meatballs in sour cream
    sauce, 254
  of asparagus, 68
  of green split peas, 67
  of mushroom, 69
  of pumpkin soup, 86
  of turnip, 71
  of turnips with
    horseradish, 311
  spinach with cream and
    melted cheese, 21

raspberries on, 545
rib roast and cream
  of turnips with
  horseradish, 316
rum pastry, 504
Tia Maria chocolate cream
  puffs, 511
Tia Maria cream
  puffs, 510
toasted almond, 504
veal chops with cream and
  cheese, 364
Creamy lobster soup, 77
Creamy pearl onion soup, 89
Crepe(s)
  and berries, 537
  Parmesan seafood, 469
  special crepe batter, 470
  suzettes, 535
Croquette(s)
  egg, 149
  chicken corn, 212
Croutons
  homemade garlic, 63
Cucumber(s)
  beef tournedos with, 332
  fresh cucumber salad, 50
  versatile cucumber
    soup, 70
Cumin stuffing, 403
  technique, 402
Curried loin of lamb, 389
Curry
  burgers, 253
  chicken curry dish, 193
  sliced pork loin with, 352
  vinaigrette, 58
Custard
  cream, 506
    technique, 507
  orange rind sauce for
    caramel, 503
  Tia Maria caramel, 500
Cutlets
  pork cutlets
    Parisienne, 354
  quick breaded, 353
  veal cutlets, prosciutto
    and cheese, 363

──────────────

D
Deboning leg of lamb, 377
Deboning loin of lamb, 386
Deboning loin of pork, 345
Deep-fried carrots, 339
Deep-fried scallops, 475
Deep-fried tiger shrimp, 472
  technique, 473
Deep-fried wings, 203
Delicious B.B.Q.
  chicken, 217
Delicious papaya, 530
  technique, 530
Delicious peppercorn filet
  mignon, 273
Delicious rum red
  snapper, 430
  technique, 431
Delicious veal kidneys, 366
Dessert
  apple cake, 526
  apple pie, 489
  baked apples, 543
  baked cheesecake, 542
  banana flambé, 534
  banana loaf, 520
  basic pie dough, 486

blueberry sandwich, 512
caramel coated cream
  puffs, 508
carrot coconut cake, 523
cheese cream puffs, 509
cheese cream puffs
  filling, 496
chocolate pears, 513
chocolate strawberry
  treats, 547
cognac cherry, 531
cognac fruit pudding, 483
cold soufflé, 537
crepes and berries, 536
crepes suzettes, 535
custard cream, 506
delicious papaya, 530
easy afternoon cake, 541
elegant fruit salad, 529
elegant strawberry
  mousse, 546
exotic fruit salad, 527
fancy blueberry tart, 493
fancy dessert treats, 544
floating island, 515
French bread treat, 484
fruit salad with
  yogurt, 528
individual blueberry
  tarts, 498
individual cherry
  tarts, 497
individual peach tarts, 499
individual strawberry
  tarts, 495
last minute blueberry
  sauce, 491
meringues, 518
orange rind sauce for
  caramel custard, 503
plums in syrup, 532
quick rice pudding, 481
raspberries on cream, 545
rhubarb cake, 519
rich chocolate sauce, 486
rum pastry cream, 504
sponge cake, 538
strawberry sauce, 485
sweet peach tart, 490
sweet pie dough, 491
Tia Maria caramel
  custard, 500
Tia Maria chocolate cream
  puffs, 511
Tia Maria cream
  puffs, 510
toasted almond
  cream, 504
Dinner
  friday night lamb
    chop, 382
Dip
  spicy cheese dip and
    vegetables, 48
Dish
  chicken curry, 193
Disjointing chicken, 175
Dough
  basic pie, 486
  chicken wrapped in, 204
  quiche, 162
  sweet pie, 491

──────────────

E
Easy afternoon cake, 541
Egg(s)
  baked, 146

baked eggs in sauce, 151
baked eggs with
  spinach, 145
baked in potatoes, 143
  technique, 144
baker's, 153
Benedict, 139
  technique, 140
boiled, technique, 152
breakfast egg treat, 158
croquette, 149
  technique, 150
farmer's omelet, 115
flat zucchini omelet, 120
fried, technique, 131
fried eggs and garlic
  bread, 134
ham omelet and maple
  syrup, 114
ham rolls, 147
  technique, 148
hard-boiled egg and ham
  quiche, 169
in cocotte, technique, 135
  the easy way, 135
in vegetables, 132
  technique, 133
last minute omelet, 113
Mexican egg brunch, 104
mushroom omelet, 118
omelet Lyonnaise, 111
omelet mousseline,
  technique, 122
omelet nouvelle
  cuisine, 117
omelet sandwich, 128
omelet soufflé with
  jam, 127
omelet soufflé with
  pears, 124
plain omelet, 108
poached, technique, 136
poached eggs
  Charron, 137
quick artichoke
  omelet, 112
quick cheese omelet, 116
salsify omelet
scrambled eggs à la
  moutarde, 104
scrambled eggs
  Archiduchesse, 103
scrambled eggs
  Cristoff, 102
scrambled eggs with
  crabmeat, 103
scrambled eggs with
  shrimps sauce, 100
scrambled eggs with
  vegetables, 99
shrimp omelet, 110
Spanish omelet, 119
stuffed with mushroom
  Duxelles, 160
  technique, 161
surprise, 156
  technique, 157
technique, 96
tips, 96
week-end omelet
  soufflé, 127
with cheddar cheese
  sauce, 141
  technique, 142
Egg noodles
  tomato soup and, 77
Eggplant
  quiche, 165

Elegant fruit salad, 529
Elegant strawberry
    chicken, 215
Elegant strawberry
    mousse, 546
Endive
    potato and endive
        salad, 45
Exotic fruit salad, 527
Eye-of-round
    roast, 268

F

Famous coquilles
    Saint-Jacques, 442
Fancy blueberry tart, 493
    technique, 494
Fancy brook trout, 429
Fancy dessert treats, 544
Farmer's omelet, 115
Farmer's potage, 76
Fava beans and zucchini, 24
Fennel roots
    braised fennel roots in
        chicken stock, 38
Filet(s)
    of sole au gratin, 413
    pike filets, mushrooms
        and shrimps, 411
    pike filets in simple caper
        sauce, 414
    sole filet rolls, 412
Filet mignon
    basic filet mignon with
        anchovy butter, 328
    delicious double
        peppercorn, 273
    olive-lover's, 327
    Parisienne, 274
Filling
    cheese cream puffs, 509
Fingers
    breaded veal, 369
    pork, 342
Fish
    aspic trout, 478
    bluefish with tomatoes
        and onions, 415
    boiling live lobster, 445
    braising, 405
    broiled bluefish with
        cheese, 417
    broiled Maine lobster, 444
    broiled scampi, 452
    brook trout with
        almonds, 424
    brook trout with
        mushroom stuffing, 427
    cherrystone clams au
        gratin, 461
    chowder, 94
        technique, 95
    cold halibut salad, 410
    cooking fresh
        mussels, 465
    cooking shrimp, 432
    coquille of shrimp and
        scallop, 439
    deep-fried scallops, 475
    deep-fried tiger
        shrimp, 476
    delicious rum red
        snapper, 430
    famous coquilles
        Saint-Jacques, 442
    fancy brook trout, 429
    filet of sole au gratin, 413
    flambéed scampi, 458

fried bluefish with
    shrimp, 418
fried frog legs, 476
fried salmon, olives and
    mushrooms, 421
fried salmon steaks with
    anchovies, 420
ginger shrimp, 435
halibut casserole, 443
Italian mussels, 467
king crab legs marinated
    in rum, 450
littleneck clams in Itaiian
    sauce, 460
lobster Newburg, 447
mussels in vermouth, 468
mussels marinière, 466
oyster stew, 462
oysters in sauce with
    cheese, 464
oysters Rockefeller, 463
Parmesan seafood
    crepes, 469
pepper shrimp, 434
pike filets, mushroom and
    shrimps, 411
pike filets in simple caper
    sauce, 414
poached bluefish with
    peppers in wine, 416
poached salmon steaks,
    new cuisine, 419
poaching fish in vegetable
    stock, 407
preparing a whole, 408
rich and creamy coquilles
    Saint-Jacques, 442
salmon steaks with
    tomatoes, 422
scallops in rice, 448
scallops vol-au-vent with
    cheese, 438
scampi, mushrooms and
    cheese, 455
seafood stick
    vol-au-vent, 437
shrimp and scallop
    vol-au-vent, 436
shrimp cocktail, 472
silver hake steaks with
    melted butter, 451
sole filet rolls, 412
steamed cherrystone
    clams, 459
steaming, 405
trout cooked in foil, 423
Flambé
    banana, 534
Flambéed scampi, 458
Floating island, 515
    technique, 516
Flat zucchini omelet, 120
    technique, 121
French boiled beef, 306
French bread treat, 484
Fresh cucumber salad, 50
Fresh fruit salad, 47
Fresh mint salad, 52
Fricassée chicken, 201
Friday night lamb chops
    dinner, 382
Fried bluefish with
    shrimp, 418
Fried chicken breasts in
    horseradish white
    sauce, 188
Fried eggs
    and garlic bread, 134
    technique, 131

Fried frog legs, 476
Fried salmon, olives and
    mushrooms, 421
Fried salmon steaks with
    anchovies, 420
Fritters
    corn, 211
Frog legs
    fried, 476
Fruit
    cognac fruit pudding, 483
    elegant fruit salad, 529
    exotic fruit salad, 527
    fresh fruit salad, 47
    salad with yogurt, 528

G

Garlic
    broccoli with, 40
    fried eggs and garlic
        bread, 134
    homemade garlic
        croutons, 63
    lamb noisettes, 393
    mustard vinaigrette, 58
Gazpacho, 91
Ginger
    seasoned wings, 229
    shrimp, 435
Goulash
    veal, 373
Grape
    cheese filled chicken with
        grape sauce, 208
Green onion
    potatoes, 264
Green peas
    cream of green split
        peas, 67
Green peppers
    stuffed, 320
Grilled salmon steaks, 220
Gruyère soufflé, 173

H

Halibut
    casserole, 443
    cold halibut salad, 410
Ham
    egg ham rolls, 147
    hard-boiled egg and ham
        quiche, 169
    omelet and maple
        syrup, 114
    sweet braised, 355
Hard-boiled egg and ham
    quiche, 169
Harvest chicken, 191
Hash
    beef hash and onions, 258
    beef hash and
        potatoes, 257
Hearty family stew, 269
    technique, 270
Hearty sausages and
    sauerkraut, 337
Hearty turkey stew with
    vegetables, 213
Helpful barbecue hints, 216
Herb mayonnaise, 474
Hollandaise sauce, 137
    technique, 138
Homemade garlic
    croutons, 63
Homemade white stock, 408
Horseradish
    cream of turnips with, 311

fried chicken breasts in
    horseradish white
    sauce, 188
rib roast and cream of
    turnips with, 316
rolled beef with
    horseradish stuffing, 297
white sauce, 178
Hot chicken strips, 236
Hunter sauce, 392

I

Individual blueberry
    tarts 498
Individual cherry tarts, 497
Individual peach tarts, 499
Individual strawberry
    tarts 495
    technique, 496
Island
    floating, 515
Italian mussels, 467

J

Jam
    omelet soufflé with, 125
Julienne vegetables, 41
    chicken with, 192
    technique, 41

K

Kebabs
    shrimp, 232
Kidneys
    delicious veal, 366
King crab legs marinated in
    rum, 450

L

Lamb
    brochettes, 223
    chops à la béarnaise, 383
    curried loin of lamb, 389
    deboning leg of, 377
    deboning loin of, 386
    friday night lamb chops
        dinner, 382
    garlic lamb noisettes, 393
    leg of lamb with
        parsley, 381
    loin of lamb, nouvelle
        cuisine, 389
    loin of lamb and garden
        vegetables, 390
    loin of lamb with
        béarnaise sauce, 387
    noisettes Milanaise, 393
    noisettes sautéed with
        cream sauce, 384
    technique, 385
    old-fashioned lamb
        stew, 380
    onion sauce for roast, 381
    quick lamb noisettes, 391
    roast leg of lamb
        jardinière, 394
    steaks, 237
    technique, 238
    stuffed leg of, 378
    stuffed loin of, 390
Lasagna
    vegetarian, 35
Last minute blueberry
    sauce, 491
Last minute omelet, 113

Leeks
    baked, 12
    sautéed potatoes and, 17
Leftover cauliflower and
    zesty tomato sauce, 39
Leg(s), chicken
    B.B.Q., 221
    cornmeal coated, 210
    sauté, 179
Leg of lamb
    deboning, 377
    roast leg of lamb
        jardinière, 394
    stuffed, 378
    with parsley, 381
Legs, crab
    king crab legs marinated
        in rum, 450
Legs, frog
    fried, 476
Lemon
    beans and mushrooms, 8
    beef, 326
    veal lemon scallops, 358
Lentil
    soup, 82
Light vegetable salad, 44
Light watercrest soup, 74
Light white sauce, 14
Linguine
    sliced chicken on, 182
Littleneck clams in Italian
    sauce, 460
Liver
    beef liver and apples, 322
    beef liver and onions, 321
    chicken liver supreme, 207
Loaf
    banana, 520
    cold vegetable, 64
Lobster(s)
    boiling live, 445
    broiled Maine, 444
    creamy lobster soup, 77
    Newburg, 447
Loin of lamb
    and garden
        vegetables, 390
    curried, 389
    deboning, 386
    nouvelle cuisine, 389
    stuffed, 390
    with béarnaise sauce, 387
Loin of pork
    deboning, 345
    sliced pork loin with
        curry, 352
London broil
    B.B.Q., 227
    in tomato and mushroom
        sauce, 249
    south of the border, 251
    technique, 250, 252
    with apples, 248

M

Mandarin sauce, 205
Maple syrup
    ham omelet and, 114
Marinade
    catsup, 225
    salmon steaks in
        wine, 234
    soya sauce, 225
    red wine, 235
Marinated beef
    Bourguignonne, 308
    technique, 309

Marinated beef on skewers, 279
  technique, 280
Marinated short ribs, 261
  technique, 262
Maryland fried chicken, 184
Mayonnaise
  herb, 474
Meal
  quick tostada, 317
Meat
  zesty meat spaghetti sauce, 318
Meatballs in sour cream sauce, 254
Meatloaf, 333
Meringues, 518
Mexican egg brunch, 104
Minestrone, 90
Mint
  fresh mint salad, 52
  veal kebabs, 367
Minute
  last minute omelet, 113
Mix
  tasty vegetable, 32
  winter vegetable, 10
Mixed vegetable soup, 83
Mousse
  elegant strawberry, 546
Moutarde
  scrambled eggs à la, 104
Mushroom(s)
  brook trout with mushroom stuffing, 426
  chicken and mushroom quiche, 172
  chicken breasts and mushroom cream sauce, 189
  cognac stuffing, 359
  cream of, 69
  Duxelles, 158
    eggs stuffed with, 160
    technique, 159
  fried salmon, olives and, 421
  lemon beans and, 8
  London broil in tomato and mushroom sauce, 249
  omelet, 118
  pike filets, mushrooms and shrimp, 411
  Provençale, 31
  scampi, mushrooms and cheese, 455
  veal and mushroom stew, 370
Mussels
  cooking fresh, 465
  in vermouth, 468
  Italian, 467
  marinière, 466
  soup à la Sonja, 89
Mustard
  garlic mustard vinaigrette, 58

N
New England boiled beef, 245
New wave curried chicken, 197
New York steaks, 219
New York steaks in green peppercorn sauce, 283
  technique, 284

Noisettes
  garlic lamb, 393
  lamb noisettes Milanaise, 393
  lamb noisettes sautéed with cream sauce, 384
  quick lamb, 391
Noodle(s)
  old time favorite chicken noodle soup, 78
  tomato soup and egg, 77

O
O'Brien potatoes, 28
Okra
  baked, 11
  soup, 72
Old-fashioned lamb stew, 380
Old time favorite noodle soup, 78
Olive(s)
  fried salmon, olives and mushrooms, 421
  lover's filet mignon, 327
  porterhouse steaks with hot olive sauce, 286
Omelet
  farmer's, 115
  flat zucchini, 120
  ham omelet and maple syrup, 114
  last minute, 113
  Lyonnaise, 111
  mousseline, technique, 122
  mushroom, 118
  nouvelle cuisine, 117
  plain, 108
  quick artichoke, 112
  quick cheese, 116
  salsify, 109
  sandwich, 128
    technique, 129
  shrimp, 110
  Spanish, 119
  soufflé with jam, 125
  soufflé with pears, 124
    technique, 125
  technique, 106
  weekend omelet soufflé, 127
Onion(s)
  beef hash and, 258
  beef liver and onions, 321
  bluefish with tomatoes and, 415
  creamy pearl onion soup, 89
  green onion potatoes, 264
  quiche, 166
    technique, 167
  sauce for roast lamb, 381
  soup au gratin, 92
Orange
  rind sauce for caramel custard, 503
Osso buco, 374
  technique, 375
Outdoor half chicken, 220
Oyster(s)
  in sauce with cheese, 464
  Rockefeller, 463
  stew, 462

P
Papaya
  delicious, 530

Parmesan
  asparagus au, 16
  seafood crepes, 469
  sliced beef, 323
  veal, 360
Parsley
  leg of lamb with, 381
Pastry
  rum pastry cream, 504
Pea(s)
  cream of green split, 67
  yellow split pea soup, 71
Peach
  individual peach tarts, 499
  sweet peach tart, 490
Peameal bacon quiche, 169
Pears
  chocolate, 513
  omelet soufflé with, 124
Pepper(s)
  poached bluefish with peppers in wine, 416
  rice, 235
  sauce, 316
  shrimp, 434
  steak, 277
  stuffed green, 320
Peppercorn
  delicious double peppercorn filet mignon, 273
  New York steaks in green peppercorn sauce, 283
Pie
  apple, 489
  basic pie dough, 486
  sweet pie dough, 491
Pike
  filets, mushrooms and shrimp, 411
  filets in simple caper sauce, 414
Pineapple chicken, 185
Plain omelet, 108
Poached bluefish with peppers in wine, 416
Poached eggs
  Charron, 137
    technique, 136
Poached salmon steaks, new cuisine, 419
Poaching fish in vegetable stock, 407
Pork
  Alfredo, 349
  and vegetables on skewers, 341
  B.B.Q. pork shish kebabs, 224
  brown sauce for, 355
  butterfly pork chops, 340
  chops with sauce charcutière, 338
  chops with sauce Roberto, 335
  cutlets Parisienne, 354
  deboning loin of, 345
  fingers, 342
  hearty sausages and sauerkraut, 337
  quick breaded cutlets, 353
  sautéed pork and vegetables, 351
  sliced pork fiesta, 350
  sliced pork loin with curry, 352
  sweet braised ham, 355
  traditional pork chops and apples, 344

Porterhouse
  steak, 287
    technique, 288
  steaks with hot olive sauce, 286
Potage
  farmer's, 76
Potato(es)
  and endive salad, 45
  baked potato skins, 29
  beef hash and, 257
  beef potato cake, 301
  boulangère, 398
  castle, 25
  eggs baked in, 143
  green onion, 264
  O'Brien, 28
  purée, 9
  puréed potato soup, 66
  rump roast and, 324
  sautéed potatoes and leeks, 17
  scalloped, 26
  sweet potato purée, 343
  tomato stuffed with castle, 36
Precooking quiche dough, 162
Preparing a whole fish, 408
Prosciutto
  veal cutlets, prosciutto and cheese, 363
Plums in syrup, 532
  technique, 533
Pudding
  cognac fruit, 483
  quick rice, 481
  Yorkshire, 311
Puffs, cream
  caramel coated cream puffs, 508
  cheese, 509
  cheese cream puffs filling, 496
  Tia Maria, 510
  Tia Maria chocolate, 511
Pumpkin
  cream of pumpkin soup, 86
Purée
  potato, 9
  sweet potato, 343
Puréed potato soup, 66

Q
Quiche
  chicken and mushroom, 172
  dough, 162
    technique, 163
  eggplant, 165
  hard-boiled egg and ham, 169
  Lorraine, 170
    technique, 171
  onion, 166
  peameal bacon, 169
  precooking quiche dough, 162
  spinach, 165
  tomato, 164
Quick arichoke omelet, 112
Quick breaded cutlets, 353
Quick cheese omelet, 116
Quick chicken soup, 80
Quick lamb noisettes, 391
  technique, 392
Quick leftover soup, 81

Quick rice pudding, 481
  technique, 482
Quick toastada meal, 317
Quick veal sticks, 368
Quick white sauce, 145

R
Rabbit
  B.B.Q., 226
Raspberries on cream, 545
Ratatouille, 34
Red snapper
  delicious rum, 430
Red wine
  capon in, 214
  marinade, 235
Rhubarb cake, 519
Rib-eye
  braised rib-eye steaks, 291
  roast, 271
Rib roast
  and cream of turnips with horseradish, 316
  with sauce, 265
    technique, 266
Rib steak
  "big apple", 306
  with beer, 278
Ribs, short
  braised short ribs in spicy sauce, 259
  marinated, 261
Rice
  chicken and rice soup, 79
  chicken broth and, 84
  classic boiled chicken and, 195
  pepper, 235
  quick rice pudding, 481
  roast chicken and rice stuffing, 202
  scallops in, 448
  steamed, 178
  stuffing, 200
Rich and creamy coquilles Saint-Jacques, 442
Rich chocolate sauce, 486
Roast
  chicken with rice stuffing, 202
  eye-of-round, 268
  leg of lamb jardinière, 394
    technique, 395
  onion sauce for roast lamb, 381
  rib-eye, 271
    technique, 272
  rib roast with sauce, 265
  sirloin roast with yellow squash, 305
Roast, rib
  and cream of turnips with horseradish, 316
  with sauce, 265
Roast, rump
  and potatoes, 324
  boneless marinated, 294
  in beer, 331
Rolled beef with horseradish stuffing, 297
  technique, 298
Rolls
  egg ham, 147
  sole filet, 412
Roquefort salad, 62
Rotini salad, 46

Rum
delicious rum red
snapper, 430
king crab legs marinated
in, 450
pastry cream, 504
technique, 505
Rump roast
boneless marinated, 294
in beer, 331
and potatoes, 324

S

Salad
aiolli with fresh
vegetables, 53
boiled beef, 56
Caesar, 60
California vegetable, 51
club, 59
cold cabbage, 41
cold halibut, 410
cold vegetable loaf, 64
curry vinaigrette, 58
elegant fruit, 529
exotic fruit, 527
fresh cucumber, 50
fresh fruit, 47
fresh mint, 52
fruit salad with
yogurt, 528
garlic mustard
vinaigrette, 58
homemade garlic
croutons, 63
light vegetable, 44
potato and endive, 45
Roquefort, 62
spicy cheese dip and
vegetables, 48
spinach, 57
rotini, 46
tomato, 49
vegetable chicken, 55
Salisbury steak, 243
technique, 244
Salmon
fried salmon, olives and
mushrooms, 421
fried salmon steaks with
anchovies, 420
grilled salmon steaks, 220
poached salmon steaks,
new cuisine, 419
steaks in wine
marinade, 234
steaks with tomatoes, 422
Salsify omelet, 109
Sandwich
blueberry, 512
omelet, 128
Sauce
baked chicken in
sauce, 186
baked eggs in, 151
béarnaise, 479
braised short ribs in
spicy, 259
brown, 397
brown sauce for pork, 355
charcutière, 339
cheese filled chicken with
grape, 208
cheese white, 20
chicken breasts and
mushroom cream, 189
chicken wings in
tomato, 181

eggs with cheddar
cheese, 141
fried chicken breasts in
horseradish white
sauce, 188
Hollandaise, 137
horseradish white, 178
hunter, 391
lamb noisettes sautéed
with cream, 384
last minute blueberry, 491
leftover cauliflower and
zesty tomato, 39
light white, 14
littleneck clams in
Italian, 460
loin of lamb with
béarnaise, 387
London broil in tomato and
mushroom, 249
mandarin, 205
meatballs in sour
cream, 254
New York steaks in green
peppercorn, 283
onion sauce for roast
lamb, 381
orange rind sauce for
caramel custard, 503
oysters in sauce with
cheese, 464
pepper, 316
pike filets in simple
caper, 414
pork chops with sauce
charcutière, 338
pork chops with sauce
Roberto, 335
porterhouse steaks with
hot olive, 286
quick white, 145
rib roast with, 265
rich chocolate, 486
Roberto, 336
scrambled eggs with
shrimp, 100
shrimp, 101
soya sauce marinade, 225
special cauliflower and
cheese, 27
strawberry, 485
Tartare, 479
thin white, 343
tomato, 399
veal scallops in sauce, 357
veal scallops in
tarragon, 359
Wellington, 314
white, 23
zesty meat spaghetti, 318
zesty tomato, 40
Sauerkraut
hearty sausages and, 337
Sausages
hearty sausages and
sauerkraut, 337
sweet B.B.Q., 233
vegetables and sausages
in foil, 218
Sauté
chicken leg, 179
**Sautéed beef Long
Island, 281**
technique, 282
**Sautéed pork and
vegetables, 351**
**Sautéed potatoes and
leeks, 17**
Scalloped potatoes, 26

Scallops
coquille of shrimp
and, 439
in rice, 448
technique, 449
deep-fried, 475
shrimp and scallops
vol-au-vent, 436
stuffed rolled veal, 363
veal lemon, 358
veal scallops in sauce, 357
veal scallops in tarragon
sauce, 359
vol-au-vent with
cheese, 438
wrapped in bacon on
skewers, 230
Scampi
broiled, 452
flambéed, 458
mushrooms and
cheese, 455
technique, 456
Scrambled eggs
à la moutarde, 104
technique, 105
Archiduchesse, 103
Cristoff, 102
technique, 98
with crabmeat, 103
with shrimp sauce, 100
with vegetables, 99
Seafood
Parmesan seafood
crepes, 469
stick vol-au-vent, 437
Shish kebabs
B.B.Q. pork, 224
vegetarian's, 231
Short ribs
braised short ribs in spicy
sauce, 259
marinated braised, 261
Shrimp
and scallops
vol-au-vent, 436
cocktail, 477
cooking, 432
coquille of shrimp and
scallop, 439
deep-fried tiger, 472
fried bluefish with, 418
ginger, 435
kebabs, 232
omelet, 110
pepper, 434
pike filets, mushrooms
and, 411
scrambled eggs with
shrimp sauce, 100
sauce, 101
technique, 101
**Silver hake steaks with
melted butter, 451**
**Sirloin roast with yellow
squash, 305**
Skins
baked potato, 29
Sliced beef Parmesan, 323
**Sliced chicken on
linguine, 182**
Sliced pork fiesta, 350
**Sliced pork loin with
curry, 352**
Sole
filet of sole au gratin, 413
filet rolls, 412
Soufflé
cold soufflé dessert, 537

Gruyère, 173
Soup
carrot, 85
cauliflower and apple, 75
chicken and rice, 79
chicken broth and rice, 84
chilled Mexican soup, 93
corn, 73
cream of asparagus, 68
cream of green split
peas, 67
cream of mushroom, 69
cream of pumpkin, 86
cream of turnip, 71
creamy lobster, 77
creamy pearl onion, 89
farmer's potage, 76
fish chowder, 94
gazpacho, 91
lentil, 82
light watercrest soup, 74
minestrone, 90
mixed vegetable, 83
mussel soup à la Sonja, 89
okra, 72
old time favorite chicken
noodle, 78
onion soup au gratin, 92
puréed potato, 66
quick chicken, 80
quick leftover, 81
tomato soup and egg
noodles, 77
versatile cucumber, 70
Vichyssoise, 87
yellow split pea, 71
Sour cream
meatballs in sour cream
sauce, 254
**South of the border London
broil, 251**
Soya sauce marinade, 225
Spaghetti
top-loin strips and, 324
zesty meat spaghetti
sauce, 318
Spanish omelet, 119
**Special cauliflower and
cheese sauce, 27**
Special crepe batter, 470
**Spicy cheese dip and
vegetables, 48**
Spicy stuffing, 379
Spinach
baked eggs with, 145
quiche, 165
salad, 57
with cream and melted
cheese, 21
technique, 22
Sponge cake, 538
technique, 539
Squash
sirloin roast with
yellow, 305
Steak(s)
"big apple" rib, 306
braised rib-eye steaks, 291
butterfly tenderloin, 228
Diane with cognac, 296
grilled salmon, 220
lamb, 237
New York, 219
New York steaks in green
peppercorn sauce, 283
pepper, 277
porterhouse, 287
porterhouse steaks with
hot olive sauce, 286

Salisbury, 243
salmon steaks in wine
marinade, 234
Swiss, 303
Tartare, 307
T-bone steaks au
cognac, 275
Steaks, salmon
fried salmon steaks with
anchovies, 420
poached salmon steaks,
new cuisine, 419
with tomatoes, 422
**Steamed cherrystone
clams, 459**
Steamed rice, 178
Steaming fish, 406
Stew
hearty family, 269
hearty turkey stew with
vegetables, 213
old-fashioned lamb, 380
oyster, 462
tomato veal, 371
veal and mushroom, 370
Sticks
quick veal, 368
Stir-fried vegetables, 30
Stock
braised fennel roots in
chicken, 38
homemade white, 409
poaching fish in vegetable
stock, 407
Strawberry
elegant strawberry
chicken, 215
elegant strawberry
mousse, 546
elegant strawberry
treats, 547
individual strawberry
tarts, 495
sauce, 485
technique, 485
Stuffed burgers, 255
technique, 256
Stuffed green peppers, 320
Stuffed loin of lamb, 390
**Stuffed rolled veal
scallops, 363**
Stuffed tomatoes, 319
Stuffed vegetables, 37
Stuffing
brook trout with
mushroom, 426
cumin, 403
mushroom cognac, 359
rice, 200
roast chicken and
rice, 202
rolled beef with
horseradish, 297
spicy, 379
eggs, 156
Sweet B.B.Q. sausages, 233
Sweet braised ham, 355
Sweet chicken wings, 211
Sweet peach tart, 490
Sweet pie dough, 491
technique, 492
Sweet potato purée, 343
Swiss steak, 303
technique, 304
Syrup
ham omelet and
maple, 114
plums in, 533

T

Tarragon
veal scallops in tarragon
sauce, 359
Tart(s)
fancy blueberry, 493
individual blueberry, 498
individual cherry, 497
individual peach, 499
individual strawberry, 495
sweet peach, 490
Tartare sauce, 479
Tasty vegetable mix, 32
T-bone
Lyonnaise, 289
technique, 290
steaks au cognac, 275
technique, 276
Technique
aiolli with fresh
vegetables, 53
anchovy butter, 329
baked cheesecake, 543
baked leeks, 13
baker's eggs, 154
banana loaf, 521
barbecued bits and
bites, 240
basic pie dough, 487
béarnaise sauce, 388
beef potato cake, 302
beef Wellington, 313
boiled eggs, 152
boiling live lobsters, 445
boneless marinated rump
roast, 295
braised chicken mama
Knox, 199
braised rib-eye steaks, 292
braised short ribs in spicy
sauce, 260
braising fish, 405
broiled scampi, 453
brook trout with
almonds, 425
brook trout
with mushrooms
stuffing, 427
carbonado of beef, 300
carrot coconut cake, 524
chocolate pears, 514
coquille of shrimp and
scallop, 440
cooking fresh
mussels, 465
cooking shrimp, 432
custard cream, 507
deboning leg of lamb, 377
deboning loin of lamb, 386
deboning loin of pork, 345
deep-fried tiger
shrimp, 472
delicious papaya, 530
delicious rum red
snapper, 431
disjointing chicken, 175
egg, 96
egg croquette, 150
egg ham rolls, 148
eggs baked in
potatoes, 143
eggs Benedict, 140
eggs in cocotte, 135
eggs stuffed with
mushroom Duxelles, 161
eggs surprise, 157
eggs vegetables, 133
eggs with cheddar cheese
sauce, 142

fancy blueberry tart, 493
flat zucchini omelet, 121
floating island, 516
fried eggs, 131
fish chowder, 95
hearty family stew, 270
Hollandaise sauce, 138
individual strawberry
tarts, 496
julienne vegetables, 41
lamb noisettes sautéed
with cream sauce, 385
lamb steaks, 238
London broil, 250, 252
marinated beef
Bourguignonne, 309
marinated beef on
skewers, 280
marinated short ribs, 262
mushroom Duxelles, 159
New York steaks in green
peppercorn sauce, 284
omelet, 106
omelet mousseline, 122
omelet sandwich, 129
omelet soufflé with
pears, 125
onion quiche, 167
osso buco, 375
poached eggs, 136
poaching fish in vegetable
stock, 407
porterhouse steak, 288
preparing a whole
fish, 408
plums in syrup, 533
quiche dough, 163
quiche Lorraine, 171
quick lamb noisettes, 392
quick rice pudding, 482
rib roast with sauce, 266
roast leg of lamb
jardinière, 394
roast rib-eye, 272
rolled beef with
horseradish stuffing, 298
rum pastry cream, 505
Salisbury steak, 244
sautéed beef Long
Island, 282
scallops in rice, 449
scampi, mushrooms and
cheese, 456
scrambled eggs, 98
scrambled eggs à la
moutarde, 105
shrimp sauce, 101
special crepe batter, 470
spinach with cream and
melted cheese, 22
sponge cake, 539
steaming fish, 406
strawberry sauce, 485
stuffed burgers, 256
sweet pie dough, 492
Swiss steak, 303
T-bone Lyonnaise, 290
T-bone steaks au
cognac, 276
Tia Maria caramel
custard, 501
tomato sauce, 400
tomato veal stew, 372
Wellington sauce, 315
Tenderloin
butterfly tenderloin
steaks, 228
Thin white sauce, 343

Tia Maria
caramel custard, 500
technique, 501
chocolate cream puffs, 511
cream puffs, 510
veal chops, 362
Toasted almond cream, 504
Tomato(es)
bluefish with tomatoes
and onions, 415
chicken breasts in, 190
chicken wings in tomato
sauce, 181
leftover cauliflower and
zesty tomato sauce, 39
London broil in tomato
and mushroom
sauce, 249
quiche, 164
salad, 49
salmon steaks with, 422
sauce, 399
technique, 400
soup and egg noodles, 77
stuffed, 319
stuffed with castle
potatoes, 36
veal stew, 371
technique, 372
zesty tomato sauce, 40
**Top-loin strips and
spaghetti, 324**
Tostada
quick tostata meal, 317
Tournedos
beef tournedos with
cucumbers, 332
**Traditional pork chops and
apples, 344**
Treat(s)
elegant strawberry, 547
fancy dessert, 544
French bread, 484
Trout
aspic, 478
brook trout with
almonds, 425
brook trout with
mushrooms stuffing, 426
cooked in foil, 423
fancy brook, 429
Turkey
hearty turkey stew with
vegetables, 213
Turnip
cream of, 71
cream of turnips with
horseradish, 311
rib roast with cream
of turnips with
horseradish, 316

V

Veal
and mushroom stew, 370
blanquette of, 373
breaded veal fingers, 369
chops Tia Maria, 362
chops with cream and
cheese, 364
chops with mixed
vegetables 361
cutlets, prosciutto and
cheese, 363
delicious veal
kidneys, 366
goulash, 373
lemon veal scallops, 358

mint veal kebabs, 367
on a bun, 365
osso buco, 374
Parmesan, 360
quick veal sticks, 368
scallops in sauce, 357
scallops in tarragon
sauce, 359
stuffed rolled veal
scallops, 363
tomato veal stew, 371
Vegetable(s)
aiolli with fresh, 53
and sausages in foil, 218
artichokes and
vinaigrette, 18
asparagus au
Parmesan, 16
asparagus with butter, 15
baked leeks, 12
baked okra, 11
baked potato skins, 29
beef and, 293
beef and vegetables mix in
sake, 325
boiled spinach, 40
braised fennel roots in
chicken stock, 38
braised white beans, 379
broccoli au gratin, 33
broccoli with garlic, 40
California vegetable
salad, 51
castle potatoes, 25
cheese white sauce, 20
chicken salad, 55
chicken with julienne, 192
Chinese cabbage, 38
cold vegetable loaf, 64
deep-fried carrots, 339
eggs in, 132
fava beans and
zucchini, 24
green onion potatoes, 264
hearty turkey stew
with, 213
julienne, 41
leftover cauliflower and
zesty tomato sauce, 39
lemon beans and
mushrooms, 8
light vegetable salad, 44
loin of lamb and
garden, 390
mixed vegetable soup, 83
mushrooms Provençale, 31
O'Brien potatoes, 28
poaching fish in vegetable
stock, 407
pork and vegetables on
skewers, 341
potatoes boulangère, 398
potato purée, 9
ratatouille, 34
sautéed pork and, 351
sautéed potatoes and
leeks, 17
scalloped potatoes, 26
scrambled eggs with, 99
special cauliflower with
cheese sauce, 27
spicy cheese dip and, 48
spinach with cream and
melted cheese, 21
stir-fried, 30
stuffed, 37

stuffed tomatoes, 320
sweet potato purée, 343
tasty vegetable mix, 32
tomatoes stuffed with
castle potatoes, 36
veal chops with mixed
vegetables, 361
vegetarian lasagna, 35
winter vegetable mix, 10
Vegetarian lasagna, 35
**Vegetarian's shish
kebabs, 231**
Vermouth
mussels in, 468
Versatile cucumber soup, 70
Vichyssoise, 87
Vinaigrette
artichokes and, 18
curry, 58
garlic mustard, 58
Vol-au-vent
seafood stick, 437
scallop vol-au-vent with
cheese, 438
shrimp and scallops, 436

W

Watercrest
light watercrest soup, 74
**Weekend omelet
soufflé, 127**
Wellington
beef, 312
sauce, 314
technique, 315
White beans
braised, 379
White sauce, 23
cheese, 20
light, 14
thin, 343
White stock
homemade, 408
Wine
capon in red, 214
poached bluefish with
peppers in, 416
red wine marinade, 235
salmon steaks in wine
marinade, 234
Wings, chicken
deep-fried, 203
ginger seasoned, 229
in tomato sauce, 181
sweet, 211
Winter vegetable mix, 10

Y

**Yellow pea
soup, 71**
Yellow split pea soup, 71
Yogurt
fruit salad with, 528
Yorkshire pudding, 311

Z

**Zesty meat spaghetti
sauce, 318**
Zesty tomato sauce
Zucchini
fava beans and, 24
flat zucchini omelet, 120

See Microwave Index next page.

A

Almonds
browning slivered, 550
**After school banana
cake, 601**
Apple
veal chops with appele
garnish, 581

B

Bacon
cooking, 552
Baked potatoes, 567
Banana
after school banana
cake, 601
Basic white rice, 594
Beans
mixed, 568
Beef
and vegetable stew, 590
Braised zucchini, 571
technique, 572
Bread
quick garlic, 563
Broccoli
salmon broccoli
casserole, 585
with cheese sauce, 558
technique, 557
Brown sugar
softening, 550
**Browning slivered
almonds, 550**

C

Cake
after school banana, 601
Casserole
chicken and vegetable, 578
salmon broccoli, 585
Cheese
broccoli with cheese
sauce, 558
scallops and cheese, 587
Cheesecake
plain, 599
Chicken
and vegetables
casserole, 578
technique, 579
cream of, 562
in sauce, 577
technique, 578
leftover chicken and
vegetables, 580
Chinese soup, 559
technique, 560

Chocolate
heavenly chocolate
pudding, 599
Chops
veal chops with apple
garnish, 581
Cod filets with parsley
sauce, 591
technique, 592
Cooking bacon, 552
Cooking vegetables, 554
Covering food, 553
with plastic wrap, 553
Cream of chicken, 562
technique, 563

D

Dinner
veal liver, 582
vegetarian's, 569

E

Easy tomato rice, 563
Egg(s)
flounder with egg
sauce, 589
scrambling, 551
Eggplant surprise, 575
technique, 574
**Everyday vegetable
soup, 560**
technique, 561

F

Filets
cold filets with parsley
sauce, 591
**Flounder with egg
sauce, 589**
technique, 590
Food
covering, 553
with plastic wrap, 553
how to arrange, 554

G

Garlic
quick garlic bread, 563

H

**Heavenly chocolate
pudding, 399**
Hot Mexican macaroni, 597
How to arrange food, 554

K

Knackwurst sausages, 565

L

**Leftover chicken and
vegetables, 580**
technique, 584
Light onion soup, 555
technique, 556
Liver
veal liver dinner, 582

M

Macaroni
hot Mexican, 597
Mixed beans, 568
technique, 568
Mock pork stir-fry, 582

O

Onion
light onion soup, 555

P

Parsley
cods filets with parsley
sauce, 591
Pasta in tomato sauce, 595
technique, 596
Plain cheesecake, 599
technique, 600
Pork
mock pork stir-fry, 582
rigatoni and leftover, 597
Potato(es)
baked, 567
salad, 583
scalloped, 566
Pudding
heavenly chocolate, 599

Q

Quick garlic bread, 564
technique, 564

R

Ratatouille
zucchini, 573
Rice
basic white, 594
easy tomato, 564
with vegetables, 594

**Rigatoni and leftover
pork, 597**

S

Salad
potato, 583
Salmon
broccoli casserole, 585
technique, 584
Sauce
broccoli with cheese, 558
chicken in, 577
cod filets with parsley, 591
flounder with egg, 589
pasta in tomato, 595
white, 598
Sausages
knackwurst, 565
Scalloped potatoes, 566
technique, 567
Scallops
and cheese, 587
technique, 588
and tomatoes, 586
technique, 587
Scrambling eggs, 551
Softening brown sugar, 550
Soup
Chinese, 559
everyday vegetable, 560
light onion, 555
Stew
beef and vegetable, 590
Stewed tomatoes, 576
Strawberry delight, 601
Sugar
softening brown, 550

T

Technique
braised zucchini, 572
broccoli with cheese
sauce, 557
chicken and vegetables
casserole, 579
chicken in sauce, 578
Chinese soup, 560
cods filets with parsley
sauce, 592
cream of chicken, 563
eggplant surprise, 574
everyday vegetable
soup, 561
flounder with egg
sauce, 590

leftover chicken and
vegetables, 580
light onion soup, 556
mixed beans, 568
pasta in tomato
sauce, 596
plain cheesecake, 600
salmon broccoli
casserole, 584
scalloped potatoes, 567
scallops and cheese, 588
scallops and
tomatoes, 586
vegetarian's dinner, 570
zucchini ratatouille, 572
Tomato(es)
easy tomato rice, 564
pasta in tomato
sauce, 595
scallops and, 586
stewed, 576
Trout for one, 593

V

Vegetable(s)
beef and vegetable
stew, 590
chicken and vegetables
casserole, 579
cooking, 554
everyday vegetable
soup, 560
leftover chicken and
vegetables, 580
rice with, 594
Vegetarian's dinner, 569
technique, 570
Veal
chops with apple
garnish, 581
liver dinner, 582

W

White rice
basic, 594
White sauce, 598

Z

Zucchini
braised, 571
ratatouille, 573
technique, 572